Charles Rau

Prehistoric fishing in Europe and North America

Charles Rau

Prehistoric fishing in Europe and North America

ISBN/EAN: 9783743349575

Manufactured in Europe, USA, Canada, Australia, Japa

Cover: Foto ©ninafisch / pixelio.de

Manufactured and distributed by brebook publishing software (www.brebook.com)

Charles Rau

Prehistoric fishing in Europe and North America

SMITHSONIAN CONTRIBUTIONS TO KNOWLEDGE.
————— 509 —————

PREHISTORIC FISHING

IN

EUROPE AND NORTH AMERICA.

BY

CHARLES RAU.

WASHINGTON CITY:
PUBLISHED BY THE SMITHSONIAN INSTITUTION.
1884.

ADVERTISEMENT.

The author of the following memoir was requested to prepare an article on "the methods and apparatus of prehistoric fishing," for the Report of the United States Commission of Fish and Fisheries; but the work grew to such proportions that it was deemed advisable to consider the propriety of its publication in the Smithsonian Contributions to Knowledge.

In accordance with the rule of the Smithsonian Institution, the work was submitted for examination to a commission of experts, consisting of Dr. DANIEL G. BRINTON, of Philadelphia, and Professor HENRY W. HAYNES, of Boston. These gentlemen having recommended its publication, it was accepted by the Institution, and is herewith presented as an important contribution to the sum of human knowledge.

The memoir, for the most part, is based on the materials contained in the archæological division (under the direction of Dr. RAU,) of the United States National Museum, of which establishment the Smithsonian Institution has the charge.

SPENCER F. BAIRD,
Secretary Smithsonian Institution.

SMITHSONIAN INSTITUTION,
Washington, December, 1884.

PREFACE.

This volume should have been written by one not only acquainted with the details of prehistoric archæology, but also well informed regarding all matters pertaining to fishing as practised in our time. Unfortunately, I cannot lay claim to any knowledge of the piscatorial art; for, after a single unsuccessful trial in angling, made in the days of my boyhood, I gave up all further attempts, and thus it happened that I never caught a fish in my life, either with hook or net. I should add that, owing to more pressing occupations, this want of practical experience has not in any way been supplemented by the study of works treating of fishing; and, as a consequence, many points doubtless have escaped my notice, which would have elicited comments on the part of an expert. Thus, in describing the ancient fish-hooks, he would have conjectured, from their form and size, what species of fishes were caught with them; the character of net-sinkers, perhaps, would have suggested to him that of the nets; and so in other instances. Yet, I must not omit to state that, while composing this work, I derived great advantage from being placed in circumstances of close association with some members of the United States Commission of Fish and Fisheries; for these gentlemen assisted me with great readiness whenever I had occasion to appeal to their knowledge of the details of fishing.

In treating of prehistoric fishing in Europe, I have used *all* the literary material within my reach; but certain data relating to the subject have doubtless been omitted—for the simple reason that the writings containing them were not at my disposal. Critical readers in Europe will bear this in mind.* If the work had been exclusively designed for the initiated, I might

---

* After the text of the first part of this work had been electrotyped, I had occasion to examine a pamphlet by Professor C. Grewingk, of Dorpat, entitled "Geologie und Archaeologie des Mergellagers von Kunda in Estland". (Dorpat, 1882). The author describes and figures a number of neolithic bone harpoon-heads extracted from marl. I would have reproduced his illustrations, if it had not been too late. I may say, however, that they present types similar to the European forms brought to the reader's notice in the first part of this volume.

The portion of the second part in which North American fish-hooks are described, also was electrotyped, when a short article by Miss Margarette W. Brooks, relative to bone fish-hooks found in a shell-heap near Narra-

have considerably abbreviated its first part by excluding much introductive and descriptive matter not immediately connected with fishing. Yet, as it probably will also be read by non-archæologists, it has been thought necessary to dwell on the differences between the palæolithic and neolithic ages, to give accounts of the tool and bone-bearing drift-beds, of cave-habitations, artificial shell-deposits, lake-dwellings, and, finally, to present a brief characterization of the bronze age. These intercalated portions were in part taken, with or without modifications, from "Early Man in Europe," a small volume embracing a series of articles, which I had written in 1875 for "Harper's New Monthly Magazine." The articles in question, notwithstanding their popular character, embodied the results of a careful study of original sources, and it is hoped that the extracts from them, utilized in the present case, will meet with the approbation of competent judges.

In the introduction to the second part of this work I have briefly stated my views concerning palæolithic man in North America. It would then have afforded me special pleasure to refer to Professor W. Boyd Dawkins's excellent article on early man in America, published in the "North American Review" (October, 1883), the more so, since his conclusions and mine point in the same direction; but the pages in which I alluded to the subject were already electrotyped before the publication of that article.

A work like that here presented must, from its very character, in a great measure be a compilation from preceding writings. There are authors who, in such cases, will slightly alter the text of their predecessors, and thus make it their own, though not without mentioning the sources from which they have drawn. I have preferred the mode of verbal quotation, not on account of being the easier one, but because I was actuated by the desire of doing full justice to those by whose labors I have profited.

I have been much assisted in my work in various ways, and it is but proper that I should express my acknowledgments. Reference was made to the advantages I derived from my acquaintance with members of the United States Fish

---

gansett Pier, Rhode Island, appeared in "Science" (Vol. 2, p. 653). There are figures of one perfect fish-hook and of fragments of three others given. The perfect one, of whose representation I would have published a copy, if it had been feasible, bears some resemblance to the original of Fig. 189 on page 127 of this work, yet is smaller and clumsier in shape. Owing to an oversight, a prehistoric Nova Scotian bone harpoon-head, figured on page 137 of Professor J. W. Dawson's "Fossil Men" (Montreal, 1880), has not been noticed in this work. Such drawbacks seem to be unavoidable.

Commission. My principal adviser among these gentlemen was Captain Joseph W. Collins, who very obligingly aided me with his great experience whenever I had occasion to ask him for an expression of his opinion. The Trustees of the Peabody Museum of American Archæology and Ethnology, at Cambridge, Massachusetts, kindly loaned for my use, at the request of the Secretary of the Smithsonian Institution, their collection of Swiss lacustrine articles employed in fishing, and I was thus enabled to extend my observations and descriptions. In connection with the Peabody Museum, I have to mention its Curator, Professor F. W. Putnam, by whom the objects, accompanied with full descriptions, were forwarded to the Smithsonian Institution.

Many other gentlemen have manifested their interest in my work by loaning me specimens, or transmitting photographs or drawings, always with the necessary—sometimes quite lengthy—explanations, and to some I am under obligations for accounts of explorations of artificial shell-deposits carried on by them. Yet, as in all instances the names of these co-laborers are given in the text, in connection with the information furnished by them, I may here confine myself to a general expression of my gratitude.

The illustrations in this work were nearly all made under my immediate supervision by the skillful artist, Mr. Charles F. Trill, and may be relied on as being either faithful copies of already published designs, or correct representations of objects specially drawn for this work, the majority of the latter being specimens belonging to the United States National Museum.* All of Mr. Trill's drawings were reproduced by the New York Photo-engraving Company (67 Park Place). In addition, I had the use of a number of cuts which had previously served to illustrate Smithsonian publications or other works. I am indebted to Messrs. Harper & Brothers for electrotypes of Figs. 29, 32, and 37, used in my small work "Early Man in Europe" (copyrighted in 1876); of Figs. 111, 112, and 113, published in Mitchell's "Past in the Present" (not copyrighted); and of Figs. 396 to 404, illustrating Squier's "Peru" (copyrighted in 1877). To these latter special reference is made in a note on page 332 of this work. To Colonel Charles C. Jones I am under obligations for the loan of the block of Fig. 337; Dr. Emil Bessels placed the cuts of Figs. 19, 20, and 21 at my disposal, and Professor Putnam accommodated me with those of Figs. 352

---

* To these illustrations the catalogue-numbers of the originals are always juxtaposited.

and 353. Electrotypes of Figs. 109, 212, 254, and 255, finally, were sent, with others, by Messrs. F. Vieweg and Son, of Braunschweig. These last-mentioned illustrations are taken from the "Archiv für Anthropologie," published by that well-known firm.

In conclusion, I would say that, whatever may be thought of this work, it will go far to illustrate anew the parallelism in the technical progress of populations totally unknown to each other, and for which only the common bond of humanity can be claimed. The designs of European and North American fishing-implements in this work bear witness to the statement. It will be noticed how slowly man in Europe arrived at the idea of barbing the fish-hook. None of the European hooks of bone or horn figured in this work is properly barbed, excepting the one shown in Fig. 91 on page 71, and this hook may postdate the neolithic period, and pertain to a time during which barbed fish-hooks of bronze were not uncommon. Among the prehistoric American fish-hooks which I was enabled to represent by designs in this publication, only one has a point armed with a barb on the inner side, namely, the deer-horn hook from New York delineated in Fig. 193 on page 128, which, as stated, is supposed to have been made after a European pattern. Yet, I would not venture to say that barbed fish-hooks had been unknown in America in ante-Columbian times; I simply state that none have fallen under my notice. Indeed, the halibut-hook of the Northwest Coast, doubtless an old aboriginal invention, may be classed among barbed fish-hooks (Fig. 9 on page 15).

Further analogies (and also differences) in the character of the prehistoric fishing-implements of Europe and America will easily be discovered by those who peruse the pages here offered.

SMITHSONIAN INSTITUTION,
    June, 1884.

CHARLES RAU.

CONTENTS.

PART I.—EUROPE.

	PAGE.
1.—PALÆOLITHIC AGE	1
General Characteristics	1
The Drift	1
Implements and Animal Remains	1
Implements used as Ice-picks (?)	4
Caves and Rock-shelters	4
Retreats of Man during the Reindeer-period	4
Fish-remains	10
Fishing and Fishing-implements	12
Delineations of Fishes and Aquatic Mammals	27
2.—NEOLITHIC AGE	32
General Characteristics	32
Artificial Shell-deposits	33
Character	33
Capture of Mollusks and Fish	36
Lake-dwellings	37
Character	37
Fish-remains	45
Fishing-implements	46
Boats	66
Fishing-implements and Utensils not found in Lacustrine Settlements	68
General Remarks	68
Double-pointed straight Bait-holders	69
Fish-hooks	69
Harpoon-heads	72
Arrow-heads	84
Sinkers	84
Boats	91
Anchor-stones	94
3.—BRONZE AGE	95
General Characteristics	95
Lake-dwellings	97
Character	97
Fishing-implements	99
Boats	105
Fishing-implements and Utensils not derived from Lake-habitations	109

CONTENTS.

PART II.—NORTH AMERICA.

	PAGE
INTRODUCTORY REMARKS	113
FISHING-IMPLEMENTS AND UTENSILS	117
Double-pointed straight Bait-holders	117
Fish-hooks	120
Harpoon and Arrow-heads	141
Nets	155
Sinkers	156
Fish-cutters	183
BOATS AND APPURTENANCES	188
Boats	188
Bailing-scoops	190
Paddles	191
Anchor-stones	192
PREHISTORIC STRUCTURES CONNECTED WITH FISHING	197
Fish-preserves	197
Fish-pens	200
REPRESENTATIONS OF FISHES, AQUATIC MAMMALS, ETC.	204
Pipes	205
Imitations in Stone and Shell	206
Clay Vessels	211
Delineations	213
ARTIFICIAL SHELL-DEPOSITS	216
Introductory Notices	216
Greenland	218
Nova Scotia	221
New Brunswick and New England	222
New York	225
New Jersey	227
Delaware	230
Maryland	235
West Virginia	239
Ohio	241
Tennessee	241
Iowa	241
Georgia	242
Florida	243
Alabama	249
California and Oregon	249
Alaska	256
EXTRACTS FROM VARIOUS WRITINGS OF THE SIXTEENTH, SEVENTEENTH, EIGHTEENTH, AND NINETEENTH CENTURIES, IN WHICH REFERENCE IS MADE TO ABORIGINAL FISHING IN NORTH AMERICA	261
Egede (Hans)	261
Crantz (David)	261
Lloyd (T. G. B.)	266
De Laet (Joannes)	267

CONTENTS.

	PAGE
De Champlain (Le Sieur)	268
Sagard Theodat (Le F. Gabriel)	268
Le Jeune (Le P. Paul)	271
Charlevoix (Father)	272
Henry (Alexander)	273
Hearne (Samuel)	274
Mackenzie (Alexander)	276
Williams (Roger)	277
[Johnson (Captain Edward)]	278
Ogilby (John)	278
Josselyn (John)	279
Van der Donck (Adriaen)	281
Kalm (Peter)	281
Morgan (Lewis H.)	282
Loskiel (George Henry)	283
De Bry (Theodorus)	284
Smith (Captain John)	287
[Beverly (Robert)]	288
Lawson (John)	289
Brickell (John)	290
Adair (James)	291
Du Pratz (M. Le Page)	293
Wyeth (Nathaniel J.)	294
Catlin (George)	295
Powers (Stephen)	296
The same	301
Stone (Livingston)	302
Dunn (John)	303
Swan (James G.)	304
The same	305
The same	310
Meares (John)	310
Cook (Captain James) and King (Captain James)	315
APPENDIX.	
NOTICES OF FISHING-IMPLEMENTS AND FISH-REPRESENTATIONS DISCOVERED SOUTH OF MEXICO	319
Nicaragua	319
Costa Rica	320
Chiriqui, State of Panama, United States of Colombia	321
State of Cauca, United States of Colombia	322
Peru	324

LIST OF ILLUSTRATIONS.

	PAGE
Fig. 1.—Drift-implement. Saint-Acheul, France	3
Fig. 2.—Double-pointed bone implement used in catching birds. Eskimos, Norton Sound, Alaska	13
Figs. 3-8.—Double-pointed bone implements. La Madelaine, France	13
Fig. 9.—Halibut-hook. Makah Indians, Cape Flattery, Washington Territory	15
Fig. 10.—Codfish-hook. Makah Indians, Cape Flattery, Washington Territory	15
Fig. 11.—Harpoon-head of reindeer-horn. La Madelaine, France	17
Fig. 12.—Harpoon-head of reindeer-horn. Bruniquel, France	17
Figs. 13-15.—Harpoon-heads of reindeer-horn. La Madelaine, France	17
Fig. 16.—Iron-headed Sioux arrow	17
Fig. 17.—Harpoon-head of reindeer-horn. La Madelaine, France	19
Fig. 18.—Harpoon-head of reindeer-horn. Laugerie Basse, France	19
Figs. 19-21.—Harpoons. Eskimos, Alaska	21
Figs. 22-23.—Harpoon or arrow heads of reindeer-horn. La Madelaine, France	23
Figs. 24-28.—Harpoon-heads of reindeer-horn (?). Kesslerloch, Switzerland	24
Figs. 29-30.—Harpoon-heads of reindeer-horn (?). Kent's Cavern, England	25
Fig. 31.—Representations of fishes and a horse on a baton of reindeer-horn. La Madelaine, France	27
Fig. 32.—Drawing of a fish on a piece of reindeer-horn. La Madelaine, France	27
Fig. 33.—Figure of a pike engraved on a drilled bear's tooth. Duruthy Grotto, France	28
Fig. 34.—Outline of a fish (*Squalius ?*) on a reindeer-jaw. Laugerie Basse, France	28
Fig. 35.—Tracing of a fish on a baton of reindeer-horn. Cave of Goyet, Belgium	29
Fig. 36.—Rude drawing of a fishing-scene on the scapula of an ox. Laugerie Basse, France	29
Fig. 37.—Outlines of two heads of the aurochs, a human figure, an eel (?), two horse heads, and three rows of marks on a piece of reindeer-horn. La Madelaine, France	31
Fig. 38.—Figure of a seal traced on a drilled bear's tooth. Duruthy Grotto, France	32
Figs. 39-40.—Double-pointed bone implements. Wangen, Baden	46
Figs. 41-43.—Double-pointed bone implements. Lake of Neuchâtel, Switzerland	46
Fig. 43.—Bone arrow-head (?). Saint-Aubin, Switzerland	47
Fig. 44.—Fish-hook of deer-horn. Wangen, Baden	48
Figs. 45-46.—Fish-hooks made of wild boars' tusks. Moosseedorf, Switzerland	48
Figs. 47-48.—Bone fish-hooks. Wangen, Baden	49
Fig. 49.—Double fish-hook (?) of deer-horn. Saint-Aubin, Switzerland	49
Figs. 50-51.—Bark floats. Robenhausen, Switzerland	50
Figs. 52-53.—Wooden implements used for recovering fishing-lines. Robenhausen, Switzerland	50
Fig. 54.—"Arpion"	50
Fig. 55.—"Devil's claw grapnel." Massachusetts	52
Figs. 56-58.—Deer-horn harpoon-heads. Saint-Aubin, Switzerland	53
Fig. 59.—Bone harpoon-head. Concise, Switzerland	54
Fig. 60.—Harpoon-head of deer-horn. Concise, Switzerland	54
Fig. 61.—Harpoon-head of deer-horn. Wauwyl, Switzerland	54
Figs. 62-64.—Harpoon-heads of deer horn. Lattringen, Switzerland	55
Fig. 65.—Arrow-head of deer-horn. Saint-Aubin, Switzerland	56
Fig. 66.—Flint arrow-head. Robenhausen, Switzerland	56
Fig. 67.—Flint arrow-head. Bodio, Italy	56
Fig. 68.—Fragment of fishing-net. Robenhausen (?), Switzerland	57
Figs. 69-70.—Stone sinkers. Allensbach, Baden	58

LIST OF ILLUSTRATIONS.

	PAGE
Fig. 71.—Stone sinker. Estavayer, Switzerland	58
Figs. 72–73.—Stone sinkers (?). Saint-Aubin, Switzerland	60
Fig. 74.—Stone sinker (?). Saint-Aubin, Switzerland	60
Fig. 75.—Clay sinker (?). Nidau-Steinberg, Switzerland	60
Fig. 76.—Clay sinker (?). Inkwyl, Switzerland	60
Fig. 77.—Bark float. Robenhausen, Switzerland	63
Fig. 78.—Wooden implement for arranging nets. Wangen, Baden	63
Figs. 79–80.—Implements made of boars' tusks. Nussdorf, Baden	64
Fig. 81.—Perforated bear's tooth. Nussdorf, Baden	64
Fig. 82.—Netting-implement. New England	65
Fig. 83.—Netting-implement. Eskimos, Nunivak Island, Alaska	65
Fig. 84.—Netting-implement. Eskimos, Chirikoff Island, Alaska	65
Fig. 85.—Netting-implement. McCloud River Indians, California	65
Fig. 86.—Boat. Robenhausen, Switzerland	66
Fig. 87.—Boat. Möringen, Switzerland	67
Fig. 88.—Flint fish-hook. Öresund, Sweden	70
Fig. 89.—Flint fish-hook. Kranke Lake, Sweden	70
Fig. 90.—Flint fish-hook (?). Scandinavia	70
Fig. 91.—Bone fish-hook. Scania, Sweden	71
Fig. 92.—Bone fish-hook. Pomerania, Prussia	71
Fig. 93.—Fish-hook of reindeer-horn. Lapland, Norway	71
Figs. 94–96.—Bone harpoon-heads. Scania, Sweden	73
Fig. 97.—Bone harpoon-head. Seeland, Denmark	73
Fig. 98.—Fish or bird-spear-head of bone. Arctic America	74
Fig. 99.—Prong of fish or bird-spear-head of bone. Scania, Sweden	74
Fig. 100.—Bone harpoon-head. Fünen, Denmark	76
Fig. 101.—Bone harpoon-head. Seeland, Denmark	76
Fig. 102.—Bone harpoon-head. Tierra del Fuego	76
Figs. 103–104.—Harpoon-heads of ox-horn. Poland	79
Fig. 105.—Bone harpoon-head. Victoria Cave, England	80
Figs. 106–108.—Javelin-heads of bone with inverted flint-flakes. Scania, Sweden	82
Fig. 109.—Javelin-head of elk-bone with inserted flakes. Eastern Prussia	82
Fig. 110.—Scanian flint-point set in wooden socket	83
Fig. 111.—Sink-stone of steatite. Shetland	85
Figs. 112–113.—Sink-stones. Wells, Shetland	86
Fig. 114.—Stone sinker. Burns, England	87
Figs. 115–116.—Stone sinkers. Ireland	88
Fig. 117.—Stone sinker. County of Down, Ireland	89
Fig. 118.—Stone sinker. County of Westmeath, Ireland	89
Fig. 119.—Stone sinker. Seeland, Denmark	90
Fig. 120.—Stone sinker. Denmark	90
Fig. 121.—Stone sinker. District of Sorö, Denmark	90
Fig. 122.—Stone sinker. District of Viborg, Denmark	90
Fig. 123.—Stone anchor (?). Bohuslund, Sweden	95
Fig. 124.—Fishing-implement (?) of bronze. Switzerland	99
Figs. 125–137.—Bronze fish-hooks. Nidau-Steinberg, Switzerland	100
Fig. 138.—Bronze fish-hook. Font, Switzerland	101
Figs. 139–140.—Bronze fish-hooks. Cortaillod, Switzerland	101
Figs. 141–143.—Bronze fish-hooks. Montellier, Switzerland	101
Fig. 144.—Bronze fish-hook. Mouth of river Scheuss, Switzerland	102
Fig. 145.—Bronze fish-hook. Lattringen, Switzerland	102
Fig. 146.—Bronze fish-hook. Romanshorn, Switzerland	103
Figs. 147–148.—Bronze fish-hooks. Unter-Uhldingen, Baden	103
Fig. 149.—Bronze fish-hook. Roseninsel, Bavaria	103
Figs. 150–153.—Bronze fish-hooks. Lake of Bourget, Savoy, France	104

LIST OF ILLUSTRATIONS.

XV

	PAGE.
Figs. 154-155.—Barbed bronze rods not yet bent into the form of fish-hooks. Peschiera, Italy	104
Fig. 156.—Barbed bronze rod not yet bent into the form of a fish-hook. Möringen, Switzerland	104
Figs. 157-158.—Barbed bronze armatures. Möringen, Switzerland	105
Fig. 159.—Barbed bronze armature. Peschiera, Italy	105
Fig. 160.—Barbed bronze armature. Roseninsel, Bavaria	105
Fig. 161.—Boat. Cudrefin, Switzerland	106
Fig. 162.—Boat. Vingelz, Switzerland	107
Fig. 163.—Boat. Mercurago, Italy	108
Fig. 164.—Bronze fish-hook. Ireland	109
Figs. 165-166.—Bronze fish-hooks. Glenluce, Scotland	109
Fig. 167.—Bronze fish-hook. Fünen, Denmark	109
Figs. 168-169.—Bronze fish-hooks in the form of baits. Germany	110
Fig. 170.—Double-pointed stone implement. Rogue River, Oregon	118
Fig. 171.—Double-pointed stone implement. Greene County, Tennessee	118
Fig. 172.—Double-pointed stone implement. Yellowstone National Park, Wyoming	118
Fig. 173.—Double-pointed grooved stone implement. Berks County, Pennsylvania	119
Figs. 174-176.—Double-pointed bone implements. Santa Cruz Island, California	120
Fig. 177.—Double-pointed bone implement. Santa Rosa Island, California	120
Figs. 178-180.—Fish-hooks composed of bone and chipped stone. Greenland	121
Fig. 181.—Bone point of fish-hook. Germany	122
Fig. 182.—Baited bone fish-hook. Kutchin Indians, Alaska	123
Fig. 183.—Bone fish-hook. Mouth of Oak Creek, Dakota	124
Fig. 184.—Bone fish-hook. Madisonville, Ohio	124
Fig. 185.—Bone fish-hook. Mississippi County, Arkansas	124
Fig. 186.—Bone fish-hook. Orleans County, New York	126
Fig. 187.—Bone fish-hook. Clarksville, Indiana	126
Fig. 188.—Bone fish-hook. Cunningham's Island, Ohio	126
Fig. 189.—Bone fish-hook. Sag Harbor, Long Island, New York	127
Fig. 190.—Bone fish-hook. Mound Lake, Cass County, Illinois	127
Fig. 191.—Bone fish-hook. Madisonville, Ohio	127
Fig. 192.—Bone fish-hook. Madisonville, Ohio	128
Fig. 193.—Fish-hook of deer-horn. Onondaga (?) County, New York	128
Figs. 194-195.—Bone fish-hooks. Santa Cruz Island, California	129
Figs. 196-199.—Bone fish-hooks. Santa Cruz Island, California	130
Fig. 200.—Bone fish-hook. Eskimos, Greenland	131
Fig. 201.—Fish-hook of reindeer-horn. Eskimos, Chesterfield Inlet, British America	131
Figs. 202-203.—Shell fish-hooks. Santa Cruz Island, California	131
Figs. 204-205.—Shell fish-hooks. Santa Cruz Island, California	132
Fig. 206.—Shell fish-hook. San Nicolas Island, California	132
Figs. 207-210.—Shell fish-hooks. Santa Cruz Island, California	133
Fig. 211.—Shell fish-hook. San Miguel Island, California	133
Fig. 212.—Series of designs illustrative of the method of making fish-hooks of shell	134
Fig. 213.—Samoan fish-hook of shell with stone sinker	135
Fig. 214.—Fish-hook of turtle-shell (?). Serle Island	136
Fig. 215.—Bone fish-hook. New Zealand	137
Fig. 216.—Copper fish-hook. Mouth of Oconto River, Wisconsin	138
Figs. 217-219.—Fish-hooks made of cactus-spines. Mohaves, Arizona	139
Fig. 220.—Honey-locust twig with spine, cut to resemble a fish-hook	140
Fig. 221.—Bone harpoon-head. Goose Island, Casco Bay, Maine	142
Figs. 222-223.—Bone harpoon-heads. San Nicolas Island, California	142
Figs. 224-225.—Bone harpoon-heads. Unalashka Island, Alaska	143
Fig. 226.—Bone harpoon-head. Greenland Cove, near Damariscotta, Maine	143
Fig. 227.—Bone harpoon-head. Livingstone County, New York	145
Fig. 228.—Bone harpoon-head. Puget Sound, Washington Territory	145
Fig. 229.—Harpoon-head of deer-horn. Onondaga County, New York	145

LIST OF ILLUSTRATIONS.

	PAGE.
Fig. 230.—Harpoon-head of elk-horn. Honeoye Falls, New York	146
Fig. 231.—Bone harpoon-head. Detroit, Michigan	146
Fig. 232.—Bone harpoon-head. Madisonville, Ohio	146
Fig. 233.—Bone harpoon-head. Atka Island, Alaska	147
Fig. 234.—Bone harpoon-head. Port Möller, Peninsula of Aliaska	147
Fig. 235.—Bone harpoon-head. Amaknak Island, Alaska	147
Fig. 236.—Bone harpoon-head. Hodgdon's Island, Maine	148
Fig. 237.—Bone harpoon-head. Muscongus Sound, Maine	148
Fig. 238.—Bone harpoon-head. Stikine River, Alaska	149
Fig. 239.—Bone harpoon-head. Fort Wayne, Michigan	149
Fig. 240.—Harpoon-head of deer-horn. Onondaga County, New York	149
Fig. 241.—Bone dart-head. Ontario County, New York	150
Fig. 242.—Bone dart-head. Goose Island, Casco Bay, Maine	150
Figs. 243-244.—Bone dart-heads. Adakh Island, Alaska	151
Fig. 245.—Bone dart-head. Amaknak Island, Alaska	151
Figs. 246-248.—Harpoon-heads of deer-horn. Elbridge, New York	152
Fig. 249.—Copper dart-head. Fond du Lac, Wisconsin	153
Fig. 250.—Copper dart-head. Waukesha County, Wisconsin	153
Fig. 251.—Copper dart head. Fond du Lac, Wisconsin	153
Fig. 252.—Copper harpoon-head. Thlinkets, Baranoff Island, Alaska	154
Fig. 253.—Modern stone sinker. Dunkirk, New York	157
Figs. 254-257.—Stone sinkers. Muncy, Pennsylvania	158
Fig. 258.—Stone sinker. Muncy, Pennsylvania	159
Fig. 259.—Stone sinker. Muncy, Pennsylvania	160
Fig. 260.—Stone sinker. Tennessee	160
Fig. 261.—Stone sinker. Santa Maria Petapa, Mexico	160
Fig. 262.—Stone sinker. Tiverton, Rhode Island	161
Fig. 263.—Stone sinker. Dos Pueblos, California	161
Fig. 264.—Stone sinker. Chilmark, Martha's Vineyard, Massachusetts	162
Fig. 265.—Stone sinker. Newport, Rhode Island	162
Figs. 266-267.—Stone sinkers. Wickford, Rhode Island	163
Fig. 268.—Stone sinker. Tiverton, Rhode Island	163
Fig. 269.—Stone sinker. Milledgeville, Georgia	163
Figs. 270-271.—Stone sinkers. Oregon	164
Fig. 272.—Stone sinker. La Patera, California	164
Fig. 273.—Stone sinker. Georgia	164
Figs. 274-275.—Stone sinkers. Columbia County, Georgia	164
Fig. 276.—Stone sinker. Mitchell County, North Carolina	165
Fig. 277.—Stone sinker. Putnam County, Georgia	166
Fig. 278.—Stone sinker. Middleborough, Massachusetts	166
Fig. 279.—Stone sinker (?). Santa Cruz Island, California	166
Fig. 280.—Stone sinker. Ohio	167
Fig. 281.—Eskimo stone sinker. Arctic America	167
Fig. 282.—Stone sinker. Mound, Licking County, Ohio	169
Fig. 283.—Sinker of specular iron. Hancock County, Illinois	169
Fig. 284.—Stone sinker. Santa Rosa Island, California	169
Fig. 285.—Cast of stone sinker. Louisiana	169
Fig. 286.—Stone sinker. Tennessee	170
Fig. 287.—Stone sinker. Morehouse Parish, Louisiana	170
Fig. 288.—Sinker of specular iron. Carroll County, Tennessee	170
Fig. 289.—Sinker of red hematite. Saint Charles County, Missouri	170
Fig. 290.—Stone sinker. Tampa Bay, Florida	171
Fig. 291.—Sinker of clay-iron stone. Shell-deposit near Mobile, Alabama	171
Fig. 292.—Sinker of specular iron. Huntington, Cabell County, West Virginia	171
Fig. 293.—Sinker of specular iron. Morehouse Parish, Louisiana	171

LIST OF ILLUSTRATIONS.

	PAGE.
Fig. 294.—Stone sinker. Mound, Henderson County, Illinois	171
Figs. 295–296.—Stone sinkers. Manatee County, Florida	172
Fig. 297.—Cast of stone sinker. Ohio	172
Fig. 298.—Stone sinker. Franklin County, Ohio	172
Fig. 299.—Sinker of specular iron. Mound, Licking County, Ohio	173
Fig. 300.—Stone sinker. Beverly, Massachusetts	174
Fig. 301.—Stone sinker. Eastport, Maine	174
Fig. 302.—Stone sinker. South Kingston, Rhode Island	174
Fig. 303.—Stone sinker. Guadaloupe, California	175
Fig. 304.—Stone sinker. Massachusetts	175
Fig. 305.—Stone sinker. Marblehead, Massachusetts	175
Fig. 306.—Stone sinker. Sarasota Bay, Florida	175
Fig. 307.—Stone sinker. Middleborough, Massachusetts	175
Fig. 308.—Stone sinker. Santa Cruz Island, California	175
Fig. 309.—Stone sinker. Santa Rosa Island, California	176
Fig. 310.—Stone sinker. Saint Croix River, Maine	176
Fig. 311.—Stone sinker. Santa Cruz Island, California	176
Fig. 312.—Stone sinker. California	176
Fig. 313.—Stone sinker (?). San Miguel Island, California	177
Fig. 314.—Sinker of specular iron. Morehouse Parish, Louisiana	177
Fig. 315.—Stone sinker. Arkansas	177
Fig. 316.—Stone sinker. San Miguel Island, California	177
Fig. 317.—Stone sinker. Chester, Illinois	177
Fig. 318.—Stone sinker. Northwest Coast	178
Fig. 319.—Cast of stone sinker. California	178
Fig. 320.—Stone sinker. Cleveland, Ohio	178
Fig. 321.—Eskimo stone sinker. Ukivok Island, Alaska	179
Figs. 322–323.—Stone sinkers. Yellowstone National Park, Wyoming	180
Fig. 324.—Copper sinker. Mound, Marietta, Ohio	181
Fig. 325.—Copper sinker. Mound, Lake County, Ohio	181
Fig. 326.—Cast of shell, prepared to serve as a sinker (?). Florida	182
Fig. 327.—Shell sinker. Sarasota Bay, Florida	182
Fig. 328.—Cast of shell sinker. Florida	182
Fig. 329.—Shell sinker (?). Shell-deposit, Blennerhassett's Island, West Virginia	182
Fig. 330.—Stone fish-cutter. Blackstone, Massachusetts	184
Fig. 331.—Cast of stone fish-cutter. Newark Valley, New York	184
Fig. 332.—Stone fish-cutter. Norristown, Pennsylvania	185
Figs. 333–334.—Stone fish-cutters, one in wooden handle. Eskimos, Norton Sound, Alaska	186
Figs. 335–336.—Iron and stone fish-cutters, that of iron inserted into a wooden handle. Makah Indians, Neah Bay, Washington Territory	187
Fig. 337.—Boat, exhumed near Savannah, Georgia	188
Fig. 338.—Wooden toy-boat. Santa Cruz Island, California	190
Fig. 339.—Wooden bailing-scoop (?). Santa Cruz Island, California	191
Fig. 340.—Paddle. Long Island, New York	191
Fig. 341.—Anchor-stone. Susquehanna River, near Sayre, Pennsylvania	193
Fig. 342.—Anchor-stone. Illinois River, near the mouth of the Sangamon, Illinois	194
Fig. 343.—" Underrunning rock." Gloucester, Massachusetts	196
Fig. 344.—" Killick." Rockport, Massachusetts	197
Fig. 345.—Earthworks in the Etowah Valley, Georgia	198
Fig. 346.—Stone fish-pen. Saratoga County, New York	201
Figs. 347–348.—Stone pipes representing a heron feeding on a fish, and an otter with a fish in its mouth. Mound near Chillicothe, Ohio	205
Fig. 349.—Clay pipe in the shape of a fish (?). Chattanooga, Tennessee	206
Fig. 350.—Piece of slate worked into the likeness of a fish. Stikine River, Alaska	207
Fig. 351.—Fish-shaped object of *Haliotis*-shell. San Nicolas Island, California	207

*3

LIST OF ILLUSTRATIONS.

	PAGE
Fig. 352.—Stone carving representing a fish. Ipswich, Massachusetts	208
Fig. 353.—Stone carving in the form of a cetacean. Seabrook, New Hampshire	209
Fig. 354.—Stone carving representing a cetacean. San Nicolas Island, California	211
Fig. 355.—Stone carving in the shape of a seal. San Nicolas Island, California	211
Fig. 356.—Clay vessel made in imitation of the sun-fish. Phillips County, Arkansas	212
Fig. 357.—Fish-shaped clay vessel. Southeastern Missouri	213
Figs. 358-359.—Fac-simile delineations illustrating Aztec navigation and fishing. From the Mendoza Codex	215
Fig. 360.—Plan showing the location of the principal shell-deposit at Keyport, New Jersey	228
Fig. 361.—Section of under-ground part of a hut. Oregon	252
Fig. 362.—Canoe of the Beothucs. Newfoundland	266
Fig. 363.—Methods of fishing practised by the Virginia Indians. After De Bry	285
Fig. 364.—Virginia Indians smoking fish. After De Bry	286
Fig. 365.—Virginia Indians engaged in boat-making. After De Bry	287
Figs. 366-367.—Bull-hide boat and paddle of poplar wood, made by Minnetarees at Fort Berthold, Dakota	295
Fig. 368.—Makah harpoon-head and line	306
Figs. 369-370.—Makah whaling-canoe and paddle	307
Fig. 371.—Makah canoe showing method of scarfing	309
Figs. 372-373.—Stone sinkers. Ometepec Island, Nicaragua	319
Figs. 374-377.—Sinkers made of fragments of clay vessels. Ometepec Island, Nicaragua	320
Fig. 378.—Stone carving in the form of a fish. Costa Rica	321
Figs. 379-380.—Fish-representations of gold. Chiriqui, United States of Colombia	322
Fig. 381.—Gold fish-hook. State of Cauca, United States of Colombia	323
Fig. 382.—Wooden mask with appended bags. Peru	325
Figs. 383-384.—Reel with line and two copper fish-hooks, and stone sinker. Peru	326
Figs. 385-387.—Copper fish-hooks. Ancon, Peru	327
Figs. 388-389.—Portions of nets. Ancon, Peru	328
Fig. 390.—Fish-shaped clay vessel. Peru	329
Fig. 391.—Fish-shaped clay vessel. Arica, Peru	330
Figs. 392-393.—Fish-shaped clay vessels. Trujillo, Peru	330
Figs. 394-395.—Clay vessel and ornamentation on it enlarged. Peru	331
Figs. 396-403.—Fish-shaped silver ornaments. From one of the Chincha Islands, Peru	333
Fig. 404.—Fish-shaped silver ornament. Gran Chimu, Peru	334
Fig. 405.—Piece of cloth with inwoven fish-designs. Pisco, Peru	335

PART I.—EUROPE.

1.—PALÆOLITHIC AGE.

GENERAL CHARACTERISTICS.

The long period during which man in Europe was not acquainted with the use of metal, and made his implements and weapons of substances less serviceable, yet more immediately offered by the hand of nature, such as wood, bone, horn, but especially stone, is generally termed the Stone Age. It has been divided into two epochs, namely, the earlier or palæolithic (old-stone) age, and the later or neolithic (new-stone) age, these divisions marking unlike conditions in the existence of the ancient inhabitants of Europe. During the palæolithic age the climate of Europe was colder than at present, owing to a refrigeration caused by glacial influences, and man then co-existed, at least in some parts of the continent, with animals forming a fauna distinct from that of later times. The evidences of his presence at that remote epoch, in the shape of relics left by him, have been derived from quaternary drift-beds and from caves, and will be more minutely considered under these heads. This age presents man under somewhat differing aspects, a separate treatment of which appears preferable to a synoptical description. As a special feature of the period, however, it should be mentioned that the stone implements pertaining to it, and nearly always made of flint, are, so far as known, simply fashioned by flaking and chipping, the practice of improving such implements by grinding and polishing being considered as characteristic of neolithic times. The art of making vessels of clay, it may also be added, appears to have been unknown to palæolithic man.

THE DRIFT.

Implements and Animal Remains.—The flint implements found in the quaternary deposits along certain rivers in France and England are the oldest objects fashioned by man of which we thus far have any positive knowledge.* These

---

* The existence of "tertiary man" in Europe, still involved in uncertainty, is not touched upon in this publication.

drift-beds, formed by layers of sand, gravel, and loam, also contain the bones of animals of that period, some of which are now extinct, like the mammoth and a few other species of elephant, several kinds of rhinoceros, the urus, and Irish elk; while others, as the hippopotamus, the cave-bear, cave-lion, and cave-hyena, may still survive under more or less modified forms. Certain quadrupeds, which have left their osseous remains in the quaternary deposits of Western Europe, still exist as before, but no longer in their ancient habitats, as, for instance, the reindeer and the musk-ox. The former inhabits now the coldest district of Europe, and the musk-ox, entirely extinct in that part of the world, is at present confined to the snow-regions bordering on Hudson's Bay. On the whole, the fauna of the European drift was richer and more varied than that of our time, for it comprised, besides the extinct mammalians, most of the now existing species. Yet, as mentioned, the temperature of Europe was lower than at present, or else such quadrupeds as the mammoth, woolly rhinoceros, reindeer, and musk-ox—all fitted for a cold climate—could not have subsisted in the latitudes where their fossil bones now occur.

The preceding condensed statements were made for the purpose of indicating, to some extent at least, the surroundings of the human beings who lived at the long-past period here under consideration. That they occupied a very low position in the scale of human development is shown by the character of the flint tools preserved in the quaternary deposits. These "drift-implements" were first discovered, about forty years ago, by M. Boucher de Perthes, in the ancient gravel-beds of the river Somme, in the neighborhood of Abbeville, in Picardy, and afterward found at Saint-Acheul, near Amiens, in the same province. They have subsequently been exhumed from corresponding deposits in other parts of France, and in various localities of England. The implements were split from nodules of flint so frequently occurring in the chalk; some of them even exhibit portions of the chalky crust which usually surrounds these flinty bodies. The prevailing forms of the flint tools are those of very roughly wrought large spear-heads, and of oval or almond-shaped flattish pieces, sharpened around their edges, and likewise exhibiting, at least in most cases, no high degree of skill on the part of their makers. The tools of the latter kind are sometimes denominated "hatchets," it being believed that a number of them were inserted in cleft sticks, and fastened with sinews or strips of hide of animals, thus fulfilling the purpose which their name implies. To these forms must be added flakes of various shapes and sizes, many of which, doubtless, were split off during the process of fashioning the more finished tools already mentioned. Others may have been detached intentionally, to serve as cutting-tools, and a few are worked into a rude scraper-form. The shape of the implements designated as spear-heads and hatchets depended, in all probability, much on the original outline of the chalk-flints from which they were manufactured. These nodules are mostly of a roundish or elongated form; and in making their tools the ancient people knocked two of them together, until flattish fragments of suitable size came off, which they brought into the required shape by blows aimed at their circumference. Hence many of the implements are not exactly of oval or spear-like forms, but present shapes intermediate between them. As a rule, the narrower or more pointed end of these instruments is the one adapted for cutting. The tools of the spear-head type usually vary in length from six to eight inches, though larger ones have been found. Many of them seem to have been used with the hand, the end opposite the pointed part being often thick and massive, to facilitate handling; and in some the lower end is not fashioned at all, but left in its original state, when the form of the flint presented a suitable handle. Others, which are worked thinner at the lower end, perhaps were fastened to poles, and thus actually served as spear-heads. Arrow-points have not been found in the drift, and hence it appears probable that the drift-people were ignorant of archery.

It can hardly be supposed that the types of implements here briefly noticed exhaust the stock of tools or weapons used by the early contemporary of the mammoth, for others, made of less durable materials, such as bone and horn, may have decayed in the gravel-beds, leaving no traces to indicate their former presence. None of the latter kind, as far as I know, have been discovered in the drift-deposits.

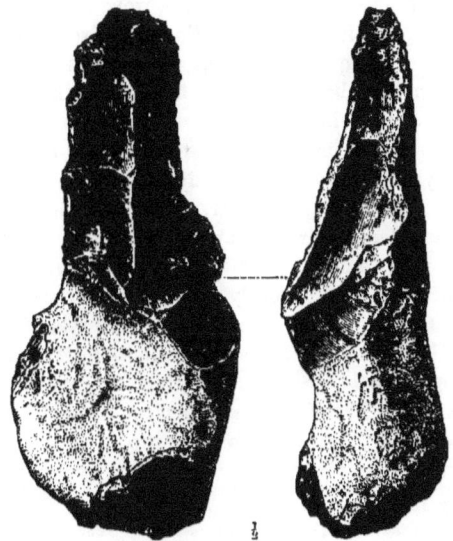

Fig. 1.—Drift-implement. Saint-Acheul. (35095).

Implements used as Ice-picks (?).—Though the savage men who formed the simple stone instruments under notice depended for subsistence on the chase and, presumably, on fishing, we are in the dark as to the methods employed by them in these pursuits. The quaternary beds have yielded no objects directly referable to fishing; yet it has been thought that some of the thick-handled pointed flint implements may have been used for making holes in the ice, in order to catch fish or aquatic mammals frequenting the great rivers at that time. In the arctic regions, it is known, the natives dig holes in the ice, and patiently wait for hours at the apertures, until the seals, coming to the surface to breathe, can be struck and secured for food. Amphibious animals, perhaps, ascended the quaternary rivers, and were captured as stated.*

I give in Fig. 1 on page 3 a representation of a drift-implement from Saint-Acheul, near Amiens, which *may* have served as an ice-pick. The lower part, or handle, as will be seen, shows the unaltered surface of the chalk-flint; the worked portion is somewhat chisel-shaped. It belongs to the series of European drift-implements exhibited in the United States National Museum.

CAVES AND ROCK-SHELTERS.

Retreats of Man during the Reindeer-period.—More definite results bearing upon the condition of the early inhabitants of Europe have been obtained of late years by the careful exploration of caves in England, France, Belgium, Germany, Switzerland, and other European countries. The caves to which I shall refer were resorted to by palæolithic man,† who has left in them such traces of his occupancy as enable us to form a more or less distinct view of his mode of life. Explorations of these early sheltering-places of man, I may state, are carried on with great energy in Europe, and already have given rise to a, literature of considerable extent. The results, however, present only local differences, while, on the whole, the conclusions arrived at are the same, namely, that in times anteceding any historical record or tradition, tribes of savage men lived in certain parts of Europe contemporaneously with various species of animals, which have either become extinct, or have migrated to other parts of Europe, or even to other continents. However, as it is not my purpose to give an account of cave-researches in Europe, but of prehistoric fishing, my observations will chiefly refer to those caves which have furnished the most abundant material for illustrating the latter subject. Among them a group situated in the valley of the

---

* Sauvage (Dr. H. E.): On Fishing during the Reindeer-Period; Reliquiæ Aquitanicæ; I, p. 219. The editor of this work, Professor T. R. Jones, adds in a note: "Some roughly dressed flints found in the quaternary gravels may have been 'sinkers' and imitation baits, such as the Eskimos use in fishing and angling."—It is questionable whether the drift-men were far enough advanced to resort to such devices.

† Some caves in Europe undoubtedly served as human habitations in neolithic times.

Vézère, an affluent of the Dordogne, which flows through a portion of Southwestern France, known in ancient times under the name of Aquitania, chiefly claims our attention. The valley of the Vézère is very rich in caves, which occur in the picturesque formations of cretaceous limestone bordering on the meandering river, and form a peculiar feature in its beautiful scenery. These caves, however, are not at all distinguished by vast proportions, some being mere hollows or "rock-shelters" (*abris* in French), owing their origin to the disintegration of soft strata which offered less resistance to atmospheric influences than the harder rocks covering them. In times long past, rude hunters and fishers used these hollowed rocks as dwelling-places, leaving there abundant tokens of their occupancy, which afford the means of judging of their conditions of existence.

The best-known of these caves and shelters—situated on both sides of the Vézère at short distances from each other, and all embraced in the Department of the Dordogne—are *Le Moustier, La Madelaine, Laugerie Haute, Laugerie Basse, Gorge d'Enfer, Les Eyzies,* and *Cro-Magnon.* They were conjointly explored by M. Edouard Lartet, a distinguished French palæontologist, and Mr. Henry Christy, an English gentleman of wealth and great scientific acquirements. Their efforts resulted in the publication of the "Reliquiæ Aquitanicæ," a comprehensive and richly-illustrated work, which, notwithstanding its Latin title, is written in the English language.*

In prehistoric times the above-named localities, or "stations," as they have been called, undoubtedly were inhabited by man for a lengthened period, during which the numerical proportion of some of the then existing species of animals seems to have undergone changes, while in the same epoch a decided progress is traceable in the mechanical acquirements of man. So much may be inferred from the animal remains and works of art found in the different caves of the Vézère.† Generally speaking, the refuse left by the cave-men, or *troglodytes*, in the caves under notice consists of bones (many of them broken for extracting the marrow), pebbles, and articles of flint, horn, and bone, intermingled with charcoal in fragments and dust: the whole often being cemented together, and forming a kind of tufa. These accumulations sometimes extend to a depth of

---

* Reliquiæ Aquitanicæ; being Contributions to the Archæology and Palæontology of Périgord and the adjoining Provinces of Southern France. By Edouard Lartet and Henry Christy. Edited by Thomas Rupert Jones. 1865-75. London, 1875.

† Sir Charles Lyell remarks, concerning the unequal representation of animal remains in the caves, as follows : "M. Lartet has founded a classification upon the prevalence of certain animals in the débris; the mammoth and cave-bear characterizing the earlier, and the reindeer the later deposits. But as the same species occur throughout, and as most of the remains were brought there by man, the abundance of any particular animal may not indicate the prevalence of that species at the time, but only the success of the hunters, or the sojourn of migratory animals in the neighborhood."—*The Geological Evidences of the Antiquity of Man;* London and Philadelphia, 1873; p. 135.

eight or ten feet, and a length of sixty or seventy feet. The cave-people of the Vézère district were more advanced and lived at a later period than the men whose implements are found in the drift-beds of the Somme and of other rivers. These conclusions have been drawn from the fauna of the caves and from the greater skill displayed by the cave-dwellers in the manufacture of their implements of war and peace. At the time when these caves served as the abodes of hunting-tribes, the mammoth, cave-hyena, cave-lion, cave-bear, gigantic Irish deer, and others, had not yet become extinct, but had apparently much decreased in number, while the reindeer, now inhabiting the northernmost portions of Europe, was prevailing,—for which reason this epoch has been styled the Reindeer-period by archæologists. Together with the reindeer, as common in the time of its preponderance, must be mentioned the horse, aurochs, ibex, and chamois, the last two of which have now left the lowlands and sought refuge in the more congenial temperature of Alpine heights. The *Antilope saïga*, an animal which now inhabits portions of Russia and Asia, belonged at that time to the fauna of Europe, as shown by a number of its bones found by M. Lartet and others. Remains of the mammoth and of the other extinct quadrupeds previously mentioned are of very rare occurrence in these caves, insomuch that it would appear doubtful whether the cave-men co-existed with them, if their representations, traced on horn and bone, or carved from such substances, had not been found in some of the caves. The character of the cave-fauna indicates a still rigid climate.

The animals most frequently hunted by the troglodytes, and furnishing their principal food, were the reindeer and the horse; the first-named quadruped being of additional value to them on account of its antlers, which they worked very skillfully into implements of various descriptions. It appears, however, that they fed on every kind of animal they could obtain by force or cunning, not excepting carnivores, such as wolves and foxes. Remains of the stag are said to be rare, and still rarer those of the wild boar. At some stations bones of birds and fishes occur abundantly. Further on I shall speak more in detail concerning the latter remains. It does not appear that these people kept any domesticated animals; neither the reindeer nor the horse seems to have been tamed by them. They had no sheep, goats, or cattle, and there were no dogs to protect the cave-men's rude dwellings or to share with them the excitement of the chase.

The reindeer-hunters of the Dordogne displayed, as has been stated, much more skill in the manufacture of implements than the people whose relics are found in the river-gravels and in the cave-deposits of earlier date. Flint continued to be the kind of stone almost exclusively used by them; but the articles made of this material show a great variety of forms, and sometimes a finish which almost assimilates them to the manufactures of the later or neolithic phase of the stone age. Yet, the people of the Vézère Valley were still ignorant of the art of grinding and polishing stone implements, no article thus improved having been discovered in the cave-deposits, excepting small boulders with a shallow cup-shaped cavity ground in on one side, which were found at several stations. They may have served as paint-mortars or for bruising vegetable substances. The accumulations in the caves contain "innumerable chips and countless thousands of blades of flint, varying in size from lance-heads, long enough and stout enough to have been used against the largest animals, down to lancets not larger than the blade of a pen-knife, and piercing-instruments of the size of the smallest bodkin."* Quite numerous are the so-called nuclei, or cores, that is, blocks of flint from which flakes have been detached, to be afterward prepared for definite uses, such as cutting, sawing, etc. Well-made spear-heads of flint have been found, and also objects resembling arrow-heads in size and shape. Flint scrapers, like those still used by the Eskimos for cleaning hides, have occurred in great number at different stations, as, for instance, at Cro-Magnon. The flint implements of Le Moustier somewhat approach the drift-types, and are generally of a ruder character than the chipped articles found at the other stations, which fact, in connection with various other circumstances, renders it almost certain that this cave was inhabited by man at a much earlier epoch than any other of the group under notice. The contents of the caves, I may state in this place, exhibit no uniformity in the products of human industry, having been inhabited by the hunters for a very long period, during which they improved perceptibly in the mechanical arts. I must refrain, however, from entering upon a detailed description of each cave or shelter, as it appears sufficient for my purpose to present a general view of troglodytic life in the valley of the Vézère.

The implements of horn and bone, which evince still more skill and patient labor than the flint tools just briefly noticed, were likewise manufactured in the caves, many unfinished articles of this class having been discovered in the rubbish. Among such relics I will mention chisels, awls, needles with diminutive holes, round and tapering lance-heads (with beveled lower ends for insertion into wooden shafts), harpoon-shaped darts, large and small,† spoon-like instruments (supposed to have served for extracting marrow from bones), whistles, and various other objects, the use of which is not always quite evident. These tools and weapons are mostly cut from reindeer-horn, a material of great hardness, and therefore well fitted for the purposes to which it was applied. Generally speaking, articles of reindeer-antler are most abundant in the caves supposed to have been the later retreats of the ancient hunters of the Vézère Valley.

There are indications that the cave-dwellers were not insensible to the charms of personal decoration. They probably painted themselves, in the fashion of still existing savage tribes, with red color, which they scraped off from pieces of soft

---

* Lartet and Christy: Reliquiæ Aquitanicæ; I, p. 21.
† To be considered hereafter.

red hematite. Such pieces, with the marks of scraping, have been found in the caves. They also employed, for ornamental purposes, shells, which they pierced with holes, in order to string them together. In the cave of Cro-Magnon* were found about three hundred pierced shells (mostly *Littorina littorea*), all belonging to still existing marine species, and probably obtained from the shores of the Atlantic Ocean. At other stations pierced fossil marine shells, doubtless derived from the *Faluns* or shell-marls of Touraine, have occurred. They further wore small oval plates of ivory, pierced for suspension, and, perhaps, as trophies of the chase or as amulets, perforated teeth of the wolf, urus, ibex, reindeer, horse, and other animals.

Strange as it appears, these people evinced, notwithstanding their otherwise low condition, a decided taste for drawing, and even for carving. Their delineations, traced with a pointed flint on horn, bone, ivory, or slate, consist occasionally of geometrical figures composed of parallel lines, rows of dots, lozenges, etc., but mostly of outlines of fishes or of quadrupeds, such as the horse, reindeer, stag, ibex, aurochs, mammoth, and others. These animals appear either singly or in groups, and often exhibit their characteristic features in a degree to render them recognizable almost at the first glance. Sometimes, however, the drawings resemble the first attempts of children at delineating animals. Such representations have chiefly been found at the stations of Les Eyzies, Laugerie Basse, and La Madelaine. Of special interest are those of the mammoth, of which several have been discovered, engraved as well as carved, and showing the characteristics of the extinct proboscidian so faithfully, that no one could have executed them who had not seen the living original.

The figures of animals are often traced on the stems or beams of reindeer-antlers, which are in such cases carefully worked, and pierced at the broader extremity with round holes, varying in number from one to four. These remarkable objects cannot have served as weapons, being too light for such an application; yet their frequent occurrence and uniformity of type show that they possessed a conventional significance, and therefore have been regarded as badges of authority or distinction worn by the chiefs or prominent men of the tribe, like the batons which in our day indicate the dignity of a marshal. The number of holes in these decorated reindeer-horns is thought by some to have been proportionate to the position occupied by the wearer. Supposing this interpretation to be correct, it would follow that the troglodytes already were sufficiently numerous to form a society in which the distinctions of rank were recognized.

Before concluding this short general account of the troglodytes who once

---

* This cave, discovered in 1868 in the course of railroad-labors, was, to judge from the different layers, first merely resorted to at different times by hunters, but afterward used as a habitation, until the accumulated rubbish gradually raised the floor so as to leave but little room between it and the roof. The cave was then abandoned by the living, but still served them as a burial-place for their dead. The remains of five individuals were found in it.

dwelled in the valley of the Vézère, it may not be out of place to review their condition of existence in a few words, in order to show in what respects they differed from later and more advanced men of the European stone age, to whom reference will be made hereafter:—

They subsisted by hunting and fishing, adding, as may be assumed, to their animal food such fruits as were spontaneously offered by nature. They had made no steps toward an agricultural state, and domesticated animals probably were entirely wanting. As dwellings they used caves, overhanging rocks, and doubtless rude huts constructed of boughs, skins, or other materials. Their tools and weapons were made, sometimes very skillfully, of stone, horn, and bone. They employed only *chipped* stone implements, and were unacquainted with the art of making vessels of clay. Their dress consisted of skins sewed together with sinews. An artistic tendency, which manifests itself in primitive attempts at drawing and carving, must be regarded as a feature distinguishing them from the populations of the later stone age.

As may be imagined, the stations of the reindeer-period, in France, are not confined to the valley of the Vézère, many others having been discovered in different parts of that country, and in Europe generally. But I know of a few only, in addition, which have yielded relics perhaps designed for fishing-purposes, and these are the "Kesslerloch," near Thayngen, in the Canton of Schaffhausen, Switzerland, and Kent's Cavern, near Torquay, Devonshire, England. The Swiss cave contained a large number of animal remains, among them those of the reindeer and alpine hare in greatest abundance, implements of flint, harpoon-heads and other objects of bone and horn, and even engraved designs of animals.

Kent's Cavern appears to have been resorted to by man at an earlier period than any of the French caves previously mentioned; for there were found in it abundantly not only the remains of the horse and reindeer, but also those of the cave-lion, cave-hyena, and cave-bear; and while bones of the mammoth are not very common, remains of the woolly rhinoceros have occurred quite frequently.* The flint implements of Kent's Cavern are not unlike those from the caves of the Vézère Valley. Only a few objects of horn and bone have come to light, three of them being harpoon-heads.

As far as I know, only one representation of an animal has been discovered in an English cave, namely, the delineation of a horse (head and fore-quarters) on a smoothed fragment of a rib. This specimen of ancient art was met with in the Robin-Hood Cave, at Cresswell Crags, Northeastern Derbyshire.

The question to what race or races the men of the palæolithic epoch belonged is yet undecided. Comparatively few human remains referable to quaternary times have been discovered, and the skulls which were in a condition to permit examination, exhibit both the brachycephalous and dolichocephalous types. The attempts to identify these men with historically known or still existing popula-

---

* Teeth of the sabre-toothed tiger (*Machairodus latidens*), first noticed in the *tertiary*, were also found.

tions, such as Lapps and Finns, are, for the present, merely speculative in character. Their surroundings compelled them to live much in the manner of the Eskimos, but this is no proof that they *were* Eskimos, as some are inclined to believe.* At any rate, they are regarded as men differing in race from those occupying Europe in the later or neolithic period, to which reference will be made in the sequel.

I now pass over to a consideration of the piscatorial pursuits carried on by the cave-men of the Vézère and of other districts, treating first of the fish-remains discovered in the caves, then of the implements supposed to have been employed by the troglodytes for obtaining fish, and lastly of the engraved delincations of fishes and aquatic mammals rescued from the cave-rubbish.

Fish-remains.—They have occurred abundantly at La Madelaine, in the cave of Les Eyzies, and particularly in the rock-shelter of Bruniquel, situated on the left bank of the river Aveyron, in the Department of Tarn-et-Garonne, and not far from Montauban. In some caves of the Vézère Valley (Le Moustier, Gorge d'Enfer, Cro-Magnon), which are supposed to have been inhabited at an early time, when the reindeer was less numerous than it became afterward, no fish-bones, and hardly any bird-remains, have been found, and these are just the stations in which barbed darts of reindeer-horn were absent. "There was not, therefore," says M. Edouard Lartet, "in the mode of living an absolute conformity between the people of these two periods, though inhabiting the same country, and in the neighborhood of the river, rich probably with fish then as now. Could it be that the more ancient people had no good fishing-implements? Or, perhaps, were they in the habit of eating their fish raw on the banks of the river, whilst their descendants, or successors of a different race, preferred to take their fish to the caves and shelters where they cooked their other articles of food? Indeed, some modern travelers tell us of existing savages living near the sea and yet ignorant of the means of obtaining fish therefrom as an article of food."†

Dr. Paul Broca, in speaking of the earlier retreats in the Vézère Valley, expresses himself quite positively on that point. "Man," he says, "hunted then the smaller animals as well as large game, but had not yet learned how to reach the fish."‡ It does not appear at all probable to me that the more ancient cave-dwellers should have neglected the practice of obtaining fish in some way. The absence of fish-bones in certain caves may be owing to causes which escape our perception at this time.

---

* The Eskimos are decidedly dolichocephalous.

† Lartet (Edouard): Remarks on the Fauna found in the Cave of Cro-Magnon; Reliquiæ Aquitanicæ; I, p. 95.

‡ Broca: The Troglodytes or Cave-Dwellers of the Valley of the Vézère; Smithsonian Report for 1872; p. 323. [Translation of an address delivered before the French Association for the Advancement of Science].

The remains of the salmon have been found abundantly in the breccia of a number of caves in the Dordogne district and in neighboring regions in the South of France, and hence it may be concluded that this species of fish served largely for food among the people of the reindeer-age. Yet, among the numerous salmon-remains, which were carefully examined by Dr. H. E. Sauvage, not a single entire skeleton has been discovered. He has seen only portions of the vertebral column, as if nothing but the edible part of the fish had been brought to the caves. Had the salmon-heads been there, they would have been as well preserved as those of the small cyprinoids which are found in the same deposits. He refers to some species of salmon common in the Northwest of America, as *Salmo quinnat*, Richardson, *Salmo Gairdneri*, Richardson, *Salmo paucidens*, Richardson, *Salmo lycaodon*, Pallas, and *Salmo proteus*, Pallas, and then continues:—

".Unfortunately we have no materials for the study and comparison of the osteology of these different salmons; hence it is impossible for us to refer any of the salmon-bones found in the reindeer-caves to one rather than another of these species. Indeed, we have been unable to recognize any difference between the salmon vertebræ from the caves and those of the living *Salmo salar*, Linné, although we have taken care to compare vertebræ from the same region and of the same size, derived from individuals presumably of the same age.

"We know that the salmon has a very wide geographical distribution, the same species being met with in Scandinavia, Russia, Germany, France, Galicia, Britain, Iceland, and in North America, according to Mitchill, Storer, Richardson, DeKay, Günther, and other naturalists; the salmon reaching very high latitudes.

"The mammalian fauna of the reindeer-age is that of the boreal regions of to-day; the birds killed by the cave-dwellers of Périgord* are the birds of this region; the shells they used for ornament, obtained from the shores of the Atlantic and Mediterranean, are such as live there still. It is therefore highly probable, not to say certain, that the existing *Salmo salar* was the common salmon of the Dordogne, affording food to the cave-dwellers of the Vézère."†

It is worthy of notice that at the present time the salmon does not come up as high as the Vézère, nor even to that part of the Dordogne, into which the Vézère empties. "A few leagues below the confluence of the two streams, not far from Lalinde," says Dr. Broca, "there exists in the bed of the Dordogne a bank of rocks, which in high water forms a rapid and at low water a regular cascade, called the *Saut de la Gratusse*. This is the present limit of the salmon, and as, in the days of the troglodytes, they did not stop here, we must conclude that the level of the Dordogne since then has lowered, either by the wearing down of the bed

---

* An old division of France, which now forms the Department of Dordogne and a part of that of Gironde.

† Sauvage: On Fishing during the Reindeer-Period; Reliquiæ Aquitanicæ; I, p. 221.

of the river, which uncovered the rocks, or by loss of a portion of the waters.* Another fish of the salmon tribe, a trout, doubtless the common trout (*Salmo fario* or *Trutta fario*), was also caught by the cave-men, but it does not seem to have been extensively used as an article of food. Remains of the pike (*Esox lucius*) are not wanting in the Dordogne caves; but they are less abundant than those of the salmon. The pike, says Dr. Sauvage, is common throughout Europe, from Scandinavia to Turkey, Northern Asia and North America, and attains a large development in cold countries.

Together with the species just mentioned, some other fishes were taken by the troglodytes of the Vézère district. Dr. Sauvage found in their hearth-stuffs the remains of the white bream (*Abramis blicca*), now common in Holland, England, France, and Germany; also bones of the bream or carp-bream (*Abramis brama*), of the dace (*Squalius leuciscus*), and of the chub (*Squalius cephalus*), all of which are now distributed from the North of Europe to the Pyrenees, and belong to the cyprinoid or carp family.

"To resume, the salmon appears to have been of great importance as food with the cave-dwellers of Périgord, and it is probable that they migrated in search of this fish; whilst in their every-day fishing they caught trout, pike, bream, white bream, dace, and chub."†

Fishing and Fishing-implements.—It seems to be a prevailing opinion that man was a fish-hunter before he became a fish-catcher, or, in other words, that the spearing and shooting of fish preceded the methods of capturing them by means of lines and nets. However that may be, there have been found in the cave-débris of Southern France bone implements which are identical in shape with a class still used for catching fishes and birds. I allude to small bone rods tapering toward both ends, and sometimes grooved around the middle, to facilitate the fastening of a line. Such a primitive fishing-utensil—it hardly can be called a fish-hook—is properly baited, and when swallowed by a fish or bird, cannot be disgorged, and the creature falls a prey to man.

These pointed rods are employed in fishing on the Northwest Coast of America, as, for instance, by the Makah Indians, who inhabit the region about Cape Flattery, in Washington Territory. "For very small fish, like perch or rock-fish," says Mr. James G. Swan, "they simply fasten a small piece of bone to a line of sinews. The bone is made as sharp as a needle at both ends, and is tied in the middle."‡

I give in Fig. 2 the representation of one of a series of double-pointed and

---

* Broca: The Troglodytes; p. 328.

† Sauvage: On Fishing during the Reindeer-Period; Reliquiæ Aquitanicæ; I, p. 225, *et passim*.

‡ Swan: The Indians of Cape Flattery, at the Entrance to the Strait of Fuca, Washington Territory; No. 220 of Smithsonian Contributions to Knowledge; Washington, 1869; p. 41.

grooved bone implements in the United States National Museum, obtained from Eskimos of Norton Sound, in Alaska, by Mr. E. W. Nelson, who went to that region in 1877, and remained there about four years, engaged in investigations

FIG. 2.—Double-pointed bone implement used in catching birds. Eskimos, Norton Sound, Alaska. (48571).

in the interest of the United States Signal Office and the National Museum. These pointed rods, Mr. Nelson informs me, are used by the natives for catching sea-gulls and murres, which they eat, using also the skins of the latter as a material for coats. A cord made of braided grass, and from fifteen to eighteen inches long, is looped to the groove of these pointed bones, and fastened laterally with the other end to a trawl-line kept extended by anchored buoys,* the bone being baited with a small fish, into which it is inserted lengthwise. The trawl-lines, with the short baited cords attached to them at intervals, are set near the breeding-places of those birds.

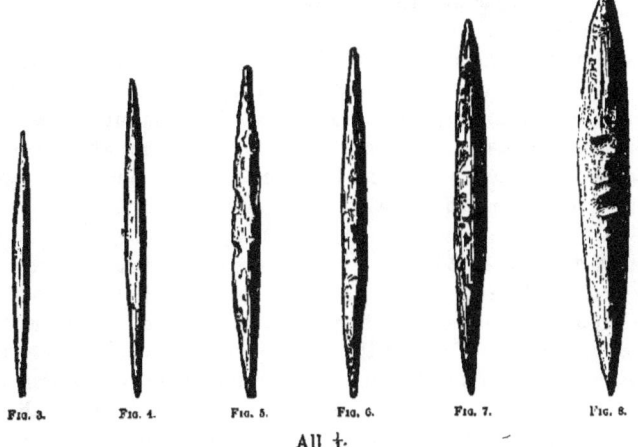

FIGS. 3-8.—Double-pointed bone implements. La Madelaine.

Similar bone rods, as stated, have occurred in French caves inhabited during the reindeer-period. Figs. 3 to 8† represent a number of such pointed implements

---

* The buoys are either worked blocks of wood or inflated bladders of seals, walruses, etc., and the anchors ordinary stones of suitable size. The stone is attached to the buoy by a raw-hide line.

† Reliquiæ Aquitanicæ; Figs. 10-15 on B Plate VI.

of different sizes, all found at the station of La Madelaine, which, however, is not the only one in Southern France that has furnished such objects. Two of those here figured show notchings, and there is at least some probability that they served in the manner before described.

M. Lartet, however, gives it as Mr. Christy's opinion "that they may have formed part of fish-hooks, having been tied to other bones or sticks obliquely; and, indeed, in the specimen Fig. 12 (here Fig. 5) there are notches made at intervals along the stem, and one of its ends is flattened on one side, so as to allow of its being laid against another piece and tied securely on."* In order to illustrate this method, M. Lartet figures† what he calls a "fishing-implement from Nootka Sound," yet without indicating for what special purpose and in what manner it was used. "Such thin tapering pieces of wood or bone are tied securely, at a certain angle, on the thicker part, and within the curve of a stick bent like a shepherd's crook. Sometimes the spikes are sharp at both ends, but more often they are blunt at the outer end."‡

The implement figured by him is a *halibut-hook*, identical in shape with one represented by Mr. Swan in his work on the Makah Indians of Cape Flattery. I give his illustration as Fig. 9, which represents the object much reduced, halibut-hooks being generally from five to ten inches long.§

"The halibut-hook," he says, "is a peculiarly-shaped instrument, and is made of splints from hemlock-knots bent in a form somewhat resembling an ox-bow. These knots remain perfectly sound long after the body of the tree has decayed, and are exceedingly tough. They are selected in preference to those of spruce, because there is no pitch in them to offend the fish, which will not bite at a hook that smells of resin. The knots are first split into small (slender ?) pieces, which, after being shaped with a knife, are inserted into a hollow piece of the stem of the kelp and roasted or steamed in the hot ashes until they are pliable; they are then bent into the required form, and tied until they are cold, when they retain the shape given them. A barb made of a piece of bone is firmly lashed on to the lower side of the hook with slips of spruce cut thin like a ribbon, or with strips of bark of the wild cherry. The upper arm of the hook is slightly curved outward, and wound round with bark, to keep it from splitting. A thread made of whale-sinews is usually fastened to the hook for the purpose of tying on the bait, and another of the same material, loosely twisted, serves to fasten the hook to the kelp line. As the halibut's mouth is vertical, instead of horizontal like that of most other fish, it readily takes the hook, the upper

---

* Reliquiæ Aquitanicæ; II, p. 58.—In a note on the same page it is said that "these bone spikes, lashed on obliquely by their middle to the beveled end of a shaft, may also have served for both point and barb of a dart, such as the Australians make out of a long stick and a kangaroo's fibula sharpened at both ends."

† Ibid.; II, p. 51.

‡ Ibid.; II, p. 55.

§ Schoolcraft figures on Plate 35 of Vol. III of his large work a similar hook from Oregon, but gives no information concerning its use.

portion of which passes outside and over the corner of the mouth, and acts as a sort of spring to fasten the barb into the fish's jaw. The Indians prefer this kind of hook for halibut fishing, although they can readily procure metal ones from the white traders. — — —

"The lines used in the halibut-fishing are usually made of the stems of the gigantic kelp. A line attached to one of the arms of the halibut-hook holds it in a vertical position, as shown in Fig. 9. The bait used is the cuttlefish or

Fig. 9.—Halibut-hook. Makah Indians, Cape Flattery.

squid (*Octopus tuberculatus*), which is plentiful and is taken by the natives by means of barbed sticks, which they thrust under the rocks at low water, to draw the animal out and kill it by transfixing it with the stick. A portion of the squid is firmly attached to the hook, which is sunk by means of a stone to the bottom, the sinker keeping the hook nearly in a stationary position. To the upper portion of the line it is usual to attach bladders, which serve as buoys, and several are set at one time. When the fish is hooked, it pulls the bladder, but cannot draw it under water. The Indian, seeing the signal, paddles out; hauls up the line; knocks the fish on the head with a club; readjusts his bait; casts it overboard; and proceeds to the next bladder he sees giving token of a fish. When a number of Indians are together in a large canoe, and the fish bite readily, it is usual to fish from the canoe without using the buoy."*

Fig. 10.—Codfish-hook. Makah Indians, Cape Flattery.

Fig. 10, also one of Mr. Swan's illustrations, shows the form of a Makah codfish-hook, which, though much simpler than the halibut-hook, is somewhat

---

*Swan: The Indians of Cape Flattery; pp. 41 and 23.

similarly constructed. Such a hook consists of a straight piece of wood, from four to six inches long, to which a bone barb is lashed on, as shown in the figure.*

I shall have more to say concerning hooks of similar make, when treating of prehistoric fishing in North America.

The questions whether the tapering bone rods from the French caves were employed either in their simple form as primitive fishing-implements, or as barbs in the construction of real hooks, or for both purposes, unfortunately cannot be positively answered at the present time, and it would not be safe to go beyond the suggestion that such *may* have been their use or uses. Possibly they were designed for other applications. Hereafter it will be seen that such pointed bones served as fishing-implements in the neolithic period.

M. Gabriel de Mortillet seems to be mistaken in attributing the character of fish-hooks to some of the bone objects found in the caves of Southern France. He says:—

"Hooks belonging to the reindeer-epoch have also been found in the caves and retreats of Dordogne, so well explored by Messrs. Lartet and Christy. Along with those of the simple form which we have just described,† others were met with of a much more perfect shape. These are likewise small fragments of bone or reindeer's horn, with deep and wide notches on one side, forming a more or less developed series of projecting and sharp teeth, or barbs. Two of them are depicted in B Plate VI of the 'Reliquiæ Aquitanicæ.'"‡

Among the figures on the plate referred to by M. de Mortillet there is not one that bears the slightest resemblance to a fish-hook, and M. Lartet, in describing the represented objects, designates none of them by that name.

While there is some doubt whether the cave-men of Southern France practised fishing with a line, it may be taken for granted that they procured fish by spearing, implements suited for that purpose having been discovered in great number in the débris of the caves. These implements, harpoon-like in character and well shaped, are generally cut from reindeer-horn, and the endurance displayed in their manufacture is really astonishing, in consideration of the stubbornness of the material, which had to be reduced to the proper shape by means of sawing, cutting, and scraping with simple tools of flint.

Figs. 11 to 15 represent characteristic forms of these harpoon-shaped dart-heads of reindeer-horn, which, whether barbed only on one side or on both, exhibit near the tapering lower end little eminences or knobs, the purpose of which will be considered hereafter. The barbs in the figured specimens are

---

* Swan: The Indians of Cape Flattery; p. 41.

† The pointed pieces of bone.

‡ De Mortillet: L'Origine de la Navigation et de la Pêche (Paris, 1867, p. 25); quoted in Figuier's "Primitive Man;" New York, 1870; p. 90.—I never saw M. de Mortillet's publication.

provided with incisions or grooves, supposed by some to have served for the reception of poison, an opinion which I hardly can share, in consideration of the fact that the arrow-shafts of many Indian tribes, such as the Sioux, Cheyennes,

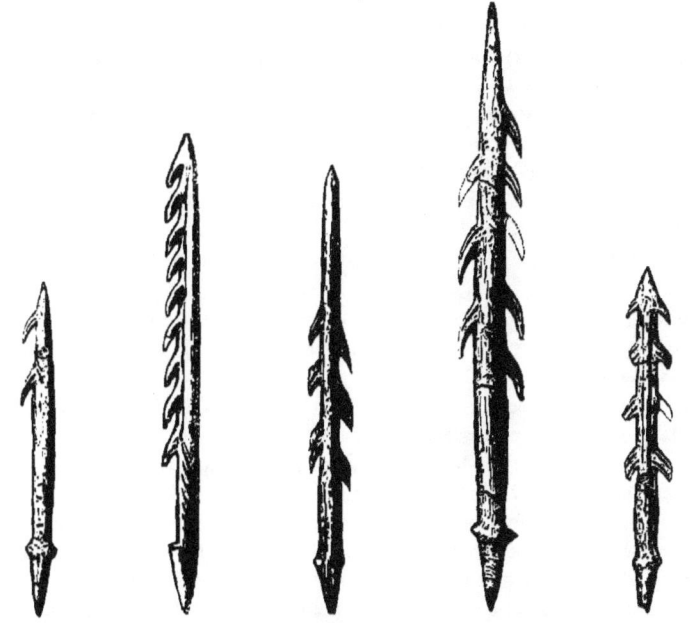

Fig. 11.—La Madelaine.   Fig. 12.—Bruniquel.   Fig. 13.—La Madelaine.   Fig. 14.—La Madelaine.   Fig. 15.—La Madelaine.
All ½.
Figs. 11–15.—Harpoon-heads of reindeer-horn.

Tonkaways, Navajos, Pai-Utes, and others, exhibit longitudinal grooves, intended to facilitate the flow of the wounded animal's blood.* There are three of these grooves, cut in at equal distances, and usually forming irregular wave lines, as shown in Fig. 16 which represents an iron-headed Sioux arrow. Of course, only one of the grooves is visible in the figure.

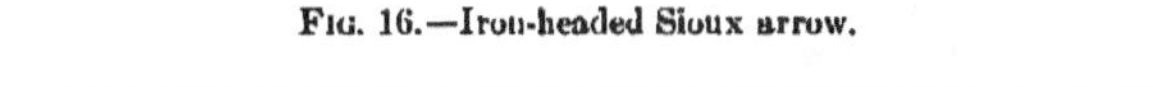

⅙

Fig. 16.—Iron-headed Sioux arrow.

* They remind one of the blood-grooves (*Blutrinnen*) on Toledo and other sword-blades.

B 3

With a similar view the troglodytes may have cut grooves in the barbs of their weapons, if, indeed, these incisions were not merely designed for ornamentation.

In describing the harpoon-like objects of reindeer-horn figured on page 17, I follow more or less M. Lartet's remarks.

Fig. 11.—This specimen exhibits only two barbs on one side. The top has been carefully tapered to a point, and the grooves of the barbs are deeply cut, especially that in the second one. The shank is slightly curved, with an evident swelling at the middle, and the knobs near the lower extremity are quite prominent. From La Madelaine.*

Fig. 12.—This fine specimen was found by M. Brun, conservator of the Museum of Montauban, under the rock-shelter of Bruniquel. Its upper point is short, and it has nine grooved barbs on one side. There is only one knob near the lower end.†

Fig. 13.—This is a perfect specimen, having its original tapering end and suddenly sharp point, and three pairs of alternating, single-grooved barbs. From La Madelaine.‡

Fig. 14.—This specimen measures nearly nine inches in length, and is one of the largest found by Messrs. Lartet and Christy. Its point is elongate and somewhat sharp, and the stem regularly rounded. The barbs, cut out symmetrically and marked with single grooves, are three on one side (left) and five on the other (right); the first on the right side is placed forward, and has none to correspond with it on the other side. The others are nearly opposite or alternate. The knobs at the lower end are very prominent. From La Madelaine.§

Fig. 15.—A distinct type,‖ with the point forming a triangle by the meeting of two barbs, which, like the others, are nearly flat, and provided with two parallel grooves on both faces. The barbs project opposite each other. The stem is marked by two longitudinal lines, between which is a somewhat raised fillet dying out at the point. The knobs at the lower end are tolerably prominent. From La Madelaine.¶

Fig. 17 represents a fragmentary harpoon-shaped object of reindeer-horn from La Madelaine, the lower part of which is not tapering, but terminates in "a butt convex on one face and nearly flat on the other," and exhibits, moreover, above the lowest pair of barbs—all that remains of them—a longitudinal, deeply-

---

* Reliquiæ Aquitanicæ; reduction of Fig. 2 on B Plate VI.

† Ibid.; reduction of Fig. 9 on p. 50, II.

‡ Ibid.; reduction of Fig. 4 on B Plate XIV.

§ Ibid.; reduction of Fig. 4 on B Plate I.

‖ "Unless," as M. Lartet says, "it was originally longer, and has been recut and sharpened after having been broken."

¶ Reliquiæ Aquitanicæ; reduction of Fig. 7 on B Plate I.

cut perforation. It is the only object of this special form figured in "Reliquiæ Aquitanicæ."* I place alongside of it Fig. 18, representing a specimen found

Fig. 17.—La Madelaine.   Fig. 18.—Laugerie Basse.

Figs. 17 and 18.—Harpoon-heads of reindeer-horn.

by M. Elie Massenat at Laugerie Basse.† Its lower extremity tapers to a point, and there is a perforation at some distance from it. The design is not sufficiently characteristic to show whether the object has a flattish or rounded form.

There can be no doubt that many of the points of reindeer-horn found in the French caves were the armatures of hunting-spears, if not of arrows, which fact, if it needed verification, is proved by the discovery, at the station of Les Eyzies, of a bone in which a broken barbed dart-head still remains fixed.‡ It would be impossible to decide at this time which of the armatures provided with barbs served as the heads of hunting-spears or of harpoons. Possibly the cavemen were not very choice in the selection, and used them as the occasion required, though it is quite probable that, in spearing fish, they preferred shafts purposely provided with heads having unilateral barbs, which, of course, penetrated with greater ease. Dr. Broca is very strict in his definition of the harpoons used by

---

* Fig. 57, I, p. 160.
† Matériaux pour l'Histoire Primitive et Naturelle de l'Homme; Vol. V, 1869, Plate 20.
‡ Figured in Figuier's "Primitive Man," p. 100.

the cave-men. "The harpoon," he says, "was a small dart of reindeer-horn, very like the large barbed arrows, except that the barbs were only on one side; a slight protuberance at the base allowed a cord to be attached, which was held in the hand of the fisherman. It has been frequently, and is still, confounded with the arrow. It is clear that an arrow barbed only on one side would be very defective in flight, as it describes a long curve; its course is necessarily affected by the resistance of the air which sustains it; but in the short flight of the harpoon this inconvenience is much less, and besides, the direction of the harpoon is downward, and it does not need to be sustained by the air. The instrument barbed only on one side is then not an arrow, and must be a harpoon. The use of its barbs was to catch and retain the fish after it was struck; but why were they all upon one side? To diminish the width of the dart so that it might penetrate more readily? I cannot say.

"One of my colleagues, M. Lecoq de Boisbaudran, in a communication before the anthropological section, makes some very interesting remarks upon the mode of action of the unilateral barbs of the harpoon. While passing through the air, these barbs do not cause the harpoon to deviate perceptibly, but as soon as it enters the water, the unequal resistance it encounters must necessarily change its direction. It would seem, then, that the fisherman who aimed straight for the fish would miss it. Now, it is well known that a straight stick appears to be broken when plunged obliquely in water; in like manner, in consequence of the refraction of the luminous rays, the image of the fish is displaced, and if direct aim were taken at this image, it would also be missed. Here are, then, two causes of error. Now, it is evident that if they can be brought to act in opposite directions, they will counteract each other, and M. Lecoq shows that when the barbed side is turned downward, the harpoon will reach its destination. This arrangement of the harpoon was then intended to rectify its course, which indicates great sagacity of observation in our troglodytes.

"The inhabitants of *Terre-de-Feu* still use a harpoon barbed on one side only."[*]

At this day, however, the Eskimos and Indians of the Northwest Coast of America use harpoons with heads barbed either on one side or on both. As an example I represent in Fig. 19 a seal-harpoon, about five feet long, used by the Eskimos of Bristol Bay, in Alaska. Fig. 20 shows its upper part enlarged. The head, made of walrus-ivory, barbed on both sides, and provided with an eye, fits with its tapering lower end into a corresponding cavity in a kind of socket, made of bone, into which the wooden shaft is inserted. An inflated

---

[*] Broca· The Troglodytes; p. 329.—A Fuegian bone harpoon-head, eight inches and five-eighths long, having a single barb on *each* side, is figured in "Reliquiæ Aquitanicæ," II, p. 179. It was obtained, with others, during the voyage of the "Beagle." Reference will be made hereafter to the fine series of bone harpoon-heads from Tierra del Fuego in the United States National Museum.

HARPOONS.   21

stomach of a seal, attached to its lower part, serves as a float or buoy. A long line of braided sinew, fastened at some distance from the end of the shaft, connects the latter with the ivory head, as shown in the figure. The line loosely

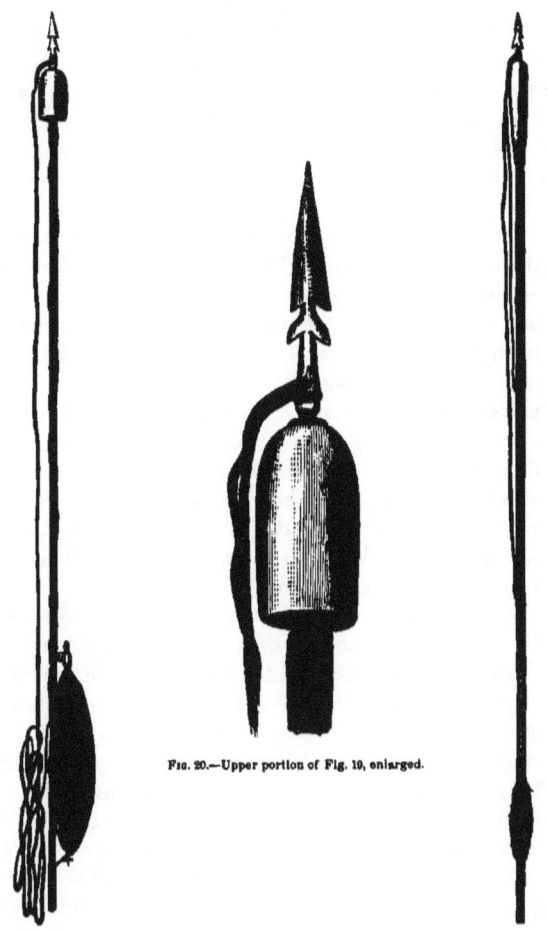

Fig. 20.—Upper portion of Fig. 19, enlarged.

Fig. 19.—Eskimos, Bristol Bay, Alaska. (11355).   Fig. 21.—Eskimos, Yukon River, Alaska. (8844).

Figs. 19–21.—Harpoons.

coiled around the shaft and closely below the socket has nothing to do with the arrangement just described, but serves to strengthen the connection of the shaft with the socket. In launching the harpoon at a seal, which is done by means of the throwing-board, the head becomes detached, remaining in the body of the animal, which dives under, pulling down the embarrassing float, but reappears after a while on the surface, when the pursuing hunters in their skin-boats (bidarkas) finally kill it with clubs. The animal is claimed by the individual who first struck it; but if two have fastened simultaneously their spears in its body, the one who wounded it nearest the head becomes the owner.

Fig. 21 represents a lighter kind of seal-harpoon, derived from Eskimos at the mouth of Yukon River, Alaska. It somewhat resembles the one just described, but lacks the buoy, and is feathered at the lower end. The hunter likewise employs the throwing-board in connection with this harpoon, which measures about five feet. The ivory head has five barbs, two on one side and three on the other. The line, passing through the eye of the head, and properly attached to it, is fastened below the socket and at some distance from the feathering. When the head is buried in the seal's body and has become detached from the shaft, the latter floats in a direction crossing that in which the animal swims or dives, and thus impedes its motions.

Arrows, in every respect similar to this kind of spear, but, of course smaller (about two feet eight inches long), and having a notch at the lower end of the shaft, are used for the water-hunt by Eskimos of the Northwest Coast, for instance by those of Bristol Bay. When the arrow has reached its victim, and the point has come off the shaft, the latter floats like that of the seal-spear just described. These arrows are shot from short bows, stiffened on the back with whalebone and sinew, and not easily bent.

I have given a somewhat detailed account of these harpoons and arrows with detachable heads, because it has been suggested the harpoon-like heads from the French caves, which nearly all show a tapering termination, served, in part at least, as detachable armatures. The projections or knobs at their lower ends, it is supposed, facilitated the fastening of a line. If such really was the case, the dart must have been inserted into a conical cavity at the upper extremity of the shaft, for no horn or bone sockets made for receiving the tapering ends of the dart-heads have been found in the French caves. It would be hazardous to assert that the cave-men of Dordogne made use of an apparatus so complicated as an Eskimo seal-spear, their attacks being chiefly directed against large fish, such as salmon and the like. No one can say whether their fish-spears had detachable or fixed points. In the latter case the knobs with which the dart-heads are provided may simply have served to hold ligatures by which the head, after being inserted into the hollowed end of the shaft, was more firmly lashed to it. Yet armatures like those represented by Figs. 17 and 18 certainly have the appearance of detachable heads.

It will be seen hereafter that certain North American Indians, in capturing salmon and sturgeon, used, and still use, a long spear with a detachable sharp bone point, connected by a string with the shaft. The point, however, is not inserted into the shaft, but the shaft is made to fit into a cavity at the upper extremity of the point.

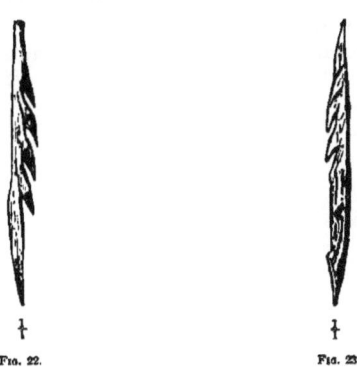

Fig. 22.   Fig. 23.

FIGS. 22 and 23.—Harpoon or arrow-heads of reindeer-horn. La Madelaine.

Figs. 22 and 23 represent small harpoon-like objects of reindeer-horn, figured in "Reliquiæ Aquitanicæ,"* and both found at La Madelaine. The first of them is thus described:—"A small specimen cut in the shape of a barbed harpoon, with a long point, which has been broken. There are four barbs on one side only, distinctly separate, sharp, and very oblique, but without the usual grooves. The lower part tapers to a point without any indication of knobs. This diminutive weapon-head may have served as an arrow-head." The description of the second, represented in Fig. 23, is as follows:—"Another minute harpoon-like head, of similar dimensions to the last, but showing only two barbs cut distinctly, whilst above them two others are indicated by shallow, oblique, unfinished notches. This specimen has preserved its sharp point. Near the pointed butt there is a kind of notch, which may have been of use in fastening this little weapon on a shaft."†

If not arrow-points, these little darts may have served as armatures of diminutive fishing-spears in the hands of juvenile cave-dwellers. They hardly resemble the barbed prongs, two or three or more of which form the heads of what are now called fish-gigs; and, indeed, in looking carefully over the plates of "Reliquiæ Aquitanicæ," I have not noticed the figure of a single specimen of a form to be thus employed.

---

* Figs. 8 and 9 on B Plate VI.   † Reliquiæ Aquitanicæ; II, p. 57, etc.

24   PREHISTORIC FISHING.

The relics found in the reindeer-hunters' retreat called the "Kesslerloch," near Thayngen, in the Canton of Zürich, Switzerland,* have been described by the discoverer of the cave, Mr. Konrad Merk, in the "Mittheilungen" (communications) of the Antiquarian Society of Zürich. The material out of which the cave-dwellers manufactured their implements, he states, was almost exclusively furnished by the antlers of the reindeer. There were found at this station only eight harpoon-like objects, differing in the execution as well as in

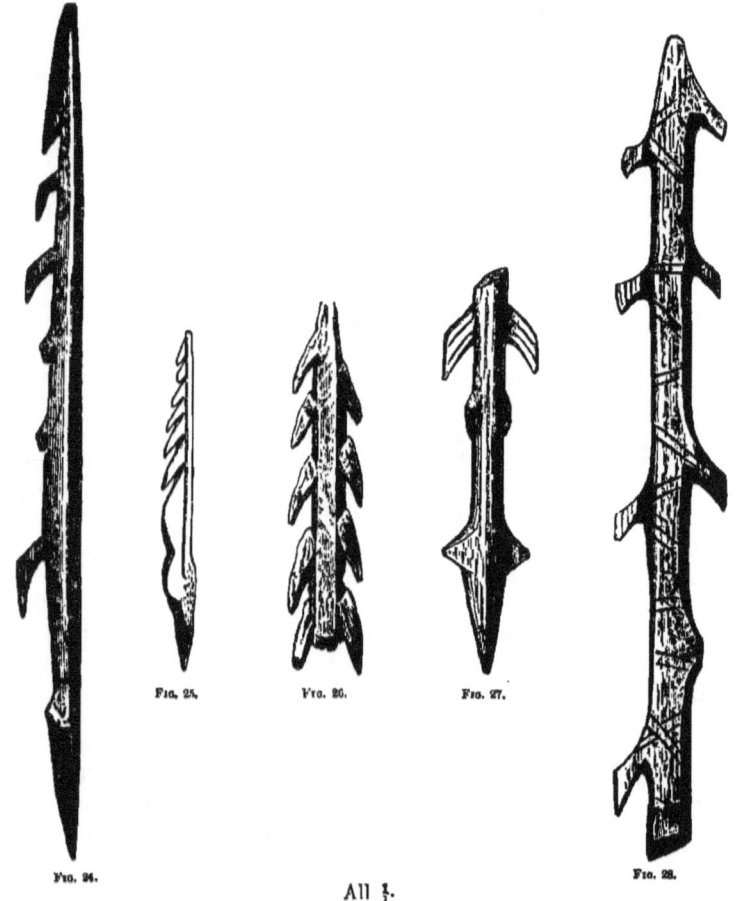

FIGS. 24–28.—Harpoon-heads of reindeer-horn (?). Kesslerloch.

---

* See p. 9.

their state of preservation. Three have unilateral barbs, while five are barbed on both sides.* The author designates these darts in the list of illustrations as *Knochenharpunen*, or bone harpoons; but in consideration of his remark that reindeer-horn was nearly always used as the material for implements, it may be inferred that the darts in question also consist of that substance.

He represents five of them, all of which are here reproduced as Figs. 24, 25, 26, 27, and 28.† The peculiarities of these dart-heads are sufficiently shown by the illustrations, and having figured and described characteristic objects of the same class from French caves, I may leave it to the reader to make his own comparisons, in order to discover analogies and differences. Mr. Merk gives it as his opinion that the dart-heads found by him served as the armatures of spears which were only thrown at birds, a view which I feel disinclined to accept. Some of them may have served in the fish-hunt.

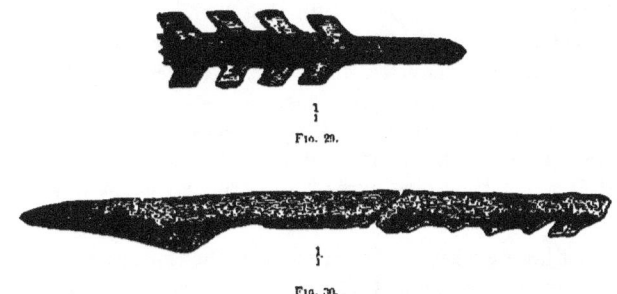

Fig. 29.

Fig. 30.

Figs. 29 and 30.—Harpoon-heads of reindeer-horn (?). Kent's Cavern.

In conclusion, I present in Figs. 29 and 30 delineations of two harpoon-heads from Kent's Cavern, near Torquay, figured by Mr. John Evans in his well-known work on the ancient stone implements, etc., of Great Britain.‡

"The harpoon-heads," he observes, " are of two kinds, some being barbed on both sides, others on one only. Of the former kind but one example has been found, which is shown in Fig. 403 (here Fig. 29). It lay in the second foot in depth in the red cave-earth in the vestibule. Above this was the black band, three inches thick, containing flint flakes and remains of extinct mammals; and above this again, the stalagmite floor, eighteen inches in thickness. It is, as

---

* Merk: Der Höhlenfund im Kesslerloch bei Thayngen (Kanton Schaffhausen); Mittheilungen der Antiquarischen Gesellschaft in Zürich, Vol. XIX, No. 1; Zürich, 1875; p. 28, etc.

† In Mr. Merk's publication, respectively, Fig. 35 on Plate IV; Fig. 49 on Plate V; Fig. 48 on Plate V; Fig. 94 on Plate VI; and Fig. 25 on Plate IV.

‡ Figs. 403 and 404 on pp. 459 and 460.

usual, imperfect, but the two and one-fourth inches which remain show the tapering point and four barbs on either side, which are opposite to each other, and not alternate. It is precisely of the same character as some of the harpoon-heads from the cave of La Madelaine, in the Dordogne, which are usually formed of reindeer-horn. The material in this instance is, I believe, the same. The striated marks of the tool by which it was scraped into form are still distinctly visible in places. Such harpoon-heads have been regarded as characteristic of the latest division in the sequence of this class of caverns, and have been found in numerous localities on the Continent.

"Of the other kind, which have the barbs along one side only of the blade, two examples have been found. One of these, though in two pieces, is otherwise nearly perfect, and is shown in Fig. 404 (here Fig. 30). It has also its analogues among the harpoon-heads found in the cave of La Madelaine and elsewhere, especially at Bruniquel. Its stem shows the projection for retaining the loop or cord by which it was connected with the shaft, though it was probably still susceptible of being detached from immediate contact with it. In this respect, as indeed in general character, these early weapons seem closely to resemble those of the Eskimos of the present day. — — —

"The other instrument of this kind, shown in Fig. 405 (not reproduced) is the terminal portion of a similar point, but with the barbs all broken off at the base. It is about three and three-fourths inches long, and was found in the black band."*

It is not known whether the cave-men of the reindeer-period in France and other parts of Europe understood fishing with nets, no prepared net-sinkers having been discovered among the débris left by them. The absence of the latter, however, is no positive proof of the non-existence of nets in palæolithic times, for pebbles without any artificial modification could have served as sinkers. It would be equally fruitless to make it a subject of inquiry whether they had boats. Referring to the cave-men of the Vézère Valley, Dr. Broca observes:—

"These antique fishermen evidently did not use nets, for with nets all kinds of fish are taken. Their sole instrument was the harpoon, with which they could only catch the large fish, and among these they chose the one whose flesh they preferred.† Had they boats for fishing? There is no evidence of it; besides, the river was then sufficiently narrow to allow the use of the harpoon from its banks."‡

---

* Evans: The Ancient Stone Implements, Weapons, and Ornaments of Great Britain; London, 1872; p. 459, etc.

† The salmon. It has been seen, however, that the troglodytes also caught smaller species of fish. Dr. Sauvage is very positive on that point. See p. 11.

‡ Broca: The Troglodytes; p. 328.

Delineations of Fishes and Aquatic Mammals.—Reference was made to the peculiar artistic *penchant* of the men of the reindeer-period, which revealed itself in the practice of engraving on horn and other substances the outlines of animals which they hunted or obtained by other means, and which, it may be assumed, were regarded with special interest on account of the advantages derived from them. The fact that a number of these sketches represent fishes seems to indicate their partiality for the spoils of the water, which, as we have seen, contributed largely to their supplies of food.

FIG. 31.—Representations of fishes and a horse on a baton of reindeer-horn. La Madelaine.

Fig. 31 represents a "baton" of reindeer-horn, one foot in length, upon which two fishes and a horse are traced, the former being very badly executed, insomuch that it would be impossible to indulge in any speculation as to the genus to which they belong. On the side opposite to that shown by Fig. 31 other fish-like figures, four in number, are drawn. This specimen was found at La Madelaine.*

FIG. 32.—Drawing of a fish on a piece of reindeer-horn. La Madelaine.

Much better is the design of a fish on a rod of reindeer-horn, here given as Fig. 32. It is thus described:—"A cylindrical piece of reindeer-horn, on which are carved two outlines of fishes, one on each side. In the figure here given, the form of the head, the shape of the gills, an obscure indication of the back-fin, and the proportions and general appearance permit us to refer this fish to one of the freshwater kind, probably of the cyprinoid (carp) family. The fragment is broken at both ends; and we can scarcely form an opinion as to its original use, and whether, indeed, it was an ornament or not."† The piece was obtained at La Madelaine.

---

* Reliquiæ Aquitanicæ; Fig. 1, B Plates III and IV.—Fig. 31 is a reduced copy.

† Ibid.; II, p. 13; representation of the engraved fish Fig. 1 on B Plate II.—The tracing on the horn is less distinct than in Fig. 32.

About eight years ago, Messrs. Louis Lartet[*] and Chaplain Duparc published in "Matériaux pour l'Histoire Primitive et Naturelle de l'Homme" an account of their exploration of the Duruthy Grotto, near Sorde, a place situated not very far from Peyrehorade, Department of Landes (Southwestern France). They discovered in the lowest deposit of the grotto—evidently a place

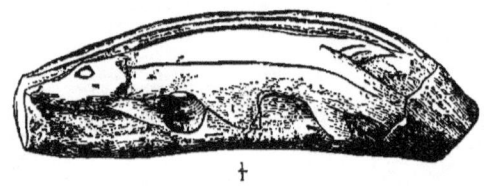

Fig. 33.—Figure of a pike engraved on a drilled bear's tooth. Duruthy Grotto.

resorted to at different times—about fifty perforated and engraved canine teeth of the bear and lion, doubtless trophies of the chase, which lay near a crushed human skull and bones, perhaps the remains of a savage hunter, whose person they once may have adorned. On one of these teeth, that of a bear, is traced the outline of a fish, which has been pronounced a pike by persons versed in ichthyology. Fig. 33, reproduced from "Matériaux,"[†] represents the incised bear's tooth.

There is in the collection of the Marquis de Vibraye a reindeer-jaw from

Fig. 34.—Outline of a fish (*Squalius?*) on a reindeer-jaw. Laugerie Basse.

Laugerie Basse, upon which is engraved the outline of a fish, supposed to be intended for a *Squalius*. Fig. 34 is a copy of the sketch.[‡]

M. Elie Massenat found at Laugerie Basse several pieces of reindeer-horn bearing fish-designs, which are figured on Plates I and II in Vol. XII (1877) of "Matériaux." The tracings represented on the first plate are rather rude, not permitting the recognition of a species; but that on the second plate is believed to be intended for a cyprinoid fish. I refrain from copying the figures, the plates being marked *Reproduction interdite*.

---

[*] Son of M. Edouard Lartet.
[†] Vol. IX, 1874, p. 142, Fig. 37.
[‡] Reliquiæ Aquitanicæ; I, p. 225.

M. Edouard Dupont has published the description and figure of a "baton" with a rough fish-design upon it, which was found in the cave of Goyet, in Belgium. The illustration is here reproduced as Fig. 35. "It is ornamented

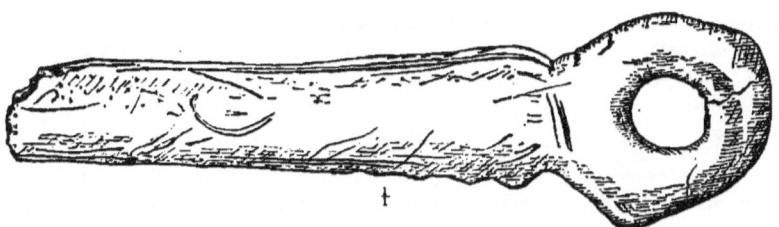

FIG. 35.—Tracing of a fish on a baton of reindeer-horn. Cave of Goyet.

on its borders and on its two faces with incised lines; I have not yet been able to discover what the ancient engraver intended to represent on one of the faces, because an important part of the design was traced on the lost portion of the object; there are seen lines which cross each other and some hatchings.

"The other face shows the figure of a fish, the posterior part of which is wanting on account of the fracture. The dots engraved on the back of the fish would seem to indicate the characteristic spots on the back of a trout."[*]

FIG. 36.—Rude drawing of a fishing-scene on the scapula of an ox. Laugerie Basse.

Fig. 36 is a reproduction of an extremely rude drawing of a fishing-scene, on the scapula of an ox, also discovered by M. Massenat at Laugerie Basse. The sketch is thus described by him :—

"This drawing represents a rudely-executed human form with an immense

---

[*] Dupont: Les "Bâtons de Commandement" de la Caverne de Goyet; Matériaux; Vol. V, 1869; p. 318; figure on Plate 16.—Professor W. Boyd Dawkins thinks this object might have been an arrow-straightener (*Cave Hunting*, London, 1874, p. 340).

arm, at least three times as long as the rest of the body. This arm, it appears, tries to seize a fin of an enormous fish, which, from the shape of the tail, easily might be taken for a cetacean. Was the draughtsman inspired by the recollection of some great maritime fishing-exploit? And why not? Have we not the certainty that the aborigines made excursions to the sea-shore? The different kinds of shells which we find in tolerable number, sometimes pierced and cut by man, among the fragments of flint and reindeer-horn are an irrefutable proof of the fact."[*]

Dr. Broca, however, gives the following explanation of the sketch:—

"It represents a man in the act of harpooning an aquatic animal. The latter, although it has the form of a fish, is so much larger than the man that it has been supposed to be one of the cetacea, probably a whale, and that the artist, in consequence, must have found his way to the Gulf of Gascogne. I am not disposed to admit this interpretation. It is hardly possible that the men of that time were sufficiently expert navigators to venture upon the ocean to harpoon the whale. It is said the tail and back suggest the form of a cetaceous animal; but may it not rather be a porpoise than a whale? Porpoises sometimes sport in the Gironde, and I saw once, in my childhood, one of these animals carried by a flood even into the Dordogne, where it was stranded between Libourne and Castillon. It was killed by fishermen with boat-hooks, and exhibited from village to village. If, as is probable, the tide rose higher in those days than now, and particularly if the Dordogne was wider and deeper, it is conceivable that a porpoise might ascend the river high enough to come within reach of the harpoons of our troglodytes, and so unusual an event would naturally inspire the enthusiasm of an artist—in this case very unskillful.

"But I am tempted to believe that this pretended cetacean is only a badly-drawn fish. The relative size of the man proves nothing, for the artist, throughout the whole sketch, has manifested entire contempt for proportion. This too diminutive man has a gigantic arm, and the harpoon he throws is proportioned to the size of the fish. We are reminded of certain jocose drawings of the present day, in which puny bodies are supplied with enormous heads. The great interest of this particular work of art consists in the unanswerable proof it gives that the troglodytes used the harpoon in fishing."[†]

The original of Fig. 37, found at La Madelaine, and evidently a part of a baton, is thus described in the "Reliquiæ Aquitanicæ":—

"The objects here represented are engraved on the face of a cylindrical rod, which our artist has rendered diagrammatically in two separate figures, so as to reproduce the whole in halves.

---

[*] Massenat: Objects Gravés et Sculptés de Laugerie Basse (Dordogne); Matériaux; Vol. V, 1869; p. 354. Sketch taken from Plate 22 of the same volume.
[†] Broca: The Troglodytes; p. 337.

"On one of these halves (represented as a flat surface) we see two heads, one after the other, evidently referable to a bovine genus. We may add that characters for a determination of the species are not altogether wanting. The

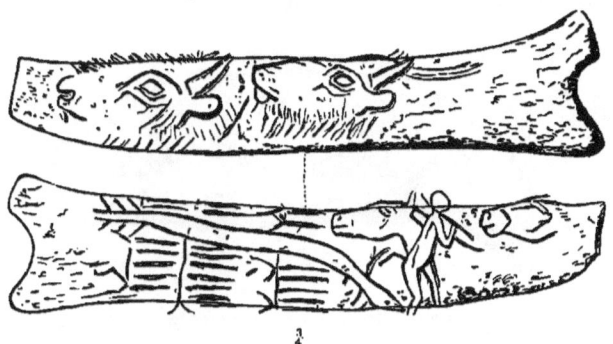

FIG. 37.—Outlines of two heads of the aurochs, a human figure, an eel (?), two horse-heads, and three rows of marks on a piece of reindeer-horn. La Madelaine.

points of attachment and the direction of the horns suffice, for themselves, to decide for the aurochs; whilst, moreover, a more significant indication could not be offered than the convexity of the forehead and the presence of hair-tufts, both on the face and under the throat.

"On the opposite side of the other half-cylinder (reproduced as a plane) we see, in a medley of figures, sometimes upside down, first, a human form, with the limbs not finished very incorrectly, although the face is without any expression—a negligence probably intentional on the part of the ancient artist, who has perfectly characterized, close by it, a horse's head and part of its chest, with their details pretty well rendered. More to the right we perceive a second horse's head, not so well cut. To the left of and behind the human form, amongst rows of dashes, or figures, of which we cannot comprehend either the intention or value, there is an outline (reversed with respect to the other figures) of a serpent, *or rather of an eel with indications of the tail-fin;** and its head, with mouth open, approaches the leg of the human figure. In this bizarre group of figures, or in the figures themselves, we avow we cannot see any intention or premeditated arrangement; and if others, more knowing, think that they here recognize the expression of an allegory, or of any symbolism, we very willingly leave to them the merit as well as the responsibility."†

---

* The italics are my own.

† Reliquiæ Aquitanicæ; II, p. 15; figure on B Plate 11, 8a and 8b.

Such is M. Edouard Lartet's comment on the engraved piece. Though, of course, it cannot be decided whether the artist intended to represent an eel, lamprey, or serpent, it was not deemed superfluous to reproduce here the group, and to transcribe the observations relating to it.

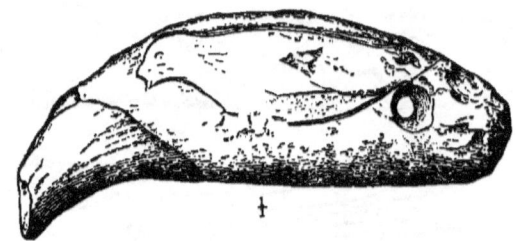

Fig. 38.—Figure of a seal traced on a drilled bear's tooth. Duruthy Grotto.

The cave-dwellers of the reindeer-period evidently had seen seals, either on the sea-coasts or in the rivers which these animals may have ascended some distance at the time of cave-inhabitation here considered. Mention is made of a representation of a seal found by M. Piette in the cave of Gourdan, Department of Haute-Garonne. I have not seen a figure of this specimen, but I am able to present in Fig. 38 a delineation of a drilled bear's tooth, upon which the outline of a seal is so distinctly traced, that the artist's intention to draw the likeness of a phocine animal cannot be doubted. The engraved tooth is one of the fifty, which, as stated on a preceding page, were discovered by Messrs. Lartet and Duparc in the lowest deposit of the Duruthy Grotto.*

2.—NEOLITHIC AGE.

GENERAL CHARACTERISTICS.

In the later or neolithic period a marked change in the condition of prehistoric men in Europe is observable. A milder temperature was now prevailing, the former climate having gradually yielded its rigor, and become more like that of our time. The mammoth, rhinoceros, hippopotamus, great bear, and hyena

---

* Matériaux; Vol. IX, 1874; p. 143, Fig. 38.

had worked out their mission in Europe, while the musk-ox, reindeer, chamois, ibex, and other quadrupeds adapted to a low temperature, had either migrated northward, or chosen the cold heights of mountains as their abodes. On the other hand, several species of animals, perhaps derived from distant countries, appear as the domesticated associates of man, who was no longer a mere savage hunter, but had become, in some districts at least, a tiller of the soil, and, consequently, a consumer of vegetable food, though still assiduously applying himself to the chase and to fishing. During the palæolithic ages, it appears, man made his stone tools and weapons almost exclusively of flint, reducing them to the intended shape by flaking or chipping alone, not having learned yet to improve their form and efficiency by the process of grinding. It was quite different in the times now under consideration. The stone implements of the neolithic period exhibit a greater variety of well-defined forms, and are no longer generally made of flint, but also of other kinds of stone, such as diorite, serpentine, basalt, quartzite, and similar suitable materials. Many of the neolithic axes, chisels, etc., are brought into their final shapes by grinding and polishing. Yet the practice of chipping flint into arrow and spear-heads, knives, scrapers, and other utensils was carried on with great industry, the articles produced in this way being not only very numerous, but also, generally speaking, of superior workmanship, insomuch that flint-chipping may be said to have assumed in this period almost the character of an art. Some of the Danish handled daggers are marvels of skill. The manufacture of clay vessels was general during this epoch; and, though always hand-made, they frequently exhibit elegant forms. The earlier megalithic monuments of Europe (dolmens, chambered tumuli, etc.), pertain to the same era.

Were the men of neolithic times the descendants of the contemporaries of the mammoth and the great bear, or immigrants from abroad, who brought with them new arts and the animals they had tamed in their old homes? There certainly exists a gap between palæolithic and neolithic implements, the gradual transition from one class to the other not being represented with sufficient distinctness by intermediate forms. It is highly probable, to say the least, that the neolithic period was inaugurated in Europe by the spreading of a new population, in which some are inclined to recognize the first wave of Aryan immigration.

ARTIFICIAL SHELL-DEPOSITS.

Character.—On the indented coasts of the Danish islands of Seeland, Fünen, Möen and Samsöe, and along the fjords of the Peninsula of Jütland there occur, mostly in the neighborhood of the sea, considerable accumulations of shells, which were formerly supposed to have been deposited by the sea at a time when the level of the land was lower than at present. It was noticed, however, that the shell-heaps showed no trace of the stratification which always characterizes marine deposits, and that they, instead of inclosing shells of mollusks of every age, contained merely those of full-grown specimens, which, moreover, belonged to a limited number of species not living together under natural conditions. Upon further examination there were found among the shells the broken bones of different species of wild quadrupeds and birds, and the remains of fishes; also implements of flint, horn, and bone, fragments of a rude kind of pottery, charcoal, and ashes, but no objects of metal whatever. The artificial origin of these accumulations being now established, they were recognized as the amassed remains of the repasts of a population that dwelled in early ages on the shores of the Baltic, pursuing the chase, but chiefly the capture of fish and shell-fish. The Danes denominate shell-heaps of this description *Kjökkenmöddinger*,* a word meaning "kitchen-refuse;" but the term "kitchen-middens" is often employed in English, *midden* being a name still used in the North of England to designate a refuse-heap. A large number of kitchen-middens have been examined conjointly by Messrs. Forchhammer, Steenstrup, and Worsaae, distinguished, respectively, for their proficiency in the departments of geology, natural history, and archæology; and the results of their investigations, contained in several reports addressed to the Academy of Sciences at Copenhagen, have added in a great measure to our knowledge of prehistoric man in the North of Europe.

Artificial shell-deposits, however, have also been discovered in other parts of Europe, as for instance, in Sweden, Norway, England, Scotland, and on the coasts of France, both north and south. Yet nowhere in Europe are they so numerous and well characterized as in the country to which my account refers.†

One of the largest kitchen-middens is that of Meilgaard, in the Northeast of Jütland. It is more than a hundred metres long, and in places three metres deep. Very extensive accumulations sometimes present an undulating surface, the refuse having been heaped up more abundantly in some points than in others; and occasionally the heaps surround an irregular free space, where the coast-people doubtless had built their huts, which may have been of the most primitive description, probably poles stuck in the ground and covered with skins. Rude hearths consisting of a kind of pavement of pebbles, not exceeding the size of a man's fist, have been discovered in the refuse-heaps. These fire-places are more or less circular, only a few feet in diameter, and surrounded with

---

* In English publications the plural form "Kjökkenmöddings" is generally applied.

† As may be imagined, shell-deposits of artificial origin are not confined to Europe, but also occur along the littoral districts of other continents. Coast-tribes, deriving their means of subsistence chiefly from the sea, necessarily will leave there the tokens of their presence. In America such shell-heaps are frequent, and have been observed from West Greenland to Tierra del Fuego, and also on the western sea-board. I shall devote a section of this publication to North American shell-deposits.

charcoal and ashes. The coast-people manufactured a kind of very primitive pottery, fragments of which are found commingled with the shells. The clay is always mixed with coarse sand, produced by the trituration of stones, and added for the purpose of preventing the cracking of the vessels while in the fire.

The Danish kjökkenmöddings have yielded a number of awls, chisels, comb-shaped articles, and other tools made of horn and bone, and in great abundance chipped flint implements, such as flakes, piercers, lance-head-shaped objects, slingstones(?), and notably axes of a peculiar shape, and therefore called "shell-mound axes." They probably served in opening bivalves. I am not aware that any objects directly referable to fishing, such as fish-hooks, harpoon-heads, sinkers, etc., have occurred among the refuse. The flint implements are mostly of a rude character, and inferior to the well-finished specimens of chipped flint so frequent in Denmark. Polished stone implements, however, are not entirely wanting in the kitchen-middens. Taking into account, additionally, the fauna of the period, presently to be considered, it may not be amiss to refer the Danish kitchen-middens provisionally to the early part of the neolithic period. Messrs. Worsaae and Steenstrup themselves are not quite in accord concerning the antiquity of the Danish kitchen-middens. While the last-named gentleman attributes them to the dolmen-builders, the former considers them as belonging to an earlier epoch.* There is no evidence that man lived in the Scandinavian North during quaternary times.†

The coast-people certainly led a very rude life, being, as it appears, unacquainted with agriculture, and compelled to subsist entirely on the spoils of the sea and the forest. No traces of carbonized cereals have been found in the kitchen-middens; but masses of what is thought to be the residue of burned eel-grass (*Zostera marina*, Lin.) occur in their immediate neighborhood. Not many centuries ago, salt was produced on the Danish sea-shores by sprinkling sea-water over burning heaps of this marine plant; and hence it is thought the ancient coast-dwellers had obtained salt by the same process. It is not quite certain whether these people inhabited the sea-board only in summer or during the whole year, though the character of the bones and antlers, which belong to animals of different ages, would favor the view that they lived there through successive seasons. Although they derived their sustenance mainly from the sea, the bones of mammals and birds scattered through the refuse show that the chase furnished a part of their provisions. The list of the former comprises the stag, roe, wild boar, urus, dog, fox, wolf, marten, otter, porpoise, seal, water-

---

* Bulletins du Congrès d'Archéologie Préhistorique à Copenhague en 1869; Copenhagen, 1872; p. 145, etc.

† "Von einer eigentlichen Besiedelung des hohen scandinavischen Nordens oder des nordöstlichen Europas überhaupt in jener Periode der Steinzeit, welche die Mammuth-und Rennthierperiode oder die 'paläolithische Zeit' genannt wird, sind noch keine Spuren nachgewiesen."—*Worsaae: Die Vorgeschichte des Nordens nach gleichzeitigen Denkmälern; in's Deutsche übertragen von J. Mestorf;* Hamburg, 1878; p. 17.

rat, beaver, lynx, wild cat, hedgehog, black bear, and mouse. Next to the sea-animals, the stag, roe, and wild boar evidently constituted the principal food of the coast-people. The dog, which is represented by a small race, seems to have been their only domesticated animal, and, as the bones show, was also eaten by them, as it is by our Indians, who keep dogs as companions, and use them as food, especially on solemn occasions. The urus (*Bos primigenius*, Boj.) has become extinct within historical times, and the wolf, black bear, wild cat, lynx, and beaver are no longer found in Denmark. No bones of the hare have occurred among the shell-heaps, perhaps for the reason that those ancient people were prevented by superstitious motives, like the Laplanders of our day, from eating that animal. The reindeer and elk are missing in the kjökkenmöddings, though their former presence in Denmark has been proved by the discovery of their bones.

Remains of aquatic birds, such as wild ducks, geese, and swans, are often met with among the shells. The great penguin or auk (*Alca impennis*, Lin.) and the capercailzie or mountain-cock (*Tetrao urogallus*, Lin.) deserve special mention. The great auk, a bird incapable of flying, being provided with mere apologies for wings, is said to have been totally exterminated everywhere by man. According to Professor Carl Vogt, it was found in Iceland, its last retreat, until the year 1842, after which it became extinct.* The capercailzie, a bird no longer found in Denmark, though still inhabiting the forests of Germany, feeds in spring chiefly on the buds of the pine, a tree not growing naturally at present in Denmark, but very common during the stone age, as has been ascertained by the examination of Danish peat-bogs. Thus it would seem that the disappearance of the pine from Denmark caused the capercailzie to leave that country. Remains of the domestic fowl, the stork, swallow, and sparrow are wanting in the kitchen-middens.

The coast-people broke all the long bones of mammals, or split them lengthwise, for extracting the marrow; those containing no marrow are left entire, but gnawed both by men and dogs, as the impressions of the teeth indicate.

Human remains, attributable to the people of this period, have not been met with among the débris.

Capture of Mollusks and Fish.—The oyster (*Ostrea edulis*, Lin.) is the species of shell-fish occurring most abundantly in the kitchen-middens, its shells sometimes constituting almost entirely their contents. Next follow, in the order of their frequency, the cockle (*Cardium edule*, Lin.), mussel (*Mytilus edulis*, Lin.), and periwinkle (*Littorina littorea*, Lin.), all of which are eaten by man at the present time. Other marine and even terrestrial shells, such as *Nassa reticulata*, Lin., and species of *Buccinum, Venus, Helix*, etc., are mentioned as occurring

---

* Vogt: Vorlesungen über den Menschen; Giessen, 1863; Vol. II, p. 114.

in the refuse; but they appear in small number, and have added but little to the bulk of the shell-heaps. In regard to the oyster, it is worthy of remark that this bivalve has disappeared from the neighborhood of the kitchen-middens, being now confined to a few localities on the Cattegat. Yet even there it never attains the large size characterizing the oysters of the old shell-beds. The cockles and periwinkles, too, though still living in the same waters, are much smaller than those of ancient times. These changes have been attributed to a diminution of the saline matter in the water of the Baltic Sea.

The crustaceans are represented in the kitchen-middens by a few fragments of crabs.

Fish-remains are quite abundant, especially those of the herring (*Clupea harengus*, Lin.); but bones of the dorse (*Gadus callarias*, Lin.), dab (*Pleuronectes limanda*, Lin.), and eel (*Murœna anguilla*, Lin.) are also quite common.

Nothing definite is known concerning the methods employed by the coast-dwellers for obtaining their prey from the sea, no implements having been discovered that afford any clue. The nature of their captures, however, indicates that they had to venture upon the open sea, in order to make them; and they probably availed themselves of small boats, perhaps formed of trunks of trees, hollowed by means of fire. That they used nets appears highly probable, though direct indications of that practice, in the shape of prepared net-sinkers, have not been found.

LAKE-DWELLINGS.

Character.—The facts hitherto considered in these pages bear rather indistinctly upon prehistoric fishing in Europe. Though we know well enough that the cave-men and the people who left the kitchen-middens practised fishing, we have scarcely any positive knowledge concerning the methods employed by them in their piscatorial pursuits, and must leave it in a great measure to imagination to supply that want. Far more precise information concerning fishing in ancient times was obtained in the course of the examinations of pile-buildings in the lakes of Switzerland and other countries of Europe. The existence of the remains of these lacustrine settlements became known in the winter of 1854, when the water in the Swiss lakes had sunk much below its ordinary level, laying bare large tracts of land along their shores. A rare chance was thus afforded to the people of the neighborhood for adding to their lands by building walls near the water's edge as a means for cutting off denuded areas. So it happened at Meilen, on the Lake of Zürich, where, during the progress of such operations, pieces of a rude kind of pottery, articles of stone, bone, and horn, hard-shelled fruits and other vegetable remains, and rows of decayed wooden piles were discovered in the mud of the lake. The late Dr. Ferdinand Keller, President of the Antiquarian Society of Zürich, who afterward acquired so much reputation by the reports in which he elucidates the subject of Swiss lacustrine settlements, proceeded to Meilen, in order to inspect the relics and the place where they had been exhumed. Being an experienced antiquarian, he recognized without difficulty the character of the relics, and, summing up his observations, concluded that the piles had served as the supports of platforms on which the ancient inhabitants of this locality erected their dwellings, thus living above the surface of the water and at some distance from the shore, with which they communicated by means of a narrow bridge. To Dr. Keller, therefore, belongs the merit of having first pointed out the true character of lacustrine remains, and of having inaugurated a series of discoveries hardly surpassed in importance by any yet made in the domain of prehistoric archæology.* It was now remembered that in times not long past, fishermen had lived in cabins built in the Limmat, a small river issuing from the Lake of Zürich. The works of modern travelers were found to contain accounts of certain Asiatic and Polynesian populations who still inhabit buildings erected on piles in the water, thus perpetuating a custom prevailing in times beyond record and tradition in the lake-regions of Switzerland, and a passage in Herodotus, relating to the Pæonians, a tribe that dwelled, 520 years before the Christian era, on Lake Prasias, in Thrace (modern Roumelia), was now often quoted as illustrative of the ancient Helvetian mode of life. There are also pile-dwellings in America.†

---

* The English version of Dr. Keller's reports bears the title: The Lake Dwellings of Switzerland and other Parts of Europe, by Dr. Ferdinand Keller, President of the Antiquarian Association of Zürich. Second Edition, greatly enlarged. Translated and arranged by John Edward Lee, F. S. A., F. G. S., Author of "Isca Silurum," etc. In two Volumes. London, 1878.—Hereafter I shall often have occasion to quote this translation.

† Alonzo de Ojeda, a Spanish nobleman, who had been a companion of Columbus on his second expedition, undertook in 1499, independently, a voyage for the purpose of exploring the northern coast of South America. He was accompanied by the Florentine, Amerigo Vespucci, who has left an account of this voyage, from which Washington Irving derived the following statement: "Proceeding along the coast, they arrived at a vast deep gulf, resembling a tranquil lake, entering which they beheld on the eastern side a village, the construction of which struck them with surprise. It consisted of twenty large houses, shaped like bells, and built on piles driven into the bottom of the lake, which in this part was limpid and of but little depth. Each house was provided with a draw-bridge and with canoes, by which the communication was carried on. From this resemblance to the Italian city, Ojeda gave the bay the name of the Gulf of Venice, and it is called at the present day Venezuela, or Little Venice; the Indian name was Coquibacoa."—*Irving: The Life and Voyages of Christopher Columbus;* New York, 1869; Vol. III, p. 28.

It is worthy of notice that in the Gulf (Lake) of Maracaibo, south of the Bay of Venezuela, and communicating with it, pile-buildings are still erected by the half-civilized Goajiro Indians. A German traveler, Mr. A. Goering, gives an account of a visit to these Indians in "Illustrated Travels" (Vol. II, p. 19-21), an extract of which, accompanied by representations of the dwellings, is contained in Keller's "Lake Dwellings" (Vol. I, p. 778-9). "The houses, with low sloping roofs," he says, "were like so many little cock-lofts perched on high over the shallow waters, and they were connected with each other by means of bridges, made of narrow planks, the split stems of palm-trees. — — — We were invited to enter one of the huts. To do this we had to perform a feat worthy of some of the monkeys in the neighboring woods, for we had to climb an upright pole by means of notches cut into its sides. Each house, or cock-loft, consisted of two parts, the pent-roof shelter being partitioned off in the middle; the front apartment served the double purpose of entrance-hall and kitchen, the rear apartment as a reception and dwelling-chamber, and I was not a little surprised to observe how clean it was kept. The floor

When the results of Dr. Keller's investigations became known by his writings, a general search for similar memorials of former times was made in the many lakes of the republic, and such unexpected success rewarded the efforts of the explorers, that more than three hundred lacustrine settlements are now known to exist in Switzerland and a part of Germany bordering on the Lake of Constance, and others have been discovered in the Lombardian lakes, in Savoy, Bavaria, Austria, Mecklenburg, Prussia, and in some districts of France, even at the foot of the Pyrenees. Hence it is evident that the habit of erecting dwellings in lakes was at one period widely spread over Europe. Nowhere, however, have these remains been found in greater number than in Switzerland, a country abounding in lakes, which naturally invited such aquatic colonies. In fact, the shore-lines of most of the Helvetian lakes are marked with the traces of these ancient habitations. In this connection should be mentioned the lakes of Neuchâtel, Geneva, Constance, Bienne, Morat, Zug, Zürich, Sempach, Pfäffikon (Canton of Zürich), Moosseedorf (near Berne), Nussbaumen (Canton of Thurgau), Inkwyl (near Soleure, or Solothurn), and Wauwyl (Canton of Lucerne).

The oldest lake-settlements date back to the neolithic period, and those, of course, are first to be considered in these pages. The pile-work at the bank of Lake Pfäffikon, near Robenhausen, for instance, has not yielded any articles of bronze, but some earthern crucibles containing lumps of melted bronze, and at Meilen only a bronze celt (or hatchet) and a bracelet of the same alloy were found; which facts demonstrate that these colonies still flourished at the time when bronze was introduced. There are many other lake-settlements in which, among hundreds of articles of stone, horn, bone, or wood, not the slightest trace of metal has occurred. These stations of the pure stone age are chiefly found in Eastern Switzerland. Most of those in the western lakes of the Helvetian republic have furnished articles both of stone and of bronze, and in some stations tools and weapons of iron, thought to be Gallic in character, and even coins and other objects of Roman origin, have come to light. It thus appears that these lacustrine colonies existed for a very long period, which was characterized by remarkable changes in the condition of man, whose progress, whatever

---

was formed of split stems of trees, set close together and covered with mats. Weapons and utensils were placed in order in the corners." Mr. Goering has also published a description of these Indian pile-dwellings in the "Gartenlaube" (1879, p. 404, etc.), with a good view of a group of the aquatic habitations. "Similar pile-buildings," he observes, "are numerous along the shores of the lake; they often form whole villages, which present a most curious aspect in a dark night, when the lighted huts are mirrored in the waters of the lake." All this tends to verify Vespucci's account. Tribes at the mouth of the Orinoco and Amazon resort to pile-dwellings more or less similar to those here described.—See also a very good article by Dr. A. Ernst, entitled " Die Goajiro-Indianer," in " Zeitschrift für Ethnologie," Vol. II, 1870; p. 328, etc.

The city of Mexico was originally a village built on piles, and other Aztec places situated near lakes were thus constructed. I am not aware that remains of aboriginal pile-dwellings have been noticed in the United States; but it would not at all be surprising to find them. Balize, a small pilot-town near the mouth of the Mississippi River, is built on piles. I saw this curious village in 1848.

its causes may have been, can be traced in an uninterrupted line. Though some of the settlements are supposed to have been abandoned toward the beginning of the Christian era, it is notable that they are not mentioned by Cæsar, who had become acquainted with the Helvetians by his wars, nor by Pliny, an author particularly fond of dwelling on details. No account, no tradition, alludes to these peculiar structures, which evidently were designed to protect their occupants from the attacks of wild beasts and human enemies.

A detailed description of the lake-dwellings pertaining to neolithic times would be out of place in this publication, which is devoted to a special subject; and I therefore confine myself to a general account of these early lacustrine structures.

They were located in shallow places, and never very far from the shore, with which each communicated by means of a narrow bridge, as before stated. The upright piles were mostly whole stems of trees growing in the neighborhood, usually from four to eight inches in diameter, and roughly pointed at the lower end by means of fire or the stone hatchet. Upon these piles, brought to a level several feet above the water, and strengthened by cross-timbers, rested the platform, often merely composed of unbarked stems lying parallel to each other, but sometimes consisting of boards two inches thick, which were fastened with wooden pegs into the frame-work, thus forming an even and solid floor. The lacustrine settlement near the German village of Wangen, on the Untersee, the northwestern detached part of the Lake of Constance, contained from forty to fifty thousand posts, and formed a parallelogram seven hundred paces long and one hundred and twenty broad; but in other lake-villages—at Robenhausen, for instance—probably twice as many piles were required. When the bottom of the lake was rocky, or afforded no sufficient hold to the stakes, stones were heaped up between and around them, in order to consolidate the erection. These stones, of course, had to be brought in boats to the designated spots. Some dwellings were not erected on piles, but on a kind of fascine-work, formed by layers of sticks and stems of trees, stones, and loam, built up from the bottom of the lake until the foundation was high enough to receive the platform. The upright piles found in these substructures only served to give them steadiness. These fascine-structures, reminding one of the Irish and Scottish *crannogs*, only occur in small lakes. The huts erected on the platforms, it has been ascertained, were mostly of a rectangular shape, and consisted of a wooden frame-work wattled with rods or twigs, and covered both inside and outside with a layer of clay from two to three inches thick. The roofs, it seems, were made of bark, straw, or rushes, the remains of which have often been found in a carbonized state. A plaster of clay mixed with gravel was spread on the floor of the hut to fill the chinks, and a rude hearth, composed of several slabs of sandstone, occupied the middle of each cabin.

During the long occupation of the lacustrine villages many objects, no doubt, fell accidentally into the water; while large quantities of refuse, such as the bones of the consumed animals and broken clay vessels, were intentionally thrown over the platforms, and, as may be assumed, through the interstices of the stems or planks forming them. These heterogeneous accumulations became imbedded in the mud, forming what are now—ages afterward—called the archæological strata or relic-beds, upon which for many years the dredging-implements of antiquaries have operated, and brought to light the evidences of a most curious, long-forgotten phase of human existence. In a number of cases the bulk of these relic-beds has been increased by the ruin of the villages themselves, some of which, there can be no doubt, were consumed by fire. These conflagrations cannot have taken place in consequence of hostile attacks, because human skeletons are exceedingly scarce in the pile-works, and therefore must be ascribed to accidental ignitions, which were likely to befall wooden straw-roofed huts, each of them provided with an open hearth, probably blazing most of the time. When such calamities happened, many articles fell into the water in a charred state, and were preserved to our days, owing to the almost indestructible nature of carbonized substances. Several Swiss lakes have much decreased in extent, and their ancient shores are fringed with formations of peat, which now inclose in some instances the remains of lacustrine villages formerly surrounded by water. Such is the case at Moosseedorf, near Berne; at Wauwyl, in the Canton of Lucerne; and at Robenhausen, on the Lake of Pfäffikon, where the owner of the celebrated pile-work, Mr. Jacob Messikommer, has been successfully engaged for years in extracting relics of the early lacustrine period from moor-ground and peat.

The builders of the early pile-works, it must be admitted, were an intelligent and industrious people, who applied to the utmost the scanty means which their primitive state of civilization offered them. They pursued hunting and fishing, but devoted themselves also to agriculture and the raising of cattle; they were skillful workers in stone, horn, bone, and wood, practised the art of pottery to a great extent, and produced very creditable tissues, employing a loom of simple construction. The various occupations of the lake-men, and the fact of their living in close communities, indicate no small degree of social order, which necessitated submission to the decrees of chiefs or a majority of the people.

They employed flint and jasper in the manufacture of arrow and spear-heads, hardly distinguishable from those found in the United States, scrapers, saws, and various cutting and piercing-tools. Some of the saws, mostly two or three inches long, still retain their wooden handles, into which they were cemented with asphaltum, a substance also employed for fastening arrow-heads in their shafts. Quite frequent are the ground celts or wedge-shaped hatchets, made of serpentine, gabbro, hornblende-rock, diorite, syenite, and other kinds of tough stone, and doubtless used for various purposes. Some, which represent chisels, were set in pieces of deer-horn, hollowed at one end for receiving the blade, and forming convenient handles. Larger ones served as axe-heads, being either inserted directly into the thick end of a wooden club, or into an intermediate deer-horn socket worked into a square form at the upper end, to fit into a corresponding cavity of the wooden shaft. These statements are not conjectural, a few complete axes, blade and shaft united, having been discovered in the pile-works. At Meilen and other lacustrine stations there have been found celts made of nephrite and jadeite, hard mineral substances, not known to occur in Europe, but not uncommon in different parts of Asia. Some, who ascribe the lacustrine settlements to new-comers from abroad, have suggested that they imported these implements, which doubtless were much valued on account of their hardness and greenish color. Various lake-villages of the stone age have furnished well-shaped stone axes pierced for the insertion of handles. Among other stone objects found in the pile-works may be mentioned slabs of hard sandstone upon which the celts, etc., were ground, grain-crushers, and flat or more or less concave slabs used in connection with them, hammers in the shape of pebbles of suitable form and little or not at all modified by art, net-sinkers, and spindle-whorls.

Most varied were the uses the lake-men made of the horns, bones, and teeth of animals. The horns of the stag were made into the handles and celt-sockets already mentioned; stout pieces of this material, perforated with holes for holding wooden handles, served, according to the manner in which their ends were fashioned, as hammers, hatchets, or hoes; and the antler was sometimes converted into a weapon or a hoe by the removal of the prongs, excepting that near the brow. Bones furnished the material for arrow and spear-heads, poniards, chisels, scrapers, piercers, needles with or without eyes, fishing-implements, and other articles. The teeth of the bear and the tusks of the wild boar were utilized for similar purposes, the latter, for instance, to serve as cutting or scraping-tools, after the inner curve had been ground to an edge. The lake-dwellers, like the men of palæolithic times, wore the perforated teeth of certain animals as trophies or amulets.

The number of objects of wood preserved in peat and water shows how extensively that material was used by the lake-dwellers. They consist of handles and shafts for implements, maces resembling that with which Hercules is usually represented, mallets used in driving the piles and for other purposes, bows, threshing-flails, ladles, dippers, bowls, tubs,[*] and boats made of a single trunk; besides knife-shaped tools, combs, primitive racks for suspending apparel and utensils, and various other objects.

That pottery was abundantly made even in the lake-settlements of earliest

---

[*] These vessels bear a great resemblance to the woodenware of the same class made at the present time.

date is proved by the great number of sherds scattered over their sites. Entire vessels also have been found, partly flat-bottomed. The material is mostly unpurified clay mixed with coarse gravel, pounded granite, small fragments of shells, or charcoal. The vessels are of rather rude appearance, and slightly baked, probably in an open fire. Yet attempts at decoration are not wanting, some of the vessels being encircled by knobs below the rim, or showing rows of impressions made with the finger* or some blunt tool; while in other cases lines are traced with an implement or by pressing a cord on the soft clay. Most of the pottery has a blackish appearance, owing to a coating with some dark pigment. There is evidence that vessels of larger size were used for storing grain, apples, and other provisions. This pottery can hardly be distinguished from that formerly made by the Indians in the eastern half of the present United States.

Not the least interesting among the lacustrine relics, preserved in consequence of their carbonization, are the twisted, plaited, and woven manufactures, which were found at various stations, but especially at Robenhausen and Wangen. A kind of short flax was cultivated by the lake-men, and used most extensively in the fabrication not only of thread, cordage, and nets for fishing, and probably for hunting, but also of different sorts of linen cloth, some with inwoven patterns, a fact proving that they employed a loom. Numerous spindle-whorls, either of stone or of clay, bear witness to the common practice of spinning. The lake-people doubtless dressed to a great extent in woven garments; but it may be assumed that they also employed the prepared skins of animals for that purpose. Indeed, fragments of leather have been found at Robenhausen.

During the early lacustrine period hunting still furnished in no small degree the means of subsistence, as shown by the large number of bones of wild animals found on the sites of the ancient lake-villages. Professor Rütimeyer, of Basel, has carefully investigated the fauna of those times, which, on the whole, corresponds to that of our days, though certain species of animals now no longer found in Switzerland then inhabited that country. The urus and aurochs, or bison, were hunted by the lake-men, or perhaps caught by them in pitfalls. The elk, an animal not known to have lived in Switzerland in historical times, still roamed through the woods; but the reindeer, it is hardly necessary to repeat, had migrated northward in search of a colder climate. The stag and wild boar, both no longer living in Switzerland, were much hunted by the lake-dwellers, and their bones indicate animals of very large size. Another species of wild hog, differing from the wild boar proper, and called the "marsh-hog" by Rütimeyer, is represented by numerous remains in the pile-works.

---

* The impressions indicate small hands. The lacustrine ceramic art, it may be assumed, was practised by women, as it was, and still is, among the North American Indians.

Bones of the roe-deer are far less abundant than those of the stag. The hare, it seems, formed no article of diet among these people, owing, perhaps, to the same prejudice which caused the men of the Danish kjökkenmöddings to abstain from its flesh. Among the carnivores may be mentioned the brown bear, wolf, and fox, the last-named of which occurs frequently in the settlements under notice, and was eaten by the lake-men, as proved by the condition of its bones. The lake-dwellers possessed a species of domestic dog of middle size, which they seem to have much valued, if the fact that it was not used as food, unless in cases of extreme need, warrants such a conclusion. Remains of the horse are exceedingly scarce in the settlements of the stone age; but two kinds of cattle were common during that period, one of them small, and called "marsh-cow" by Professor Rütimeyer; the second species, larger in size, is supposed by this author to have descended from the urus. The other domesticated animals were goats and sheep. Traces of the tamed hog are almost entirely wanting in the oldest settlements of the stone age; but they become more numerous in later periods of lacustrine occupancy. It has been ascertained beyond doubt that the tamed animals were brought for shelter to the lake-villages, where they were kept in stalls distributed between the huts. The large bones of quadrupeds are nearly always broken or split for extracting the marrow. Remains of domestic fowl have not been discovered. The wild birds which have left their traces in the deposits around the piles, all pertaining to the present fauna of Switzerland, are wild ducks, geese, swans, water-hens, grouse, and some other species of the feathered tribe. They evidently were objects of the chase. The amphibians are represented by the common water-turtle (*Cistudo europæa*), still occasionally found in Swiss lakes, two species of frog and one of toad. The remains of fishes, which, as may be expected, are numerous, will be considered in a separate section, in accordance with the plan adopted in this publication.

Carbonized vegetable remains have been preserved in great abundance and variety, to assist, as it were, in elucidating the mode of life of those ancient lake-villagers. They undoubtedly raised barley, wheat, and millet, several kinds of each of these cereals having been found in the lacustrine deposits. Some of these species of grain were cultivated in Egypt, and therefore are believed to have found their way from that country to Switzerland. Rye was not known to the colonists, and oats not before bronze had come into use. Barley and wheat appear either in grains, sometimes in considerable quantities, or, more rarely, in the shape of ears; and even carbonized wheat-bread, in which the bran and the imperfectly-crushed grains can be distinctly seen, has been found at Robenhausen and Wangen. This unleavened prehistoric bread, which is very coarse and compact, mostly occurs in fragments, but sometimes in the form of roundish cakes, about an inch or an inch and a half thick, and four or five inches or more in diameter, and was doubtless baked by placing the dough on hot stones, and covering it over with glowing ashes. Millet was employed in a similar manner for making bread. It is probable, however, that the lake-people consumed their farinaceous food chiefly in the shape of porridge.

Carbonized apples of small size, identical with those growing wild in the woods of Switzerland, have been found abundantly, and in a tolerable state of preservation. They are often cut in halves, more rarely in three or four parts, and were evidently dried for consumption during winter. Whether a larger kind of apple, found at Robenhausen, was a cultivated or a wild-growing species, remains undecided. Professor Oswald Heer, of Zürich, who has published an interesting work on lacustrine vegetable remains, inclines to the former view. Wild pears were treated in the same manner; but they are far less common than apples, which must have formed a much-sought article of diet. Among other vegetable remains accumulated in the lake-mud may be mentioned hazel-nuts and beech-nuts, both in great plenty; also water-chestnuts, which doubtless were collected and eaten by the lake-men, as they are in Upper Italy at this day. Their present occurrence in Switzerland appears to be restricted to a tarn in the Canton of Lucerne. There have further been found the stones of sloes, bird-cherries and wild plums, and seeds of the raspberry, blackberry, and strawberry, showing that these fruits of the forest were used as food. Excepting peas, no culinary vegetables have appeared in the stone-age settlements. Allusion having been made to the cultivation of flax, it may further be stated that hemp was totally unknown to the lake-dwellers, even to those of a later period.

According to Dr. Keller, the lake-colonists of the stone age drew their sustenance chiefly from the vegetable kingdom. Their animal food was acquired by hunting rather than by the breeding of cattle, considering that in the accumulations around the piles the bones of wild animals outnumber those of the domestic species. In the bronze-yielding pile-works, it will be seen, the proportion is reversed.

Fish-remains.—People living upon lakes plentifully stocked with fish, it can be imagined, availed themselves of all means in their power for capturing them, and the numerous remains of fishes discovered on the sites of the ancient lacustrine villages bear witness to the extent of their efforts in that direction. Not only the bones of fishes, but also their scales, the latter even in a good state of preservation, have been extracted from the lake-mud. "With respect to fishes," says Professor Rütimeyer, " many species were found which are now the most abundant in our lakes and rivers."[*] The following are mentioned:—

The salmon (*Salmo salar*, Lin.), the pike (*Esox lucius*, Lin.), the perch (*Perca fluviatilis*, Lin.), the carp (*Cyprinus carpio*, Lin.), the dace (*Cyprinus*

---

[*] Keller: Lake Dwellings; Vol. I, p. 537.

leuciscus, Lin.), the chub (*Cyprinus dobula*, Nilss.), the nase (*Chondrostoma nasus*, [Lin.] Agass.), the burbot (*Lota vulgaris*, Jen.), and the rud (*Scardinius erythrophthalmus*, [Lin.] Bon.).*

Pike of very large size are mentioned. Fish-remains were most abundant at the stations of Robenhausen and Moosseedorf.

Fishing-implements.—The relics directly referable to fishing, which have been discovered in the lacustrine relic-beds, render it certain that the ancient lake-dwellers fished with the line and with nets, and there can hardly be any doubt that they speared fish. Their mode of life rendered the use of boats necessary, and some of them, indeed, have been preserved to our time.

Such pointed bone rods as probably were used during the reindeer-period, instead of real fish-hooks, occur frequently in the deposits around the piles of ancient lake-villages, and no doubts are entertained as to their use. Dr. Keller, in treating of the antiquities found at Wangen, describes them in these words:—

"Fishing-implements made of bone. These occur very abundantly. A straight pin or shank is cut away a little, or has an incision round it in the middle, to which the fishing-line is attached, and then the little pin is quite covered over with the bait; when swallowed it cannot easily be got rid of by the fish. This plan is now in use on the Untersee for catching ducks."†

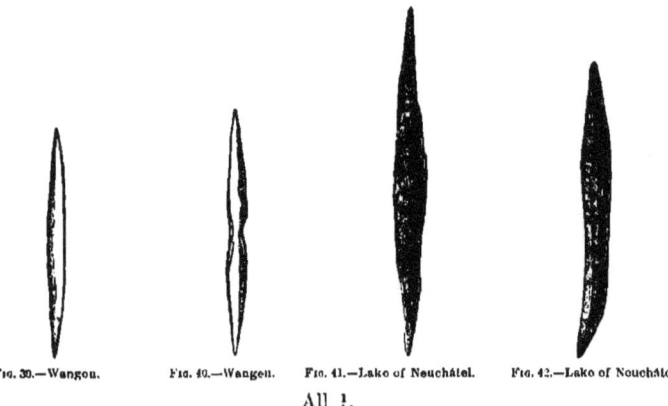

Fig. 39.—Wangen.   Fig. 40.—Wangen.   Fig. 41.—Lake of Neuchâtel.   Fig. 42.—Lake of Neuchâtel.

All ½.

Figs. 39–42.—Double-pointed bone implements.

---

* Keller: Lake Dwellings; Vol. I, p. 544.

† Ibid.; Vol. I, p. 71.—"M. de la Blanchère tells us that in France a similar form of instrument is used for catching eels. A straight piece of elder is taken, a needle pointed at both ends is passed through it; this is baited, and so eels are caught."—*Barnet Phillips: Transactions of the American Fish Cultural Association*, New York, 1879; p. 53.

The lake-people may have used them for catching fish as well as aquatic birds.

Figs. 39 and 40 represent such fishing-implements from Wangen.* Their character is so plainly expressed by the illustrations that a description becomes superfluous. There are several pointed bones of this character in the archæological collection of the United States National Museum. I give in Figs 41 and 42 representations of two of them, which were obtained from one of the pile-works in the Lake of Neuchâtel. However, I would not assert that their application really was that of bait-holders, considering the absence of notches or grooves in the middle.

FIG. 43.—Bone arrow-head (?). Saint-Aubin.

M. Henri Le Hon believes that somewhat curved specimens of this class served as arrow-heads, being attached to the end of the shaft in a manner to form both point and barb, as indicated by Fig. 43, which is copied from his work.† The original, he states, was obtained from the stone-age settlement near Saint-Aubin, in the Lake of Neuchâtel. If it really is as represented, all doubts as to its use must cease; but the design, for aught I know, may show an imaginary connection of point and shaft.

Real fish-hooks, made of horn, bone, and boars' tusks, approaching modern forms, and, in some cases, objects of less characteristic shapes, but supposed to represent fish-hooks, are not wanting in the lacustrine deposits of early date. Yet they appear to occur in limited number, only a few being figured in Dr. Keller's work. Fortunately I derive some aid from the reports on the International Fishery Exhibition, held at Berlin in 1880, in which delineations of some Swiss hooks are given.

---

* Keller: Lake Dwellings; Vol. II, Plate XIV, Figs. 23 and 24.
† Le Hon: L'Homme Fossile en Europe; fifth edition; Brussels and Paris; 1877, p. 215. (See p. 14, first note).

Fig. 44 is a reproduction of one of the represented specimens characterized as fish-hooks.* It was found at Wangen, and is said to consist of bone.† If, indeed, the object was applied as a fish-hook, it can, of course, only have served for catching larger kinds of fish.

Fig. 44.—Wangen.   Fig. 45.—Moosseedorf.   Fig. 46.—Moosseedorf.

Figs. 44–46.—Fish-hooks of deer-horn and boars' tusks.

The original of Fig. 45 is described by Dr. Keller as "a fish-hook made of the tusk of a wild boar."‡ To judge from the illustration, the specimen, which was obtained at Moosseedorf, is in its present form of rather unpromising appearance; but it seems that a portion of the hook has been removed by fracture. While complete, it may have fulfilled its purpose well enough.

There can be no doubt as to the character of the original of Fig. 46, which was also found at Moosseedorf, and is thus described:—"Fish-hook made of a boar's tusk; it was manufactured in the following manner: two holes were bored through it, the space between them was cleared away, and the whole was then finished by scraping-tools."§

Figs. 47 and 48 are reproductions of designs representing two well-defined bone fish-hooks from Wangen, somewhat resembling that just described. The shanks, however, show no incision for the attachment of a line, as in the preceding case. They were exhibited at Berlin in 1880.‖

---

* Amtliche Berichte über die Internationale Fischerei-Ausstellung zu Berlin, 1880.—Wissenschaftliche Abtheilung. Geschichte der Fischerei (von E. Friedel); Berlin, 1881; p. 128, Fig. 82.

† The material is doubtless deer-horn.

‡ Keller: Lake Dwellings; Vol. 1, p. 38; Vol. II, Plate V, Fig. 14.

§ Ibid.; Vol. 1, p. 39; Vol. II, Plate XXII, Fig. 5.

‖ Amtliche Berichte; p. 128, Figs. 80 and 81.

FISH-HOOKS.

The original of Fig. 49, which is copied from Keller's "Lake Dwellings,"* has been regarded as a double fish-hook. This specimen, made of deer-horn, was found at the station of Saint-Aubin. I will not attempt to decide whether it served as a fishing-implement or for some other purpose.

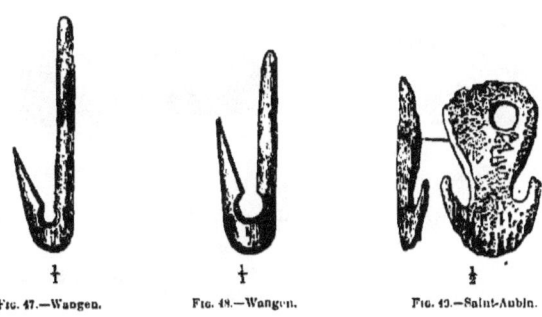

Fig. 47.—Wangen.   Fig. 48.—Wangen.   Fig. 49.—Saint-Aubin.

Figs. 47–49.—Bone and deer-horn fish-hooks.

None of the hooks here represented are barbed, though the perforations in Figs. 46, 47, and 48 leave projections which partake to some extent of the character of barbs.

The lake-men unquestionably used stone sinkers for deep-water fishing with hook and line; but as it is in many cases impossible to draw a line of demarcation between line and net-weights, I shall subsequently refer to them when treating of the objects characterized as sinkers.

Small pieces of bark of oval or rectangular, and sometimes of rather irregular, outline, pierced with one hole, or with two, which have been called floats for nets, are not unfrequent in some of the lacustrine relic-beds. The objects of this class figured in Keller's "Lake Dwellings" apppear to be too small to have been used for floating nets, and the same holds good for the specimens in the collection of the United States National Museum as well as in my own, which latter were obtained at Robenhausen, and sent to me by Mr. Messikommer, many years ago, among a series of relics from that locality. Larger ones, however, suitable for buoying nets, are in the collection of the Peabody Museum of American Archæology and Ethnology, at Cambridge, Massachusetts, and one of them will be described by me hereafter. I am of opinion that the smaller objects of the class here considered were employed as floats for fishing-lines, taking the place of the cork floats used in our days. Figs. 50 and 51 represent specimens in my collection. The original of Fig. 50

---

* Vol. II, Plate XLIII, Fig. 14.

50 PREHISTORIC FISHING.

is a flat piece of bark, not quite three-eighths of an inch in thickness, and pierced with a hole nearly in the middle. Fig. 51 shows a form like that of a boat with truncated ends. In this instance a hole is placed near each extremity.

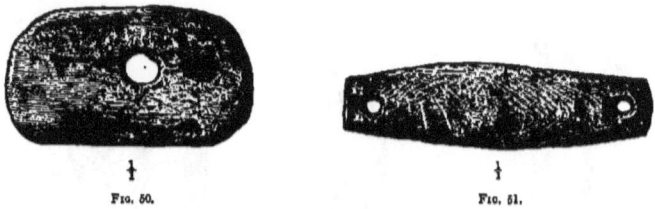

FIG. 50. FIG. 51.

FIGS. 50 and 51.—Bark floats. Robenhausen.

The lower surface is flat, the upper one, seen in the figure, irregularly convex. The two holes would have facilitated the sliding of the float along the fishing-line, before fastening it at the desired distance from the hook. There are two bark floats of this shape in the archæological collection of the United States National Museum, both likewise from Robenhausen.

FIG. 52.—Robenhausen. FIG. 53.—Robenhausen. FIG. 54.—"Arpion."

FIGS. 52–54.—Wooden implements used for recovering fishing-lines.

In connection with the line-fishing of the lake-men I have to describe a rather numerous class of simple wooden implements which bear much resemblance to the twirling-sticks used in making chocolate. They consist of a piece of a small tree-stem with the stumps of the lateral branches projecting from its lower end. Fig. 52 represents an object of this kind from Robenhausen, which is apparently much better preserved than others from the same locality.* I

---

* Keller: Lake Dwellings; Vol. II, Plate X, Fig. 12.

possess myself two of them and have seen others, all of which present a much rougher appearance than the specimen here figured. I place alongside of it, as Fig. 53, the representation of one, also from Robenhausen, which was sent to the Berlin Fishery Exhibition in 1880.* It shows the character of these objects much better than Fig. 52.

"These implements, which are not at all uncommon at Robenhausen, are of peculiar interest; at first they were considered as implements used for the churning or manufacturing of butter, but M. Rochat Maure, the engineer of Geneva, in the following notice, has clearly shown that they are to be considered as fishing-implements:—

'The fishermen who at the present day use implements of this kind live, while the fish are going up, on the banks of the river Arve, well known for its cold and rushing stream. They pass the night almost like savages, under huts made of twigs, and their small subsistence is extremely precarious. They catch the fish in the following manner:—To one end of a cord, the length of a stone's throw, they fasten a roundish flat stone, and to the other end a heavier stone of any convenient form. To this main cord they tie at intervals thinner strings with hooks at the end, and from three to five feet long. The heavy stone is then let down into the water from the boat at the side of the bank, but the other stone is thrown as far as possible straight across the stream towards the opposite bank. Early in the morning these cords are drawn up and examined, the implement used for this purpose being exactly like those found at Robenhausen. It is in fact the top of a young fir-tree with the branches springing from the main stem like radii. A cord is fastened to the upper end of this kind of hook, and in order to make it sink, some leaden rings or hooks are fastened to the main stem: it goes by the name of *arpion* amongst the fishermen. It is thrown into the water from the boat, and when drawn up, brings with it the thinner cords which have the hooks at the end. As the settlers at Robenhausen had no lead, it is possible that the perforated stones found in that settlement may have been used to sink these implements. — — — This implement is of great interest with respect to the history of civilization, for it proves that implements which have actually derived their origin from the highest antiquity are at the present moment used in precisely the same manner."†

Fig. 54 represents the arpion, which measures about eight inches in length.‡

Nearly related to this simple appliance in form and function, though more complicated and entirely made of iron, is the "devil's claw grapnel" (Fig. 55), used by New England fishermen to recover fishing-lines from the bottom of the

---

* Amtliche Berichte; p. 180, Fig. 96.
† Keller: Lake Dwellings; Vol. I, p. 53.
‡ Ibid.; Vol. 1, p. 54.

sea, when the buoys marking the position of the set lines or trawls have been lost or submerged by the action of violent winds and waves. It is generally employed on the outer fishing-banks lying off the East Coast of North America, in depths varying from twenty-five to over one hundred fathoms. The operation is as follows: one end of a long line—generally six-thread Manilla hemp buoy-line—is fastened to the long link at the extremity of the apparatus. This done, the implement is thrown out of the boat, and so much line veered out that the grapnel will "hug" the bottom, while the dory is being pulled along. Ordinarily two men row the boat during this operation of dragging for the lost gear, while another sits at the stern with his hand on the line, in order to be able to tell more surely than he otherwise could when the trawl-line is hooked. If the depth of water exceeds fifty fathoms, it is generally necessary to fasten an additional weight on the line, two or three fathoms distant from the grapnel, for the purpose of keeping the latter close to the bottom.*

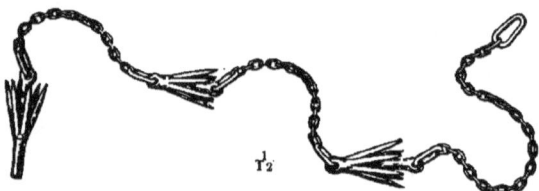

Fig. 55.—"Devil's claw grapnel." Massachusetts. (54342).

It has been stated that the lake-people doubtless obtained fish by the method of spearing—a supposition based upon the discovery of lacustrine barbed dart-heads of horn and bone, well suited for that purpose. Some of them may have been the armatures of hunting-spears, although, as we have seen,, the lake-dwellers were experts in the fabrication of weapon-heads of flint and jasper.

The original of Fig. 56, made of stag-horn, certainly bears the character of a harpoon-head. This specimen was found at the station of Saint-Aubin, and belonged to the collection of M. de Mortillet.†

Fig. 57 represents another harpoon-head of deer-horn, likewise found at Saint-Aubin, and formerly in the possession of Dr. Clement, whose collection was acquired by the Peabody Museum. It appears that Professor Desor considers this specimen as a fish-hook, an opinion which I can hardly share.‡

* For this information I am indebted to Captain Joseph W. Collins, of the United States Commission of Fish and Fisheries.

† The illustration is reproduced from "Reliquiæ Aquitanicæ," II, p. 51, Fig. 11.

‡ Desor: Palafittes, or Lacustrian Constructions, in the Lake of Neuchâtel; Smithsonian Report for 1865; p. 357. Fig. 57 is a reproduction of Fig. 11 a on the same page.—I could not identify this specimen among the Swiss harpoon-heads sent to me for examination by the trustees of the Peabody Museum.

HARPOON-HEADS.

Mr. Friedel figures a lacustrine object of almost the same shape, which he designates—correctly, I think—as a harpoon-head. To its shank still adheres the bituminous substance by which it was fastened into a shaft.* Fig. 58 repre-

FIGS. 56-58.—Deer-horn harpoon-heads. Saint-Aubin.

sents a fine deer-horn harpoon-head of kindred character from Saint-Aubin, which is preserved in the Peabody Museum (No. 5232. C). A smaller one, four and one-fourth inches in length, derived from the same locality, and likewise in

---

*Amtliche Berichte; p. 180, Fig. 97.

the above-named institution, has adhering to its shank a small fragment of the wooden shaft into which it was inserted.

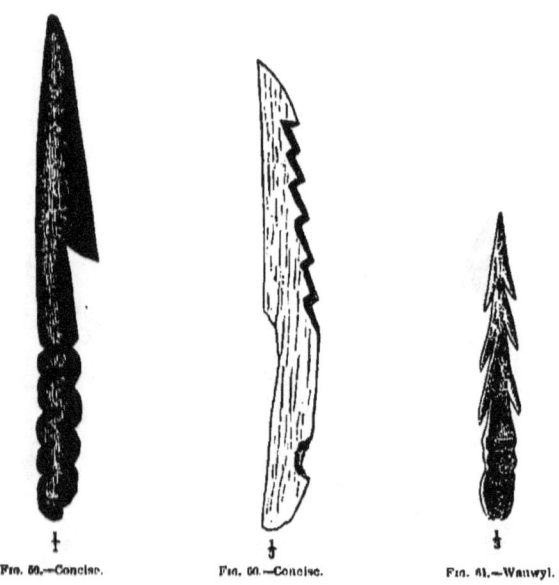

Figs. 59–61.—Harpoon-heads of bone and deer-horn.

Fig. 59 shows a very carefully worked bone harpoon-head, exhibited at Berlin in 1880.* The locality from which the specimen was derived is not named; but the same object, it appears, is figured, with other similar ones, on a smaller scale, in Dr. Keller's work,† as well as in that of M. Fréd. Troyon.‡ They are there denominated bone arrow-heads, and the Concise settlement in the Lake of Neuchâtel is mentioned as the locality where the specimens were obtained. These objects are attributed to the stone period, though the lake-village in question still flourished after the introduction of bronze. The shank of Fig. 59, it will be seen, is very artistically notched, and if its form is cylindrical or rod-like, as the delineation suggests, the notches may have served for the reception of bitumen by which the head was fastened in a socket-like cavity at the end of the shaft. There are, indeed, no very strong indications that the

---

* Amtliche Berichte; p. 128, Fig. 85.
† Keller: Lake Dwellings; Vol. II, Plate CIII, Figs. 16, 17, and 18.
‡ Troyon: Habitations Lacustres des Temps Anciens et Modernes; Lausanne, 1860; Plate VI, Figs. 3, 4, and 5.

lake-men used harpoons with detachable heads; but they may nevertheless have employed them.

The armatures thus far described exhibit only a single barb; in Fig. 60 a series of unilateral barbs is seen. The specimen, made of deer-horn, was found at Concise.*

Passing over to harpoon-like armatures with bilateral barbs, I give in Fig. 61 the representation of a specimen of deer-horn, found at Wauwyl. It shows three sharply-cut barbs on each side, and appears to be of a flattish form.†

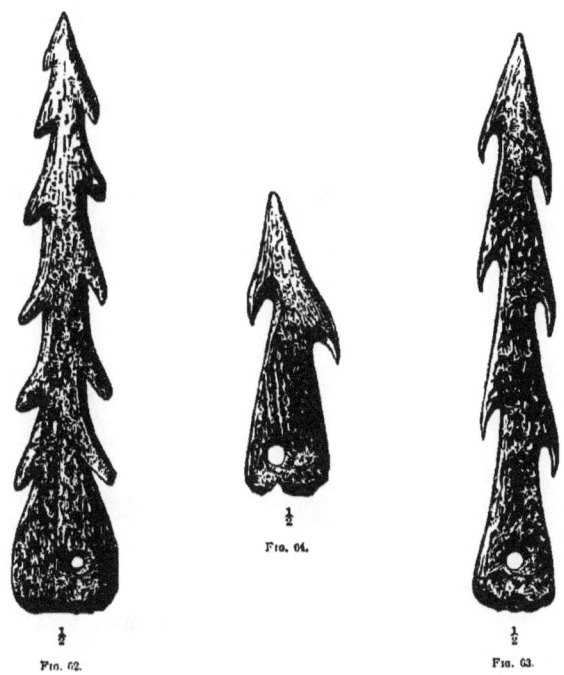

Figs. 62–64.—Deer-horn harpoon-heads. Lattringen.

Figs. 62, 63, and 64 are delineations of deer-horn harpoon-heads obtained by Dr. Gross from the Lattringen stone and bronze-age settlement in the Lake of Bienne. They are all perforated at the lower ends, which terminate abruptly.

---

* Troyon: Habitations Lacustres; Plate VI, Fig. 25.
† Keller: Lake Dwellings; Vol. II, Plate XX, Fig. 26.

The original of Fig. 62 is characterized by Dr. Gross as "a large harpoon, nearly eight and three-fourths inches long; it has eleven barbs, is perforated at the base, and has been skillfully made out of a fragment of stag's horn."[*] The barbs are rather blunt. Fig. 63 represents a very fine specimen, thus described by Dr. Gross in "Matériaux": "A large harpoon of deer-horn, twenty-two centimeters in length, provided with six very sharp barbs, and perforated at the base for being fastened to a wooden shaft by means of a peg (*cheville*)."[†] Dr. Gross, consequently, does not regard these harpoon-heads as detachable armatures. If the perforations had served for receiving a line they probably would not have been placed so near the lower end. Fig. 64 shows a shorter harpoon-head of similar character, with only one barb on each side. A deer-horn harpoon-head resembling very much the original of Fig. 64, and nearly of the same length, is preserved in the Peabody Museum. It was found at Saint-Aubin, and belonged to the Clement collection.

It may be assumed that one of the methods employed by the lake-people for obtaining fish was that of shooting them with arrows—barbed points of bone, horn, and stone, well suited to form the armatures of such arrows, having been found on the sites of the ancient lake-villages.

FIG. 65.—Saint-Aubin.   FIG. 66.—Robenhausen.   FIG. 67.—Bodio.

FIGS. 65–67.—Arrow-heads of horn and flint.

An arrow-head from Saint-Aubin, consisting of stag-horn, and according to the illustration, still connected with a portion of the shaft, is represented by Fig. 65.[‡] It has only one barb, and is certainly of a shape suggestive of fish-shooting. Fig. 66 shows the form of a barbed flint point from Robenhausen, which might have been used with advantage as the head of an arrow designed

---

[*] Keller: Lake Dwellings; Vol. I, p 450; Vol. II, Plate XLII, Fig. 1.

[†] Gross: Dernières Trouvailles dans les Habitations Lacustres du Lac de Bienne; Matériaux; Vol. XV, 1880; p. 10. Representations of the two harpoon-heads on Plate II, Figs. 1 and 2.

[‡] Keller: Lake Dwellings; Vol. II, Plate XLIII, Fig. 12.

for the fish-hunt.* I am uncertain whether Figs. 65 and 66 are drawn in full or fractional size, no statements indicating the scale being made in the translation of Dr. Keller's work.† In Fig. 67 I present the delineation of a similar flint arrow-head from the stone and bronze-yielding station near Bodio, on the Lake of Varese, in Lombardy. In this instance, too, the size is not mentioned; but it is probably the natural one.‡ It hardly need be remarked that the stone arrow-heads here figured may just as well have belonged to hunting, or, perhaps, even to war-arrows. I have simply dealt in probabilities in guardedly assigning to them another use.

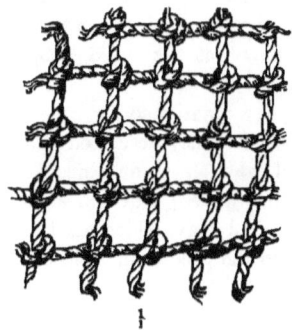

FIG. 68.—Fragment of fishing-net. Robenhausen (?).

There can be no doubt that the lake-dwellers fished with nets. Owing to peculiar circumstances, known to the reader, many fabrics of flax have been preserved in the relic-beds, and among these are fragments of nets made exactly like those used in our time. But even in the absence of these fragments the occurrence of real net-sinkers would furnish sufficient ground for the assertion. "Of netted manufacture," it is said, "the most simple form are the nets, which vary considerably, both in the strength of the cord and in the size of the meshes, according to the purposes for which they were designed, and yet they seem all to have been made in the same manner."§ It would be strange, indeed, if primitive people had employed different methods in making nets, whatever their destination might have been. There are but two delineations of net-fragments given in Dr. Keller's work, one of which is here reproduced as Fig. 68.‖ The meshes of this

---

* Keller: Lake Dwellings; Vol. II, Plate XIII, Fig. 13.
† Unfortunately this is too often the case in that publication, and greatly diminishes its scientific value.
‡ Keller: Lake-Dwellings; Vol. II, Plate CLXII, Fig. 1.
§ Ibid.; Vol. I, p. 510.
‖ Ibid.; Vol. II, Plate CXXXVI, Fig. 2.

58 PREHISTORIC FISHING.

net, which is made of strong cord, are not quite three-eighths of an inch in width, and hence it was well suited for fishing-purposes. The other figured fragment of a net has meshes no less than two inches wide, and is therefore—with good reason, I believe—designated as a remnant of a hunting-net. The plate from which Fig. 68 is copied shows designs of flax fabrics from Robenhausen and Wangen, but the locality where each object was obtained is not specialized, either on the plate or, as far as I could discover, in the text and the list of illustrations.

Of course, any attempt at speculating on the character of the nets employed by the lake-dwellers would be fruitless. The few remaining fragments certainly give us no clue. It is likely that they used the primitive and almost universal seine-net while fishing near the shore; in deep water they may have followed other methods. We only know that they used *nets*, and must be satisfied with that information.

Net-sinkers are frequently mentioned in the translation of Dr. Keller's work, but in many cases not sufficiently described and rarely figured. There are sometimes doubts expressed whether stone objects of a certain form are to be considered as sinkers or sling-stones; and the same vagueness prevails with regard to pierced cones of baked clay, which are thought to have served either as net-sinkers or as weights in the process of weaving.

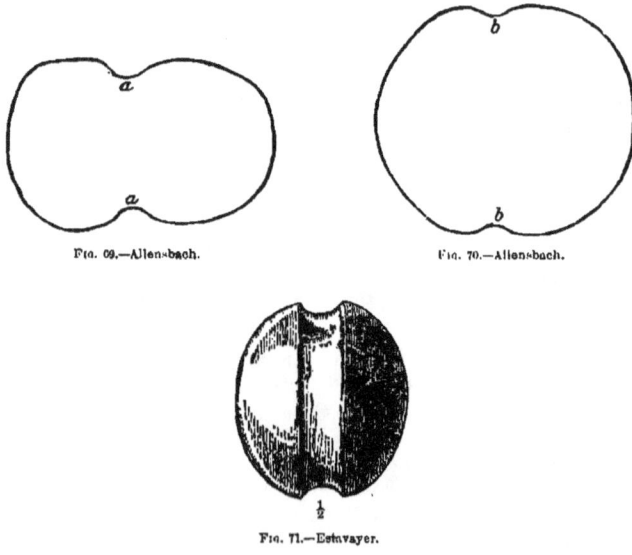

FIG. 69.—Allensbach.   FIG. 70.—Allensbach.

FIG. 71.—Estavayer.

FIGS. 69–71.—Stone sinkers.

SINKERS.

Before entering upon a description of lacustrine sinkers, I would draw attention to the fact that only such as are found in settlements of the pure stone age can with certainty be regarded as neolithic, provided they occur under circumstances excluding the possibility of later intrusion. Those from stations pertaining to the ages of stone and bronze may belong to either. It is evident that the transition from stone to bronze would not have changed the character of the sinkers. Indeed, net-weights of stone and clay are even at present in use among uncivilized and civilized peoples.

Allusion was already made to the difficulty, or rather impossibility, of distinguishing in many instances between sinkers for lines and such as served as net-weights. Yet European archæologists mostly refer to net-sinkers only.

I have no doubt that the originals of Figs. 69 and 70* were used as sinkers. They certainly resemble the commonest North American aboriginal net-weights, consisting of water-worn flat pebbles notched on opposite sides, the notches being produced by blows. The originals of Figs. 69 and 70, which are derived from the stone-age station of Allensbach, on the Untersee (Baden), are described as "flat, almost unworked rolled stones, from four to five lines thick and from three and a half to four inches in length, showing no further traces of workmanship than the hollows or furrows at a and b."† It is not even stated whether the indentations are produced by blows or by grinding, and the designs—here faithfully copied—consist of mere outlines, which fail to indicate the precise character of the specimens.

The original of Fig. 71,‡ from the stone and bronze-age station near Estavayer, on the Lake of Neuchâtel, is mentioned as one of the stones commonly called "sling-stones."§ Yet there are undoubted North American sink-stones of exactly the same form; and quite similar ones found in Europe, apart from lake-dwellings, are pronounced sinkers by competent archæologists, as will be shown in the sequel. I would unhesitatingly ascribe that character to the figured specimen.

A few stone discs or disc-like pebbles, with a central perforation, which may have served as net-sinkers, are figured in Keller's "Lake Dwellings;" but instead of copying any of his illustrations, I give in Figs. 72 and 73, on the following page, designs of originals in the Peabody Museum, at Cambridge. Fig. 72 is an irregular flat disc of gray sandstone, half an inch in thickness, and exhibiting a rough surface, which latter circumstance renders it difficult to decide whether the stone has been artificially modified or not. The hole in the middle

---

* Keller: Lake Dwellings; Vol. II, Plate XXIV, Figs. 1 and 4.

† Ibid.; Vol. I, p. 90.

‡ Ibid.; Vol. II, Plate XCVII, Fig. 12.

§ Ibid.; Vol. I, p. 265.

is drilled from both sides. This specimen (No. 4991. A) was obtained at the Saint-Aubin station. The original of Fig. 73 (No. 4991. B) is a somewhat flat-

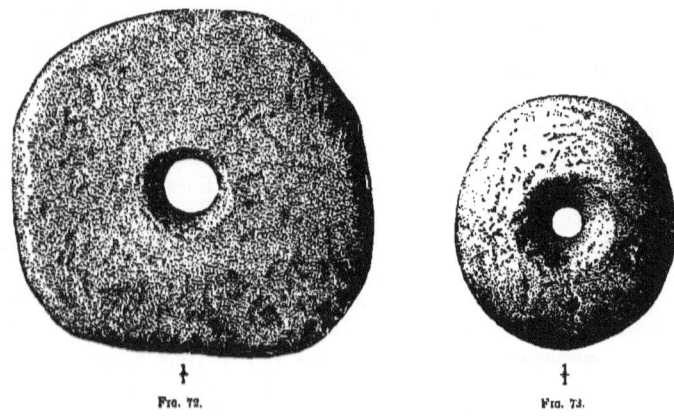

FIGS. 72 and 73.—Stone sinkers (?). Saint-Aubin.

tish oval pebble of compact gray sandstone (molasse), with a central perforation sunk from both sides, and of bi-conical form. It was likewise found at Saint-Aubin.

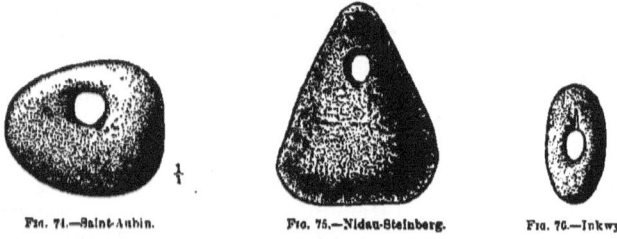

FIG. 74.—Saint-Aubin. FIG. 75.—Nidau-Steinberg. FIG. 76.—Inkwyl.

FIGS. 74-76.—Sinkers (?) of stone and clay.

There are in the Peabody Museum smaller pebbles, perforated, but not in the centre, which are almost too light to have served as net-sinkers, but which may have been used in connection with fishing-lines, if they were not designed for other purposes. One of them (No. 4991. G), found at Saint-Aubin, is here represented as Fig. 74. It is a small water-worn stone of pale-gray color and calcareous character, pierced with a straight cylindrical hole.

In Fig. 75 I represent one of the clay cones to which reference was made.*

---

* Keller: Lake Dwellings; Vol. II, Plate XXXVIII, Fig. 16.

It belongs to the large series of objects derived from the important Nidau-Steinberg settlement in the Lake of Bienne. "Many objects of stone, bone, and pottery which have been obtained there, and which mark the commencement of the civilization of man in our districts, show that it was a settlement in the earliest period; but its existence was prolonged up to the time when bronze was commonly employed for implements; nay, it even outlasted this period, and reached that when iron came into use."* The clay cones are thus described:— "The things which commonly go by these names—sink-stones (*sic*) or weights—are about four and a half inches high, of a conical form, and are about four or four and a half in diameter at the base; they were made without any care and of common clay. The fact that they are perforated towards the point of the cone and that they were found at a fishing-station, seems to argue for the correctness of the common designation; but subsequent investigations have proved that many at least of these clay cones were simply weights used in weaving."† This theory was first advanced by Mr. Paur, a ribbon-manufacturer of Zürich, who constructed a weaving-apparatus by which he made the various kinds of linen cloth found in the lake-settlements. "And, as a further proof, he showed from indubitable evidence that the clay cones are to be considered as constituent parts of the looms of the lake-dwellings. If further proof were wanting, it may be given in the fact that in several rooms lately excavated by Mr. Messikommer at Robenhausen, at least half a dozen of these clay cones were found in each, so that weaving must have been carried on there to a great extent."‡

This sounds very plausible, but it does not carry conviction with it. Mr. Paur's reconstructed loom,§ which, by the way, bears a striking resemblance to one in the Archaeological Museum at Copenhagen,‖ is by no means an absolutely simple contrivance, but rather complicated when compared with the simple looms of modern Indians of the West, who produce textile fabrics certainly as good as those of the Swiss lake-men. The Pima Indians on the Gila River, for instance, make very creditable and really ornamental tissues, employing a loom that consists only of a few sticks, which they carry about in a small bundle.¶ The loom of the ancient Mexicans,** was far less complicated than that constructed by Mr. Paur, and yet the inhabitants wove cotton cloth which excited the admiration of the Spanish conquerors. A number of such primitive Indian

---

* Keller: Lake Dwellings; Vol. I, p. 139.

† Ibid.; Vol. I, p. 151.

‡ Ibid.; Vol. I, p. 514.

§ Ibid.; Vol. I, p. 516, Fig. 40.

‖ This mediæval loom, obtained from one of the Færöe Islands, is figured in Worsaae's "Nordiske Oldsager i det Kongelige Museum i Kjöbenhavn;" Copenhagen, 1859; p. 159, Fig. 558.

¶ Emory: Notes of a Military Reconnoissance, etc.; Washington, 1848; p. 85.

** Represented in the Mendoza Codex.

looms, with a commenced piece of cloth on them, may be seen in the United States National Museum. In these looms a stick serves as a warp-stretcher.

In various lacustrine stations have been found rings of baked clay, to which the character of net-sinkers is now and then attributed. "These rings," it is stated, with reference to those found at Nidau, "are made of clay mixed with little stones and pieces of charcoal, but they are imperfectly burnt, and very little care has been bestowed upon them; they vary in external diameter from three and a half to nine and a half inches; the hole in the middle is from seven lines to two and a half inches wide, and the thickness of the ring itself varies from one inch to upwards of two inches. Various opinions have been expressed as to the use of these rings. The idea that they were net-weights is now abandoned. It seems now ascertained that they were used as supports for the vessels which either had no base at all, or one so small that they would not stand. There can be no doubt also that they were used in a similar way as supports for pipkins with a conical base when placed on the hearth. Many of these rings have become friable from the action of violent heat, but it is not always certain whether this happened on the hearth or when the settlement was burnt down."* The view that these rings served as supports for vessels seems to me correct, and they belong, as far as I can judge, more properly to the era of lacustrine life when bronze was in use, and during which many vessels with convex or even conical bottoms were made. I have one of these clay rings, which was sent to me, with many other lacustrine relics, by the late Professor Desor. The specimen in question, obtained at Auvernier, Lake of Neuchâtel, is rather carelessly made, and answers well the description just given. Even the little stones and pieces of charcoal are not wanting. The ring is not quite four inches in diameter, and the central hole is a little more than an inch and a half wide. It shows no wear indicative of use as a net-sinker, but distinct traces of exposure to fire. On the accompanying label is written by Professor Desor: *Bronzezeit. Ring von gebrannter Erde zum Aufstellen der Vasen.*

Yet some of the clay rings actually seem to have been used as net or line-sinkers, as, for instance, the original of Fig. 76 on page 60, which was found in the stone-age settlement of the Lake of Inkwyl.† "This specimen has the furrow still remaining which was worn by the cord. It seems now clear that these smaller rings were net-weights, while most of the larger ones were supports for the conical-footed earthenware vessels."‡ The size of the specimen is not mentioned. It is probably double the size of the figure.

According to Mr. E. Frank, net-sinkers consisting of pieces of pottery with

---

* Keller: Lake Dwellings; Vol. I, p. 150.

† Ibid.; Vol. II, Plate XXXIX, Fig. 2.

‡ Ibid., Vol. I, p. 445.

FLOATS. 63

incisions or notches on opposite sides have occurred in large number at the lacustrine settlement of Schussenried, in the basin of the Feder-See, in Würtemberg.* This station, which belongs to the stone age, was particularly rich in pottery. There are in the United States National Museum some Central-American net-sinkers of the same kind, to which reference will be made in the appendix to this work.

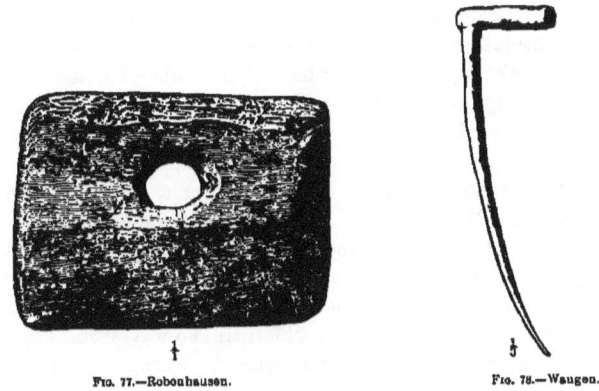

FIG. 77.—Robenhausen.   FIG. 78.—Wangen.

FIGS. 77 and 78.—Bark float and wooden implement for arranging nets.

It was stated on a preceding page that a few of the lacustrine bark floats in the Peabody Museum appear to be of sufficient size to have been used for buoying nets. Fig. 77 (No. 3238) represents one of them, which was found in the Robenhausen lake-settlement. It is of rectangular shape and provided with a rude perforation. The lake-men, for aught we know, may have used for their nets floats of wood—a material still frequently employed for the same purpose. Yet in the translation of Keller's work, bark is always mentioned as the material of which they are made.

A wooden implement from Wangen, represented in Fig. 78,† is described in a satisfactory manner as "a fishing-implement made of the branch of a shrub and its offshoot, and intended for drawing together and arranging the nets when dried. Exactly similar implements are now in use amongst fishermen."‡ I am unable to say whether several of these utensils have been preserved; but the recovery of even a single one appears of interest, in so far as it demonstrates

---

* Keller: Lake Dwellings; Vol. I, p. 583.
† Ibid.; Vol. II, Plate XXII, Fig. 6.
‡ Ibid.; Vol. I, p. 71.

that the ancient fishermen applied such simple contrivances tending to facilitate their work.

It cannot now be decided whether the lake-men made their nets "on a frame by knotting the string at each point of intersection," as M. Figuier conjectures,* or employed netting-needles. The latter are repeatedly alluded to in the work from which I derive the principal facts bearing upon prehistoric fishing in the Swiss and other lakes. But the notices relating to these implements are vague and not calculated to throw any light on the method of net-making. Among the antiquities found at the stone-age station near Nussdorf, on the Ueberlinger See, the northwestern branch of the Lake of Constance (Baden), are mentioned "netting, hair, or clothes pins, made out of boars' tusks, and consequently curved; they have a sharp point, and are sometimes notched at one end, probably caused by the use to which they were applied. The pins for making fishing-nets were made out of the corner tooth of a bear and perforated."† I reproduce in Figs. 79, 80, and 81 the representations serving to illustrate the above descriptions.‡ Figs. 79 and 80 certainly bear no resemblance to any netting-implements with which I am acquainted; and as for the pierced bear's tooth (Fig. 81), there is no statement made in support of the view that it served as a pin for making fishing-nets. It differs in no way from the pierced teeth worn as trophies or charms by the prehistoric Europeans as well as by still existing savage tribes. Pointed ribs found at some lacustrine stations have been regarded as netting-implements; but it is not at all certain that they were thus employed.

Figs. 79–81.—Implements made of boars' tusks, and perforated bear's tooth. Nussdorf.

---

* Figuier: Primitive Man; p. 186.
† Keller: Lake Dwellings; Vol. I, p. 119.
‡ Ibid.; Vol. II, Plate XXVIII, Figs. 16, 17, and 15, respectively.

In order to show the appearance of netting-needles at present used in North America, both by the civilized and uncivilized, I insert here representations of such implements.

Fig. 82.—New England. (25593).

Fig. 83.—Eskimos, Nunivak Island, Alaska. (16171).

Fig. 84.—Eskimos, Chirikoff Island, Alaska. (16296).

Fig. 85.—McCloud River Indians, California.

All ½.

Figs. 82–85.—Modern netting-implements.

Fig. 82 illustrates the shape of the ordinary wooden netting-needle still in use among fishermen in New England, although nets are now to a great extent manufactured there by machinery. Fig. 83 represents a netting-implement of bone, derived from the Magemut Eskimos in Nunivak Island, Alaska. A similar wooden implement used by the Eskimos of Chirikoff Island, Alaska, is represented in Fig. 84; and in Fig. 85, lastly, I show the form of the simple tool employed for netting by the McCloud River Indians in California. It consists of two slightly curved and pointed sticks, bound together with vegetable fibre. Sometimes they use a stick bifurcated at both ends.

PREHISTORIC FISHING.

Boats.—Lacustrine life would hardly have been possible without the means of locomotion on the water, and hence we may assume that there was no lack of boats among the lake-men. Many boats, indeed, have been found imbedded in the mud on or near the sites of former lake-settlements. Excepting a few, these ancient boats are made of a single tree, and hollowed out by means of stone or metallic implements, according to the period in which they originated. In times anteceding the introduction of bronze, fire doubtless was an efficient aid in the manufacture of these boats. Such primitive vessels, corresponding to the dug-outs in this country, are still in use on some of the Swiss lakes, as, for instance, on those of Lucerne, Zug, and Aegeri, in the Canton of Zug, in which district they are manufactured to the present day. A boat of this description is called *Einbaum* (one-tree) in Switzerland.

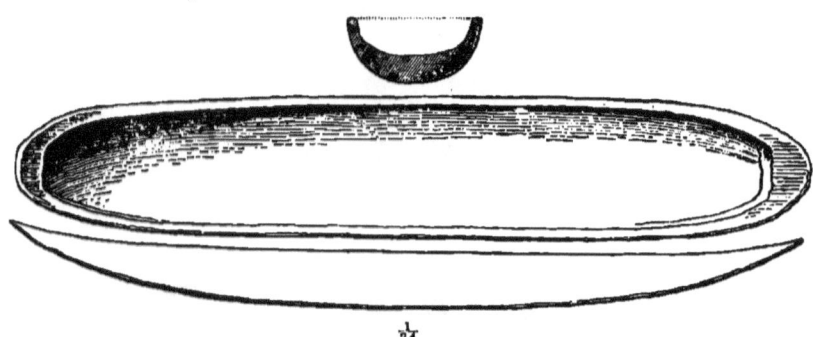

FIG. 86.—Boat. Robenhausen.

An ancient boat, found at Robenhausen by Mr. Messikommer, and, I believe, still in existence—notwithstanding the difficulty of preserving such objects when out of the water—is represented in Fig. 86.* It is twelve feet long, two feet and a half wide, and five inches deep.† I find no statement concerning the kind of wood of which it is made. The illustration (upper view, side-view, and cross-section) renders any further description unnecessary. As Robenhausen is a station of the stone age, this boat can with safety be attributed to that period.

Professor Desor speaks of a number of such pirogues in the Lake of Bienne, one of which can be seen near Saint Peter's Island (*Île de Saint-Pierre*), projecting from the mud of the lake, and still holding the cargo of stones with which

---

* Keller: Lake Dwellings; Vol. II, Plate X, Fig. 8.
† Ibid.; Vol. I, p. 53.

it had foundered.* It is made of the trunk of an oak, scarcely less than fifty feet long, by three and a half to four feet in width.† "According to M. Desor," says M. de Mortillet, "the lake-dwellers of the stone age, in order to consolidate the piles designed to support their habitations, wedged them up (*les calaient*) with stones which they gathered in boats on the shore, the bottom of the lake being totally free of them. The pirogue of Saint Peter's Island, therefore, would appear to be a vessel sunk with its load of stones at a date reaching as far back as the epoch of polished stone."‡ As it is well known that maritime tribes have hollowed out very large canoes without metallic tools, M. de Mortillet's view may be correct; but it is equally possible that the boat in question belongs to a later time.

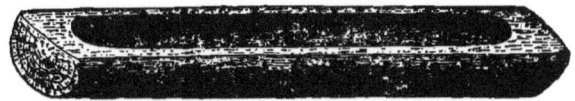

FIG. 87.—Boat. Möringen.

Fig. 87 illustrates the form of one of several dug-outs found at the station of Möringen, Lake of Bienne.§ It certainly has a very primitive appearance, and may belong to the stone age; but, considering that the Möringen settlement has furnished objects of stone, bronze, and iron, it is impossible to assign to it a definite place in lacustrine chronology. Strangely enough, the dimensions of this boat are not indicated in the translation of Dr. Keller's reports, and I would not even know that it consists of oak-wood, if the fact were not mentioned in M. Troyon's "Habitations Lacustres" (page 165).

Mention is made, and a figure given, of a toy-boat of fir-wood, nine inches long and one and a half wide, found at the settlement of Gerolfingen (Gérofin), in the Lake of Bienne, and characterized as "merely a reproduction of the lacustrine canoes of the stone period."‖ But having been found associated with objects of metal, its antiquity is uncertain.

I am not aware that any contrivances for propelling boats (paddles, etc.) have been discovered among the lacustrine remains of Switzerland or other countries. An anchor-stone from Nidau is described and figured in Lee's translation. Its origin, however, is of comparatively recent date, and therefore

---

* Desor: Palafittes; p. 359.
† Troyon: Habitations Lacustres; p. 166.
‡ De Mortillet: Origine de la Navigation et de la Pêche; Matériaux, Vol. III, 1867; p. 47.
§ Keller: Lake Dwellings; Vol. II, Plate XL, Fig. 4.
‖ Ibid.; Vol. I, p. 452.

beyond the compass of my present observations. According to Professor Gastaldi, a wooden anchor came to light in the peat-covered small pile-work at Mercurago, near Arona, on Lago Maggiore. This station, from the objects there found, is supposed to pertain to the time when bronze began to take the place of stone. The wooden anchor was more than a meter in length, terminated at one end in two hooks, and was perforated at the other, to receive the rope.* No further description, or figure, is given, and it remains doubtful to what period the object belongs.

I shall have to refer to lacustrine boats again, when treating of fishing during the bronze period.

The abstracts of reports on lake-settlements in Austria, Bavaria, etc., contained in the translation of Dr. Keller's work have furnished no additional details bearing upon fishing in the neolithic age. Unfortunately, the original treatises are not at my command.

FISHING-IMPLEMENTS AND UTENSILS NOT FOUND IN LACUSTRINE SETTLEMENTS.

General Remarks.—The above title sufficiently explains the purport of this section, in which a limited number of objects will be described. It appears to me that not many isolated fishing-implements have been discovered in Europe; for, if they were frequent, more would be said concerning them in archæological works. Yet, not a few may be in existence of which I have no knowledge, notwithstanding my endeavors to follow the progress of prehistoric archæology in Europe as closely as distance and other adverse circumstances permit. In the main, however, I believe my observation regarding the comparative scarcity of neolithic antiquities bearing upon fishing to be correct. I will mention an example in point. In August, 1880, there was in the city of Berlin an exhibition of archæological finds (*Funde*) made in Germany, to which nearly all public and private collections of the empire had contributed their shares, and it doubtless represented not only all types of German prehistoric antiquities, but also their numerical proportion. The exhibited objects are enumerated in a printed catalogue of 619 octavo pages, to which a supplement of 128 pages is added. In examining the catalogue, I was struck with the scarcity of fishing-objects mentioned in it, there being specified only a number of flints pointed at both ends and supposed to have been used like fish-hooks, two bone fish-hooks, one bone harpoon-head, two bone darts (*Fischstecher*)—one with inserted splinters of flint—

---

* Gastaldi: Lake Habitations and Prehistoric Remains in the Turbaries and Marl-Beds of Northern and Central Italy; translated by C. H. Chambers; London, 1865; p. 102.

and seventeen net-weights, some of them marked doubtful. A number of these sinkers may not belong to neolithic, but to later, times. There are further enumerated, I will add, a fish-hook of bronze, one of iron, and two or three other objects.* It will be admitted that these few articles formed but an insignificant fraction of the many thousands of antiquities exhibited at Berlin.

I will now proceed to describe the fishing-implements referred to at the beginning of this section, classifying them according to the use to which they were applied.

Double-pointed straight Bait-holders.—Reference has been made on preceding pages to bone rods tapering toward both ends, which were, and still are, used in lieu of fish-hooks. It appears that in neolithic times such simple implements for catching fish were made of flint. I never have seen any of them, and therefore have to rely on the statements of others. Mr. Friedel alludes to one in the Fishery Department of the Berlin Provincial Museum, of which he is in charge. He says:—"Upon these stone spindles, chipped to a point at each end, and attached in the middle to a line, the bait was fastened, in order to be swallowed entire by the fish intended to be caught."† The specimen in question was found on an island in the river Havel, near Berlin. Several, obtained from the Island of Rügen, in the Baltic Sea, were exhibited by Mr. Rosenberg at Berlin in 1880. He considers them well suited for catching pike.‡ Mr. Rosenberg speaks of another class of flint implements from Rügen, which present a peculiar form, and served, as he thinks, in the construction of fish-hooks.§ I shall revert to them hereafter, when treating of a peculiar class of fish-hooks from Greenland.

Fish-hooks.—Two entire fish-hooks of flint, preserved in the Museum of Lund, Sweden, are described and figured by Professor Sven Nilsson. I reproduce on the next page his designs as Figs. 88 and 89.|| The Swedish archæologist gives the following account of the specimens:—

"The first of these (here Fig. 88) was found near Lomma, on the shore of the Sound (Öresund). It is in length, from the middle of the end of the shaft to the bend of the hook, about one inch and five lines, and in breadth, from the

---

* Among fish-remains are mentioned those of the pike from a pile-work on the Roseninsel (Island of Roses) in Lake Starnberg, Bavaria, and of the *Wels* (*Silurus glanis*, of the cat-fish family) and pike from Schussenried, in Würtemberg.

† Friedel: Führer durch die Fischerei-Abtheilung des Märkischen Provinzial-Museums der Stadtgemeinde Berlin; Berlin, 1880; p. 1.

‡ Such implements of stone, bone, or bronze are called *Spitzangeln* in German.

§ (Voss): Katalog der Ausstellung prähistorischer und anthropologischer Funde Deutschlands — — — zu Berlin (August, 1880); Berlin, 1880; p. 364.

|| Nilsson: The Primitive Inhabitants of Scandinavia; translated by Sir John Lubbock; London, 1868; Plate 11, Figs. 28 and 29.—Fig. 29 is also to be found in Worsaae's "Danmarks Oldtid oplyst ved Oldsager og Gravböie;" Copenhagen, 1843; p. 10.

outside of the shaft to the outside of the hook, about one inch and four lines. At the top it is thick and broken off straight, and below the thick end there is a scarcely noticeable incision, or neck, round which to tie the line. It tapers downwards to the point, and has been *chipped on both sides* towards the front and back; it has, therefore, as we see, been fashioned with some skill to answer its purpose.

"Nobody who has seen the fish-hooks of bone, wood, or shell, made by savages, can entertain the least doubt that this one has been used for the same purpose. It is even possible to say with tolerable accuracy, judging from its size and the place where it was found, what description of fish was principally caught with it. Amongst the fish indigenous to the Sound (Öresund), on the shore of which it was picked up, it would have been too large for the mouth of eels, flounders, or whiting, but it is suitable in every way for the Öresund cod-fish (*Gadus callarias*, Lin.), and this species of fish is still caught by hooks, here and elsewhere. There is little doubt, therefore, that the said flint fish-hook was used in ancient times for cod-fishing in the Sound. The other fish-hook of flint (here Fig. 89) was found on the bank of the Kranke Lake, near Silfåkra. It is smaller, the length scarcely exceeding one inch and one line, and the breadth, from the outside of the shaft to the outside of the hook, not quite six lines. It has likewise been chipped in front and back, and the shaft widens at the top to allow the line to be tied to it. It has been used for catching smaller fish than the former. The Kranke Lake is still stocked with perch and eel, and an experienced angler has assured me that one would still be able to catch these kinds of fish with this very hook."*

Fig. 88.—Öresund.   Fig. 89.—Kranke Lake.   Fig. 90.—Scandinavia. (5275).

Figs. 88-90.—Flint fish-hooks.

Mr. John Evans makes the following statement with regard to flint fish-hooks:—"Fish-hooks formed entirely of flint, and found in Sweden, have been engraved by Nilsson, and others, presumed to have been found in Holderness,

---

* Nilsson: Primitive Inhabitants; p. 22, etc.

by Mr. T. Wright, F. S. A. The latter are, however, in all probability, forgeries."*

I introduce on the preceding page (not without some misgivings) Fig. 90, representing a chipped flint hook found either in Sweden or Norway, and presented to the National Museum by Professor Jillson, a gentleman of Scandinavian nationality. The hook is two inches and one-eighth long, and made of a flattish flake, on an average about one-eighth of an inch in thickness, the somewhat rude chipping being confined to the outline. The point terminates rather sharply. No doubt can be entertained as to the genuineness of the relic, its appearance betokening great antiquity. Of course, it remains undecided whether this hook was designed for catching fish or for some other purpose, though experts in angling have admitted the *bare possibility* that it may have been a fish-hook. The width of the shank and of the curved portion, however, lessen its fitness for that purpose.

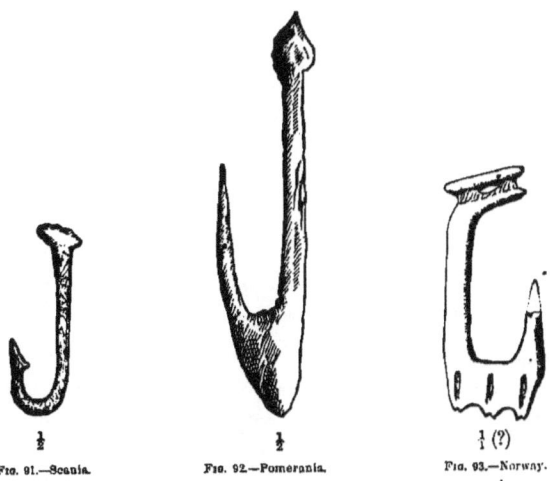

FIG. 91.—Scania.   FIG. 92.—Pomerania.   FIG. 93.—Norway.

FIGS. 91–93.—Fish-hooks of bone and reindeer-horn.

Professor Nilsson gives the description and figure of a fine barbed bone fish-hook (here Fig. 91) which possibly belongs to the neolithic age.† "It has been found," he says, "in one of the old peat-bogs in the South of Scania. It is three inches long, and about six-eighths of an inch from the point of the barb to the bar. The bar and the bend are nearly round, and flattened a little

---

* Evans: Ancient Stone Implements; p. 265.

† The lacustrine fish-hooks of bone, etc., it will be remembered, are unbarbed.

towards the top, which is broad, for the purpose of fastening the line. It was found in a bog containing fresh water, and has no doubt been used for catching pike, of which enormously large skeletons have been found in the bogs of Scania. I know no other fresh-water fish in Scania for which such a large-sized hook could have been used."*

A bone fish-hook of more primitive appearance, preserved in the collection of the Society for Pomeranian History and Archæology, at Stettin, is represented on the preceding page in Fig. 92. This specimen was found imbedded in marl, fourteen feet below the surface, near Reddies, District of Rummelsburg, Pomerania. It is figured and described by Mr. Christensen.†

Fig. 93, on the same page, is copied from "Matériaux." It shows the form of a fish-hook of reindeer-horn, preserved in the Museum of Christiania, Norway, and taken from a grave in the Norwegian part of Lapland. These graves, situated on the Island of Kjelmöe, in the Waranger Fjord, close to the Russian frontier, contained corpses wrapped in bands of willow-bark. With them, or scattered over the surface of the soil, were found pottery, reminding one of that of the dolmens, pieces of asbestus (use unknown), and a large number of objects made of reindeer-bone, such as combs, arrow and lance-heads, fish-hooks, spoons, etc. The age to which these antiquities belong has not yet been established.‡ Though, in all probability, they are post-neolithic, I did not deem it amiss to give a figure of that curiously-shaped fish-hook. The representation presumably shows the object in natural size.

Harpoon-heads.—Several ancient harpoon-heads of bone are described by Professor Nilsson in his work on the primitive inhabitants of Scandinavia.§

---

* Nilsson: Primitive Inhabitants; p. 24.

† Christensen: Zur Geschichte des Angelhakens; Deutsche Fischerei-Zeitung; Stettin, March 22, 1881; p. 95.

‡ Cazalis de Fondouce: Compte-rendu du Congrès International d'Archéologie et d'Anthropologie Préhistoriques de Copenhague; 2ᵉ Partie; Matériaux; Vol. VI, 1870; p. 221; figure on the same page.

§ It should be stated that some of the bone darts to be described may be of post-neolithic origin. In Sweden, for instance, bone-headed javelins were still used at a time when bronze was known. Professor Nilsson furnishes the following proof:—

"When, about thirty years ago, a level piece of ground near the village of Tygelsjö, in the South of Scania, was to be cultivated, there were found, close under the surface of the earth, a number of skeletons of human beings, who had been interred there, and round each skeleton was a row of stones forming an elongated square seven feet by three. This manner of interring the dead occurs only amongst those nations who used weapons of bronze, and probably not amongst the poor, never amongst people who used only stone weapons. As a further proof that these skeletons belonged to a tribe which, when settling in the South of Sweden, were in possession of bronze, I may mention that one of the skeletons, probably that of a woman, had round one of the arm-bones a spiral ring made of semi-circular bronze wire, such as was worn by the people of the bronze age.

"The skull of one of the skeletons was pierced with a javelin of bone, made from the point of the antler of an elk, which, when it came into my hands, was mutilated, but, when found, had been quite perfect; about seven inches long, round, having the smaller end pointed, the thicker cut off straight, and about an inch in diameter."— *Primitive Inhabitants;* p. 171.

"The harpoon," he says, "is a common fishing and hunting-implement among those savages who inhabit islands and the sea-coast. It can be used only in the water, where it is thrown in order to fasten in the animal which is to be caught. Its purpose is not to kill the prey, but to check its career in the water, so that it may be more easily approached and killed with another weapon—the spear.*

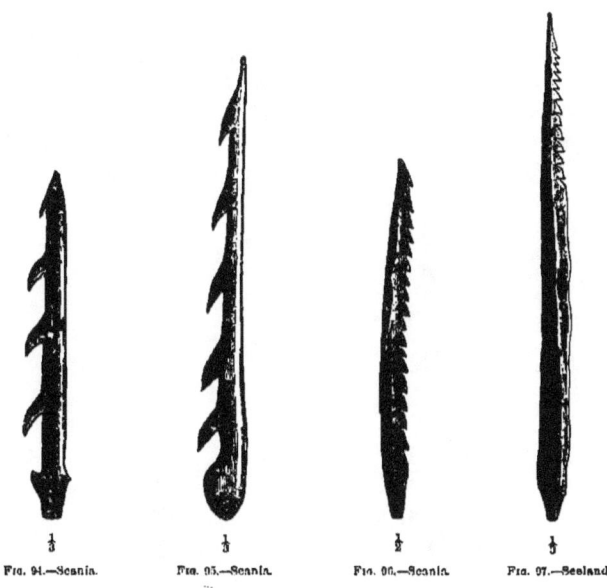

FIGS. 94-97.—Bone harpoon-heads.

"Harpoons of bone, sharp-pointed, with barbs on one side, are occasionally found in our ancient peat-bogs in Scania. Such a one is seen on Plate IV, Fig. 71 (here Fig. 94). This harpoon-point appears, like those from Greenland, to have been fastened to its long shaft in such a manner as to be disengaged therefrom when it stuck fast in the harpooned animal, because above the point of attachment is a projection over which the strap or line seems to have been tied. It was found in Scania, in a bog near the sea-coast. It may have been used for hunting seals or small whales or other similar animals. Meanwhile, it is very remarkable that amongst the objects which Messrs. Christy and Lartet have found in the caves of Périgord, and which may be considered as being among

---

* Nilsson: Primitive Inhabitants; p. 26.

74   PREHISTORIC FISHING.

the most ancient traces of man in Europe, are harpoons of bone, which seem to have been helved in the same manner."*

The Swedish archæologist figures another bone harpoon-head, here Fig. 95. on the preceding page, found in a Scanian bog, and "showing traces of having been helved in a somewhat different manner, namely, by the point of bone being fastened to the handle."†

Alongside of it he represents a somewhat similar harpoon-head from Tierra del Fuego, many of which, he says, are in the British Museum, labeled *Heads of Fishing-spears used by the Natives of Tierra del Fuego*. In addition, he represents two harpoon-heads of bone, Figs. 96 and 97 on page 73, which were likewise found in bogs, the original of Fig. 96 in the South of Scania, that of Fig. 97 in Seeland.‡ The type shown by Fig. 96 will be considered hereafter.

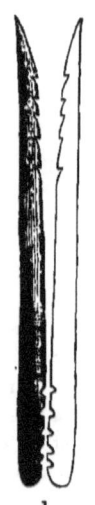

Fig. 98.—Arctic America.   Fig. 99.—Scania.

Figs. 98 and 99.—Fish or bird-spear-heads of bone.

---

* Nilsson : Primitive Inhabitants ; p. 29.
† Ibid. ; p. 80, Plate IV, Fig. 69.
‡ Ibid.; p. 80, Plate IV, Figs 73 and 74.

Professor Nilsson represents in his work what he calls a *leister*, or fish-spear, from the Northwest Coast of America. He sketched this implement in 1836 in the Museum at Bristol. He also gives illustrations of another similar implement, obtained north of Hudson's Bay, and preserved in the Ethnological Museum at Copenhagen.* I reproduce as Fig. 98 his design of the upper part of the last-named implement. His other figure shows the whole object on a smaller scale. The implements are thus described by him :—

"On the top of a long pole are fastened two tolerably long sharp-pointed bones, the points bent a little outwards and the inner side provided with teeth pointing backwards, to hold the fish securely when struck. These bones are fastened to the shaft in such a manner that each, independently of the other, is in some way movable inwards and outwards; their sides are therefore flat at the other end, and the inner edge provided with one or more teeth, pointing forwards, in order to be tied fast, so that they cannot be torn away by the fish; and, in order to prevent their being bent too much apart, they are tied together by means of a strap at a short distance from the handle."†

Speaking of the dart here represented (Fig. 98), he says :—

"Its entire length is thirty-eight inches, of which the wooden shaft measures thirty-one inches and three-fourths; the bone points, in all eleven inches long, are, to a length of five inches, fastened to the shaft, and consequently protrude six inches beyond it. The shaft is round, about half an inch in diameter, somewhat compressed in front of the lower end, the end itself cut off diagonally with an incised broad round notch, showing that a thick bow-string has been resting thereon; at the end three feathers are fastened lengthwise. It appears, however, that this implement was made rather for shooting birds on the wing than for spearing fish in the water.‡

"But be this how it may, it is nevertheless very remarkable that the half of an implement, evidently similar to this last-mentioned one, has been found in the peat-bog of Felsmosse, about three English miles from Lund, in the province of Scania. I have sketched this on Plate IV, Fig. 79 (Fig. 99, opposite page). This bone dart is seven inches long, round, and compressed; the back a little thicker, pointed towards the top end, round, and bent outwards a little; the inner side somewhat compressed, with five broad incisions forming teeth, bent backwards; the lower end broader and also compressed, the inner edge provided with oblique notches forming teeth, pointing forwards, which thus prevent the dart from being drawn forward. But what still more shows the

---

* Nilsson: Primitive Inhabitants; Plate IV, Figs. 75, 77, and 78.
† Ibid.; p. 38.
‡ Ibid.; p. 34.

76 PREHISTORIC FISHING.

perfect likeness between the North American and the Scanian instrument is, that if we carefully examine the latter, we shall find it scratched transversely in two places, the one at the place where the strings on the American one attach the points to the shaft, and the other a little way higher up, where the shaft ends in the American implement, and where the points are tied round; the Scanian dart is in other respects entirely even and smooth.

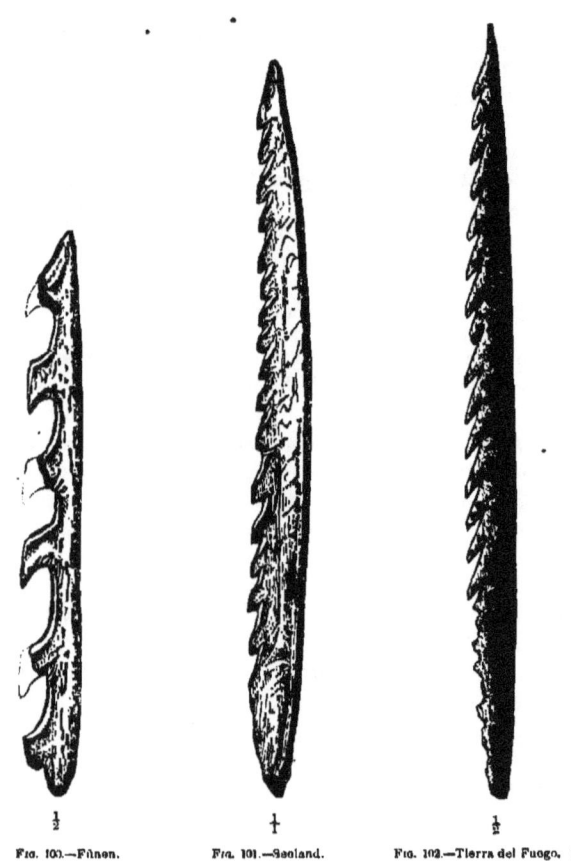

Fig. 100.—Fünen.   Fig. 101.—Seeland.   Fig. 102.—Tierra del Fuego. (5724).

Figs. 100–102.—Bone harpoon-heads.

"Thus we see that the Scanian implement was constructed exactly in the same manner as the American, and it is difficult for us to understand how implements so complicated could have been constructed so completely alike by the Eskimos of the present day, living in the most northern part of North America, and by the aborigines in the most southern part of Scandinavia, between which two races, so very dissimilar in origin, and so widely separated as to locality, we cannot suppose any relationship to have existed. That implements so simple in construction as the flint arrow should be alike in most countries, even in Scania and Tierra del Fuego, can be explained by a kind of instinct in man, *as man*, everywhere, as long as he stands at the very lowest point of civilization; but the perfect similarity between implements so complicated as those now in question, I look upon as one of the great, still unsolved, enigmas of ethnological science."*

I must confess that the case does not appear to me as having such an extraordinary bearing. As soon as man, in any part of the world, had conceived and carried out the idea of constructing a dart with two or three prongs for fishing or hunting purposes (a plan very simple in itself), a short practice would have taught him the desirability of rendering the prongs movable to a certain extent, and hence he would naturally have been led to fasten the ligatures in a way to bring about the change for the better. Professor Nilsson's discovery, however, is very interesting.

I find on Plate 40 of Captain A. P. Madsen's beautifully illustrated work "Antiquités Préhistoriques du Danemark. L'Âge de la Pierre" (Copenhagen, 1873) representations of three bone harpoon-heads (Figs. 6, 7, and 8), each of them showing a different type. One of these darts (Fig. 6, not reproduced), which measures a trifle less than ten inches, was found in a bog in Jütland. It shows two broken unilateral barbs, the first forming the downward continuation of the point, the second projecting two inches below the first. Another (Fig. 7), of which Fig. 100 on the opposite page is a reduced copy, shows much more elaborate workmanship. It was found near Odense, in the Island of Fünen. The third (Fig. 8), of which Fig. 101 on the opposite page is a copy, was extracted from a bog in the District of Frederiksborg, Seeland. It closely resembles in shape Fig. 96, copied from Professor Nilsson's work. Javelins with bone armatures of this shape, but larger, are still in use among the poor inhabitants of Tierra del Fuego. Fig. 102 represents one of a number obtained during the United States Exploring Expedition under Lieutenant Wilkes, and now in the United States National Museum. The longest of these dart-heads, which exhibit very creditable workmanship, measures nearly sixteen inches.

Not long ago Count Jan Zawisza, of Warsaw, was kind enough to send me No. IV of a Polish publication entitled "Wiadomości Archeologiczne"† (War-

---

* Nilsson: Primitive Inhabitants; p. 34, etc.

† Archæological News.

saw, 1882), to which number Prince J. T. Lubomirski has contributed an interesting article relating to the discovery of fishing-spear-heads on the banks of the Uświata River. The article, for a translation of which I am indebted to Mr. Louis Solyom, of the Library of Congress, is illustrated with two representations of harpoon-heads, of which Figs. 103 and 104 on the opposite page are copies. It follows here in full:—

"It is now generally known that prehistoric man selected the vicinity of water for his place of abode. Water being one of the necessaries of life, and the art of well-digging probably unknown, this choice followed as a natural consequence. Nor do those miss the truth who assert that it was done with a view to facilitate locomotion, the communication across large tracts of land being then much impeded by swamps and virgin forests. Fishing, also, furnishing palatable and healthy food, was another inducement to select such situations, and that fish was duly appreciated as an article of diet is sufficiently proved by the fish-remains discovered in places inhabited by prehistoric man.

"But who can explain their mode of fishing? Were fishing-nets known and used? It is often asserted that the discs of burned clay which are frequently found served as weights for nets. Yet net-fishing was probably not the first method resorted to by primitive man. Those who have observed how fish are caught during spring, when they enter shallow waters to deposit their spawn, probably will accept the conclusion that spearing, which is considered a barbarous mode at present, though still practised, was probably the first attempt at fishing made by prehistoric man. It was during the pairing-season of fish, in shallow waters, that he had the first opportunity for observing them closely, and the first chance to get possession of them, until he discovered that they could be caught all the year round in lakes and rivers. In winter, for instance, they could be captured by means of baskets let down through openings cut in the ice, the fish crowding near these apertures, impelled by the necessity of breathing fresh air. According to Herodotus, this method was practised by the people who occupied pile-dwellings in Lake Prasias.

"Nevertheless, it is most probable that the first fishing-implement was a spear similar to that used at the present time, and hence spear-heads are found in all prehistoric localities where fish formed an important food-article.

"Madsen has published in his work 'Antiquités Préhistoriques du Danemark' designs of spear-heads found in that country ('Âge de la Pierre,' Plate 40, Figs. 6, 7, and 8), which he calls bone arrow-heads, yet erroneously, considering that some of them reach a length of fifteen centimeters, a size not only unnecessary, but even inconvenient for arrow-heads. We therefore incline without hesitation to the opinion of Oscar Montelius, expressed in the 'Antiquités Suédoises' (Vol. I, p. 14, No. 53), where he gives representations of bone

HARPOON-HEADS. 79

spear-heads, calling them harpoons, and mentioning the fact that they were found at the bottom of Hästefjorden Lake, among other articles of bone. The place of discovery of these implements indicates their use.

"They also occur in Russia, as we learn from the work of Count Uwarov, recently published, and devoted to the prehistoric times of Russia. He describes there a bone spear-head found near the river Oka.

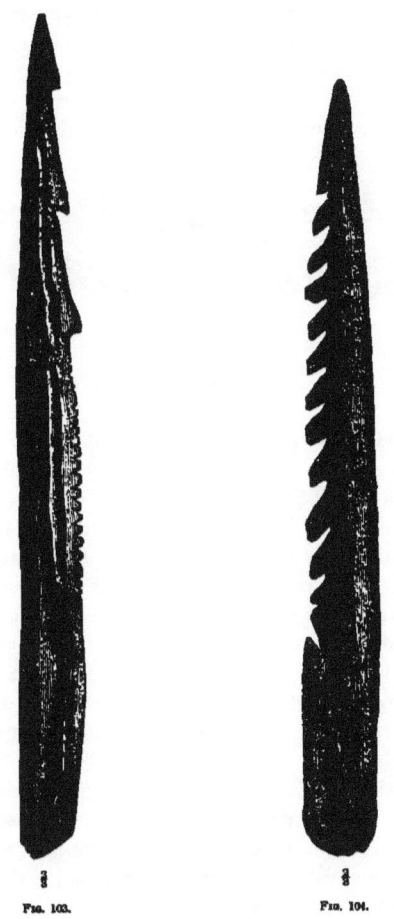

Fig. 103. Fig. 104.

Fig. 103 and 104.—Harpoon-heads of ox-horn. Poland.

"Heretofore these implements had not been met with among the relics of the stone age within the limits of ancient Poland. It therefore affords me much pleasure to announce the discovery of two specimens of the implements under notice, found in the district of Orszan, on the bank of the small river Uświata, which empties into the left shore of the Dniepr. At the time of this discovery the land drained by the Uświata was the property of the learned Dr. Zeckert, now deceased.

"Both heads are made of ox-horn, and very well preserved, though discolored by the action of time. One is almost black, the other yellowish-brown. Our illustrations show the objects reduced to two-thirds of their actual size. Length of one, twenty-four centimeters; of the other, twenty-three centimeters. They are at present in the collection of antiquities at Mala wieś, near Groice."

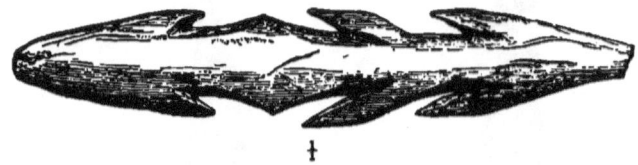

Fig. 105.—Bone harpoon-head. Victoria Cave.

A bone harpoon-head of peculiar shape, represented in Fig. 105, was discovered in the neolithic stratum of the Victoria Cave, near Settle, Yorkshire, England. "The harpoon," says Professor W. Boyd Dawkins, "is a little more than three inches long, with the head armed with two barbs on each side, and the base presenting a mode of securing attachment to the handle, which has not before been discovered in Britain. Instead of a mere projection to catch the ligatures by which it was bound to the shaft, there is a well-cut barb on either side, pointing in a contrary direction to those which form the head. Ample use for such an instrument would be found in Malham tarn, some three miles off, and very probably also in that which formerly existed close by at Attermire, but which has been choked up by peat, and is now turned into grass-land by drainage."*

Having alluded to the javelins in use as hunting-implements among the Kurile Islanders and the Greenlanders, Professor Nilsson describes a class of North European armatures considered by him as javelin-points, giving on Plate VI of his work several illustrations, of which I reproduce Figs. 124, 125, and 126 as Figs. 106, 107, and 108 on page 82.

---

* Dawkins: Cave Hunting; p. 111.

"We find now and then in our peat-mosses," he says, "implements which have evidently been used in the same manner as the javelin from the Kurile Islands, above described. These implements are of bone, six to ten inches long, two and one-fourth to two or three lines broad, occasionally round, but generally rather compressed, tapering to a point towards both ends, and either provided along both sides with a deeply indented groove, into which thin sharp flakes of flint are inserted, and fastened by means of black putty resembling pitch, or the groove with the flint flakes is found only along one side.* The front end is pointed, and behind, the point is occasionally widened, in shape like a spear-point, so that the whole bone represents a spear in miniature, with its long shaft; the groove holding the flint-splinters does not reach quite to the point. Such is the implement in its *original* form, but, by degrees, as it wears out and is again sharpened to a point, the spear-shaped expansion disappears and the point is worn down to the grooves. The hinder end is likewise sharp-pointed, and has evidently been inserted in a wooden shaft. Generally this end is to a certain distance less smooth than the remainder of the bone, and sometimes the resin, by means of which it has been cemented in the shaft, remains up to a little more than an inch. This implement is principally found in bogs in the South of Scania; also in the province of Bohusland, on Tjörn (west coast of Sweden); it is said to have been also found in the Island of Öland. In the Museum of the Academy of Antiquities, in Stockholm, there is a specimen, the longest which I have seen (ten inches in length), found during the digging of the Götha Canal, between Påfvelstorp and Tåtorp, in peat-earth, under a bed of clay, and eight feet under ground. But where there is peat-earth there must have been water; consequently, everything that is found on, and especially under, peat-earth, has sunk to the bottom in some water. It is probable, therefore, that the implements in question, while being used on the water, have dropped therein and gone to the bottom. In order to form a correct idea of the manner in which these implements were used by the Scandinavian aborigines, we ought to enquire how they are employed amongst the nations where they are still in use.

"The Greenlander uses this weapon *only* on the water, in the pursuit of aquatic birds. It is provided with a shaft five feet in length, ending at the back with some ornament, generally a reindeer-foot or something of that kind, and is thrown by hand at birds while they are resting on the water. It strikes usually at the distance of from fifty to sixty paces, and Egede relates that the Greenlander can hit his prey at a tolerably long distance, as surely as a good shot could do it with a fowling-piece. From his early childhood the Greenlander begins to practise throwing the bird-javelin. It is thrown by means of a

---

* These darts remind one by their construction of the Mexican *maquahuitl*, which the Spaniards called *espada*, or sword.

throwing-stick or board with such force that it flies whizzing through the air, and with such wonderful skill that it generally pierces the head of the duck.

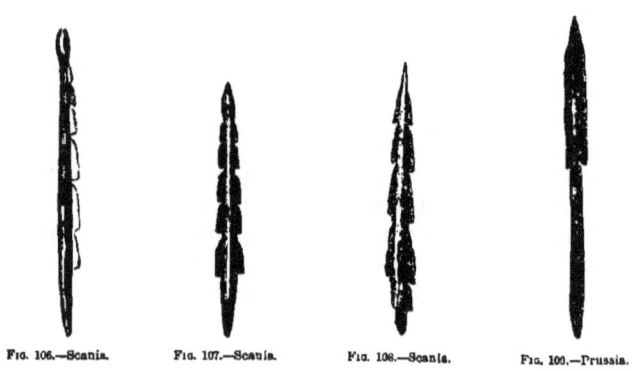

Fig. 106.—Scania.   Fig. 107.—Scania.   Fig. 108.—Scania.   Fig. 109.—Prussia.

All ¼.

Figs. 106–109.—Javelin-heads of bone with inserted flint flakes.

"There is scarcely any doubt that the darts here sketched have been the same kind of hunting-implements, and that they have been employed in the same way. That they have been, and were intended to be, thrown by hand, we can easily see, because they could have been used only on the water; for if thrown on land, they must infallibly have been broken to pieces and destroyed. They are, therefore, found only in peat-bogs, which in former times were open waters, sometimes of considerable extent. They occur not unfrequently in the South of Sweden. Our museums contain a great number of them; but in Denmark they are rare."*

Professor Nilsson's statements seem to be correct in every particular; yet these darts, on account of their jagged sides, were also serviceable as heads of implements used in the fish-hunt, and for this reason I have given the preceding extract from Nilsson's work.

The peat-bogs of Eastern Prussia likewise have yielded a limited number of these bone-and-flint darts, which are preserved in the collection of northern antiquities in the New Museum at Berlin. They were described by Mr. Friedel in an article entitled "Ueber Knochenpfeile aus Deutschland," which appeared in "Archiv für Anthropologie" (Vol. V, 1872, page 433). Fig. 109 is one

---

* Nilsson: Primitive Inhabitants; p. 46, etc.—Madsen figures a number of Danish specimens of this kind on Plate 40 of his "Antiquités Préhistoriques du Danemark."

of his illustrations, showing a dart of elk-bone* with flint-splinters set closely together and disposed in two rows. I present this figure simply with a view to show the appearance of a bone-and-flint dart somewhat differing in type from those described by Professor Nilsson.

Stone points, we may assume, were also used as armatures for harpoons in neolithic times; but Professor Nilsson's suggestion that some may have been inserted in sockets of bone or wood, and thus connected with the shaft, is not supported by any evidence, provided my opinion that no such sockets have been discovered is correct. Those of wood, of course, could not have resisted decay; while sockets of bone or horn, if they had been used, would be still in existence, like the much older horn and bone objects of the reindeer-period.

FIG. 110.—Scanian flint point set in wooden socket.

Nilsson figures (Plate X, Fig. 203) a well-chipped flint point found in the earth near the sea-shore of the Sound of Lomma, in Scania, which he considers as a harpoon-head. "A person who had long resided in Greenland," he says, "recognized it at once as such; and in order to show me the way in which the stone point had been fastened to the harpoon, and the harpoon to the shaft, he provided it with a piece of wood as represented in the sketch, Plate III, Fig. 49 (here Fig. 110). At the lower end of this piece of wood is an indentation into which the shaft of the harpoon enters. Below is the loop by which the harpoon is attached to the shaft as well as the strap, to the end of which a bladder is tied."† He designates various other European flint points figured by him as harpoon-heads used in this manner; but he is not very positive in his statements, and finally expresses his own doubts in the following remark:—"It

---

* The European elk corresponds to the American moose.
† Nilsson: Primitive Inhabitants; p. 29.

ought, however, to be observed that it is difficult to draw a line of demarcation between the stone points which have been harpoons, and those which have belonged to arrows, because the same stone point could have been adapted either to a harpoon or to an arrow."†

On the other hand, it may be taken for granted that shafts with chipped stone points of suitable size and shape *immediately* attached to them, formed fishing-darts at the period under consideration. It would be impossible, however, to single out the points thus employed, though such as are provided with barbs seem particularly fitted for that purpose. Mr. John Evans, in his well-known work on the ancient stone implements of Great Britain, figures (page 340, etc.) several chipped flint points of this class, small and large, that might well have served as armatures for fishing-spears, and others are represented on the plates of Captain Madsen's work on the prehistoric antiquities of Denmark; but, in view of the uncertainty as to their use, I refrain from copying any of these illustrations.

Arrow-heads.—With regard to arrows used in shooting fish—a method most probably practised during the period here treated—I have nothing to add to my statements on page 56. An arrow employed in hunting quadrupeds or birds would also on occasion serve to kill a fish, and hence an attempt at specification must necessarily prove fruitless.

Sinkers.—The objects of this class obtained from the lacustrine settlements of the stone age may in general be considered as neolithic relics; but the antiquity of such as have been found on or below the surface of the soil, in water, swamps, etc., is doubtful, to say the least, considering that line and net-sinkers of stone are used in Europe at the present time. Only particular circumstances of association would favor the recognition of the period to which such stray specimens pertain. In a late work Dr. Arthur Mitchell, of Edinburgh, makes some observations bearing on this subject, which are of sufficient interest to be given here in full. I also insert the illustrations accompanying his remarks.

"There is a class of stone objects," he says, "which are nearly always to be seen in collections of antiquities, and which are now correctly called sinkers. They have been often found under circumstances which indicate a great age. Worsaae figures them among the antiquities of the stone age in Denmark. They vary much in form and in character. Most of them are simply bored stones— generally with one hole roughly picked or ground through them, but occasionally with two. Sometimes they have a groove cut down one face of the stone and running over its end, and another similar groove cut transversely to this; or the

---

† Nilsson: Primitive Inhabitants; p. 82.

groove may run round the circumference of a flattish ovoid water-worn pebble, giving it somewhat the appearance of a ship's block.

Fig. 111.—Sink-stone of steatite from Shetland; weight, 14 ounces.

"These stone sinkers I have frequently seen in use. As regards the first type, those which are simply bored stones, I have seen the same man with one of them at the end of one line, and at the end of the other a sinker of lead cast in a mould and tastefully shaped. Usually the bored sinkers are water-worn stones, selected for suitability of shape; but sometimes they are made of a piece of stone roughly flaked into a proper form; while at other times, where the soft soapstone is found, there is more or less neatness in their design, and they may even be found imitating the form of the leaden sinker, or having rudely cut on them the initials of their owner (see Fig. 111). It may happen again that they are entirely natural stones; that is, both their form and the hole through them may be due to natural agencies. A sinker of this last kind I once saw with a Shetlander. It was of flint, and he said he had brought it from 'foreign parts,' because he thought it would be useful at home as a sinker.

"Of one of the types of sinkers, that showing the two grooves crossing each other, there was some difficulty in seeing the exact way in which the line and hooks were made fast to the stones, and what purpose the grooves served. Some stones of this kind have been found in circumstances indicating great age; and I remember hearing a distinguished antiquary, no longer alive, speculating ingeniously as to whether they could really have served so commonplace a purpose as that of sinking a fisherman's line. But I have been able to set the question at rest by procuring two specimens from the parish of Walls, through the Rev. James Russell, with all the appliances on them exactly as they were when actually in use a few years ago (see Figs. 112 and 113 on the following page). Sinkers of this form vary in size. They are generally, I think, larger than those of the bored form; and I understand that this is explained by the fact that they are chiefly used when fishing in deep waters.

"It is not solely, however, in those districts of our country which we regard as outlying and remote that we encounter fishermen using stone instead of lead or other materials for the manufacture of sinkers. On the Tweed to this day the nets are weighted by bored stones, and specimens of these are placed in museums of antiquities, not because they are themselves objects of antiquity, but because their history being accurately known, they teach lessons of caution in dealing with objects not very dissimilar, about the history and use of which we have no accurate knowledge."*

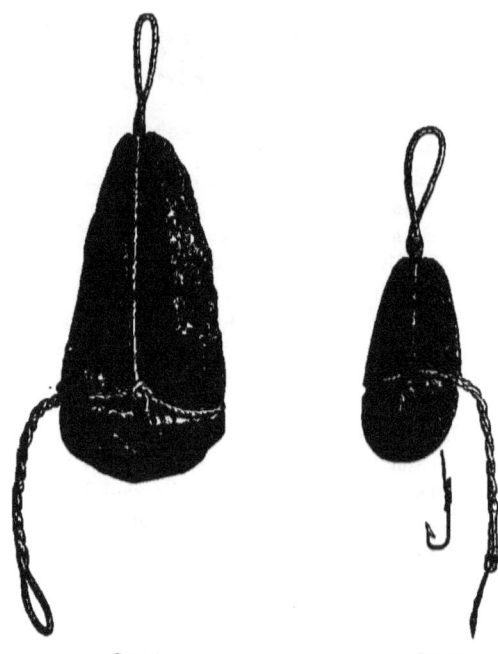

Figs. 112 and 113.—Sink-stones from Walls, in Shetland. The larger is a roughly-flaked piece of sandstone, and the smaller a water-worn beach-stone. In order to make the cord grasp these stones securely, grooves are roughly cut in them in the way indicated by the woodcuts. The larger stone is 8 inches long, and weighs 43 ounces; the smaller, to which the hook is still attached, is 5 inches long, and weighs 11 ounces.

If, under these circumstances, I describe and figure some sinkers, I do it with the mental reservation which the foregoing observations necessarily imply.† I would also refer again to the difficulty of making a proper distinction between line and net-sinkers, for even at present heavy line-sinkers and light net-sinkers are used, and *vice versa*.

---

* Mitchell: The Past in the Present—What is Civilization? New York, 1881; p. 141, etc.

† The scrutinizing reader, I hope, will not find fault with me for describing, while treating of the neolithic period, objects which may be of much later date. The possibility that some of them may be neolithic will be accepted as my excuse.

Sinkers in their simplest, I am almost tempted to say natural, form are like that in possession of the fisherman mentioned by Dr. Mitchell, namely, naturally perforated nodules of flint, which, according to Dr. Klemm, "are so frequent and sometimes of such large size on the shores of Heligoland and Rügen, that the inhabitants use them as net-weights and even as anchors."* There are several net-sinkers and anchor-stones of this kind in the Berlin Provincial Museum, one of the latter having been obtained by Dr. Friedel in the Island of Rügen from a fisherman who actually used it as an anchor.† Such weights doubtless were employed in very early times; but, of course, no one would attempt to speculate on the antiquity of this class of relics, or rather on the time in which they were utilized. Some of these natural formations considered as sinkers may in reality never have been applied to any use by man.

Mr. John Evans, having described the grooved hammers found in Great Britain, continues as follows:—

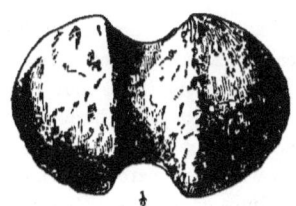

Fig. 114.—Stone sinker. Burns.

"Closely connected in form and character with the mining hammers, though as a rule much smaller in size, and in all probability intended for a totally different purpose, are the class of stone objects of which Fig. 149 (here Fig. 114) gives a representation, reproduced from the 'Archæological Journal.' This specimen was found with two others at Burns, near Ambleside, Westmoreland; and another, almost precisely similar in size and form, was found at Perry's Leap, and is preserved in the Museum of Antiquities at Alnwick Castle. Another, from Westmoreland, is in the Mayer Collection at Liverpool, and they have, I believe, been found in some numbers in that district. A stone of the same character, but more elaborately worked, having somewhat acorn-shaped ends, was found by the Hon. W. O. Stanley, F. S. A., at Old Geir, Anglesea. They were originally regarded as hammer-stones, but such as I have examined are made of a softer stone than those usually employed for hammers, and they

---

* Klemm: Allgemeine Culturwissenschaft; Werkzeuge und Waffen; Leipzig, 1854; p. 12.
† Friedel: Führer durch die Fischerei-Abtheilung; p. 1.

are not battered or worn at the ends. It seems, therefore, probable that they were used as sinkers for nets or lines, for which purpose they are well adapted, the groove being deep enough to protect small cord around it from wear by friction. They seem also usually to occur in the neighborhood either of lakes, rivers, or the sea. A water-worn nodule of sandstone, five inches long, with a deep groove round it, and described as probably a sinker for a net or line, was found in Aberdeenshire, and is in the Antiquarian Museum at Edinburgh; and I have one of soft grit, about the same length, given me by Mr. R. D. Darbishire, F. G. S., and found by him near Nantlle, Carnarvonshire. Many of these sink-stones are probably of no great antiquity."

Mr. Evans refers in the same place to "sink-stones, weights, or plummets formed by boring a hole towards one end of a flattish stone." He mentions several specimens, but gives no illustrations of them. While in Sweden, he saw the leg-bones of animals used as weights for sinking nets.*

"In Ireland," Sir William Wilde observes, "sink-stones, for either nets or fishing-lines, are by no means rare, as they continue in use even at the present day; and quoit-like discs, of sandstone, from four to six inches in diameter and with a hole in the centre to attach them to the bottom-rope of a net, are not uncommon in localities where lead is scarce. ——— But, besides these rude implements, we find others formed with more care, and which are generally supposed to have been attached to either lines or nets."† He gives three illustrations of such stones, Figs. 77, 78, and 79, of which I reproduce the first two as Figs. 115 and 116. The original of Fig. 115 is described as being composed of soft white

FIG. 115.   FIG. 116.

FIGS. 115 and 116.—Stone sinkers. Ireland.

sandstone traversed by a vein of quartz, and encircled by a groove round the long axis for retaining a string or thong. Fig. 116 represents "a plummet-like piece of sandstone, three inches and a half long, with a hole at the small extrem-

---

* Evans: Ancient Stone Implements; p. 211.

† Sir W. Wilde: A Descriptive Catalogue of the Antiquities in the Museum of the Royal Irish Academy: Vol. 1, Dublin, 1863; p. 94.

SINKERS. 89

ity." Yet, Sir W. Wilde, while admitting that these stones would form useful sink-stones, thinks there is no direct authority bearing on the subject. Indeed, the stone represented by Fig. 115 has been regarded by some as one of the "flail-stones" attached by a thong to a stick, used in early Irish warfare, and to which some allusion is made in ancient records. As for the object shown in Fig. 116, he thinks it might have been used as a plummet, or the weight for a steelyard or ouncel, "an implement in much more frequent use than a beam and scales in the western parts of Ireland up to a very recent period."*

I have little doubt that Fig. 115, at least, represents a sinker.

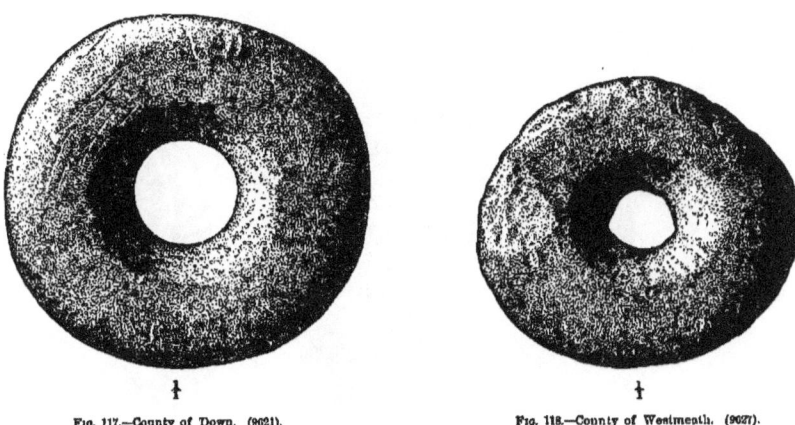

FIG. 117.—County of Down. (9021).   FIG. 118.—County of Westmeath. (9027).

FIGS. 117 and 118.—Stone sinkers (?).

I present in Figs. 117 and 118 delineations of two of the quoit-like discs with a hole in the centre, to which Sir W. Wilde draws attention. They were sent, in 1870, with other Irish antiquities, to the Smithsonian Institution by Mr. Robert Day, Jr., of Cork County. The material of these specimens, which certainly have the appearance of being very old, is fine-grained sandstone. They were found, respectively, in the counties of Down and Westmeath.

Passing over to Danish specimens, I give in Fig. 119 on the following page a somewhat enlarged copy of one figured by Mr. Worsaae,† who classes it, doubtless for good reason, among the relics of the stone age. He informs me that it was dug up in a bog in the Island of Seeland.

---

* Sir W. Wilde: Catalogue; p. 95.
† Worsaae: Nordiske Oldsager; Fig. 88, p. 18.

Figs. 120, 121, and 122 are copied from Plate 30 of Captain Madsen's work, before cited.*

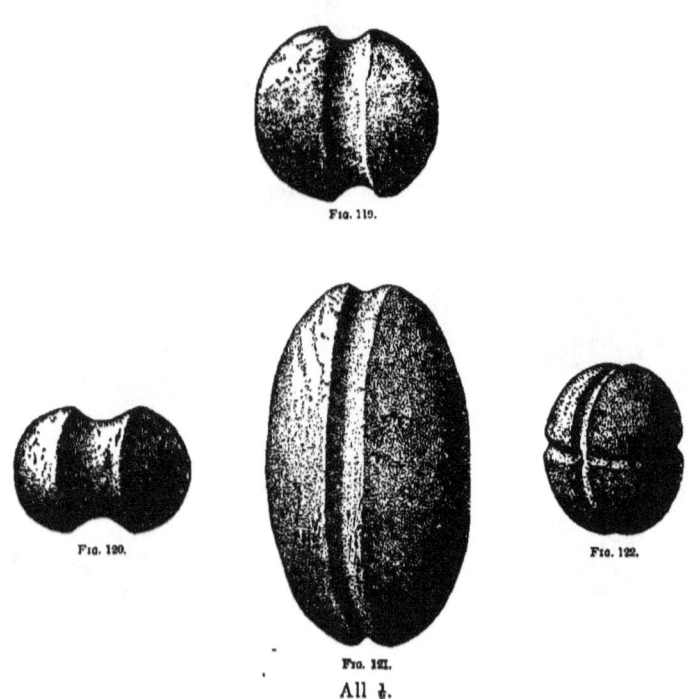

FIGS. 119-122.—Stone Sinkers. Denmark.

The Danish locality where the original of Fig. 120 was found is not specified. The object shown in Fig. 121 was ploughed up in the District of Sorö, and that represented by Fig. 122, exhibiting two grooves crossing each other, was obtained in the District of Viborg. All these Danish specimens are preserved in the Museum of Northern Antiquities at Copenhagen.

Professor Nilsson describes and represents several sink-stones, one of them, like the Danish specimen, provided with two grooves crossing each other (Fig. 122). Concerning this class of sinkers he observes:—"These plummets are generally large, and have probably been used as weights for trolling-nets, etc. They are still occasionally picked up in islets and reefs on the coast of Bohus-

---

* They are there Figs. 18, 17, and 16, respectively.

Län (west coast of Sweden).* He also figures a number of sinkers with single grooves.

To the figures of sinkers here presented others could be added, but I have selected only such as most probably *were* sink-stones; for, without entering into details, I will confess that I have my doubts as to several other figured specimens to which that character is attributed.

Professor Virchow alludes to ancient clay net-sinkers, chiefly obtained from pile-works in Prussia, which, however, are of comparatively late origin, being referable to the close of pagan times. The largest and most recent of the sinkers, from Boissin Lake near Belgard (Pomerania) are described as large flat round discs with a hole in the centre, and, as a rule, rather slightly burned. Of special interest is Professor Virchow's observation that such clay net-weights, burned entirely black (*ganz schwarz gebrannt*), are still used in Eastern Prussia.†

Boats.—Quite a number of ancient boats, discovered under circumstances favoring preservation, have been described by various authors, but most of them doubtless belong to post-neolithic times. There is in the Provincial Museum at Berlin an oaken dug-out, formed like a shallow trough, and hollowed out by means of fire, while its outside is rudely shaped with stone instruments. It measures, in its present shrunken state, eight meters in length and about forty centimeters in width. This boat was found near Berneuchen, in the District of Landsberg on the Warthe (Brandenburg), two meters imbedded in peat.‡ It may be a relic of the stone age.

I find no reference to existing stone-age boats in such publications on Danish and Scandinavian antiquities as are within my reach. Professor Nilsson treats of boats in a transient way, merely alluding to the probable method of their manufacture. "These (the boats) seem to have been excavated trunks of trees, for the broad gouge has evidently been used for excavating wood."§

Sir W. Wilde describes several ancient Irish boats still in existence, though without giving any clue as to the time from which they may date. "So far as we yet know," he observes, "two kinds of boats appear to have been in use in very early times in the British Isles—the canoe and the curragh‖—the one formed out of a single piece of wood, the other composed of wicker-work, covered with hide. No ancient specimen of the curragh could, however, have come down to modern times. The single-piece canoe is generally formed of oak, and may be divided into three varieties, viz., a small trough-shaped one, square at the

---

* Nilsson: Primitive Inhabitants; p. 26.
† Circulare des Deutschen Fischerei-Vereins im Jahre 1873; Berlin, 1873; p. 149.
‡ Friedel: Führer durch die Fischerei-Abtheilung; p. 2.
§ Nilsson: Primitive Inhabitants; p. 101.
‖ Coracle.

ends, from eight to twelve feet long, round at the bottom, and having projecting handles at either extremity, apparently for the purpose of transporting it from place to place. Such a boat could be used either in fishing or as a means of transport upon the inland lakes and rivers. This, in common with the two other varieties, is very shallow, so that those who used it must have sat flat upon the bottom, and progressed themselves by means of light paddles—probably one used in either hand; this is further confirmed by the total absence of all appearance of row-locks. The second variety generally averages twenty feet in length and about two in breadth, is flat-bottomed, round at the prow, and nearly square at the stern. — — — The third variety of ancient Irish canoe is sharp at both ends."*

He refers to the discovery of a boat of the first-mentioned kind in Monaghan County, but furnishes no illustration. It may or may not be a boat made during the stone age. The two other kinds are represented by specimens in the Dublin Museum, and Sir W. Wilde gives figures of them, which I will not reproduce, because the originals appear to belong to more or less recent periods.

"A single-piece canoe," he says, "has been discovered either upon or in the vicinity of all the crannoges which have been carefully examined. They have also been found in bogs and in the beds of rivers, as the Boyne, the Brosna, and the Ban, etc. Ware says that single-piece canoes were in use on some rivers in Ireland in his time. The curragh or coracle is still employed: upon the Boyne it is formed of wicker-work, covered with hide; and in Aran the framework is formed of light timber, fastened together with great ingenuity, and covered with canvas."†

While treating of "Upheaval since the Human Period of the Central District of Scotland," Sir Charles Lyell gives a highly interesting account of boats imbedded in silt bordering the estuary of the river Clyde; and though his observations refer to boats of different periods, I cannot resist the temptation of inserting here the distinguished investigator's valuable information:—

"It has long been a fact familiar to geologists, that, both on the east and west coasts of the central part of Scotland, there are lines of raised beaches, containing marine shells of the same species as those now inhabiting the neighboring sea. The two most marked of these littoral deposits occur at heights of about forty and twenty-five feet above high-water mark, that of forty feet being considered as the more ancient, and owing its superior elevation to a longer continuance of the upheaving movement. They are seen in some places to rest on the arctic shell-beds and boulder clay of the glacial period.

---

* Sir W. Wilde: Catalogue; p. 202, etc.
† Ibid.; p. 204.

"In those districts where large rivers, such as the Clyde, Forth, and Tay, enter the sea, the lower of the two deposits, or that of twenty-five feet, expands into a terrace, fringing the estuaries, and varying in breadth from a few yards to several miles. Of this nature are the flat lands which occur along the margin of the Clyde at Glasgow, which consist of finely laminated sand, silt, clay, and gravel. Mr. John Buchanan, a zealous antiquary, writing in 1855, informs us that in the course of the eighty years preceding that date, no less than seventeen canoes had been dug out of this estuarine silt, and that he had personally inspected a large number of them before they were exhumed. Five of them lay buried in silt under the streets of Glasgow, one in a vertical position with the prow uppermost as if it had sunk in a storm. In the inside of it were a number of marine shells. Twelve other canoes were found about a hundred yards back from the river, at the average depth of about nineteen feet from the surface of the soil, or seven feet above high-water mark; but a few of them were only four or five feet deep, and consequently more than twenty feet above the sea-level. One was sticking in the sand at an angle of forty-five degrees, another had been capsized, and lay bottom uppermost: all the rest were in a horizontal position, as if they had sunk in smooth water. Within the last few years (1869) three other canoes have been found in the silts of the Clyde, between Bowling and Dumbarton, and are preserved for inspection in the adjacent grounds of Auchentorlie. Two of these had been exhumed from the bed of the river near Dunglass. They were found lying abreast of each other, embedded in tenacious clay, containing water-worn boulders, overlaid by a deposit of alluvial mud.

"Almost every one of these ancient boats was formed out of a single oak-stem, hollowed out by blunt tools—probably stone axes—aided by the action of fire; a few were cut beautifully smooth, evidently with metallic tools. Hence a gradation could be traced from a pattern of extreme rudeness to one showing great mechanical ingenuity. Two of them were built of planks, one of the two, dug up on the property of Bankton in 1853, being eighteen feet in length, and very elaborately constructed. Its prow was not unlike the beak of an antique galley; its stern, formed of a triangular-shaped piece of oak, fitted in exactly like those of our day. The planks were fastened to the ribs, partly by singularly shaped oaken pins, and partly by what must have been square nails of some kind of metal; these had entirely disappeared, but some of the oaken pins remained. This boat had been upset, and was lying keel uppermost, with the prow pointing straight up the river. In one of the canoes a beautifully polished celt or axe of greenstone was found, in the bottom of another a plug of cork, 'which,' as Professor Geikie remarks, 'could only have come from the latitudes of Spain, Southern France, or Italy.'

"There can be no doubt that some of these buried vessels are of far more ancient date than others. Those most roughly hewn may be relics of the stone period; those more smoothly cut, of the bronze age; and the regularly built boat of Bankton may perhaps come within the age of iron. The occurrence of all of them in one and the same upraised marine formation by no means implies that they belong to the same era, for in the beds of all great rivers and estuaries, there are changes continually in progress, brought about by the deposition, removal, and redeposition of gravel, sand, and fine sediment, and by the shifting of the channel of the main currents from year to year, and from century to century. All these it behooves the geologist and antiquary to bear in mind, so as to be always on their guard, when they are endeavoring to settle the relative date, whether of objects of art or of organic remains embedded in any set of alluvial strata."*

M. de Mortillet mentions several dug-outs extracted from peat, gravel, etc., in France.† Yet, from his descriptions, which are otherwise sufficiently minute, I cannot infer that a single one of them pertains to the stone age.

I am not aware that paddles or other boat-propelling implements of wood referable to the neolithic era have come to light. Several broken paddles are preserved in the Dublin Museum, and one of them is figured by Sir W. Wilde. "They are all of black oak, and present the appearance of great antiquity."‡

Anchor-stones.—The anchor in its simplest form—next to a naturally perforated heavy nodule of flint—doubtless was a stone of proper form and weight, attached to some sort of rope. A groove cut around the stone for holding the rope in place rendered this primitive anchor more serviceable. Such stones, however, may belong to any age, and I allude to them merely for indicating the probable character of a neolithic anchor.

Mr. Friedel mentions an *Ankerstein* from the District of Angermünde (Brandenburg), exhibited in the Berlin Provincial Museum. It is of sandstone, about the size of a man's head, and encircled by a deep groove.§

I have no illustration of such a stone to present.

Professor Nilsson figures on Plate IX (Fig. 189) a perforated stone object with four pointed arms, forming a sort of cross. It is here reproduced as Fig. 123. This specimen, found in the Province of Bohusland and preserved in the Antiquarian Museum of Lund, has been considered as an anchor-stone, and Nilsson formerly shared this opinion; but subsequently he thought it more probable that it had been the head of a battle-axe, though he is by no means

---

* Sir C. Lyell: Antiquity of Man; p. 50, etc.

† De Mortillet: Origine de la Navigation et de la Pêche; Matériaux; Vol. III, 1867; p. 48, etc.—This is not, as the title would indicate, M. de Mortillet's entire publication, but only one of its chapters.

‡ Sir W. Wilde: Catalogue; p. 204, etc.

§ Friedel: Führer durch die Fischerei-Abtheilung; p. 1.

certain. A nearly similar object, on which zigzag-lines are engraved, was likewise found in Bohusland, and is now in the Museum of Göteborg. Professor Nilsson observes that he has not yet found this form among weapons used by modern savages.* The Peruvians, I will mention, used star-shaped perforated weapon-heads of stone, copper, or bronze. M. Cazalis de Fondouce, who saw the original of Fig. 123 at Lund, considers it too unwieldy to have served as suggested by the Swedish archæologist.†

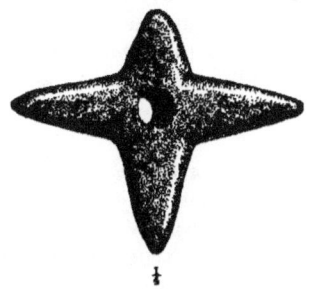

FIG. 123.—Stone anchor (?). Bohusland.

3.—BRONZE AGE.

GENERAL CHARACTERISTICS.

It would be beyond the scope of this treatise to discuss to any length the question by what agencies implements and ornaments of bronze gradually found their way to those European countries in which the use of metal previously had been unknown. I shall offer only a few observations, though for the purposes here in view it would almost suffice to state that bronze in the form of cast articles appeared there, first sparsely, and afterward in greater abundance, insomuch that the ordinary implements hitherto made of stone, etc., could be replaced by more serviceable ones of bronze. This transition, however, must have been slow, especially in its beginning stage, the costly composition‡ being

---

* Nilsson: Primitive Inhabitants; p. 75.

† Cazalis de Fondouce: Compte-rendu du Congrès International d'Archéologie et d'Anthropologie Préhistoriques de Copenhague; Matériaux; Vol. VI, 1870–'71; p. 235.

‡ The ordinary bronze of that period is an alloy of nine parts of copper and one of tin.

then, as may be assumed, accessible only to the wealthy, while the poor had to content themselves with non-metallic tools and implements as before. In fact, a period in which bronze was exclusively used never existed, as the examination of bronze-age tumuli has revealed; for in many of them objects of bronze and stone were found in close juxtaposition. Even in times when iron was employed, stone implements had not yet entirely fallen into disuse.

Some believe in immigrations of bronze-producing Asiatics—for Asia is generally considered as that part of the world where bronze had its origin—among them the distinguished Danish archæologist, J. J. A. Worsaae, who draws attention to the circumstance that after the appearance of bronze a change in the mode of burial took place; for, while the men of neolithic times buried their dead unburned, those of the bronze period mostly disposed of them by cremation.*

The inhabitants of the Mediterranean countries probably were, in consequence of their commercial relations, earlier in possession of bronze than the populations of more northern countries, who, it may be conjectured, received their first supplies from the South.† Yet there can be no doubt that the people who obtained objects of bronze first by importation, manufactured them afterward; for in different districts different types of the same class of articles are observable, insomuch "that a practised archæologist can in almost all cases, on inspection of a group of bronze antiquities, fix with some degree of confidence the country in which they were found."‡ The bronze objects themselves present a great variety of tools, weapons, and ornaments, which I will specify, following Mr. John Evans's classification. He enumerates:—celts (flat, flanged, winged, socketed), chisels, gouges, hammers, sickles, knives, razors, daggers, rapiers, halberds, maces, leaf-shaped swords, arrow and spear-heads, shields, bucklers, helmets, trumpets, bells, pins, torques, bracelets, rings, ear-rings, and many other personal ornaments; finally, vessels, caldrons, etc. It should be understood that this list of the classes of antique bronze articles found in Great Britain and Ireland includes some which probably pertain to a period more recent than the bronze age. Mr. Evans is careful to make his comments in every doubtful case.

As the most useful among the bronze articles may be considered the edged tools, such as hatchets, chisels, knives, etc., by means of which work of various kinds, especially wood-work, could be done in far shorter time than before their introduction. The bronze relics in general present remarkably elegant forms, even the celts, spear-heads and other smaller articles, and many are ornamented

---

* Worsaae: Die Vorgeschichte des Nordens nach gleichzeitigen Denkmälern; p. 50.

† This theory, however, may not hold good for Hungarian bronze antiquities, which exhibit marked peculiarities of form. They probably came directly from the East.

‡ Evans: The Ancient Bronze Implements, Weapons, and Ornaments of Great Britain and Ireland; New York, 1881; p. 24.

with punched lines of divers patterns. The pottery of this period, though made without the application of the lathe, is superior to that of preceding times. It is obvious that the men of the bronze age, who showed so much appreciation of art, were considerably advanced in culture, when compared with the stone-using people hitherto considered. Some observations on bronze-age civilization, as it appears in a special district of Europe, will be made in the following section.

LAKE-DWELLINGS.

Character.—The bronze-yielding lake-settlements of Switzerland were generally of greater extent than those of the preceding period, and, being farther distant from the shore, stood in deeper water. The piles supporting the platform were split stems, from five to six inches or more in thickness, and pointed with bronze hatchets. The huts, it seems, resembled in their construction those of the stone-age colonies. As for the occupation of the lake-men of this period, it may be safely inferred that, like their predecessors, they were agriculturists, hunters, and fishers. They cultivated the cereals previously mentioned, and, in addition, oats, which, however, only appears at the stations of later date. They probably used deer-horn or wooden hoes for preparing the ground, and, perhaps, employed a plough of simple form. To the list of animals already domesticated in the preceding period must be added a pony-like horse and a dog somewhat larger than that of the earlier settlements; there are also traces of a smaller species of dog. They hunted the wild boar, stag, roe, and brown bear. The first-named of these animals still existed in large numbers, as its bones testify, while the stag appears less frequently than in former times. Remains of the hare are wanting, probably because, as formerly, it was not eaten, owing to superstitious motives. The ibex, elk, urus, and bison were not as much hunted as in the earlier period, having, perhaps, farther retreated from the abodes of man. The bones of domesticated animals found on the sites of the bronze-age pile-works outnumber those of the wild species, a fact which would indicate a decline in hunting and a more vigorous application to husbandry. Fishing evidently was eagerly pursued, as I shall have occasion to show.

The bronze tools and implements in use among the lake-people were celts or hatchets of every description, hammers with sockets for the insertion of crooked handles, chisels, gouges, knives (often of elegant form, the blades being curved in the direction of a wave-line), razors, sickles (designed to be provided with wooden handles)[*], fish-hooks, sewing-needles, and engraving-instruments. Among the weapons are to be mentioned leaf-shaped, short-handled swords and

---

[*] Some of these handles have been found, which are carved with great ingenuity to fit the grip of the hand.

daggers, both rare, socketed lance-heads, often ornamented, and barbed arrowheads with a stem for insertion into the shaft, rarely socketed. A few bridle-bits of bronze, indicative of horsemanship, have been found, but no horse-shoes.

The bronze ornaments, which are very numerous, comprise hair and dress-pins, armlets, neck-rings, finger-rings, ear-rings, fibulæ, buttons, and various other objects designed for personal adornment. The pins, sometimes very long, are generally provided at the upper end with knobs of different, mostly really tasteful, patterns; some terminate in rings. Flattish rings, about three-fourths of an inch in diameter, are supposed to represent the money of the period. Moulds of stone, clay, or bronze, for casting various objects, have been found; other articles may have been obtained by trade from abroad, especially certain pieces of superior workmanship.

Numerous clay spindle-whorls bear witness to the extensive production of flax-thread, undoubtedly much used in the manufacture of linen cloth designed for garments. Skins, it may be supposed, served in their stead during the cold season.

The clay vessels of this period betoken a considerable progress in the ceramic art. The clay of large pots serving for the preservation of provisions is strongly mixed with quartz sand; that of the smaller vessels, which often exhibit elegant shapes, is purified, and forms a homogeneous mass. Some vessels have convex or even conical bottoms, and had to be supported by those coarse clay rings previously mentioned, which are peculiar to the bronze period. There have been found plates which may be considered as an innovation, as they are absent in the stone-age pile-works; and clay lamps with two ears for suspension denote another progress in the civilization of the lake-people. The ornamentation of the pottery, like that of the bronze articles, consists of dots, incised parallel lines, rows of triangles, concentric circles, frets, and other geometric designs. Many of the vessels have a coating of black paint, but different colors were sometimes employed for displaying ornamental designs, such as triangles and circles. A black-ware dish from the Cortaillod settlement (Lake of Neuchâtel) is decorated with regularly-cut, thin sheets of tin, which are rendered adhesive by means of a resinous substance. Curious objects of clay, shaped like a crescent supported by a foot—rudely made, and yet exhibiting some form of decoration—have caused much speculation, being regarded either as head-rests or as symbols connected with moon-worship.

It is supposed that the lake-people of this period disposed of their dead both by interment and cremation.

According to Professor Desor's conjecture, the introduction of bronze in Switzerland took place eight hundred or a thousand years before the Christian era.*

---

* Most of the facts mentioned in this short résumé are taken from an excellent little work, entitled "Die Blüthezeit des Bronzealters der Pfahlbauten in der Schweiz, dargestellt von Prof. E. Desor; Referat von Dr. A. Jahn; Bern, 1875.

FISH-HOOKS.

Fishing-implements.—Excepting bronze fish-hooks, hardly any fishing implements have come to light, which can be safely referred to the period characterized by the knowledge of bronze. The lake-men of these times doubtless used sink-stones and floats like those previously described, and nets of the same make, though their methods of net-fishing may have undergone changes for the better. Of this, however, we know nothing. It is even possible that the use of bone-headed harpoons was continued, for some time at least, and there is some likelihood that the one or the other of the bone harpoon-heads described in these pages, which were obtained from stone and bronze-yielding settlements, may in reality pertain to the age of bronze.

FIG. 124.—Fishing-implement (?) of bronze. Switzerland.

The pointed pieces of bone or flint serving as bait-holders, which are by this time familiar to the reader, also seem to have been copied in bronze. Mr. Friedel, at least, figures a double-pointed bronze object thus classed by him,* stating at the same time that such specimens are extremely rare. I reproduce his representation as Fig. 124. The locality where the original, of course a lacustrine relic, was found is not specified.

Real fish-hooks of bronze, on the other hand, are very frequent in some stations, exhibiting a great variety in form and size, and doubtless shaped in accordance with the character of the kind of fish to be caught with them. The smaller hooks are made of wire, either rounded or more or less square in the section; the larger ones seem to be cast.† Some of the hooks bear so close a resemblance to those used at the present time that an expert in angling might have occasion to indulge in comments on their special applicability.

Figs. 125 to 137, on the following page, represent, in half-size, a series of thirteen hooks obtained at the Nidau-Steinberg settlement,‡ where the late Colonel Schwab collected so many valuable relics, which he bequeathed to the city of Bienne. Figs. 125 to 128 show unbarbed hooks, having the upper part of the shank bent over, so as to form an eye for the attachment of the line. Figs. 129 to 134 illustrate barbed specimens, all with shanks bent at the upper extremity into the shapes of hooks or eyes. Fig. 135 shows the shank notched for giving a hold

---

* Amtliche Berichte; p. 126, Fig. 64.

† I must state, however, that I have not seen specimens of the larger kind.

‡ Keller: Lake Dwellings; Vol. II, Plate XXXVI, Figs. 25, 32, 31, 26, 29, 30, 23, 21, 22, 24, 20, 28, 27, respectively.

to the line. In Figs. 136 and 137 forms of unbarbed double hooks are given. Thus it will be seen that hooks of this character are no recent invention.

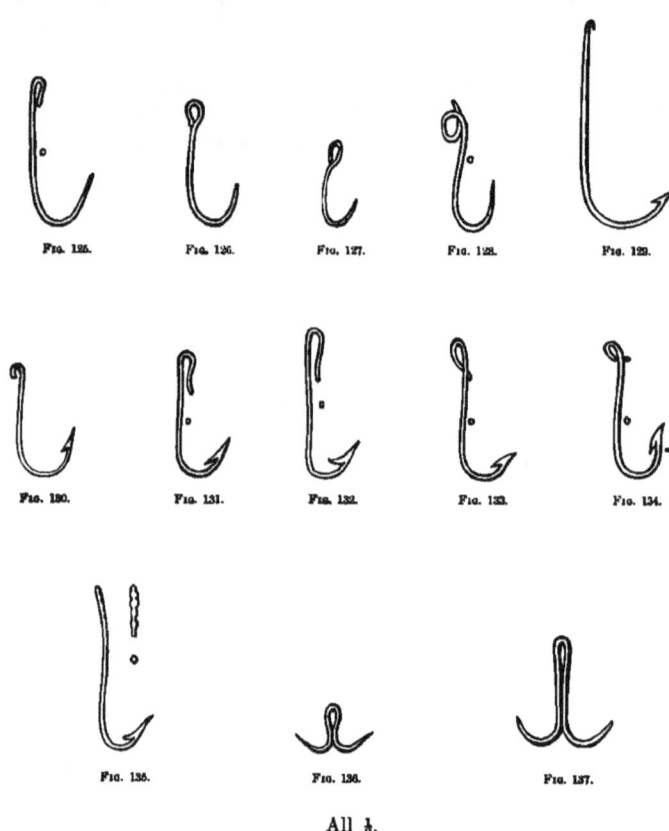

FIGS. 125–137.—Bronze fish-hooks. Nidau-Steinberg.

The second group, comprising Figs. 138, 139, and 140, illustrates forms of hooks from the stations of Font and Cortaillod, in the Lake of Neuchâtel. The originals, formerly belonging to the Clement collection, are now in the Peabody Museum (Nos. 6069.S, 26471, and 6096.Z). The unbarbed hook shown in Fig.

138 is remarkable on account of the unusual form of the eye; Figs. 139 and 140 represent barbed double hooks.*

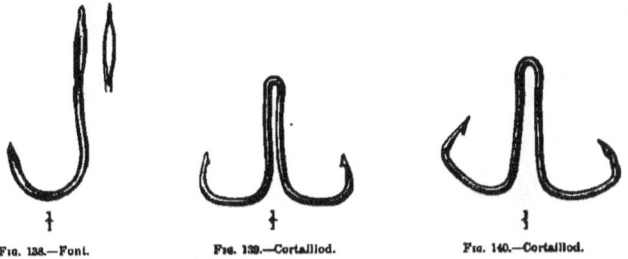

Fig. 138.—Font.   Fig. 139.—Cortaillod.   Fig. 140.—Cortaillod.

Figs. 138-140.—Bronze fish-hooks.

Figs. 141, 142, and 143† show forms of fish-hooks from the station of Montellier, Lake of Morat or Murten, in the Canton of Freiburg (Fribourg). As the illustrations fully exhibit the character of the specimens, further explanations are not needed.

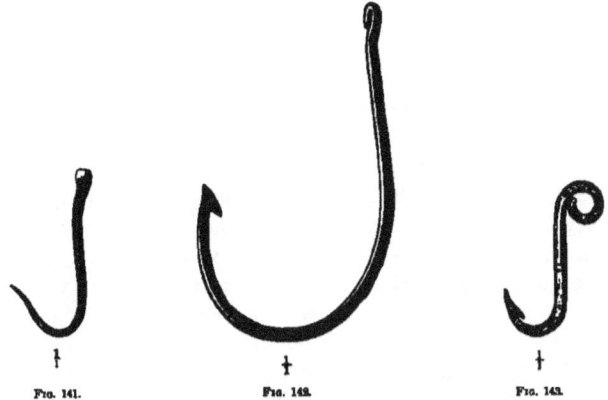

Fig. 141.   Fig. 142.   Fig. 143.

Figs. 141-143.—Bronze fish-hooks. Montellier.

The next group, composed of Figs. 144 and 145, on page 102, exhibits designs of two bronze fish-hooks, obtained, respectively, at the mouth of the

---

* Not a single *barbed* double hook is figured in the translation of Dr. Keller's work.

† Keller: Lake Dwellings; Vol. II, Plate C, Figs. 21, 20, and 22, respectively.

small river Schouss, which empties into the northeastern end of the Lake of Bienne, and at the Lattringen station in the same lake. These two illustrations probably represent the objects in natural size; but nothing relative to it is said in Mr. Lee's translation of Dr. Keller's reports, from which the figures are taken.*

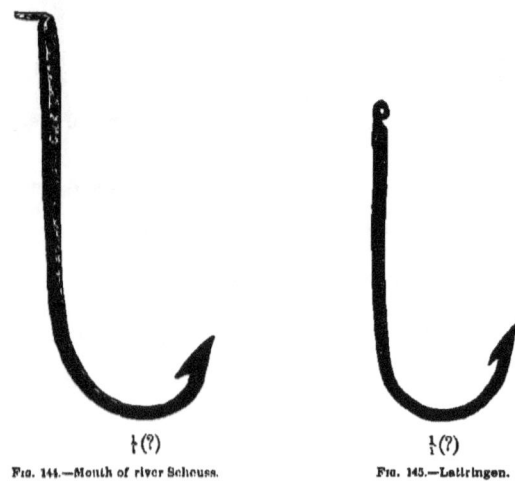

½ (?)   ½ (?)

Fig. 144.—Mouth of river Schouss.   Fig. 145.—Lattringen.

Figs. 144 and 145.—Bronze fish-hooks.

The very fine and large specimen of which Fig. 146 shows the form and size, belonged to the series of lacustrine relics sent by the Antiquarian Society of Zürich to the International Fishery Exhibition, held, as stated, in the year 1880 at Berlin, and the figure is copied from the volume treating of that exhibition.† It was found at Romanshorn, on the Swiss side of the Lake of Constance. Though there is, as far as I can discover, no pile-work at Romanshorn, such constructions existed in the neighborhood, and the specimen is considered as a relic of the lake-men.‡ The originals of Figs. 147 and 148§ were obtained at the station of Unter-Uhldingen in the Ueberlinger See (Baden), and that of Fig. 149,‖ a large unbarbed double hook, is a relic from the Roseninsel, in Lake Starnberg, Bavaria.

---

* Keller: Lake Dwellings; Plate XC, Figs. 12 and 13.

† Amtliche Berichte; p. 127, Fig. 74.

‡ The frontispiece represents a still larger lacustrine bronze fish-hook. Copied from Plate LXVIII of Keller's "Lake Dwellings."

§ Keller: Lake Dwellings; Vol. II, Plate XXIX, Figs. 21 and 22.

‖ Ibid.; Vol. II, Plate CLXXXI, Fig. 7.

FISH-HOOKS.

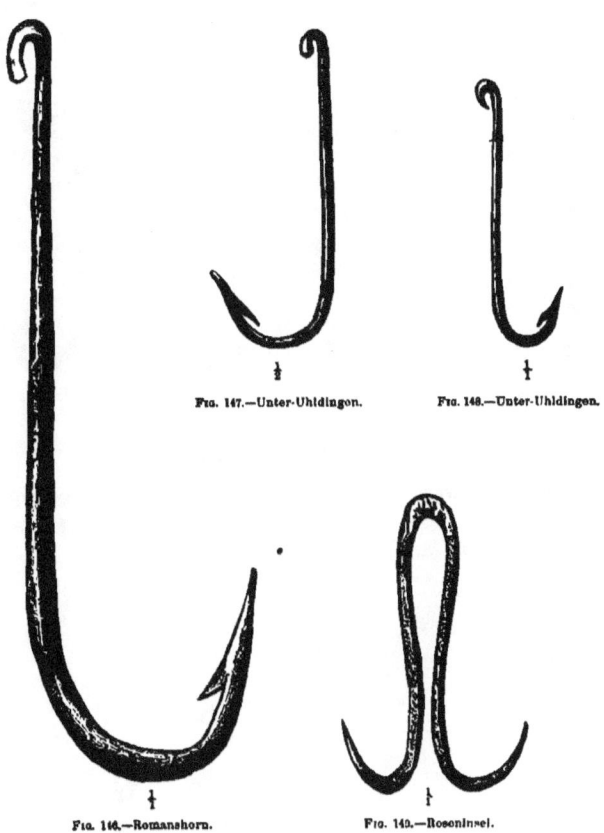

FIG. 146.—Romanshorn. FIG. 147.—Unter-Uhldingen. FIG. 148.—Unter-Uhldingen. FIG. 149.—Roseninsel.

FIGS. 146–149.—Bronze fish-hooks.

Lastly, I present on the following page in Figs. 150 to 153[*] a group of bronze fish-hooks, barbed and unbarbed, from settlements in the Lake of Bourget, Savoy. The original of Fig. 150 is certainly of very clumsy make, and its shape suggestive of some doubt as to its use as a fish-hook.

The originals of Figs. 154 and 155, also on page 104, obtained at the pile-work of Peschiera, on Lake Garda, are designated as small harpoons.[†] They cer-

---

[*] Keller: Lake Dwellings; Vol. II, Plate CLVII, Figs. 13, 12, 18, and 19, respectively.
[†] Ibid.; Vol. II, Plate CXIX, Figs. 1 and 3

tainly are too diminutive for such a use, and Fig. 154, moreover, is curiously curved, and has an eye at the upper extremity. I conjecture that the originals of

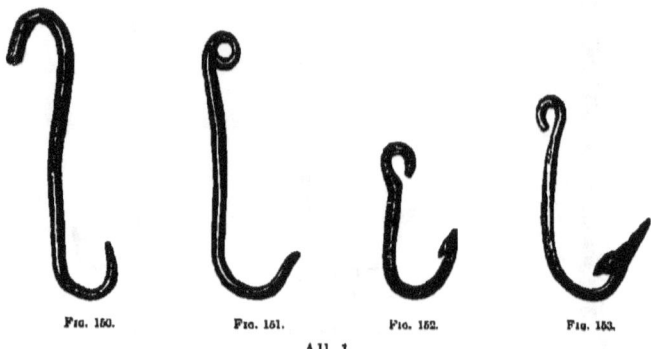

Figs. 150–153.—Bronze fish-hooks. Lake of Bourget.

both, Figs. 154 and 155, were fish-hooks not yet brought into the proper form by bending, and I have the same opinion with regard to the object represented by Fig. 156, a specimen from Möringen, figured by Mr. Friedel.*

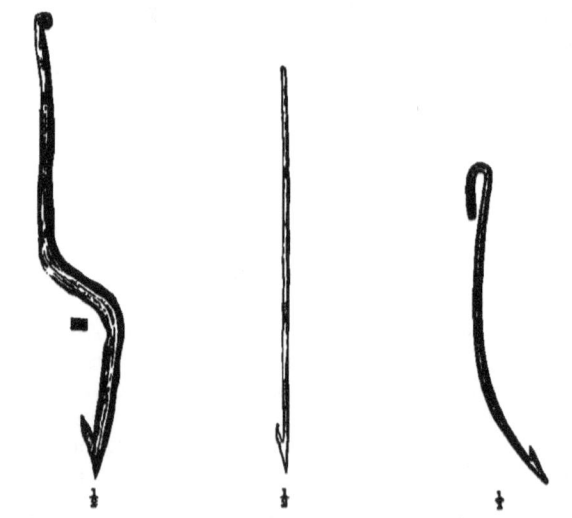

Fig. 154–156.—Barbed bronze rods not yet bent into the form of fish-hooks.

* Amtliche Berichte; p. 128, Fig. 64.

Bronze points, however, which may possibly have been the armatures of harpoons and arrows for shooting fish have occurred, and I give illustrations of a few. Figs. 157 and 158 show barbed points from Möringen, the one stemmed, the other socketed.* Fig. 159 represents a socketed specimen from Peschiera,† and Fig. 160 another one from the Roseninsel, in Lake Starnberg.‡ Yet the use of bone and flint points may have long continued after the introduction of bronze.

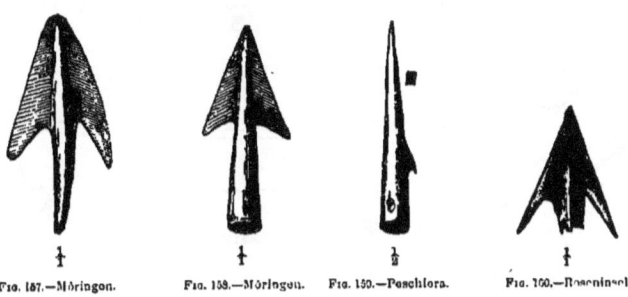

Fig. 157.—Möringen. Fig. 158.—Möringen. Fig. 159.—Peschiera. Fig. 160.—Roseninsel.

Figs. 157–160.—Barbed bronze armatures.

Boats.—The possession of bronze hatchets enabled the lake-dwellers of this period to produce better dug-outs than those made by their predecessors, who were restricted to the use of stone implements. Many of the boats, however, have been found under circumstances which render it difficult to determine their antiquity, as in the case of those discovered in bronze-yielding pile-works inhabited up to the time when iron was used. Such may be either of bronze or iron-age origin.

A curious boat was found in the settlement near Cudrefin, in the Lake of Neuchâtel. In the translation of Keller's work reference is made to the extent of this station and its numerous piles, and it is further mentioned that " pottery has been found here and a boat made out of a single stem."§ From this scanty information it is impossible to draw any conclusion as to the antiquity of the last-named object. At any rate, I reproduce as Fig. 161 on the next page the three views illustrating the appearance of this boat,|| which is certainly of a remarkable form, and, being provided with a sort of handle at one end, reminds

---

* Keller: Lake Dwellings; Vol. II, Plate XLVII, Figs. 9 and 11.
† Ibid.; Vol. II, Plate CXIX, Fig. 2.
‡ Ibid.; Vol. II, Plate CLXXXI, Fig. 6.
§ Ibid.; Vol. I, p. 462.
|| Ibid.; Vol. II, Plate LXXXVII, Figs. 3, 4, and 5.

one of a class of ancient Irish boats mentioned by Sir W. Wilde (page 62 of this publication). This dug-out, which was with great difficulty taken in several pieces out of the water, is thus described by Professor Grangier:—

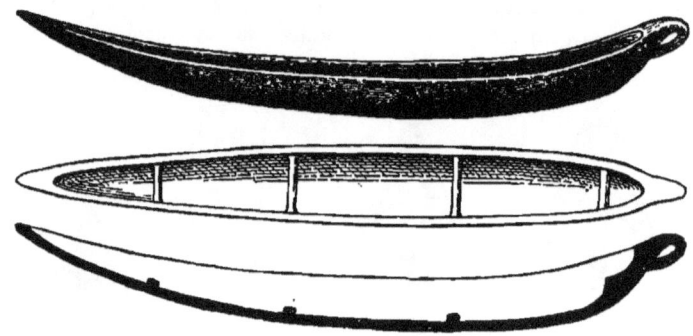

Fig. 161.—Boat. Cudrefin.

"The Cudrefin canoe is about thirty-six and a half English feet long, and about two feet nine inches in its broadest part. The height in the middle is about two feet, the depth nearly one foot six inches, the thickness of the sides is three inches, and that of the bottom rather more than four inches. At the bottom of the boat there are four cross-ribs, made out of the same piece of oak timber as the boat, and at a distance apart of eight or nine feet; that at the prow is an actual seat, and is about one foot wide and eight inches high; the three others are about three inches high and seven inches wide. They were probably intended to strengthen the bottom. — — — As it would have been rather difficult, with my small experience in these matters, to give an idea of the different pieces which together make up this vessel, I have thought it best to draw it, not just as it is at the present moment, but as it was before it was taken out of the water. The most remarkable things about it, according to my ideas, are the part like a handle and the prow, which are in very good preservation."*

M. Edmond de Fellenberg succeeded in recovering two boats near the station of Vingelz, in the Lake of Bienne. One of them is referred by him to the bronze age. The first, an oaken dug-out strengthened by cross-ribs at the bottom, measured a little over forty-three feet in length. A crack extended from one end to the other, and it had been kept together in olden times by *iron*

---

* Keller: Lake Dwellings; Vol. I, p. 282.

cramps, remnants of which still remained in place. M. de Fellenberg ascribes it to the pre-Roman iron period.

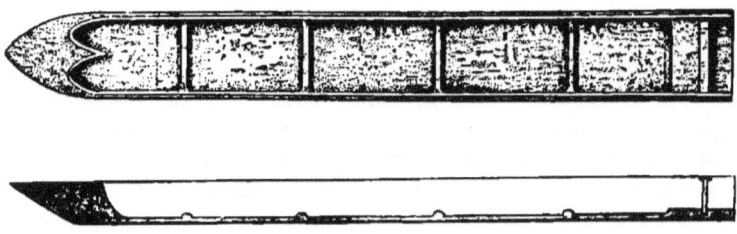

FIG. 162.—Boat. Vingelz.

Fig. 162 is a reduced copy of the representation of the second boat brought to light by him.* He thus describes it :—

"When I was engaged in excavating the large canoe at Vingelz, one of the visitors informed me that the stem of a tree, apparently cut into a conical form, was projecting a little from the bottom of the lake; it lay about thirty paces on one side of the great canoe. When we had secured the large boat, I had this conical stem uncovered, and found, to my no small delight, that we had unexpectedly fallen in with a second canoe, for the conical piece of wood soon appeared as if cut off smoothly above, and after a few minutes' work we brought to light the complete sides of a small but still perfect 'Einbaum,' or 'dug-out' canoe. I had the whole canoe carefully uncovered, and there were so many peculiarities in it that it may be considered as one of the most interesting boats of its kind. It lay with its massive conical end towards the lake, tolerably parallel with the great canoe, and, like it, nearly a hundred feet distant from the ancient bank; that is, from the vineyards below Vingelz. The massive conical end was the highest part, and the canoe sank gradually into the mud, so that the other end was buried two feet deep. This canoe had one remarkable peculiarity: at the hinder part it is cut off quite square, both sides and bottom, and about eight inches from the end a board about an inch thick, and worked with the hatchet, is fastened in on the bottom and between the sides as a kind of makeshift. It seems from this, either that the front portion of this primitive boat had, by some accident, been destroyed, and that the canoe had been made again available by the insertion of this board instead of the stern part, or that the stern portion of the boat, in its usual rounded form, had never existed, and that this singular arrangement was the intentional termination of the boat. In

* Koller: Lake Dwellings; Vol. II, Plate LXXXVII, Figs. 1 and 2.

the latter case it is difficult to understand the prolongation of the bottom and sides for eight inches, or the additional thickness of the wood just at this end from about the fifth rib down to the part cut off. One would almost have thought that this was the middle of the canoe.*

"The canoe, in its present state, is a trifle more than nineteen English feet long, from the extreme point of the conical end to the part cut off. The circumference is somewhat round, so that the sides project beyond the bottom and slope very gradually downwards; thus the boat has somewhat the shape of a trough. It is strengthened at the bottom by five cross-ribs, which rise nearly two and a half inches from the bottom, but do not reach the sides. There is a peculiar beak-shaped projection in the massive conical bow, which stretches about eight inches into the hollow of the canoe and divides the extreme end into two parts. The sides are very thin at the edge, and this is also the case with the bottom, except near the part where it is cut off, where it is twice as thick as elsewhere. It was unfortunately impossible to preserve this very perishable canoe, as it was of poplar, and fell to pieces as soon as it was exposed. — — —

"If we ask the age of this interesting boat, it will itself return the answer; for in fact we found lying on the bottom in the middle of the canoe, a quantity of pieces of pottery belonging to three different earthenware vessels. This pottery is of half-baked clay in two instances, mixed with a quantity of quartzose sand. One has the edge ornamented with impressions similar to those common at Nidau-Steinberg and Möringen. One piece belonged to a shining black thin vessel, and very decidedly indicates the *bronze age*, and to this age we may consider the canoe to belong. It may probably have hailed from Nidau-Steinberg."†

Fig. 163.—Boat. Mercurago.

A boat from the pile-work in the turbary of Mercurago (see page 68 of this publication) is described and figured by Professor Gastaldi.‡ His illustration, here given as Fig. 163, shows the boat in a fragmentary state, only one meter and ninety centimeters of its length remaining; it is about a meter wide, and thirty centimeters in depth. The station in question, it will be remembered, is

---

* This appears plausible enough. But a dug-out, twenty-two feet long, with a stern-piece placed exactly as in the Swiss boat, was found in the lake-dwelling at Buston, near Kilmaurs, Scotland. It is described and represented in Dr. Robert Munro's "Ancient Scottish Lake Dwellings or Crannogs" (Edinburgh, 1882; p. 200, etc.). He mentions in his work several Scottish canoes, but does not seem to assign to them any great antiquity.

† Keller: Lake Dwellings; Vol. I, p. 224, etc.

‡ Gastaldi: Lake Habitations; p. 102, Fig. 30.

considered as belonging to the transition from stone to bronze, and the dug-out may be of bronze-age origin.

FISHING-IMPLEMENTS AND UTENSILS NOT DERIVED FROM LAKE-HABITATIONS.

Under this head I have so little to say that subdivisions appear entirely superfluous; for, though many non-lacustrine bronze-age objects bearing upon fishing may be in existence, my scanty literary material will not permit me to go beyond an allusion to a few fish-hooks and boats.

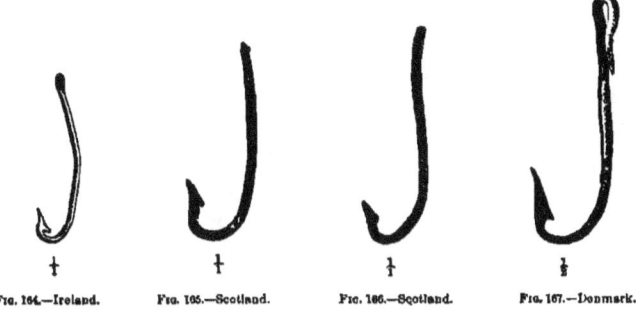

FIG. 164.—Ireland. FIG. 165.—Scotland. FIG. 166.—Scotland. FIG. 167.—Denmark.

FIGS. 164-167.—Bronze fish-hooks.

Mr. John Evans states in his excellent work on the bronze age that he knows only of one bronze fish-hook found in the British Islands, namely, the Irish specimen figured by Sir W. Wilde.* It is here represented as Fig. 164. In this specimen, it will be seen, the upper end of the shank is flattened out for the attachment of the line, just as in modern fish-hooks. There are, however, in the National Museum of Antiquities of Scotland five bronze hooks from Glenluce, Wigtonshire, two of which have been figured. Figs. 165 and 166 are copies.† Mr. Worsaae figures only one Danish fish-hook of bronze in his catalogue of the antiquities in the Copenhagen Museum.‡ His representation is here copied as Fig. 167. He informs me that this fish-hook was found in the Island of Fünen, adding that several others are in the Copenhagen Museum, one of them belonging to a large find of bronze-age antiquities in a tumulus

---

* Sir W. Wilde: Catalogue; p. 526, Fig. 403.

† Proceedings of the Society of Antiquaries of Scotland, 1880-'81; Edinburgh, 1881; Figs. 10 and 11 on p. 273.

‡ Worsaae: Nordiske Oldsager; p. 60, Fig. 277.

in Fünen. Bronze hooks were found in the foundry of Larnaud (Jura) and in the hoard of Saint-Pierre-en-Châtre (Oise),* but the works in which mention of them is made are not at my disposal.

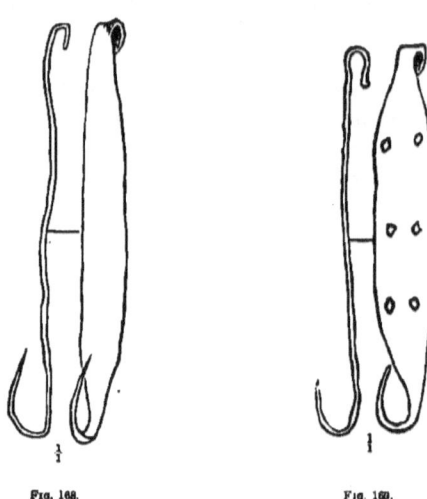

FIG. 168.   FIG. 169.

FIGS. 168 and 169.—Bronze fish-hooks in the form of baits. Germany.

There are in a museum at Lübeck (*Culturhistorisches Museum*) three fish hooks made of thin sheet bronze, and having sharp points and somewhat fish-shaped shanks. Mr. Christensen, who describes and represents them in the article quoted on page 72,† is of opinion that they were thus formed in order to serve as artificial baits. Figs. 168 and 169 are fac-simile copies of two of his rather uncouth illustrations. If these hooks were employed as baits, which seems probable, it was chiefly their metallic lustre which attracted the fish, while iron hooks of the same shape, on account of their less shining appearance, probably would have been useless. These Lübeck specimens, therefore, may have purposely been made of bronze at a time when iron was the common metal.

Mr. Friedel describes a bronze-age dug-out preserved in the Provincial Museum at Berlin. It is made of an oak-stem, four meters long and eighty centimeters wide, and was found in a turbary near Linum, in the District of

---

* Evans: Ancient Bronze Implements; p. 192.

† Deutsche Fischerei-Zeitung; March 22, 1881; p. 95.

East Havelland (Brandenburg), on sandy soil covered by a layer of peat exceeding three meters in thickness.*

Two Danish oaken dug-outs—or rather their remnants—in the Copenhagen Museum, which probably belong to the bronze age, are represented in Worsaae's catalogue. Yet the distinguished archæologist is not altogether certain as to their antiquity, for the word *Broncealderen* with an interrogation-mark after it forms the heading of the page on which they are figured.†

Here I bring my account of prehistoric fishing in Europe to a close.

---

* Friedel: Führer durch die Fischerei-Abtheilung; p. 8.

† Worsaae: Nordiske Oldsager; p. 66, Figs. 294 and 295.—On page 65 of his catalogue Mr. Worsaae represents in Fig. 293 a bronze-age coffin, consisting of the excavated half of an oak-stem with truncated ends. Below the figure the word *Liigkiste* is printed, which means *Leiçhenkiste* in German, and *corpse-chest* in English. M. Gabriel de Mortillet erroneously refers to it as a Danish canoe of the bronze age (Matériaux, Vol. III, 1867; p. 48).

PART II.—NORTH AMERICA.

INTRODUCTORY REMARKS.

While there is no difficulty in comprehending the term "prehistoric," when applied to the antiquities of Europe, the same word assumes an altered significance in its connection with the artefacts left by the former inhabitants of this country. Here, by general consent, all objects are considered as prehistoric, which occur in mounds and other burial-places of early date, on and below the surface of the ground, in caves, shell-heaps, etc.—in fact all articles of aboriginal workmanship that cannot with certainty be ascribed to any of the tribes which are either still in existence, or have become extinct within historical times, or, to speak more distinctly, within the recollection of the white successors of the Indians. Thus, a collection of North American relics may contain specimens of very high antiquity as well as others of comparatively recent date; yet there is no way of suggesting accurate discrimination. Moreover, it cannot be doubted that some, or even many, of the objects classed with our antiquities originated after the arrival of Europeans in this country; for, though the natives were not slow in recognizing the superiority of the white man's tools and other implements, and endeavored to obtain them by barter from the immigrants, the less favored ones among them—for not all could be supplied at once—were still compelled to manufacture, according to old usage, various articles, which, when discovered, are placed in collections of North American antiquities.

It certainly would be a mistake to attribute aboriginal relics from any given district positively to the Indians who occupied it when the whites arrived. Though these natives doubtless left many manufactures on the soil of their special country, it cannot be decided, at least not in most cases, whether an object there discovered is to be assigned to the last occupants, or to invaders, or to predecessors of a different lineage.*

If all these circumstances are taken into account, there arises a probability that the one or the other object hereafter described by me may be of more or less recent origin, and even post-date the advent of the Caucasians in this country.

---

* These observations refer immediately to the long-settled eastern regions of North America; but they can with equal force be applied to the western districts which have lately been colonized by the whites.

Was there a palæolithic age in North America?

During a number of years, Dr. Charles C. Abbott, of Trenton, New Jersey, has published papers in which he describes rude implements found by him in the undisturbed gravel-beds of the Delaware Valley at Trenton, and he finally sums up his experiences, together with those of others, in the thirty-second chapter of a late work treating of the aboriginal relics of the northern Atlantic sea-board of America. The implements in question resemble in shape more or less those from the drift of France and England; yet while the latter consist of cretaceous flint, the material of the New Jersey specimens is argillite.* I have seen but three of them, which were sent to me by Dr. Abbott, and these are unmistakably fashioned by the hand of man. They were all found, he informs me, by himself in the gravel-bluff facing the Delaware River at Trenton, at a depth of thirteen feet from the surface. "The purplish-colored one was underneath a boulder and could never have been above it, since the deposition of the boulder." Dr. Abbott's illustrations of Trenton implements likewise leave no doubt as to the artificial shaping of the originals. He admits that, "having been seriously misled by the various geological reports that purport to give, in proper sequence, the respective ages of the several strata of clay, gravel, boulders, and sand, through which the river has finally worn its channel to the ocean-level, he has probably, in previous publications, ascribed too great an antiquity to these implements, although what is now known to be a substantially correct history of the various deposits in the river-valley does not dissociate these traces of man from a time when essentially glacial conditions existed in the upper valley of the Delaware River, though they occurred subsequently to the existence of the great continental glacier, when at its greatest magnitude.

"It was not until the surface geology of the Delaware River Valley was carefully studied by Mr. Henry Carvill Lewis, of the Second Geological Survey of Pennsylvania, that we were in possession of all the facts necessary to enable us to recognize the full significance of those early traces of man, discovered in one of the latest geological formations of this valley."†

The conclusions drawn by Mr. Lewis from his investigation are, that the Trenton gravel is a true river-gravel, and is the most recent of all the formations in the valley of the Delaware River; that it is apparently post-glacial; and that the stone implements of palæolithic type, which this gravel contains, indicate the existence of man in a rude state, at the time of its deposition.‡ It remains to be seen whether this is the last verdict in the case.

---

* Only one spear-head-like implement of flint has thus far been noticed. It was taken, within the city of Trenton, from the gravel, at a depth of six feet below the surface.

† Abbott: Primitive Industry: or Illustrations of the Handiwork, in Stone, Bone and Clay, of the Native Races of the Northern Atlantic Seaboard of America; Salem, Mass., 1881; p. 471.

‡ Ibid.; p. 551.

There has been discovered at Trenton, about fourteen feet below the surface, the tusk of a mastodon, covered with partly stratified gravel and stones. Alluding to this circumstance, Dr. Abbott observes:—"When we consider that not only the remains of the mastodon, but those of the bison, have been found in this gravel, and that within a few yards of the spot where the tusk of the mastodon mentioned by Professor Cook, was found, palæolithic implements have been gathered, one at the same, and three at greater depths, it is apparent that we here have evidence of man's contemporaneity, on the Atlantic coast, with the large mammals mentioned."* Bones of the reindeer also have been met with, though sparingly, in this gravel.

Finally, Dr. Abbott strongly inclines to the view—not an unusual one—that the Eskimos formerly extended far to the southward in North America, and, indeed, were the makers of the rude tools found by him in the Trenton gravel.

Professor Henry W. Haynes, of Boston, who has studied the stone age for six years in Europe and Northern Africa, lately visited, in company with Professor W. Boyd Dawkins and other gentlemen, the region in question, and became fully convinced of the palæolithic character of the Trenton argillite tools. On this occasion, it should be stated, several implements were taken by his companions, either from the gravel or the talus on the river-bank, in his presence, and he found five himself.

"It has been my good fortune," he says, "to find palæolithic implements in Europe in several localities, both where they have been accompanied by the characteristic fossil bones, and where these have been wanting. I have thus had the opportunity of making myself familiar with the general character of such localities and the appearance of the country in the vicinity, together with the nature and quality of the gravels in which the implements are found. I have especially studied the gravel-beds of the valley of the Seine, in the vicinity of Paris, and of the Tiber, near Rome, for several successive years, and in a very great number of visits, and from both these localities I have obtained fossil bones of the mammoth, the rhinoceros, the hippopotamus, the bos antiquus, the great extinct elk, the horse, the reindeer, etc. Accompanying these fossil bones were found the characteristic palæolithic implements. I have also visited the famous locality of Saint-Acheul, and the well-known gravel-pits near Salisbury, England, in both of which spots have occurred numerous finds of palæolithic implements, accompanied by similar fossil bones. In another locality, near Dinan, in Normandy, where the pleistocene deposits no longer exist, as is also the case in the valley of the Nile, I have found a large quantity of palæolithic implements made out of quartzite. From these various experiences I feel myself warranted in stating that the general appearance of the country and the character of the

---

* Abbott: Primitive Industry; p. 482.

gravels at Trenton, New Jersey, present a most striking resemblance to what I have seen in the various localities in the Old World to which I have referred. There is the same rudely-stratified mingling of coarse materials marked by a similar absence of clay. It is true that in the gravels of New Jersey thus far not many fossil bones have been discovered, but only a few of the mammoth, the bison, the reindeer, and the walrus, some of which, like the animals of Europe under similar circumstances, have since migrated to the colder regions of the north. But the fact remains that fossil animal bones have actually been discovered in these gravels, and when we call to mind to what a limited extent they have as yet been examined, we may reasonably expect more to be found hereafter.

"I limit myself to a general statement like this in regard to the marked resemblance of the locality, and the precisely similar character of the gravels at Trenton, New Jersey, to what I have seen in many localities in Europe, which have yielded true palæolithic implements, and I leave in more competent hands the discussion and determination of the true geological character of the gravels of the Delaware Valley.

"Speaking then merely from an archæological stand-point, I do not hesitate to declare my firm conviction that the rude argillite objects found in the gravels of the Delaware River, at Trenton, New Jersey, are true palæolithic implements."*

This is certainly a strong vindication of Dr. Abbott's claims.

I have elsewhere expressed my belief that man is an exotic element in America; but that the present American continent received its first population at a very remote period, when, perhaps, the distribution of land and sea was different from what it is now. The earliest immigrants, I further stated, may have been so low in the scale of human development that they lacked the faculty of expressing themselves in articulate language, as it is difficult to account in another way for the totally diverse characteristics of the numerous linguistic families of America.

In accordance with these views, I do not deem it improbable that implements analogous in character to those of the European drift should occur under corresponding circumstances in North America.

I cannot express a similar opinion with regard to "pliocene" man in America. Admitting, for instance, the correctness of the reports on the polished stone implements said to have been taken from a bed of Table Mountain in Tuolumne County, California, older than the European drift, it would follow that man lived in America in a polished-stone age, before the contemporary of

---

* Haynes: The Argillite Implements found in the Gravels of the Delaware River, at Trenton, N. J., compared with the Palæolithic Implements of Europe; Proceedings of the Boston Society of Natural History; Vol. XXI, January 19, 1881; p. 136, etc.

the mammoth in Europe fashioned his rude implements of flint. An inference of such stupendous bearing should not be accepted without incontrovertible proofs, and these, it seems to me, have not yet been furnished. If, ultimately, what now appears almost incredible, should become an established fact, all doubts, of course, will be removed.

While treating of prehistoric fishing in Europe, I was enabled to divide the subject into different sections, devoting each of them to a special phase of human existence. But such a mode of proceeding would hardly be applicable to North America, and I prefer describing, in proper succession, such relics bearing upon fishing as may be called prehistoric, according to the explanation of the term as given on a preceding page.

The abundance of fish in the rivers and lakes of North America—not to speak of the sea-boards—excited the astonishment of the early European colonists, who found the natives well acquainted with various modes of fishing, which could only have been acquired by long-continued pursuits. Taking them as a whole, they practised fishing by spearing and shooting, with hook and line, and nets of various kinds, and they even knew how to stupefy fish by throwing intoxicating substances into the water. They constructed traps, weirs, fish-pens, and fish-preserves, and, finally, navigated, for the purpose of fishing, the streams, lakes, and seas with boats varying greatly in size and make.

All this will subsequently be set forth in a series of extracts from authors who describe the natives of North America as they were when first observed, or when their habits had not been materially changed by intercourse with the whites.

For the rest, I abstain from giving any details concerning Indian mode of life. The indigenous American still belongs to the present, and it may be presupposed that his characteristics are known to the reader of this work.

FISHING-IMPLEMENTS AND UTENSILS.

Double-pointed straight Bait-holders.—Among the many thousand North American articles of flint and other stone exhibited in the United States National Museum there is not one to which the above application could with any degree of safety be assigned. Only a few among them possibly might have thus been employed; but these constitute a fraction by far too small to form a type, or, in other words, to represent a class of objects made for a common purpose. Nevertheless I will describe some of them.

The original of Fig. 170, on the following page, is a chipped implement of dark-gray jasper, found by Mr. Paul Schumacher near Rogue River, Oregon. It is slender, and the points are rather blunt, apparently not from use, but in consequence of exposure, the specimen showing a kind of polish evidently produced by contact with other bodies. It looks as though it had been drifted in water.

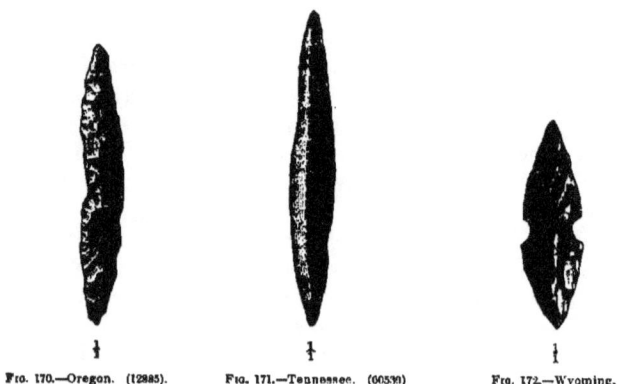

Fig. 170.—Oregon. (12885).   Fig. 171.—Tennessee. (60539).   Fig. 172.—Wyoming.

Figs. 170-172.—Double-pointed stone implements.

Fig. 171 shows the form of a somewhat similar object, in this instance brought into shape by grinding. This specimen, presented by Professor W. A. Kite, is not flattish like the one first described, but almost round in the cross-section, and terminates in tolerably sharp points. It consists of a blackish kind of stone, apparently argillite, and was found nearly opposite the mouth of Middle Creek, in Greene County, Tennessee.

Fig. 172 is taken from the "Fifth Annual Report of the Superintendent of the Yellowstone National Park" (Washington, 1881, Fig. 16 on page 37). It is not distinctly stated whether the original, which belongs to a series of stone implements collected in the National Park by Superintendent P. W. Norris, consists of flint or obsidian. This, however, is of little consequence, as the shape alone is the noticeable feature, and that is certainly exceptional and suggestive of the application here considered. The notches would have facilitated the attachment of a line, and the implement, inserted into a fish and swallowed by a larger one, could not easily have been disgorged by the latter. But, nevertheless, it probably was prepared for a totally different purpose.

I give in Fig. 173 the delineation of a rather large polished implement, found in Berks County, Pennsylvania, and presented to the Smithsonian Institution by the Hon. G. H. Keim. I figure this specimen for the simple reason that it has been regarded by some as a bait-holder, an opinion in which I cannot concur. The material is a greenish-gray argillite. The illustration shows its form distinctly, and I have only to add that a cross-section laid through the middle would present a somewhat flattened oval. I am inclined to regard this specimen as a ceremonial weapon in which the usual perforation for the reception of a handle is replaced by a groove. It weighs three ounces and a half.

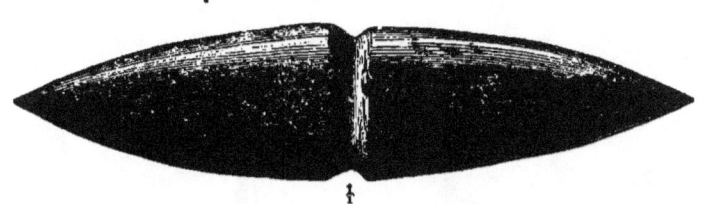

FIG. 173.—Double-pointed grooved stone implement. Pennsylvania. (6627).

Straight bone rods tapering toward both ends are not wanting in the archæological division of the National Museum. They were chiefly obtained in the course of explorations of the Californian Santa Barbara group of islands and their neighborhood, undertaken in the interest of the United States National Museum by Messrs. Paul Schumacher and Stephen Bowers. These explorations extended over the islands of San Miguel, Santa Cruz, San Nicolas, and Santa Catalina, and various points on the main-land, embraced in the counties of San Luis Obispo and Santa Barbara. A place called Dos Pueblos in the last-named district has furnished many remarkable objects.*

Figs. 174, 175, and 176, on page 120, represent specimens of pointed bone rods found by Mr. Bowers on Santa Cruz Island; the original of Fig. 177 was obtained by him on Santa Rosa Island. Some of the specimens on exhibition in the National Museum show traces of asphaltum in the middle. They are of a somewhat compressed form and generally well made, and their number in the Museum is sufficient to form a class. If they were grooved or notched in the middle, as shown in Fig. 2 on page 13, I would have little doubt as to their use as bait-holders, though the grooves or notches are not absolutely necessary features. As

---

* The relics were found in graves as well as on the surface, and while many of them are evidently very old, others betoken a more recent origin, and some of the latter have occurred in association with articles of European manufacture, such as iron blades, objects of brass, beads of glass and enamel, etc., proving that they are referable to the natives whom the whites found in possession of the islands and the neighboring coast. The islands have been totally vacated by the Indians, the last of whom, a few in number, were removed, nearly fifty years ago, to the Santa Barbara Mission.

Accounts of the explorations were published by Dr. H. C. Yarrow and Mr. Paul Schumacher, and more than half of Vol. VII of the "United States Geographical Surveys West of the One Hundredth Meridian, in charge of First Lieutenant George M. Wheeler" (Washington, 1879), is devoted to a minute description of the localities and the objects there obtained.

it is, they may have served in the manner indicated, or as parts of fish-hooks, or in some other way not yet explained.

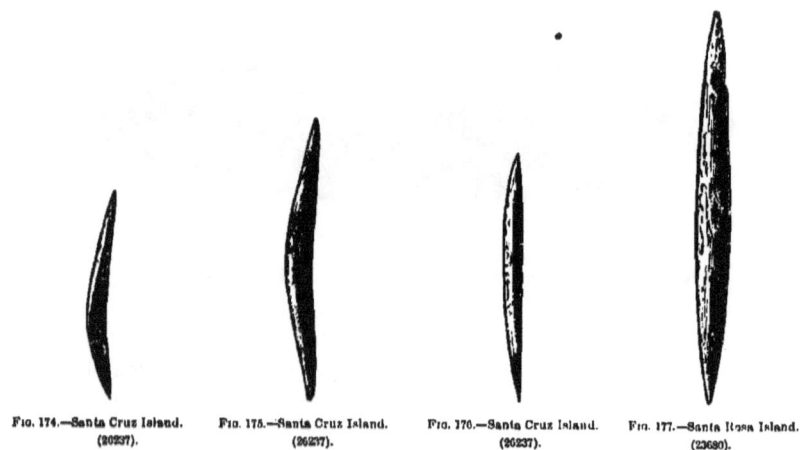

Fig. 174.—Santa Cruz Island. (20237).   Fig. 175.—Santa Cruz Island. (26237).   Fig. 176.—Santa Cruz Island. (20237).   Fig. 177.—Santa Rosa Island. (23680).

All ½.

Figs. 174–177.—Double-pointed bone implements.

Fish-hooks.—It does not appear that fish-hooks entirely made of silicious material, like those described by Professor Nilsson, have been found in North America; but hooks constructed of flint or chalcedony and bone have occurred in Greenland. Dr. Gustav Klemm describes and represents such a specimen obtained from an old grave in that country. Fig. 178 is a reproduction of his illustration. The curved bone shank and piece of worked flint are bound together with a narrow strip of whalebone, and the line attached to the upper end of the shank consists of twisted vegetable fibre.*

Another somewhat similar specimen from a grave in Southern Greenland is in the Ethnological Museum at Copenhagen. It attracted the special attention of Dr. Emil Bessels during a visit to that city in 1881, and the distinguished artist, Captain A. P. Madsen, made for him a drawing of the object. That gentleman's design is here copied as Fig. 179. The shank, pierced with four holes, and nearly cylindrical in its upper part, but worked flat lower downward, is made from a bone of some quadruped, and shows a brown coloration, like bones extracted from peat-bogs. The chipped hook consists of bluish-white chalcedony. Both shank and hook were found together, but without ligature, this connecting medium having yielded to the effects of decay. The re-uniting of the two parts

---

* Klemm: Allgemeine Culturwissenschaft; Werkzeuge und Waffen; Leipzig, 1854; p. 61, Fig. 101.

by means of twine is the work of Mr. C. L. Steinhauer, Inspector of the museum just mentioned.

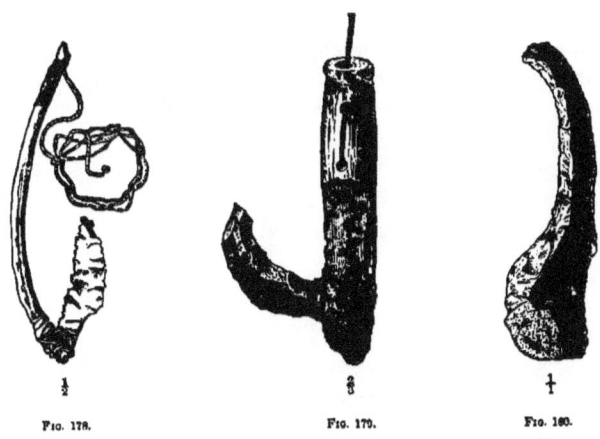

FIGS. 178–180.—Fish-hooks composed of bone and chipped stone. Greenland.

Dr. Bessels obtained on the same occasion a very fine specimen from Greenland, namely, a well-chipped piece of transparent bluish-gray chalcedony, which apparently formed, or was designed to form, a part of a fish-hook of the kind here noticed. Fig. 180 shows its appearance. This object is triangular in the cross-section, the portion not seen in the illustration being flat and but little chipped.

It is doubtful whether flint was thus prepared by the former inhabitants of the present United States, to serve in the construction of fish-hooks, for not a single specimen of the required form is to be found among the thousands of flint objects in the National Museum. Articles of this description, however, appear to occur in Germany, and a number of specimens derived from the Island of Rügen, and thought to belong to this class, were presented for inspection by Mr. Rosenberg during the exhibition of prehistoric German relics, held at Berlin in 1880. To judge from the description, they are not brought into a definite shape by chipping, but are simply flakes (*Spleisse*) of suitable form, some of them but little modified for the attachment to a shank. Their size being considerable, they could only have served in the construction of hooks designed to catch the large species of fish.*

---

* (Voss): Katalog der Ausstellung prähistorischer und anthropologischer Funde Deutschlands; p. 368.

A similar statement is made by Mr. Christensen in the article already quoted in two instances. He says there are sometimes found in Germany flint splinters with curved points, occasionally fashioned at the thicker end for attachment to a shank. These specimens are regarded by him as component parts of fish-hooks. In addition, he represents a *bone* object of a form suggestive of the same use, preserved in the collection of the antiquarian association "Prussia" in Königsberg, Prussia. I copy here his illustration as Fig. 181.*

Fig. 181.—Bone point of fish-hook. Germany.

After this short digression I resume the subject of North American prehistoric fish-hooks.

In the first place I have to allude to their great scarcity in the eastern portion of North America, and to state that those which have been found within that area are almost exclusively made of bone. They occur more frequently on the Pacific Coast, especially in Californian latitudes, and there they consist either of bone or of shell. I refer here to real fish-hooks, and not to relics which possibly were parts of hooks. Bone fish-hooks are occasionally mentioned by the early authors on North America, as a perusal of the "Extracts" at the end of this publication will show.† The hooks used by the Indians of Virginia are thus described by Captain John Smith:—"Their hookes are either a bone grated as they noch their arrowes in the forme of a crooked pinne or fish-hooke, or of the splinter of a bone tyed to the clift of a little sticke, and with the end of the line they tie on the bait." From this short, but eminently graphic, description we learn that the Indians of a certain Atlantic district used fish-hooks made entirely of a fragment of bone, and others consisting of two parts joined together. The latter class of hooks is still in use among some North American tribes. The Makah codfish-hook, Fig. 10 on page 15, is similarly constructed, and I present, additionally, in Fig. 182 the form of a fish-hook used by the Kutchin Indians, who inhabit the territory between the Mackenzie River and Norton Sound. "The hooks," observes Mr. Strachan Jones, "are made and baited in

---

* Deutsche Fischerei-Zeitung; March 22, 1881; p. 95.

† See "Extracts:" Captain Smith, Ogilby, Sagard, Kalm, etc.

the following manner:—The pinion of a goose is taken, and the smaller bone is sharpened and fastened hook-shape to the larger; a piece of fish-skin is cut in the shape of a fish and sewed on the hook; that part representing the head is at the point of the hook; that representing the tail is where the bones have crossed each other; a line is then knotted to the larger bone, and all is complete."[*]

FIG. 182.—Baited bone fish-hook. Kutchin Indians, Alaska.

Prehistoric fish-hooks of this kind, as far as known to me, have not been preserved. After the decay of the ligature the constituent parts of such a hook would become separated, and, when discovered, their real character probably would escape recognition in most cases. Mr. A. T. Gamage, of Damariscotta, Maine, informs me that he has found in the artificial shell-deposits near that place quite a number of double-pointed bone rods, which, he suggests, were parts of fish-hooks.

I now pass over to a description of North American fish-hooks made of a single piece of bone or horn.

Fig. 183 (on page 124).—The original of this bone hook was presented to the National Museum by Dr. W. J. Hoffman, of the Bureau of Ethnology. It is as simple a form of a fish-hook as could be conceived; there is not even a distinct notch at the upper end of the shank, only a faint trace of one being visible. The surface of the hook shows the striæ produced by the scraping-instrument used in fashioning it. Dr. Hoffman has furnished me with the following account relating to its discovery:—

"Traces of aboriginal settlements occur quite abundantly along the valley of the Missouri River, north of the mouth of Oak Creek, at the former location of Grand River Agency, Dakota. The latter stream (Oak Creek), emptying into

---

[*] Jones: The Kutchin Tribes; Smithsonian Report for 1866, p. 324; figure on the same page.

the Missouri from the west, has formed a point of the prairie-terrace, upon which are visible numerous low heaps or mounds of earth and clay, varying from several inches to a foot in height, and from two to ten feet in diameter. Some of these consist underneath almost entirely of bones of the larger mammals, while at various other points the soil seems to have been washed away, leaving the bones, sturgeon-scales, etc., lying around promiscuously. The bones in no instance presented the effects of fire, but always exhibited the sharp, irregular appearance of having been cracked for the removal of the marrow.

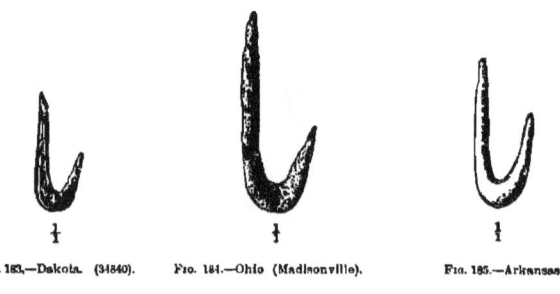

Fig. 183.—Dakota. (31840).   Fig. 184.—Ohio (Madisonville).   Fig. 185.—Arkansas.

Figs. 183–185.—Bone fish-hooks.

"Upon digging into one of these smaller earth-heaps, the fish-hook was found in the end of a fractured thigh-bone of a buffalo. Fragments of pottery were very abundant, while arrow-heads, hammer-stones (such as are used at this day for driving down tent-pins, etc.), and small blue beads were not uncommon.

"Black Eye, chief of the Upper Yanktonnais, informed me that the Arikara were defeated and driven from that identical spot by the Dakotas, under the command of his father, in 1818. The hillocks present every appearance of having once been earth-lodges, though smaller than found at this day at Fort Berthold."

Fig. 184.—The original of this much-corroded hook was found in one of the so-called ash-pits of the great cemetery near Madisonville, Hamilton County, Ohio. The depressions at the upper end of the shank are the result of decay, small particles of the bone having come off in that place. The hook is in possession of the Hon. Joseph Cox, of Cincinnati, who kindly sent it to the National Museum to be drawn.*

---

* The results of an exploration of this cemetery, carried on under the auspices of the Madisonville Literary and Scientific Society, are presented in three illustrated reports by Mr. Charles F. Low, published in the "Journal of the Cincinnati Society of Natural History" (Vol. III, 1880, p. 40–68; p. 128–139; p. 203–220); and Dr. F. W. Langdon has given in the same journal (Vol. IV, 1881, p. 237–257) an account of the osteological characteristics of the skeletons there exhumed. In addition, the subject has been treated in several articles. I subjoin a

Fig. 185.—A bone fish-hook preserved in the collection of the Davenport Academy of Natural Sciences. Mr. W. H. Pratt, Corresponding Secretary and Curator of that association, had the kindness to send it to me for examination. The specimen is polished on both sides; that not seen in the illustration exhibits a portion of the marrow-cavity of the bone. The point is not very sharp, and, owing to the curvature of the bone, not in the same plane with the shank, the upper part of which shows some slight indentations for the attachment of the line. I am informed by Mr. Pratt that this specimen was taken, together with a bone awl, from a small clay mound on the Craighead farm, Mississippi County, Arkansas, opposite the mouth of the Big Hatchie River. The mound was about two feet high, and three feet below its surface the skeleton of a boy, about twelve years old, the bone hook and awl, some shell beads, and a quantity of fish-bones and turtle-shells were found. Mr. Pratt learned these details from Captain W. P. Hall, a resident of Davenport, who presented the fish-hook to the Academy.

Fig. 186 (on page 126).—The original was found by Mr. F. H. Cushing, of the Bureau of Ethnology. It is made of deer-bone, and beautifully polished, especially at the point. The shank expands a little at the upper end where there are some slight grooves. Viewed horizontally from the lower end, this hook shows in a slight degree the cavity of the bone. It was discovered in an accumulation of débris, eighteen inches below the surface, near the centre of an old circular earthwork in the township of Shelby, Orleans County, New York. With it, Mr. Cushing informs me, occurred various other remains, such as broken bones of animals, rudely-ornamented pot-sherds, flint implements, awls, spatulæ, portions of weapons and ornaments of bone and deer-horn, shell and stone beads, etc.

Fig. 187 (on page 126).—A hook of larger size, remarkable for its straight base. It shows the marrow-cavity of the bone on the side not exposed to view in the figure. A slight contraction below the end of the shank allowed the line to be firmly tied on. This apparently old specimen, of a yellowish-brown color, belongs to Dr. John Sloan, Secretary of the Society of Natural History at New Albany, Indiana,

---

short notice from a letter by Mr. Cox:—

"The cemetery is located in a dense wood of perhaps seventy-five or a hundred acres, which has been left intact since white men took possession of the Miami country. The trees are very thick, from three to five feet in diameter. So far as we have sounded, there are fifteen acres covered by these graves. We have exhumed about seven hundred skeletons, and apparently the whole fifteen acres are covered with the same average number of graves as the space we have opened. Thus the interments would reach the number of ten thousand. The graves are about two and a half feet deep, and under them, running down through hard clay, are circular ash-pits, as we call them, three feet in diameter, and from two to six feet in depth. These holes are filled with ashes and earth, inclosing different kinds of stone and bone articles: pipes, axes, arrow-heads, deer and elk-horns, worked and unworked, bone awls and needles, and fish-hooks and harpoon-heads of the same material. We have opened over four hundred of these in the cemetery. From ordinary calculation of the growth of trees on the graves, we estimate the trees to be from two to three hundred years old. How old the graves are, or the ash-pits, or for what purpose the latter were made, we have no conjecture."

who obligingly loaned it to me for the purpose of having it drawn. The hook, I am informed by that gentleman, occurred in the "Indian grave-yard" at Clarksville on the Ohio River, two miles and a half above New Albany, nearly opposite Louisville. The graves, being situated at a bend of the river, become

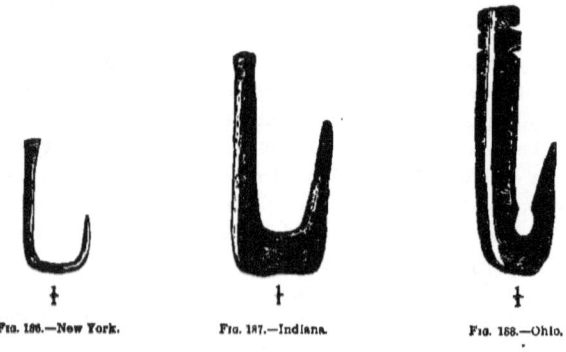

Fig. 186.—New York.   Fig. 187.—Indiana.   Fig. 188.—Ohio.

Figs. 186–188.—Bone fish-hooks.

exposed after the spring-freshets by the crumbling away of the bank, and have yielded many relics, the commercial value of which is well appreciated by the residents. Of late years, however, comparatively little has been found.

Fig. 188.—This illustration shows the form of a rather uncouth bone fish-hook, which, nevertheless, bears a general resemblance to some of the lacustrine hooks represented on pages 48 and 49 of this work. It has been figured by Schoolcraft, who states that it was found within an earthen inclosure on Cunningham's Island, in Lake Erie (Ohio). "Within these inclosures have been found stone axes, pipes, perforators, bone fish-hooks, fragments of pottery, arrow-heads, net-sinkers, and fragments of human bones."*

Fig. 189.—This figure, representing a large bone hook, is taken from Dr. C. C. Abbott's "Primitive Industry," before quoted.† The specimen is in possession of Mr. W. Wallace Tooker, of Sag Harbor, Long Island, New York, and was found by him in a shell-heap in the neighborhood of Sag Harbor. It is the only object of this kind discovered by that gentleman in the course of his explorations of shell-heaps in Long Island.

Fig. 190.—The original, a fine bone hook with deeply-notched shank, belongs to Dr. J. F. Snyder, of Virginia, Cass County, Illinois. I am indebted to him

---

* Schoolcraft: Historical and Statistical Information, respecting the History, Condition and Prospects of the Indian Tribes of the United States; Vol. II, Philadelphia, 1852; p. 87; Fig. 4 on Plate 38.

† Fig. 193 on p. 208.

for a drawing of the specimen. "It was found," he states, "some years ago, at the base of a long mound on the edge of Mound Lake, in Cass County, in one of the numerous heaps of camp-rubbish there seen, consisting of mussel-shells, ashes, charcoal, and earth, interspersed with many fragments of pottery, flint chips, and bones of deer, buffalo, wild turkey, raccoon, opossum, etc., the whole covered with sand and silt deposited by the inundations of ages.

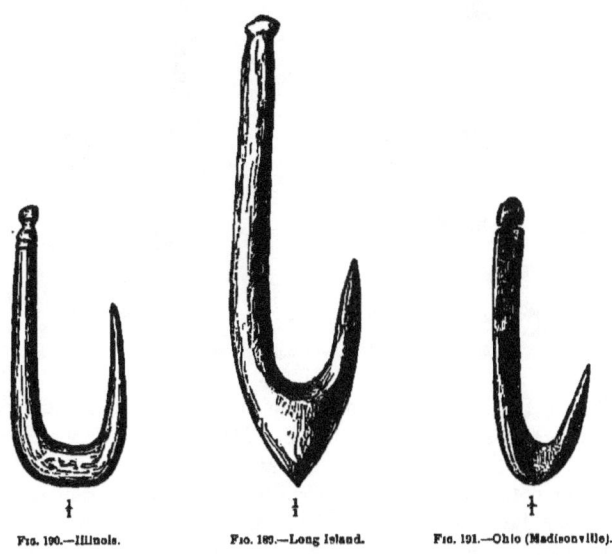

Fig. 190.—Illinois.   Fig. 189.—Long Island.   Fig. 191.—Ohio (Madisonville).

Figs. 189–191.—Bone fish-hooks.

"Mound Lake—like all the other lakes and sloughs of the Sangamon Bottom—is merely a stretch of one of the ancient beds of the Sangamon River, and communicates with it by a short outlet; and is now, as it probably was centuries ago, the habitat of innumerable pike, buffalo, cat, and other species of fine fish. I can find no evidence to sustain the idea that the ancient tribes of this region understood the art of catching fish with nets;* but this bone hook proves that they practised at least one method of fishing."

Fig. 191.—This hook presents a perfectly fresh appearance, being almost white, and is of excellent workmanship and well polished. The upper part of the shank, including that above the well-cut groove, is four-sided. The figure

---

* Dr. Snyder found no net-sinkers in that neighborhood.

shows a portion of the marrow-cavity of the bone. This specimen, found in one of the Madisonville ash-pits or graves, was sent to the National Museum, with a view to further my work, by the Hon. Joseph Cox. Its possessor is the Hon. Samuel F. Covington, of Cincinnati.

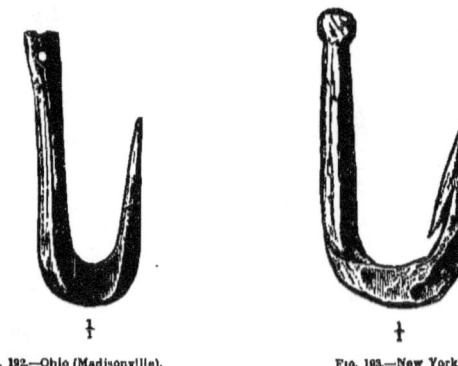

FIG. 192.—Ohio (Madisonville).   FIG. 193.—New York.

FIGS. 192 and 193.—Fish-hooks of bone and deer-horn.

Fig. 192.—Another fine specimen from the Madisonville cemetery, and, like the original of Fig. 191, owned by Mr. S. F. Covington. This carefully-worked and polished hook is somewhat flattish at the upper end of the shank, while the remaining portion, excepting the curve where the marrow-cavity appears, presents a roundish form. I have not seen any other bone fish-hook found in the United States which is pierced for suspension. The hole is placed near the extremity of the shank, and carefully drilled from both sides. This specimen shows a yellowish color.

Fig. 193.—The figure, representing a deer-horn fish-hook, is copied from a drawing kindly sent by the Rev. W. M. Beauchamp, of Baldwinsville, Onondaga County, New York. This specimen was found, in 1880, by a laborer on what is called the Atwell Site, in Pompey Township, Onondaga (or Madison) County, New York,[*] and is in possession of Mr. L. W. Ledyard, of Cazenovia, in Madison County of that state. The hook being provided with a barb, Mr. Beauchamp thinks that it was made, in imitation of the European fish-hook, by an Onondaga Indian in the seventeenth century. There was an earthwork and ditch on the site, which has yielded deer-horn forks or combs, bone punches, awls of deer-horn, clay pipes, some of them exhibiting curiously intertwined human

---

[*] "The site," says Mr. Beauchamp, "is commonly described as being on Lot 44, Pompey, Onondaga County, but is more strictly in Madison County." These counties, of course, are contiguous.

faces, pottery with human faces at the angles of the rims, and many other objects. The specimen here figured is the only regularly barbed fish-hook of aboriginal manufacture known to me, and Mr. Beauchamp's view as to its recent origin appears very plausible.

In California, as stated, fish-hooks have have been found in greater number than in the eastern part of North America.

FIG. 194.   FIG. 195.

FIGS. 194 and 195.—Bone fish-hooks. Santa Cruz Island. (26240).
shell ?

· Figs. 194 and 195.—They represent bone hooks from Santa Cruz Island, which were obtained by Mr. Stephen Bowers. In these specimens the outer curve is rounded, the inner rather angular until it reaches the shank, which presents a conical shape, and is destitute of any device for holding a line. The end of the line was tightly wound around the shank and fastened on with asphaltum, portions of which can still be seen in both specimens. Even the impressions produced by the line are visible. The peculiar feature of these fish-hooks, and, indeed, of nearly all other Californian specimens in the National Museum, is the close approach of the curved point to the shank—a feature which actually has induced some to doubt their use as fishing-implements. I hope I shall succeed in removing these doubts.

Figs. 196 to 199 (on page 130).—These figures show the appearance of bone fish-hooks of more developed forms. They were collected by Mr. Paul Schumacher on the Island of Santa Cruz. In the original of Fig. 196 the end of the shank is grooved a short distance on both sides, and farther down notched on the outside, thus offering a firm hold to the line. Where the shank ends, slight traces of asphaltum are perceivable. In the three other specimens the fastening of the line was performed in a similar manner; but the groove on both sides of the shank is carried around it. The four hooks in this group have a much fresher appearance than the preceding ones, and in the last three the shanks are thickly covered with asphaltum. The barb-like projection on the outer curve, which

R 17

characterizes these specimens, probably was only intended to hold the bait in place.

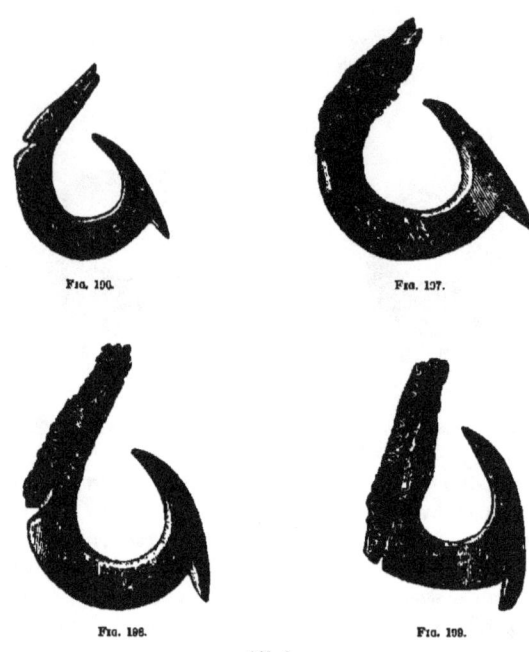

Figs. 196–199.—Bone fish-hooks. Santa Cruz Island. (18188).

The same feature characterizes New Zealand fish-hooks,* and it is observable in two hooks from Arctic America, preserved in the United States National Museum, and represented by the following figures.

The original of Fig. 200 is a large bone hook from Greenland, presented by the Copenhagen Museum. This hook is unbarbed, and exhibits the outer projection, though not very prominently. The upper end of the shank is pierced with two holes. The appearance of the bone indicates that this hook is rather old.

The other specimen, represented by Fig. 201, is barbed and provided with a barb-like point on the outside. It was presented to the National Museum by Dr. Emil Bessels, to whom it had been given by Captain H. C. Chester, of the United States Commission of Fish and Fisheries. The latter informed me he

---

* See Fig. 215 on p. 137.

had obtained it from Eskimos near Chesterfield Inlet, in the northern part of Hudson's Bay. This hook, which shows a peculiar contrivance for fastening the line, namely, a cavity sunk from the top of the shank met by a lateral one, seems to consist of reindeer-horn.

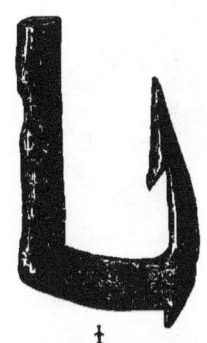

Fig. 200.—Eskimos, Greenland. (45903).   Fig. 201.—Eskimos, Chesterfield Inlet. (72600).

Figs. 200 and 201.—Fish-hooks of bone and reindeer-horn.

There are modern bone fish-hooks from tribes of the Northwest Coast and other northern regions of America in the Ethnological Department of the United States National Museum. These, however, are composed of different parts, and the originals of Figs. 200 and 201 are the only specimens consisting of a single piece.

I now pass over to Californian fish-hooks made of shell.

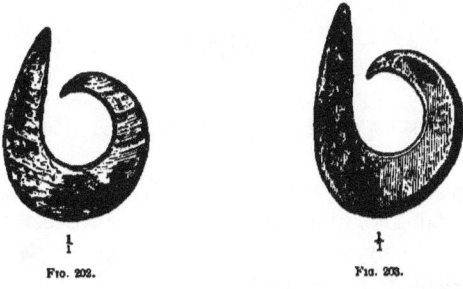

Fig. 202.   Fig. 203.

Figs. 202 and 203.—Shell fish-hooks. Santa Cruz Island. (26252).

Figs. 202 and 203 (on the preceding page).—Two hooks cut from the shell of *Mytilus Californianus*, and exhibiting on both sides the natural surfaces of the valve, which is from one-eighth to one-fourth of an inch in thickness. They resemble so much the originals of Figs. 194 and 195 that a further description is unnecessary. Traces of asphaltum are seen on the shanks of these hooks. They were found by Mr. Stephen Bowers on Santa Cruz Island.

FIGS. 204 and 205.—Shell fish-hooks. Santa Cruz Island. (26252).

Figs. 204 and 205.—Of the same material, and also obtained at Santa Cruz Island by Mr. Bowers, are the hooks represented by these two figures, which show with sufficient distinctness in what manner the line was fastened.

FIG. 206.—Shell fish-hook. San Nicolas Island. (20406).

Fig. 206.—This specimen, cut from a piece of the *Haliotis*, is apparently very old, yet still retains the beautiful iridescence of that shell. Both curves are cut angularly. The point is broken off, and the upper portion of the shank damaged. The thickness is about three-sixteenths of an inch. This specimen was obtained by Mr. Schumacher on San Nicolas Island.

FISH-HOOKS. 133

Figs. 207 to 209.—In this group are represented three fish-hooks of *Haliotis*-shell, obtained on Santa Cruz Island by Mr. Schumacher.

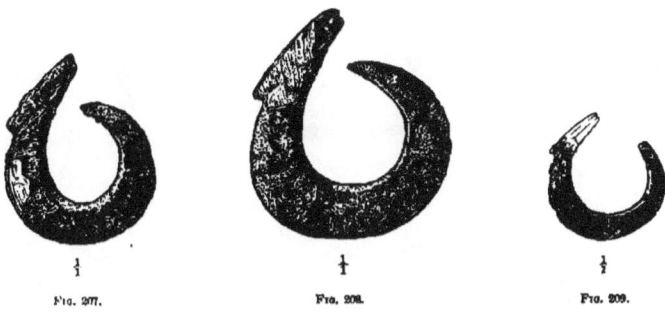

FIGS. 207–209.—Shell fish-hooks. Santa Cruz Island. (20407).

Fig. 210.—A tolerably well preserved hook of *Haliotis*-shell from Santa Cruz Island, found by Mr. Schumacher.

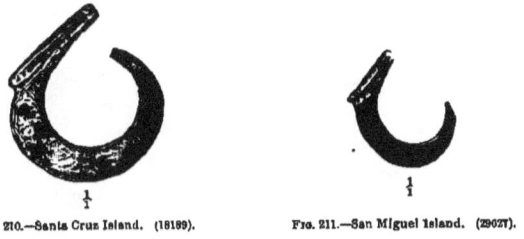

FIG. 210.—Santa Cruz Island. (18199).   FIG. 211.—San Miguel Island. (29027).

FIGS. 210 and 211.—Shell fish-hooks.

Fig. 211.—This figure represents a small specimen cut from the *Mytilus Californianus* in such a manner that the original surfaces of the shell have totally disappeared. The specimen, obtained by Mr. Bowers on San Miguel Island, hardly has suffered from the effects of time, and shows the purple color of the inner mass of the shell.—The barb-like projection on the outer curve, characteristic of some of the Californian bone fish-hooks, is absent in the shell hooks from the same region, at least in the specimens in the National Museum.

Mr. Schumacher discovered on Santa Cruz Island a grave which probably was that of a maker of shell fish-hooks, for it contained the tools used in their manufacture as well as the material in all stages of fabrication.

134　　　　　　　　　PREHISTORIC FISHING.

In Fig. 212 representations of a series of objects illustrating the process of manufacture are grouped together. A piece of *Haliotis*-shell was first reduced to a rude disc-form (a), and then pierced with a hole in the centre (b) by means

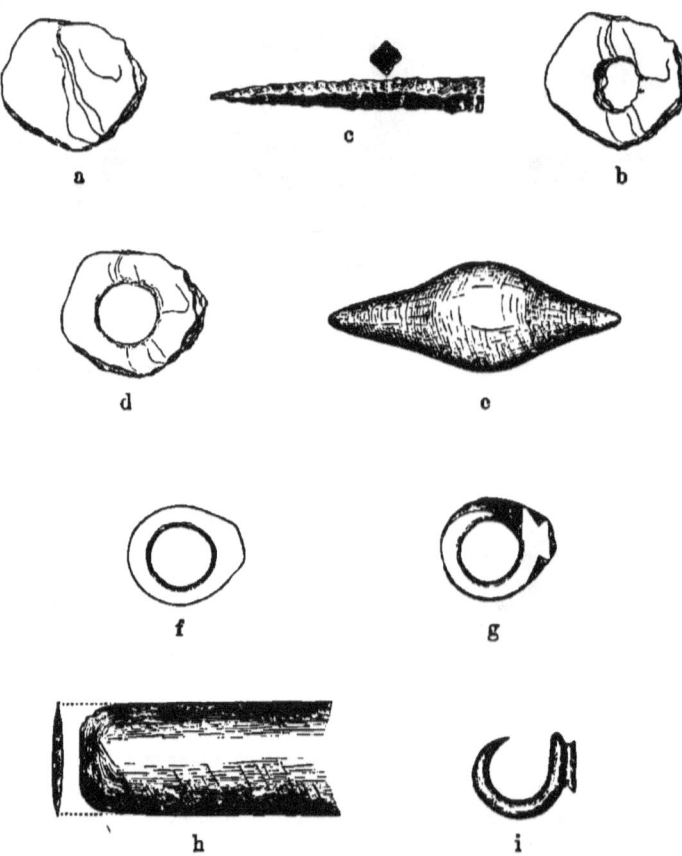

FIG. 212.—Series of designs illustrative of the method of making fish-hooks of shell.

of a four-sided pointed flint implement (c). The enlarging and rounding of the hole (as shown in d) was performed with a double-pointed borer of hard, coarse sandstone (e), and an ordinary flat piece of sandstone served to grind the perforated disc into a ring-like form (f). By the removal of certain portions of this ring (hatched in g) with a sort of double-edged stone knife (h) and some further touches a fish-hook (i) was produced. This brief account is an abstract from one of the interesting articles published by Mr. Paul Schumacher.*

Allusion was made to the short distance between the point and shank in nearly all Californian hooks, and it was added that on this account their suitableness for fishing-purposes had been doubted. It is difficult, if not impossible, to perceive how fish could have been caught with hooks of this form, unless it is assumed that they swallowed both bait and hook. The latter, however, may have served the double purpose of hook and bait. Yet there can hardly be any doubt as to their use, considering that similar fish-hooks (or, perhaps more properly, baits or bait-holders) are still employed by islanders of the Pacific Ocean. In the following figures I represent two fish-hooks obtained during Lieutenant Wilkes's circumnavigation of the globe, and preserved in the National Museum, with the other objects of ethnological interest collected in the course of that voyage. The illustrations can be relied on as perfectly accurate.

Fig. 213.—Samoan fish-hook of shell with stone sinker. (3399).

---

* Schumacher: Die Anfertigung der Angelhaken aus Muschelschalen bei den früheren Bewohnern der Inseln im Santa Barbara Canal; Archiv für Anthropologie; Vol. VIII, 1875; p. 223, etc. (Also: Bulletin of the United States Geological and Geographical Survey of the Territories; Vol. III, No. 1; Washington, 1877; p. 42, etc.).

136 PREHISTORIC FISHING.

The original of Fig. 213, on the preceding page, was procured on one of the Samoan Islands. It shows the hook, which is made of nacreous shell, connected with the sinker by means of vegetable fibre, both plaited and twisted with great care. The sinker is an entirely unaltered, somewhat porous pebble, apparently of volcanic origin.

FIG. 214.—Fish-hook of turtle-shell (?). Serle Island. (3676).

Fig. 214 exhibits the form of a hook derived from natives of Serle Island, one of the coral isles of the Low Archipelago, not far from the Society Islands. This identical hook is mentioned by Dr. Charles Pickering, who belonged to the scientific staff attached to the United States Exploring Expedition. Among the articles obtained from the islanders, he says, was " a large fish-hook (perhaps of turtle-bone), in form and tie similar to those we afterwards saw at the Disappointment Islands."*

In the originals of Figs. 213 and 214 the point approaches the shank so close that the idea of *hooking* a fish with them must be abandoned; and yet they are actual fish-hooks, acquired, many years ago, by barter from islanders of the South Sea.

FIG. 215.—Bone fish-hook. New Zealand.

Fig. 215, representing a fish-hook from New Zealand, is copied from an excellent little work, entitled "The New Zealanders," which was published as a volume of "The Library of Entertaining Knowledge" (London, 1830). I have selected the figure from a group of fishing-implements on page 189. The hook, it will be seen, exhibits not only the close proximity of point and shank, but also the outside barb for fastening a bait. Nothing is said concerning its size.

For the purpose of further elucidation, I extract from Ellis's "Polynesian Researches" a few passages bearing on fishing with hook and line among the Society Islanders:—

"They use the hook and line both in the smooth water within the reef, and in the open sea; and in different modes display great skill. In this department they seldom have any bait, excepting a small kind of oobu, a black fresh-water fish, which they employ when catching albicores and bonitos. *Their hooks usually answer the double purpose of hook and bait.*† Their lines are made with the tough elastic romaha, or flax, twisted by the hand.

"In no part of the world, perhaps, are the inhabitants better fishermen; and considering their former entire destitution of iron, their variety of fishing-apparatus is astonishing. Their hooks were of every form and size, and made of wood, shell, or bone—frequently human bone. — — —

---

* Pickering: The Races of Man; London, 1872; p. 48.

† The italicizing in these extracts is my own.

"The hooks made with wood were curious: some were exceedingly small, not more than two or three inches in length, but remarkably strong; others were large. The wooden hooks *were never barbed, but simply pointed, usually curved inwards at the point*, but sometimes standing out very wide, occasionally armed at the point with a piece of bone. — — —

"The shell, or shell and bone hooks, were curious and useful, and always answered the purpose of hook and bait; *the small ones are made almost circular, and bent so as to resemble a worm*."*

Of this special form are the Californian hooks represented by Figs. 194, 195, 203, 204, and others. They probably were intended to imitate worms, and to be swallowed entire by the fish.

It appears to me that those ethnologists who claim an affinity between the Californians and Malays might use the similarity in the fish-hooks among these peoples as an argument in favor of their theory.

The former inhabitants of this country, it is well known, made to some extent implements and ornaments of native copper, which they brought into shape by hammering, their supplies of the virgin metal being in all probability chiefly derived from the district of Lake Superior, where the traces of primitive mining-operations are abundant. Among the copper articles hitherto discovered are a few fish-hooks, harpoon-heads, and sinkers. Though I knew of the existence of several copper fish-hooks in the United States, I could obtain only one specimen for inspection and representation. It belongs to Mr. Charles L. Mann, of Milwaukee, and was for a short time obligingly placed at my disposition by that gentleman. Fig. 216 shows it in full size.

FIG. 216.—Copper fish-hook. Wisconsin (Oconto River).

Mr. Mann describes its mode of manufacture so well that I will quote his own words:—"It is made of copper, hammered thin, and rolled up just as one

---

* Ellis: Polynesian Researches; Vol. I, London, 1853; p. 145, etc.—The author speaks from personal observation, having been engaged in missionary labors in Polynesia from 1816-'24. The first edition of "Polynesian Researches" appeared in 1828.

would roll up a piece of paper by carefully beginning at the edge. It is not only an entirely unique and heretofore unnoticed method of aboriginal workmanship, but also in the nature of corroborative evidence that all our copper implements were produced by hammering." The swelling of the shank was perhaps produced intentionally, for the purpose of affording a hold to the line. Mr. Mann has a copper awl fashioned by a similar process. "These two implements," he says, "along with others not made in the same way, and many unworked small bits of copper, were found in loose white sand, near the mouth of the Oconto River, Green Bay, Wisconsin. The consistency of the soil accounts for the unusually good preservation."

Considering that fishing with hook and line was commonly practised by the North American tribes at the time of their first contact with Europeans, the comparative scarcity of fish-hooks in the territory formerly occupied by them is remarkable. May not the natives also have made fish-hooks out of substances more liable to decay than bone, horn or shell, not to speak of copper, which was but rarely used? The people of the Northwest Coast, for instance, make even at present hooks for catching halibut and other fish entirely of spruce-wood; and the Mohaves in Arizona, until lately, utilized bent cactus-spines as fish-hooks. A number of these were sent to the National Museum by Dr. Edward Palmer, three of which are represented in Figs. 217, 218, and 219.

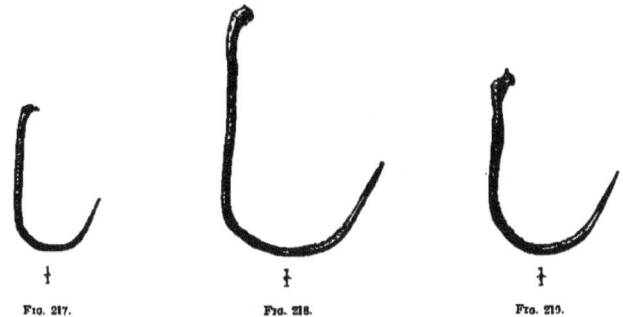

FIGS. 217-219.—Fish-hooks made of cactus-spines. Mohaves, Arizona. (24133).

He thus describes their manufacture:—

"Questioning some old Indians about their native fish-hooks, I found that they used the spine of a cactus for this purpose. Having made a bargain with one to allow me to see him make the hooks, he returned in a few hours with a plant and a number of the spines of *Echinocactus Wislizeni*. He commenced by placing the spines in water for a short time, in order to render them pliable, at the same time wrapping the thumb and first finger of his right hand with rags. He then made a small torch about half the size of one's little finger by twisting some pieces of rags together rather tightly. Selecting a spine from the water and placing it between the ends of the wrapped thumb and finger, the torch was lit and held in the left hand close to the spine, the workman dexterously changing the position so as to impart the same amount of heat to all portions at once. Occasionally he moistened the spine in his mouth. By this application of heat and moisture he tempered the spine, and at the same time applying a gentle pressure by the end of the wrapped finger, he was soon able to produce a very fair and strong hook. As soon as a sufficient curvature is obtained, it is secured by fastening a string from the point to the shaft.

"The fish of the Colorado River, eaten by the Mohaves, do not nibble the bait, but bolt it, hook and all, and are killed by the wounds which are made in their gills. This cactus-spine hook would be of no use in catching fish that nibble, as there is no barb. The Indians fasten the bait below the hook before throwing it into the water. The iron hooks obtained from the whites now take the place of their old-fashioned ones."*

This "bolting," as Dr. Palmer calls it, throws some light on the applicability of the Californian fish-hooks.

The eastern Indians, of course, could not employ cactus-spines, but they had thorny brushes and trees, which might have furnished them the material for fish-hooks.

Fig. 220.—Honey-locust twig with spine, cut to resemble a fish-hook.

By way of illustration, I present in Fig. 220 the delineation of a hook which I cut from the thorn-bearing portion of a stem of the honey-locust (*Gleditschia*

---

* Palmer: Fish-Hooks of the Mohave Indians; American Naturalist; Vol. XII, 1878; p. 403.

triacanthos, Lin.), growing in the District of Columbia. This hook, consisting of tough wood, probably would make just as efficient a fishing-implement as the Kutchin hook figured on page 123, or as Captain Smith's " splinter of bone tyed to the clift of a little sticke."

The sinkers used in connection with line-fishing will be considered under the general head of "Sinkers."

I am not cognizant of the existence of any prehistoric North American objects to which the character of floats can be attributed.

Harpoon and Arrow-heads.—As in the first part of this work, the description of harpoon-heads follows that of the implements used in angling—a succession by no means intended to convey the idea that harpooning was a later practice than line-fishing. Man, in the opinion of many, hunted fish before he caught them. Yet, a harpoon, more especially one with a detachable head, is a rather complicated contrivance, and its later developments may, generally speaking, post-date the invention of a primitive angling-apparatus. A double-pointed bone rod attached to a line, though requiring a bait, is certainly a very simple device, that may have been resorted to in the earliest times. The question of priority, therefore, cannot be decided with absolute positiveness, and thus it matters little whether I treat harpoon-heads after fish-hooks, or *vice versa*.

There can be little doubt that among the immense number of dart-heads of chipped silicious material, which are found everywhere in this country, many served as the armatures of spears and arrows used in the capture of fish. Indeed, there is hardly a collection of such articles from which barbed specimens suitable for such applications could not be selected; even unbarbed ones are thought by some to have served as the heads of darts employed in the fish-hunt. I could figure a series of such specimens; but in view of their well-known character, and of the circumstance that the use of any given object of this class in connection with fishing is absolutely problematical, I refrain from presenting illustrations.*

The Greenland Eskimos sometimes used, as discoveries in ancient sepulchres have shown, blades of chipped flint or ground slate for pointing the detachable harpoon-heads, somewhat in the manner shown by Fig. 110 on page 83. The Eskimos of the more eastern parts of North America likewise provided their detachable harpoon-heads with ground slate points; but at present they insert, like the Greenlanders, blades of iron, in consequence of the increased facilities of obtaining that metal.† In general, however, their harpoon-heads are entirely made of bone or walrus-ivory.

---

* I am aware of the existence of a few stemmed flint points which are barbed only on one side. It appears probable that they were the armatures of arrows used in shooting fish.

† I have seen some harpoons from the Northwest Coast, in which the head terminated in a blade of sheet copper.

142   PREHISTORIC FISHING.

We learn from the early accounts of North America that bone-headed harpoons were in use among the Indians inhabiting the Atlantic region. Captain Smith, in treating of the Virginians (1629), speaks of "staues like vnto Iauelin, headed with bone." Josselyn (1674) describes the harpoon of the New England Indians as "a kind of dart or staff, to the lower end whereof they fasten a sharp jagged bone;" yet he states at the same time that iron points were superseding those of bone. Roger Williams, in referring to the same Indians (1643), mentions "an harping Iron or such like Instrument." The Southern Indians employed harpoons made of cane until the middle of the last century, and, perhaps, in more recent times.*

Considering that bone, on account of its toughness, was an excellent material for pointing fishing-darts, the comparatively small number of old bone heads thus far discovered in the United States would be somewhat surprising, if their

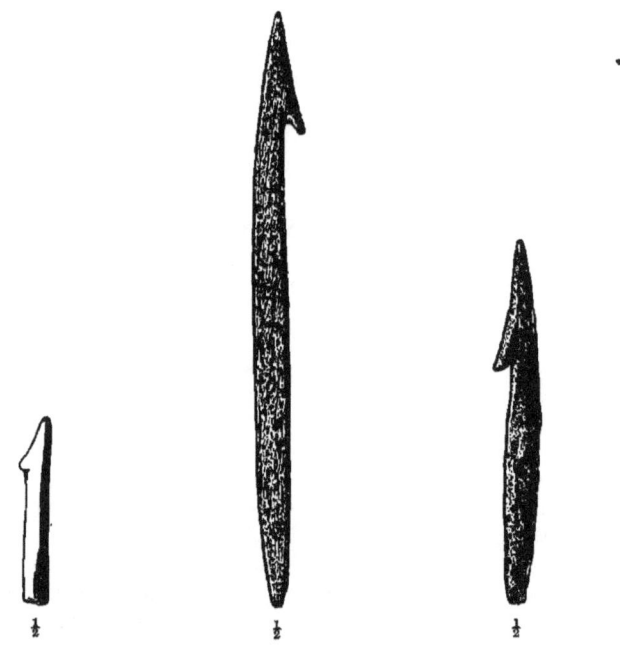

FIG. 221.—Maine (Casco Bay).   FIG. 222.—San Nicolas Island. (20527).   FIG. 223.—San Nicolas Island. (20527).

FIGS. 221–223.—Bone harpoon-heads.

---

* See "Extracts:" Captain Smith, Josselyn, Roger Williams, Brickell, Adair, Bartram, etc.

scarcity could not be accounted for by their undoubtedly frequent loss in the water of the sea, of lakes, and rivers.

Among the twenty-eight heads of bone and horn, presently to be figured and described, twenty are provided with unilateral, and only eight with bilateral barbs. I believe that most of them were armatures for fishing-darts, though I would not attempt to decide in each case whether the specimen formed the point of a spear-like implement or of an arrow used in shooting fish. The objects under notice, being mostly cut from hollow bones, are generally flattish, and often exhibit, like the bone fish-hooks, on one side a portion of the marrow-cavity.

Fig. 221.—This figure is reduced from one given by Professor Jeffries Wyman.* The original occurred in a shell-deposit on Goose Island, Casco Bay, Maine, and is described as a flattened piece cut from a long bone, and showing the cancellated structure on one side. The point and barb appear to be rounded by friction. This specimen is in the Peabody Museum.

Fig. 222.—A harpoon-head with a rather sharp point and a single barb. Its lower end is tapering and fitted for insertion into a shaft. This specimen appears to be very old, its surface being much corroded and bleached by exposure. Its longitudinal curve (not perceivable in the illustration) renders it probable that it was cut from a rib, perhaps that of a cetacean. Obtained by Mr. Schumacher on San Nicolas Island.

Fig. 223.—A smaller specimen of the same character, found by Mr. Schumacher with the original of Fig. 222.

FIG. 224.—Unalashka Island. (16083).   FIG. 225.—Unalashka Island. (16083).   FIG. 226.—Maine (Damariscotta).

FIGS. 224-226.—Bone harpoon-heads.

---

* Wyman: An Account of some Kjœkkenmœddings, or Shell-Heaps, in Maine and Massachusetts; American Naturalist; Vol. I, 1868; Plate 15, Fig. 13; described on p. 583.

Fig. 224 (on page 143).—This figure represents one of a series of bone dart-heads collected by Mr. W. H. Dall in shell-heaps on the Aleutian Islands. He has published an account of his examination of these artificial shell-deposits, accompanied by illustrations of the relics found in them.* Mr. Dall comes to the conclusion "that the people who first populated the islands were more similar to the lowest grades of Innuit (so-called Eskimo) than to the Aleuts of the historic period; and that while the development of the other Innuit went on in the direction in which they first started, that of the Aleuts was differentiated and changed by the limitations of their environment; that a gradual progression from the low Innuit stage to the present Aleut condition, without serious interruption, is plainly indicated by the succession of the materials of, and utensils in, the shell-heaps of the islands; that the stratification of the shell-heaps shows a tolerably uniform division into three stages, characterized by the food which formed the staple of subsistence and by the weapons for obtaining, and utensils for preparing, this food, as found in the separate strata; these stages being—I. the littoral period, represented by the echinus-layer; II. the fishing-period, represented by the fish-bone layer; III. the hunting-period, represented by the mammalian layer."†

This extract will suffice for my purposes.

The original of Fig. 224 was found in the lower mammalian layer, on Ulakhta Spit, Unalashka Island. This single-barbed specimen has suffered much from the effects of time, and lost its point. The lower part is comparatively thin, and presents on one side a shoulder for fastening the line. It probably was a detachable head.

Fig. 225 (on page 143).—A somewhat similar bone harpoon-head of much fresher appearance than the one just described. It was taken by Mr. Dall from the upper fish-bone layer of a shell-heap in Unalashka Island. Its point has been artificially rounded, evidently for serving a secondary purpose. The lower part, from the indentations downward, has a chisel-like shape, and it terminates in a blunt edge. There is some reason for conjecturing that the specimen formed a detachable point.

Fig. 226 (on page 143).—A bone harpoon-point with two barbs, from a shell-heap at Greenland Cove, near Damariscotta, Maine. Found by Mr. A. I. Phelps, in 1882, and given by him to the Peabody Museum (No. 29234). It is made from a piece probably cut from the leg-bone of a deer or moose, slightly flattened on one side, and has the natural rounded surface on the other. The base shows slight signs of wear, as if from insertion into a shaft. Thickness of the base

---

* Dall: On Succession in the Shell-Heaps of the Aleutian Islands; Contributions to North American Ethnology; Vol. I, Washington, 1877; p. 41–91.

† Ibid.; p. 49.

HARPOON-HEADS. 145

two-eighths of an inch. The figure is made after a drawing sent by Professor F. W. Putnam.

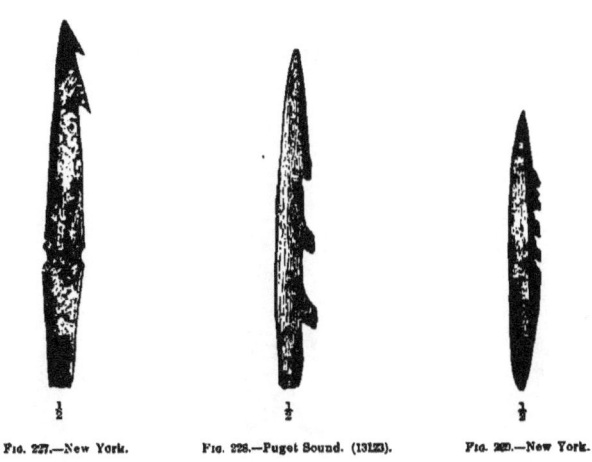

Fig. 227.—New York.   Fig. 228.—Puget Sound. (13123).   Fig. 229.—New York.

Figs. 227-229.—Harpoon-heads of bone and deer-horn.

Fig. 227.—This harpoon-head, figured by Mr. E. G. Squier, shows two well-defined unilateral barbs, and farther below two opposite notches for attaching the line which connected it with the shaft. It is said to have been made of the ulna of a deer. Found in Livingstone County, New York.* I am unable to state where this specimen is preserved.

Fig. 228.—A well-worked, flattened bone point with three barbs on one side. The lower end is damaged. Obtained by Mr. J. G. Swan, with another specimen of nearly the same form, and likewise broken at the lower extremity, from a shell-heap on Puget Sound, Washington Territory.

Fig. 229.—The figure is made after a drawing by the Rev. W. M. Beauchamp. It represents a deer-horn harpoon with a good point and a number of partly damaged barbs on one side. The lower extremity terminates in a blunt point. The original, in possession of Mr. Otis M. Bigelow, of Baldwinsville, Onondaga County, New York, was found in an Indian grave, excavated in gravel, at Lock's Reefs, near Elbridge, Onondaga County. This grave contained two other harpoon-heads, to which reference will be made.

---

* Squier: Aboriginal Monuments of the State of New York; Smithsonian Contributions to Knowledge; Vol. II, Washington, 1849; p. 79, Fig. 26.

146   PREHISTORIC FISHING.

Fig. 230.—A fine single-barbed harpoon-head of elk-horn, in an excellent state of preservation. It measures nearly ten inches and a half in length, and has a thickness of about half an inch in the middle. The broad lower part shows two shoulders, but its base, instead of being worked thin, is more than one-fourth of an inch thick. The head, nevertheless, may have been detachable. This specimen was presented to the National Museum, with other valuable relics,

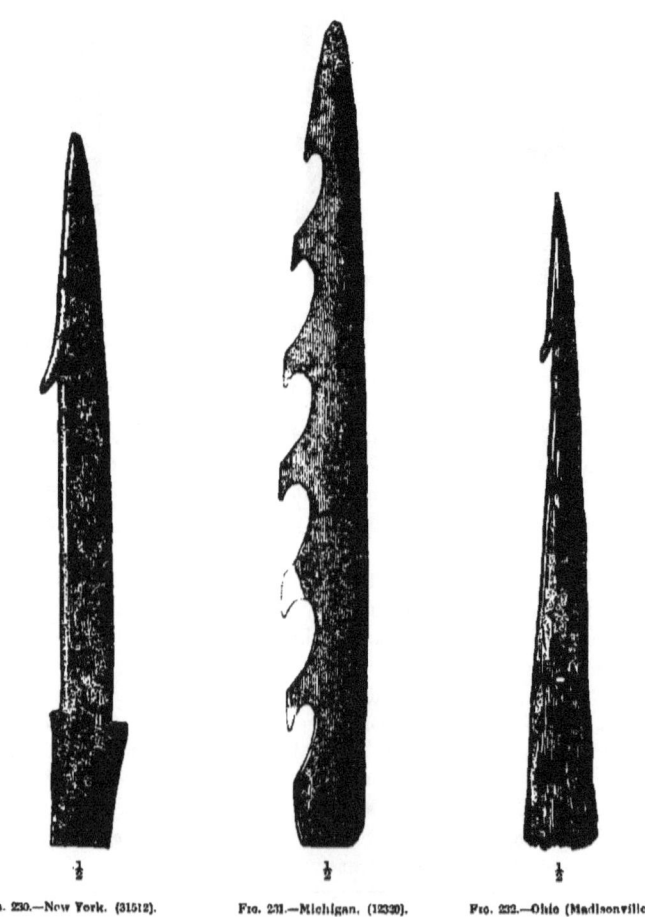

Fig. 230.—New York. (31512).   Fig. 231.—Michigan. (12330).   Fig. 232.—Ohio (Madisonville).

Figs. 230-232.—Harpoon-heads of elk-horn and bone.

by the late W. M. Locke, of Honeoye Falls, Monroe County, New York. His son, Mr. F. M. Locke, of Rochester, New York, informed me by letter that he had found it himself about two miles south of Honeoye, on the old Indian reservation called the Ball Farm. "It lay on the surface where there had been a great many camp-fires, and the clayish ground was covered with ashes, preserving the spear and other relics that might have decayed, had it not been for the ashes and clay."

Fig. 231.—Another remarkable harpoon-head, about a foot in length, not quite half an inch thick in the middle, and exhibiting six well-cut unilateral barbs, partly damaged. It is made of a long bone of some large animal. The perfect lower part is comparatively thin, and fitted for insertion into a shaft or socket. This specimen, which appears to be very old (the bone having lost its animal matter) was found, according to the Smithsonian record, near Detroit, Michigan, and presented by Mr. J. W. Paxton.

Fig. 232.—A single-barbed harpoon-head of peculiar form, being broadest at the base, and tapering gradually to the point. About the middle it is three-eighths of an inch thick. The side exposed to view shows the striæ produced by the instrument with which the dart was finished; on the opposite side a small portion of the marrow-cavity can be seen. In forming the base, a cut was made all around to a certain depth, and the remaining part of the bone broken off. At a distance of two inches and three-eighths from the lower end is an oval hole, designed to connect the dart, perhaps a detachable one, with the shaft. This specimen, which is of a yellowish color and well preserved, was found in the Madisonville cemetery, and belongs to the Hon. Joseph Cox, to whom I am indebted for its loan.

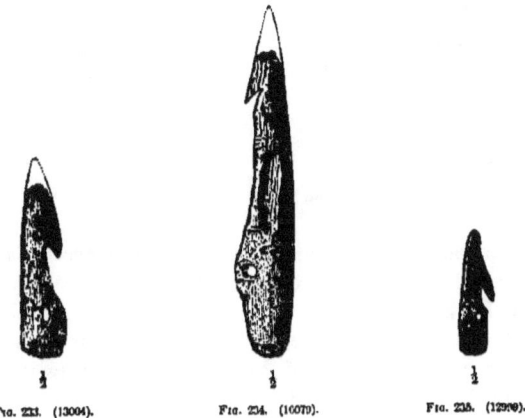

Fig. 233. (13004).   Fig. 234. (10079).   Fig. 235. (12930).

FIGS. 233–235.—Bone harpoon-heads. Alaska.

148   PREHISTORIC FISHING.

Fig. 233 (on page 147).—This harpoon-head, of very old appearance, has lost its point and is broken at the lower part, which shows a roughly executed perforation. It was probably detachable. Obtained by Mr. Dall from the lower mammalian layer of an ancient rock-shelter in Atka Island, Alaska.

Fig. 234 (on page 147).—A larger specimen, in a better state of preservation, but likewise lacking its point. The base forms an edge like that of a blunt chisel, and the hole is carefully drilled. On both sides a cavity of elongated oval form is worked out between the hole and the barb. This dart, it appears, separated from the shaft, when used. It was found by Mr. Dall in the lower mammalian layer at Port Möller, Peninsula of Aliaska.

Fig. 235 (on page 147).—This diminutive dart-head, of excellent workmanship and fresh appearance, probably was not designed for practical use, but may have served as the armature of a toy-harpoon, by means of which a juvenile hunter qualified himself for the more serious work of later years. The point is rounded and polished like the whole object. The base of the barb shows a straight ornamental incision, and below the blunt point a small nick has been cut out. It is one of the specimens collected by Mr. Dall. He discovered it in the upper fish-bone layer in a cave of Amaknak Island, Captain's Bay, Unalashka.

Fig. 236.—Maine (Hodgdon's Island).

Fig. 237.—Maine (Muscongus Sound).

Figs. 236 and 237.—Bone harpoon-heads.

Fig. 236.—A bone harpoon-head resembling in general character the specimens just described, but derived from the Atlantic coast-region. It is probably made from the leg-bone of a deer. One side shows the natural rounded surface of the bone, the other its internal cavity. Thickness about three-eighths of an inch. This dart was found in 1882 by Mr. A. T. Gamage in a shell-heap on Hodgdon's Island, Damariscotta River, Maine, and presented by him to the Peabody Museum (No. 29279).

Fig. 237.—This harpoon-head has lost its upper part, but probably terminated as indicated in the dotted restoration, which is justified by the fact that there is a smooth cut at the place marked *a*. It was found in 1882 in a shell-heap at Keene's Point, Muscongus Sound, Maine, by Mr. A. I. Phelps, and is now in the Peabody Museum (No. 29234). This figure and the preceding one were made after drawings sent by Professor F. W. Putnam, to whom I am also indebted for descriptions of the specimens. This dart-head, like that represented in the preceding figure, appears to have been detachable.

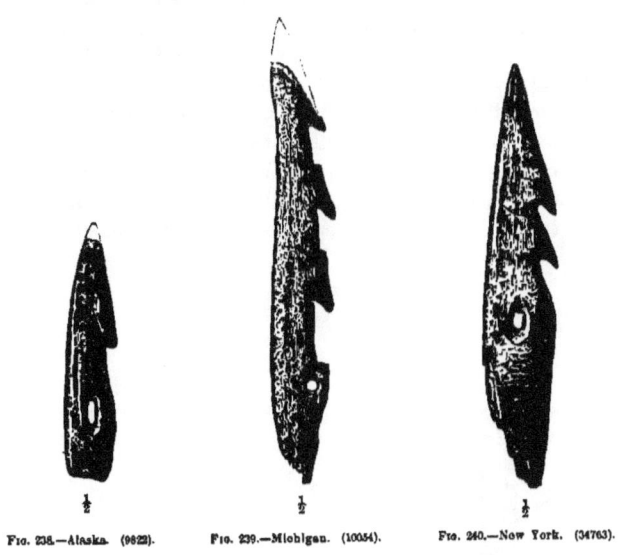

Fig. 238.—Alaska. (9822).   Fig. 239.—Michigan. (10054).   Fig. 240.—New York. (34763).

Figs. 238-240.—Harpoon-heads of bone and deer-horn.

Fig. 238.—A specimen of ancient appearance, with damaged point and base, and one blunt barb. It is rather thick in proportion to its size, measuring half an inch above the elongated eye. Found near Stikine River, Alaska, by Lieutenant F. W. Ring, U. S. A.

Fig. 239.—This specimen, a bone harpoon-head with three unilateral barbs, is likewise broken at both extremities. The two lower barbs are of peculiar shape, being provided with a kind of shoulder. The side seen in the illustration exhibits the natural roundness of the bone; the lower one is nearly flat. Thickness in the middle nearly half an inch. This dart-head was found in an Indian grave at Fort Wayne, near Detroit, Michigan, and presented by Dr. J. D. Irwin, U. S. A.

Fig. 240 (on page 149).—A harpoon-head of deer-horn, tolerably well preserved, but unfortunately broken at the lower extremity. The point and the two barbs are carefully finished; the perforation, sunk in from both sides, is of irregular form. A cross-section above it would form an elongated ellipse with a shorter axis of nearly half an inch. Found by Mr. F. H. Cushing in a shell-heap in Onondaga County, New York.

This dart is the last in my available series of *perforated* specimens made of bone or horn, which, I believe, were mostly intended to separate from the shaft when launched. It probably has been noticed that these pierced dart-heads have all unilateral barbs; those with barbs on both sides, it will be seen, are not perforated, but may also, in part at least, have been detachable. Perhaps it is only owing to accident that none of the bilaterally barbed heads at my disposition is perforated. The Eskimos of the Northwest Coast, it will be remembered, use to this day walrus-ivory harpoon-heads with barbs on both sides and an eye for receiving the line which connects the head with the shaft.* Some of the bone points presently to be described may have been armatures for arrows used in shooting fish.

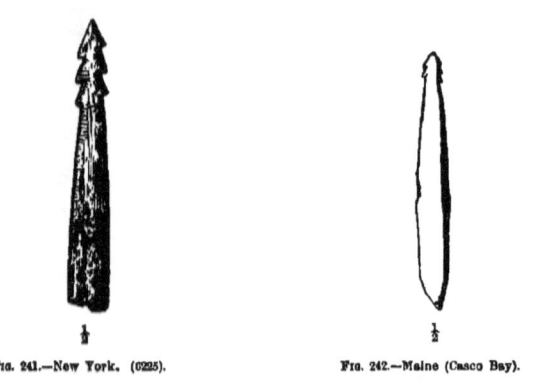

Fig. 241.—New York. (0225). Fig. 242.—Maine (Casco Bay).

Figs. 241 and 242.—Bone dart-heads.

Fig. 241.—A dart-head with three small barbs on each side, so placed that they alternate. The upper side is rounded; on the lower one the cavity of the bone reaches from the broken lower end to the lowest barb. I would not venture to say more concerning the use of this dart-head, than that it probably was employed in the fish-hunt. Obtained in Ontario County, New York, and presented by Colonel E. Jewett.

---

* See Figs. 19, 20, and 21 on p. 21.

Fig. 242.—This figure represents a bone dart-head with bilateral barbs, two on one side and three on the other. It is made of a long bone, showing the internal cavity on one side. The pointed and barbed part is remarkably narrow in proportion to the width of the dart, insomuch that the method of its application is not quite obvious. This specimen, like the original of Fig. 221, was obtained on Goose Island, during Professor Wyman's exploration of shell-heaps in that locality. It is in the Peabody Museum.[*]

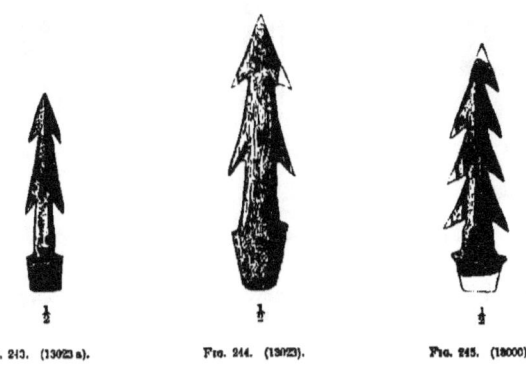

Fig. 243. (13023 a).   Fig. 244. (13023).   Fig. 245. (18000).

Figs. 243–245.—Bone dart-heads. Alaska.

Fig. 243.—A very fine and well-preserved bone point with two sharp barbs on each side and a broad flat lower termination for insertion. This specimen is altogether the neatest North American bone dart-head that has fallen under my notice, being equally well worked on both sides, which show a regular slight convexity. Its length, however, is not more than two inches and seven-eighths. Found by Mr. Dall in the upper mammalian layer on Adakh Island, Alaska.

Fig. 244.—A larger specimen of corresponding form, but less perfect workmanship, and somewhat damaged in various places. The object is a little curved, apparently on account of being cut from a rib. It was taken by Mr. Dall from the middle mammalian layer on Adakh Island.

Fig. 245.—This dart-head has four sharp barbs on one side and three on the other, the latter having all lost their points. Both extremities of this specimen are likewise defective. A deep groove is cut out longitudinally, and slighter grooves mark the places from which the barbs project. These grooves are in all probability purely ornamental. The opposite side is worked smooth, but shows

---

[*] Figured and described in Professor Wyman's article quoted on p. 143.

the cellular structure of the bone. The object was taken by Mr. Dall from the lowest mammalian layer in a cave on Amaknak Island, Alaska.

Figs. 246-248.—Harpoon-heads of deer-horn. New York.

Figs. 246 to 248.—These figures were made after drawings sent by the Rev. W. M. Beauchamp. The specimens, all consisting of deer-horn, belong to Mr. Otis M. Bigelow, already mentioned. The original of Fig. 246, broken at the base, was found, with other relics, in a gravel-bed on Charles Bidwell's lot, Elbridge, Onondaga County, New York. The originals of Figs. 247 and 248 occurred in the same grave which contained the specimen represented in Fig. 229 (on page 145).

In conclusion, I have to describe the few ancient harpoon-heads of copper known to me. They all belong to the State Historical Society of Wisconsin (at Madison), which is particularly rich in prehistoric objects of copper, the State of Wisconsin, on account of its proximity to the source of the virgin metal, having furnished a large number of relics of this material.

Fig. 249.—A small dart-head, perhaps the head of an arrow for shooting fish. Professor James D. Butler, in his jocose mode of expression, refers to it as follows:—" We hope for special aid from *Germans*, for we have had it. Most of our specimens bear the names of German finders. History will repeat itself. Three great German inventions begin with the letter P., Printing, Powder, and Protestantism. Let us have one more, namely, Prehistorics. But all nationalities will aid us. They have. Our French inhabitants are few, but one of them, M. de Neveu, of Fond du Lac, has just presented a copper quite unlike any other in our cabinet. We call it a spear with a unilateral barb. Those like it have been found in France and on the Island of Santa Barbara, and are now used in Tierra del Fuego. Meeting with unequal resistance in water, it will not go

HARPOON-HEADS.

straight. So it seems of an absurd pattern, but it is found that if aimed at a fish it will hit him, for, owing to the refraction of light, he is not where he looks as if he were. One barb is then better than two, and we are the fools after all."*

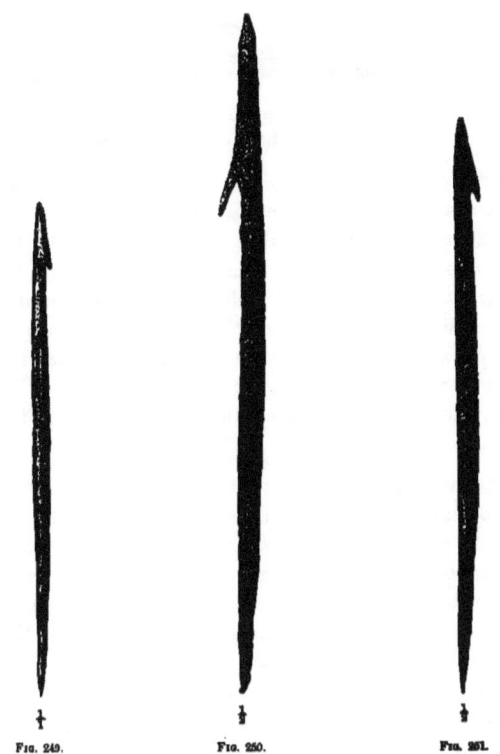

Figs. 249. Fig. 250. Fig. 251.

FIGS. 249-251.—Copper dart-heads. Wisconsin.

Afterward the Society was enriched with two additional copper harpoon-heads of similar form, but much larger size. The illustrations representing them were made after photographs kindly procured for me by Professor Butler.

Fig. 250.—A single-barbed copper harpoon-head, measuring nine inches and three-fourths in length. It was found in Waukesha County, Wisconsin, in 1877, and presented to the Society by Dr. John A. Rice, of Merton, in the same county.

---

* Butler: Prehistoric Wisconsin; Annual Address before the State Historical Society of Wisconsin, in the Assembly Chamber, February 18, 1876; p. 18.—Fig. 249 is copied from one of the plates accompanying this pamphlet.

Fig. 251 (on page 153).—Another single-barbed specimen, eight inches and one-half in length. Found in the neighborhood of Fond du Lac, and presented to the Society in 1876 by M. de Neveu.

FIG. 252.—Copper harpoon-head. Alaska.

Until comparatively recent times harpoon-heads were hammered out of native copper by certain Indians of Alaska. There are several specimens in the United States National Museum, contributed by Mr. Dall and Dr. T. T. Minor, and one of them, obtained by the last-named gentleman from the Thlinkets on Baranoff Island (Sitka), is represented in Fig. 252. It is a well-worked flattish harpoon-head, three-sixteenths of an inch thick, with five sharp unilateral barbs and an eye in the expanding lower part, and strikingly similar in shape to some of the specimens of bone heretofore described.

I am indebted to Mr. Dall for the following details concerning the use of native copper in Alaska :—

"The earliest ethnological fact recorded by Steller, the first white man who set foot on these coasts, at Kayak Island, near the mouth of the Atna or Copper River, July 20, 1741, was the discovery (among other things) of a whetstone on which copper knives had been sharpened. The Atna River contains in the gravels of its bed waterworn masses of native copper, of which I purchased one (now in the National Museum) from the natives living near this river during their annual visit to Port Etches, in 1874. They have been from time immemorial in the habit of bringing down the pieces of copper to trade to the coast-natives, who made of them knives, arrow and harpoon-points, shields, and amulets, specimens of which are in the collection of the National Museum, or have been seen by me in use. The Indians about Sitka, after the Russians became established there, discarded copper for iron, which they bought from the Russians and from English and American traders. Occasionally they obtained pieces of yellow sheathing-metal, which is harder than copper. But the old implements were preserved with veneration or because they were 'lucky'; yet they have now mostly passed into the hands of collectors.

"It would be absurd for people who can buy iron to continue the manufacture of implements of soft copper. As a matter of fact, its use was given up very soon, wherever intercourse with the whites became habitual. In unfrequented localities near the source of the copper its use continued until lately. It is now nearly or quite obsolete."

Nets.—I am not aware that remains of nets, to which the term "prehistoric" can be applied, are in any of the collections in the United States, for causes tending to their preservation, as in the case of the Swiss lacustrine woven fabrics, do not seem to have operated in this country. A few meshes of net, however, are said to have been found, with other articles, in the Mammoth Cave, Kentucky. The reference occurs in a note accompanying a number of these objects (including the net-fragment) sent by Mr. Gratz, formerly the owner of the Mammoth Cave, to Dr. Samuel L. Mitchill, of New York. The note is thus worded:—

"There will be found in this bundle two mocasons, in the same state they were when dug out of the Mammoth Cave, about two hundred yards from its mouth. Upon examination, it will be perceived that they are fabricated out of different materials; one is supposed to be made of a species of *flag*, or *lily*, which grows in the southern parts of Kentucky; the other, of the bark of some tree, probably the *pappaw*.

"There are, also, in this packet, a part of what is supposed to be a *kinniconecke* pouch, two meshes of a fishing-net, and a piece of what we suppose to be the raw material, and of which the fishing-net, the pouch, and one of the mocasons are made. All of which were dug out of the Mammoth Cave, nine or ten feet under ground; that is, below the surface or floor of the cavern."[*]

"This," says Professor F. W. Putnam, "is the only statement we have of articles of this character being found in the Mammoth Cave, and it is very probable that they are some of the missing articles belonging to the body found in Short Cave."[†] He refers to the so-called "Mammoth Cave Mummy," which has attracted so much attention in past years. This desiccated human body was found in 1814, if not earlier, in Short Cave, situated about eight miles from Mammoth Cave, and had been taken to the latter place for the purpose of exhibition. Professor Putnam has established these facts in the course of investigations made *in loco*.[‡] The body belonged formerly to the American Antiquarian Society, but is now in the National Museum. After the foregoing statement, it is hardly necessary to add that the net-fragment is not among the articles accompanying the body.

In the earliest works on North America the fishing-nets of the Indians are mentioned, but not described. Cabeza de Vaca, the first European who gave an account of the interior of the country, refers in various places, though in a transient manner, to the nets of the natives whom he met during his long wanderings. The Spaniards under Pamphilo de Narvaez, after their landing in

---

[*] Archæologia Americana; Vol. I; Worcester, Massachusetts, 1820; p. 328.

[†] Putnam: Archæological Researches in Kentucky and Indiana, 1874; Proceedings of the Boston Society of Natural History; Vol. XVII, 1875; p. 331.

[‡] Ibid.; p. 321.

Florida (1528), he says, found in one of the large houses, or *buhios*, a golden bell among nets (*hallamos alli una Sonaja de Oro, entre las Redes*); and in speaking of the Marcames, he states that if they wanted to marry, they bought wives from their enemies, paying for each wife the best bow they could procure and two arrows; but that in default of these weapons they gave a square net measuring a fathom either way (*i si acaso no tiene Arco, una Red, hasta una braça en ancho, i otra en largo*).* His other references to nets are of little moment. The two principal authors who have left accounts of De Soto's expedition for the conquest of Florida (1539–'43), Garcilasso de la Vega and the anonymous Portuguese gentleman, called the Knight of Elvas, likewise say little concerning the nets of the Indians. The latter relates, however, that the Spaniards, while at a place near the Mississippi called Pacaha (Capaha, according to Garcilasso) caught fish in a lake with nets furnished by the Indians.† Later authors are more explicit in their statements concerning Indian net-fishing, as an examination of the "Extracts" given later on will show.

Sinkers.—It scarcely need be specially affirmed that the natives of North America, like the primitive fishermen in all parts of the world, weighted their nets by means of stones. In our time the Indian and Innuit tribes of the Northwest Coast and of other northern regions of America use pebbles, either unaltered, if of suitable form, or notched or grooved, as sinkers for their different kinds of nets, and the same is done by whites in many districts of this country. Those, for instance, who pursue the trade of fishing along the Susquehanna and its North Branch, use stone sinkers for their set-lines and nets, the stones employed by them being usually not notched or grooved, but having naturally two opposite sides curved inwardly, around which a string can be firmly tied. They carefully select the stones which present this form.

The original of Fig. 253 was given to Mr. F. H. Cushing by a white fisherman at Dunkirk, on Lake Erie (New York). It is a nearly circular pebble, not quite an inch thick in the middle, and notched on opposite sides. The string which connected it with the net is still in place. Such stones, Mr. Cushing informed me, are prepared and extensively used for weighting gill-nets by fishermen along the shores of the great lakes.

Sinkers of this simple character were most commonly employed by the indigenous inhabitants of North America, and they are represented in the National Museum by specimens from Rhode Island, New York, Pennsylvania,

---

* Naufragios de Alvar Nuñez Cabeza de Vaca, etc.; Barcia: "Historiadores Primitivos de las Indias Occidentales;" Vol. I, Madrid, 1749; pp. 8 and 20.—The original work appeared at Valladolid in 1555.

† Narratives of the Career of Hernando de Soto in the Conquest of Florida, as told by a Knight of Elvas, and in a Relation by Luys Hernandez de Biedma, Factor of the Expedition; translated by Buckingham Smith; New York, 1866; p. 112.—There will be occasion to refer again to this passage in another connection.

Ohio, Tennessee, Indiana, Utah, California, Oregon, and the Aleutian Islands. According to Dr. C. C. Abbott, they occur in New Jersey by the hundreds in the valley of every creek and along the river-shores. "In the summer of 1878," he says, "a series of these notched pebbles was found in the wasting northern shore of Crosswick's Creek, about two miles from its mouth, at Bordentown, New Jersey. They were in an irregular heap, in some instances one just above the other, but in contact. They were twenty-two inches below the surface of the meadow, which is composed of a fine, sandy mud, that has been slowly accumulating at this point for centuries. There were seventy-three in the series, and supposing them to have been placed at a distance of a foot apart, they would have supplied a net just long enough to stretch across the creek at this point."*

FIG. 253.—Modern stone sinker. Dunkirk.

About ten years ago, a large series of such sinkers was sent to me by Mr. J. M. M. Gernerd, who had collected them on both banks of the Susquehanna River, near his place of residence, the town of Muncy, in Lycoming County, Pennsylvania.

Figs. 254 to 257, on the following page, illustrate a group of such objects. The smallest (Fig. 257) measures two inches in its longer diameter, and weighs only one ounce; but I have one weighing not more than half an ounce. A number of these small modified pebbles may have served to weight the bottom-line of a net. Some of them, perhaps, were employed as sinkers in connection with hook and line.

My largest specimen, represented in Fig. 258 (on page 159), is a flat stone of irregular outline, eight inches wide across the broadest part, and one inch and three-eighths thick in the middle. It weighs two pounds and fourteen ounces.

---

* Abbott: Primitive Industry; p. 288.

This specimen is unusually large, and heavy enough to have served for weighting a set-net.* The ordinary size of these sinkers is from three to five inches, with a corresponding weight of from six to ten ounces.

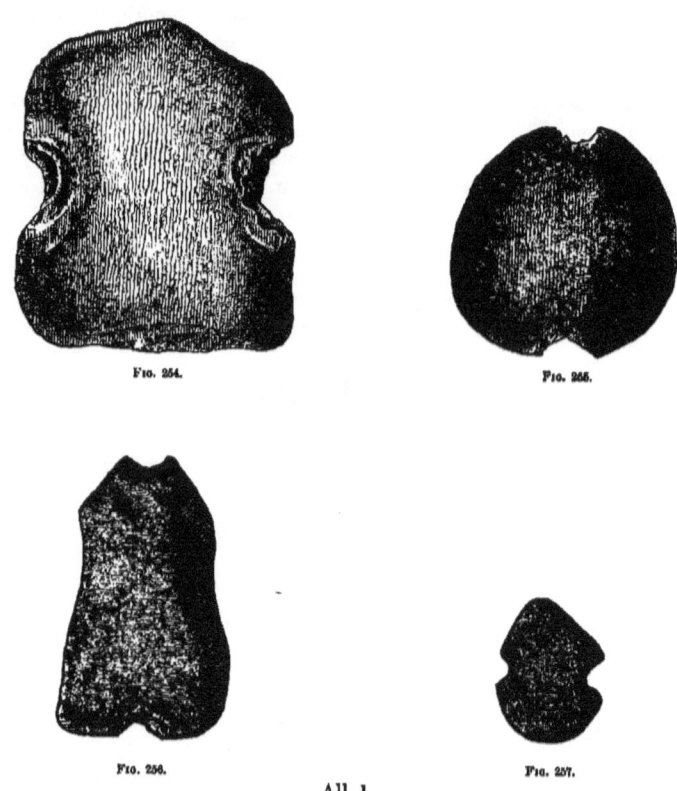

Figs. 254–257.—Stone sinkers. Susquehanna Valley (Muncy).

---

* Such heavy notched pebbles have been noticed by Dr. Abbott. "In June, 1879," he says, "while relic-hunting in the Delaware Valley, with Professor F. W. Putnam, of the Museum at Cambridge, Massachusetts, the author found a very large notched pebble on the shore of the river, a short distance above the Water Gap, in Monroe County, Pennsylvania, which, judging from the size and the fact of its having four notches, was used as an anchor or set-weight. This example measures eight inches square, and weighs nearly five pounds. To secure a net, which was placed in the stream, as gilling-nets and fykes are now set, such a weight would have been frequently a necessity, especially where there was a swift current, as there is in the river at the point where this specimen was found; but it is evidently impossible that such a stone could have been used, as one of a hundred or more, in dragging a sweep-net through the water. Aside from their weight, stones of such size would constantly be caught by obstructions in the bed of the stream, and thus render the free movement of a net impracticable."— *Primitive Industry*; p. 241.

SINKERS.

Sinkers with four notches (Fig. 259 on the following page) also have been found, though not frequently, near Muncy, and in these cases the notches are so placed that the stone was encompassed crosswise by the strings or thongs which connected it with the net. One of the specimens in possession of Mr. Gernerd is even provided with seven notches.

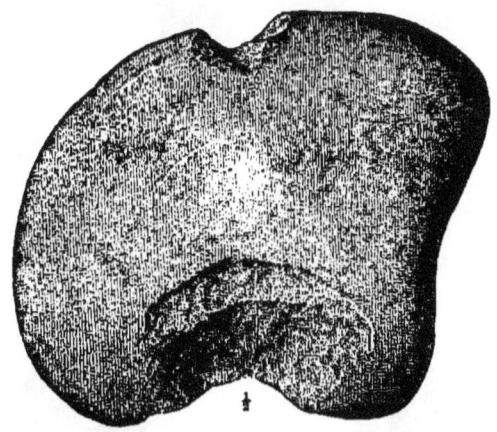

FIG. 258.—Stone sinker. Susquehanna Valley (Muncy).

The material of these sinkers is almost exclusively graywacke, a kind of rock belonging to the geological formation of Muncy, and also occurring in numerous pebbles in the neighboring creeks which empty into the Susquehanna. The frequency of sinkers in this vicinity indicates that the Indians were much engaged in fishing at this point. The Susquehanna is here about nine hundred and fifty feet wide, very deep in some places, and well stocked with fish, such as perch, pike, sun-fish, cat-fish, and eels. There existed formerly a shad-fishery near Muncy, before the river was obstructed by dams. Formerly, however, fish were still more abundant, and the locality, therefore, afforded the aborigines great advantages as a fishing-station. The first white settlers found on or near the site of Muncy a village of the Minsi or Munsey Indians, the Wolf clan of the Lenni-Lenape or Delaware nation, and hence the name "Muncy." These Indians probably made and used the sinkers found in the vicinity.

The notched flat pebbles here described consist of graywacke, as stated, being derived from one locality. In North America generally, however, any kind of pebble of convenient form was notched and utilized as a sinker, the native fishermen availing themselves of the suitable material nearest at hand.

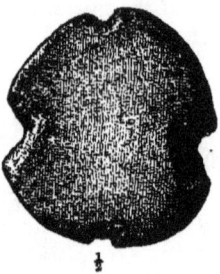

Fig. 259.—Stone sinker. Susquehanna Valley (Muncy).

There are other sinkers exhibiting notches not produced by blows, but by cutting or grinding.

Fig. 260.—Tennessee. (59239). Fig. 261.—Mexico. (61035).

Figs. 260 and 261.—Stone sinkers.

Fig. 260 shows such a specimen from Tennessee, made of a piece of potstone and provided with two deeply-cut notches. It was sent by Mr. C. L. Stratton. I represent in Fig. 261 a nearly oval pebble, five-eighths of an inch thick in the middle, and apparently consisting of fine-grained graywacke. The notches are carefully ground, and form sharp angles. This sinker, presented to the National Museum by Mr. August Shmedtie, of Washington, D. C., was found, with other relics, in a cave near Santo Domingo, a place not far distant from Santa Maria Petapa, on the Isthmus of Tehuantepec, Mexico. The cave was examined during the survey of the isthmus in 1851, and has been described by Mr. J. J. Williams.*

---

* "Santo Domingo, a mile and a half westerly from Petapa, once constituted a part of the old city; at present it contains 900 inhabitants, who annually produce a considerable quantity of vanilla, indigo, and sarsaparilla. The chief attractive features of this vicinity are the mountain-caves, which merit some attention from their connection with the past history of the indigenous people. The entrance to the principal cave, called that of Santo

SINKERS. 161

Sink-stones encompassed by a groove form a rather numerous class of North American prehistoric relics. They are very often rounded pebbles, showing no other artificial modification but the groove, which is mostly produced by pecking, but in some cases by pecking and additional grinding. In soft material the groove is cut out. Now and then the form of the stone, if not suitable in its natural state, has been somewhat modified by art; and there are specimens, especially small ones, in which the original surface of the stone has totally disappeared in the process of fashioning it.

Fig. 262.—Rhode Island. (17813).

Fig. 263.—California. (18507).

Figs. 262 and 263.—Stone sinkers.

Domingo, is elevated about seven hundred feet above the base of a limestone mountain, a mile north from the village, and is accessible only by a steep path. The mouth to this cave has an arch spanning eighty feet by twenty in height, and the plane of its floor cuts the horizon at an angle of thirty degrees, until reaching a depth of one hundred feet below the entrance. At the foot of this slope is a magnificent apartment, some three hundred feet in diameter and fifty in height, with its sides ornamented with stalactites and stalagmites of every conceivable form and variety. The floor is quite level; and at one extremity is a sparkling pool of clear, cold water. Beyond this ante-chamber, the cave extends into the mountain for a distance of more than two thousand feet, sometimes expanding into large halls, or forming regular arched passage-ways, several hundred feet in length, alternately ascending and descending into ridges and valleys. On the walls, at the extreme end of the cave, are several circular paintings, rudely executed with red ochre, and probably intended to represent the sun and moon. There are also several representations of the human hand, done in black. Immediately fronting these drawings, in the floor of the cave, is a small aperture through which, by means of ropes, access is obtained to an apartment beneath. In this are fragments of arrow-heads, human bones, and antique pottery."—*The Isthmus of Tehuantepec: being the Results of a Survey for a Railroad to connect the Atlantic and Pacific Oceans, made by the Scientific Commission under the Direction of Major J. G. Barnard, U. S. Engineers*; New York, 1852; p. 243, etc.

R 21

The pebbles out of which, as stated, such sinkers are made, generally present a more or less compressed oval form, and vary in size from less than an inch to six inches and more in the greater diameter. Most of these specimens in the National Museum, particularly the larger ones, have been obtained from the New England States; Oregon has furnished quite a number of small ones, and the others came from Pennsylvania, Tennessee, Ohio, Kentucky, the District of Columbia, and California.

Fig. 262 (on page 161).—A large pebble of oval outline, measuring two inches and three-fourths in its thickest part, and surrounded by a pecked groove. The material is a granitic rock, in which feldspar prevails. This specimen was found at Tiverton, Newport County, Rhode Island, and belongs to a collection of New England relics obtained from Mr. J. H. Clark.

Fig. 263 (on page 161).—A specimen of similar form, but of greater thickness, being nearly circular in the section crossing the groove, which is rather rudely pecked, and forms the only alteration of the sandstone pebble. Found at Dos Pueblos, California, by Mr. Schumacher.

FIG. 264.—Massachusetts. (17818).   FIG. 265.—Rhode Island. (17834).

FIGS. 264 and 265.—Stone sinkers.

Fig. 264.—This specimen shows a carefully pecked groove, and its longitudinal sides also have been shaped by pecking. It has in the middle (near the groove) a thickness of two and a half inches. The material is like that of the original of Fig. 262. From Chilmark, Island of Martha's Vineyard, Massachusetts. Clark collection.

Fig. 265.—A smaller object of the same shape and material. The groove appears to be the only modification of the pebble. From Newport, Rhode Island. Clark collection.

SINKERS. 163

Fig. 266.—A smooth gneissoid pebble, grooved and shaped at the shorter sides by pecking. Thickness an inch and five-eighths. From Wickford, Washington County, Rhode Island. Clark collection.

FIG. 266. (17846).   FIG. 267. (17834).

FIGS. 266 and 267.—Stone sinkers. Rhode Island.

Fig. 267.—This sinker is derived from the same locality. It exhibits two grooves crossing each other, and appears to have been shaped altogether by artificial means. Thickness an inch and one-half. The material is a garnetiferous mica-schist. Clark collection.

FIG. 268.—Rhode Island. (17814).   FIG. 269.—Georgia. (10473).

FIGS. 268 and 269.—Stone sinkers.

Fig. 268.—A rather smooth pebble, syenitic in character, but containing very little hornblende. Its form is that of a slightly flattened globe. The groove shows traces of grinding. Found by Mr. Clark at Tiverton, Rhode Island.

Fig. 269.—A piece of compact potstone, worked into an approximately globular form, and provided with a narrow, deep groove, produced by cutting.

Found in the neighborhood of Milledgeville, Georgia, and sent by Mr. W. McKinley.

Fig. 270.—Oregon. (13222).   Fig. 271.—Oregon. (12893).   Fig. 272.—California. (12255).   Fig. 273.—Georgia. (21294).

All ½.

Figs. 270–273.—Stone sinkers.

Fig. 270.—This is a small oval sandstone pebble, with a groove produced by grinding. The specimen was found in Oregon, and presented by Mr. A. W. Chase.

Fig. 271.—Another specimen from Oregon, of more elongated shape, and ornamented with incised lines. The material is fine-grained sandstone. It was sent by Mr. Schumacher. There are several small unornamented specimens of the same form, likewise found in Oregon, in the National Museum.

Fig. 272.—This object, obtained by Dr. H. C. Yarrow at La Patera, Santa Barbara County, California, consists of greenstone and is carefully worked into a bi-conoid shape, and polished. The narrow groove is rather shallow. A similar specimen from Ohio, of more elongated form, and provided with a somewhat deeper groove, has been figured by Messrs. Squier and Davis.* It consists of hematite. A specimen of specular iron ore, almost identical in form with that just mentioned, but a trifle larger, and likewise from Ohio, is in the National Museum. Being very heavy, it would make an excellent sinker for a fishing-line.

Fig. 273.—The original, carefully made of chlorite, has the form of a sinker, but is almost too small and light for that application. Perhaps it served as an ornament. Sent from Georgia by Mr. M. F. Stephenson.

Fig. 274.   Fig. 275.

Figs. 274 and 275.—Stone sinkers. Georgia.

Fig. 274.—This specimen belongs to a class of sinkers quite frequent in

---

* Squier and Davis: Ancient Monuments of the Mississippi Valley; Vol. I of Smithsonian Contributions to Knowledge; Washington, 1848; p. 235, Fig. 3 (erroneously marked as Fig. 5). Also figured in Stevens's "Flint Chips"; London, 1870; p. 501. The specimen is now in the Blackmore Museum, at Salisbury, England.

Georgia. They are made of pieces of potstone and have no definite forms, being recognizable as sinkers only by the groove that surrounds them. Colonel Charles C. Jones has drawn particular attention to these relics.* Indeed, the original of Fig. 274 was presented to me by that gentleman, who found it, with many objects of a similar character, in a relic-bed at the junction of the Great Kiokee Creek and the Savannah River, in Columbia County of the above-named state.

Fig. 275.—A smaller specimen, perhaps used as a sinker for a fishing-line. It was found by Colonel Jones on the right bank of Keg Creek, near its confluence with the Savannah, in Columbia County, and belongs to his collection.

He also found in Georgia notched potstone sinkers (like the original of Fig. 260), and quite a number of perforated ones, made of the same easily-worked material. These latter generally consist of flat, smooth pieces of indefinite, but mostly roundish, outline, which are an inch or less in thickness, and measure from three to six inches in diameter. Each has a single perforation, either in the centre or near the edge of the stone. The holes are usually drilled from two sides, and narrowing in the middle, where they measure about half an inch in diameter. Specimens of this kind have been found almost in all parts of the United States where potstone occurs; but they were also made of other materials.

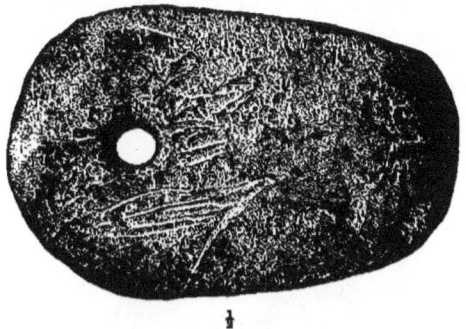

FIG. 276.—Stone sinker. North Carolina.

Fig. 276.—A specimen of the class of relics usually considered as sinkers. It is a water-worn, flat piece of potstone, approaching an oval in outline, and not quite an inch thick near the hole, which is placed an inch and three-fourths from the broader end, and drilled from both sides. It was obtained in Mitchell County, North Carolina, and presented by General J. T. Wilder.

---

* Jones: Antiquities of the Southern Indians, particularly of the Georgia Tribes; New York, 1873; p. 338.

Fig. 277.—In this rather irregular piece of potstone the carelessly drilled hole is placed nearly in the centre. It was found in the bottom of the Oconee River, in Putnam County, Georgia, and presented by Mr. McKinley.

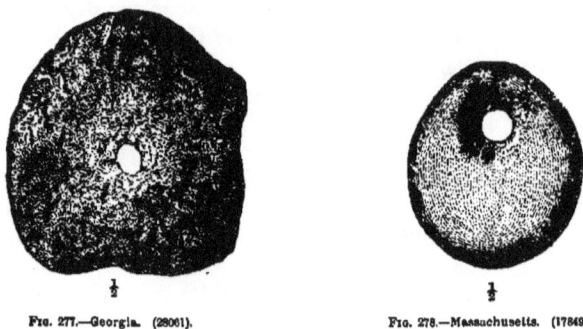

Fig. 277.—Georgia. (28061).   Fig. 278.—Massachusetts. (17849).

Figs. 277 and 278.—Stone sinkers.

Fig. 278.—A very flat, smooth pebble of oval shape, pierced with a round hole near the edge. The perforation was sunk from both sides, and the slanting cavities show traces of additional grinding. This specimen, consisting of a kind of potstone of very compact structure, probably served as a sinker. From Middleborough, Plymouth County, Massachusetts. It was obtained from Mr. Clark.

Fig. 279.—Stone sinker (?). California. (18300).

Fig. 279.—One of the many pierced stone discs from the Santa Barbara group of islands, collected for the National Museum by Messrs. Schumacher, Bowers, and Harford. It is a flat pebble of micaceous schist, having in the centre a perforation, flaring on both sides, and carefully finished by grinding. Thickness in the middle seven-eighths of an inch. Sent by Mr. Schumacher from Santa Cruz Island. This object would have done good service as a sinker, and may have been employed as such. It is known that the Indians of that region used seine-nets.

Another class of sinkers consists of egg-shaped or roundish pebbles, perforated near the edge with an oblique hole, which is drilled from two sides, and generally forms an obtuse angle where the perforations meet. Such specimens are rare; but they occur in sufficient number to constitute a type. Those which have fallen under my notice were rather small, and evidently designed for sinking fishing-lines.

Fig. 280.—Ohio. (12198).   Fig. 281.—Eskimos, Arctic America. (10117).

FIGS. 280 and 281.—Stone sinkers.

Fig. 280.—A specimen of this kind from Ohio. It is made of a sandstone pebble. Presented by Mr. T. Rhodes. In this specimen the perforations are larger than in others which I have seen.

Fig. 281.—An Eskimo sinker, made of a small, roundish quartzite pebble, and showing a similar perforation. There are slight grooves extending from the orifices across the corresponding sides of the stone. Obtained by Captain C. F. Hall. If there were any doubts as to the application of the original of Fig. 280, and of similar specimens, the character of this Eskimo sinker would set them at rest.

I now pass over to the description of a numerous and well-known class of North American relics to which several names have been given, and different purposes assigned. In view of their varied shapes, it is rather difficult to define the character of these objects, which are known as pendants, plumbs, plummets, sinkers, etc. Most of them may be designated as pear-shaped, though that expression must not be taken in its strictest sense. They consist of red or brown hematite, specular iron, quartzite, serpentine, greenstone, and other heavy materials capable of a good polish. Suspension was in many cases facilitated by a groove, a knob, or a perforation at one end, generally the more tapering one; some of them, however, exhibit forms requiring other methods of fastening.

Many of these objects show really elegant forms, are fashioned with the utmost precision, and beautifully polished; and hence they were formerly, when comparatively few had been collected, and their wide distribution was not yet known, regarded as articles of ornamental character, as, for instance, by Messrs. Squier and Davis.[*] Mr. J. W. Foster is inclined to consider them as weights used in weaving, "to keep the thread taut," and tries also other explanations, none of which carries conviction with it.[†] The opinion that they were used by the mound-builders as plumbs to aid in the construction of earthworks is hardly tenable, for they are found as well in districts where these monuments abound, as in such where they are entirely absent. A close examination of the large series of such objects in the United States National Museum has led me to consider them as sinkers for fishing-lines, a view which does not exclude the possibility that some of them may have been differently used. Such relics occur throughout the whole breadth of the United States, from New England to California, and the specimens obtained from this extensive territory show, notwithstanding the variety of their forms, a conformity in general character, which, according to my judgment, points to the same mode of application.

The theory of their use as sinkers is met by the objection that too much care has been bestowed on the manufacture of many of them to risk their loss while employed. But this argument can easily be overcome by an examination of the angling-implements still in use among uncivilized, yet somewhat advanced, tribes. These people take great pains in the production of their weapons and other accoutrements, as any one can perceive who devotes his attention to a collection of such articles. The western Eskimos, for instance, excel in the production of fishing-tackle of every kind, and I will mention, with special reference to the question here treated, that they employ at the present time carefully-made pear-shaped line-sinkers of stone and ivory, and risk to lose them while angling; and if, by accident, they are deprived of them, they make new ones.

An elongated pear-shape, it must be admitted, is the form best adapted for a line-sinker, and, indeed, is commonly given to the leaden sinkers found in every hardware-store, where apparatus for angling is sold.

The sinkers which I am now about to describe mostly would present a circular horizontal section, and any deviation from this form will be mentioned.

Fig. 282.—A specimen made of dark-greenish argillite, regular in outline, and well polished. Found in a mound in Licking County, Ohio, and presented by Mr. W. Anderson.

Fig. 283.—A larger specimen of similar form, made of specular iron, and carefully polished. From Hancock County, Illinois. Presented by Mr. M. Tandy.

---

[*] Squier and Davis: Ancient Monuments; p. 285.
[†] Foster: Prehistoric Races of the United States of America; Chicago, 1873; p. 230, etc.

As these two specimens are not specially prepared for the attachment of the line, it must be assumed that it passed around the tapering ends and along the sides of the objects. This operation was easily performed, as I have found out by experiment.

Fig. 282.—Ohio. (11486).   Fig. 283.—Illinois. (59580).   Fig. 284.—California. (23662).   Fig. 285.—Louisiana. (10624).

All ½.

Figs. 282–285.—Stone sinkers.

Fig. 284.—A specimen of very slender form, made of fine-grained mica-schist. The surface is tolerably smooth, but not polished. Both ends are covered with asphaltum, which shows the impression of strings. Obtained by Mr. Bowers on Santa Rosa Island, California. There are other Californian specimens of the same kind in the National Museum, some of them likewise encrusted with asphaltum at the extremities, and one of them, moreover, has a distinct groove passing around the more pointed end. It measures more than eight inches in length.

Fig. 285.—A cast of an apparently well-polished stone object, which was in 1871 in the Louisiana State Seminary, at Baton Rouge. It does not strictly belong to the kind of relics just described, being provided with a smooth, nearly semi-circular indentation at the lower part; but I notice it in connection with those specimens, because it comes nearest to them in other respects. The indentation would have presented a firm hold for the line. However, I am not at all convinced that it really was a sinker, as it may have been a tool for rounding and smoothing articles of yielding material, such as wood, etc.

R 22

The next group shows four sinkers encircled by a groove near the narrower extremity.

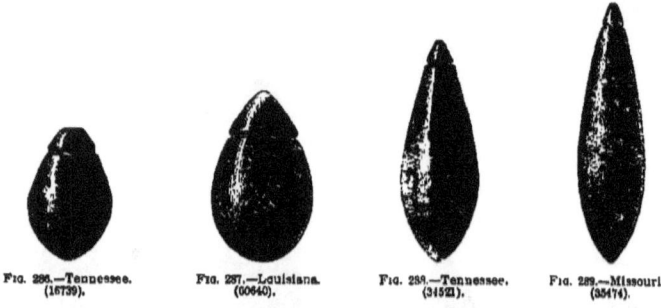

Fig. 286.—Tennessee. (16739). Fig. 287.—Louisiana. (00640). Fig. 288.—Tennessee. (34521). Fig. 289.—Missouri. (35474).

All ½.

FIGS. 286–289.—Stone sinkers.

Fig. 286.—This specimen is made of a brown ferruginous stone, neither hematite nor clay-iron stone, and softer than ferruginous quartz. It exhibits a tolerably regular pear-shape, is slightly truncated at the upper end, and polished. From Tennessee. Presented by the Rev. E. H. Randle.

Fig. 287.—A pear-shaped sinker with somewhat rounded apex, from which the groove is farther distant than in the other specimens of similar form. It consists of yellowish-brown quartzite. The object is regularly shaped, and its surface smoothed. It was found in Morehouse Parish, Louisiana, and belongs to a series of sinkers and other relics presented to the National Museum by Mr. B. H. Brodnax, of Plantersville, in Morehouse Parish.

Fig. 288.—This specimen, obtusely pointed at both ends, is made of specular iron, and highly polished. Like other sinkers of this kind, yet to be described, it is as symmetrical in form as though it had been turned in a lathe. Obtained in Carroll County, Tennessee, and presented by Mr. Randle.

Fig. 289.—This object, made of red hematite, resembles in shape the original of Fig. 288, but is more slender, and not so well polished. It was found in Saint Charles County, Missouri, and sent by Mr. G. A. Slatery.

The following series comprises five sinkers truncated at the upper end.

Fig. 290.—A quartzite sinker found near Tampa Bay, Florida. It is of a flattened pear-shape, and though tolerably well worked, appears somewhat rude, when compared with the other specimens of this group. Sent by Mr. S. T. Walker.

Fig. 291.—This specimen, of elegant form and good workmanship, consists of brown clay-iron stone, composed of concentric layers, the outer of which has become detached in some places. From a shell-deposit a few miles north of Mobile, Alabama, between the Mobile and Tensas Rivers. Presented by Mr. K. M. Cunningham.

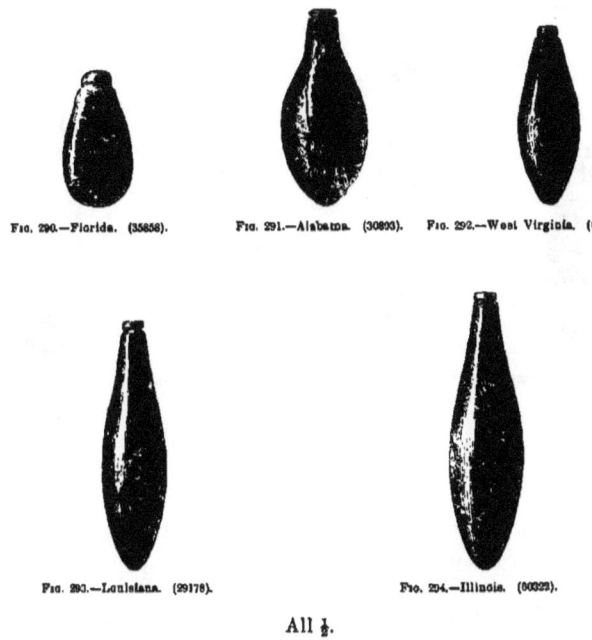

Fig. 290.—Florida. (35858). Fig. 291.—Alabama. (30893). Fig. 292.—West Virginia. (00745).

Fig. 293.—Louisiana. (29178). Fig. 294.—Illinois. (60322).

All ½.

Figs. 290-294.—Stone sinkers.

Fig. 292.—The material of this most carefully fashioned and polished sinker is specular iron. Found thirty feet below the surface, at Huntington, in Cabell County, West Virginia. Presented by Mr. W. J. Haller.

Fig. 293.—A larger specimen of similar form and excellent finish, and likewise composed of specular iron. It belongs to the series of sinkers from Morehouse Parish, Louisiana, sent by Mr. Brodnax.

Fig. 294.—Another specimen of absolutely symmetrical and tasteful shape. It is made of whitish limestone. About an inch and a half below the flattened upper extremity is a small hole filled with oxidized copper, probably the end of the drill, which broke during the operation. On the opposite side, but only one inch below the narrow end, is another hole of the same diameter, shallow and without any traces of copper. It is not quite evident for what purpose these holes were drilled, unless it was with a view to ornamentation. From a mound in Henderson County, Illinois. Presented by Mr. M. Tandy.[*]

The specimens figured next are of rather heterogeneous shapes, but have the groove in common.

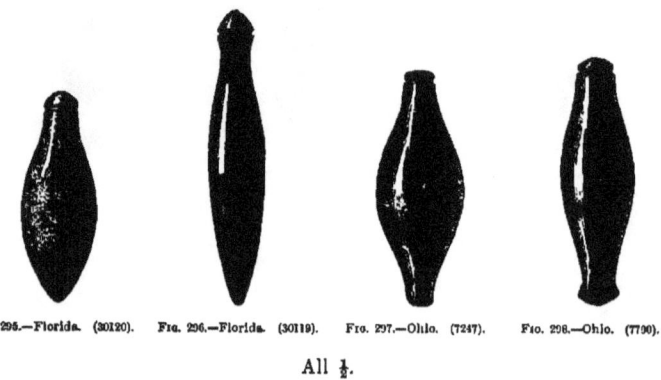

Fig. 295.—Florida. (30120).   Fig. 296.—Florida. (30119).   Fig. 297.—Ohio. (7247).   Fig. 298.—Ohio. (7790).

All ½.

Figs. 295–298.—Stone sinkers.

Fig. 295.—This object, consisting of a dark-colored serpentine-like material, is of regular outline, and polished. The part above the groove has a conoid form. It was found in Manatee County, Florida, and sent by Mr. J. P. Wall.

Fig. 296.—A specimen derived from the same locality, also presented by Mr. Wall. It is of a very graceful, slender form, contracting below the groove, and terminating in a conoid above it. The surface is beautifully polished, and entirely free of scratches and other marks indicative of use. The material is like that of the original of Fig. 295.

---

[*] This mound, located a mile and a half from Dallas City, in Hancock County, Illinois, is remarkable for the abundance of human remains and artefacts it contained; but having been dug into by different parties, a minute record of the manner of their disposition is not extant. More than a hundred skeletons are said to have been inclosed in this mound; a tree, twenty inches in diameter, had spread its roots among the bones, and impeded the operations, until removed. The bodies, all belonging to adults, had been placed closely together, as it seemed, in a doubled-up position. Curiously enough, many of the skulls exhibit a small round perforation in one of the temporal bones, generally the left; and several skulls were found with a flint perforator sticking in the aperture, and evidently driven into the head after death, perhaps in pursuance of some superstitious motive. Across the mound, from east to west, a streak of ashes and charcoal was noticed. The east side of the mound inclosed a grave made of stone slabs, and containing a skeleton stretched out at full length, with the head to the south. In this grave were found two sinkers and a shell. The relics taken from this mound consist of sinkers of stone and iron ore (sixteen in number), arrow and spear-heads, pipes, beads, and other ornaments of shell, perforated teeth of animals, bone awls, and fragments of hematite, lead ore, copper, deer and elk-horn. It is probable that the burials in this mound belong to different periods. Many of the relics here found were presented to the National Museum by Mr. M. Tandy, of Dallas City, and others who had exhumed them.

SINKERS. 173

Fig. 297.—Cast of a specimen formerly belonging to Dr. E. H. Davis, and now in the Blackmore Museum, at Salisbury, England. It is figured by Mr. Stevens and described by him as " a plummet-like object of talc, grooved at one end, and with the other end worked to a corresponding point."* Squier and Davis represent a similar specimen of more graceful form. They call these relics " pendants," and state that they " are of frequent occurrence in the vicinity of the ancient works, though seldom found, if indeed found at all, in the ancient mounds themselves."† The original of Fig. 297 was found in Ohio.

Fig. 298.—This specimen bears some resemblance to the original of Fig. 297, but it bulges less in the middle, and its lower end expands and terminates in a conoid. The material of this well-polished object is a dark-green, compact kind of greenstone, somewhat porphyritic in structure. It belongs to a collection of relics from Madison Township, in Franklin County, Ohio, which were presented to the National Museum by Mr. W. R. Limpert, of Groveport, in the same township. They were not taken from mounds, but were found by farmers while ploughing.

FIG. 299.—Stone sinker. Ohio. (16034).

Fig. 299.—A well-polished sinker of specular iron, provided with two grooves, the lower one of which runs in an oblique direction. It was taken from a mound in Licking County, Ohio, and presented by Mr. W. Anderson.

The following class comprises sinkers in which the upper part is worked into the shape of a knob.

Fig. 300 (on page 174).—This sinker is of a flattened pear-shape, being one inch and three-eighths thick in the middle, and apparently made of fine-grained granite. The surface is entirely decomposed and rough. From Beverly, Essex County, Massachusetts. Presented by Mr. Levi Cole.

Fig. 301 (on page 174).—A specimen of more regular form, consisting of feldspathic rock. The surface is rough, in consequence of weathering. Found at Eastport, Washington County, Maine, and presented by the Rev. E. Vetromile.

---

* Stevens: Flint Chips; p. 500.
† Squier and Davis: Ancient Monuments; p. 235.

Fig. 302.—This object, of a somewhat flattened shape, consists of a dark metamorphic slate. It expands considerably in the middle, and the lower part shows four ground facets terminating in a point, like the apex of a four-sided pyramid. From South Kingston, Washington County, Rhode Island. It belongs to the Clark collection.

Fig. 300.—Massachusetts. (6508). Fig. 301.—Maine. (11621). Fig. 302.—Rhode Island. (17876).

Figs. 300–302.—Stone sinkers.

Fig. 303.—In this specimen, which has a tolerably regular form, the knob is not sufficiently expanding for permitting a line to be tied firmly below it. But the sinker, composed of sandstone, is much weathered, and the knob may have gradually dwindled away. If, however, the object presents its original form, we must assume that the line also passed around its lower part. From Guadaloupe, Santa Barbara County, California. Sent by Mr. Bowers.

Fig. 304.—A very large sinker of granite, probably suspended in the manner suggested in the preceding case. The side not exposed to view in the figure is partly flat. This sinker may have been used in connection with a large hook for catching cod or halibut. From Massachusetts. Presented by General J. H. Devereux.

Fig. 305.—A specimen of unusual form, made of a pebble of elongated shape, somewhat resembling a four-sided prism. The neck is produced by pecking, and there are also traces of work noticeable on the left side and at the lower end. The material is a greenish-gray metamorphic slate. Obtained at Marblehead, Essex County, Massachusetts, and presented by Mr. J. J. H. Gregory.

Fig. 306.—A well-shaped sinker with flattened knob. The surface is much corroded, and has a slightly porous appearance. The stone out of which this sinker is made effervesces when treated with an acid, and consequently consists of, or contains much, carbonate of lime. Obtained at Sarasota Bay, Manatee County, Florida, and presented by Mr. J. G. Webb.

SINKERS. 175

Fig. 307.—A quartzite sinker of conoidal form, with a knob traversed by a groove, which doubtless was intended to facilitate the adjustment of the line. From Middleborough, Massachusetts. Presented by Professor J. W. P. Jenks.

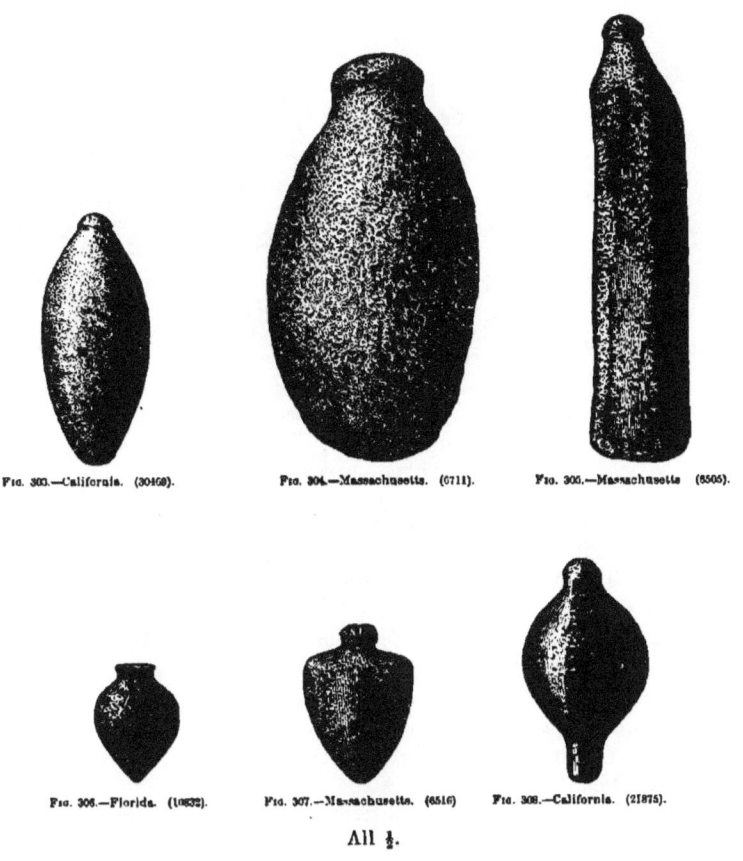

Fig. 303.—California. (30469).   Fig. 304.—Massachusetts. (6711).   Fig. 305.—Massachusetts. (8505).

Fig. 306.—Florida. (10532).   Fig. 307.—Massachusetts. (6516).   Fig. 308.—California. (21875).

All ½.

Figs. 303-308.—Stone sinkers.

Fig. 308.—This specimen, which consists of serpentine, exhibits an almost globular bulge. In this sinker, as in others already described, the neck portion of the knob is hardly narrow enough to allow a firm attachment of the line, for which reason it may be supposed that the latter passed around both the knob and the opposite extremity. Found by Mr. Schumacher on Santa Cruz Island.*

In the four specimens forming the next group there are no knobs, properly speaking, and other forms appear in their stead.

FIG. 309.—California. (12130).   FIG. 310.—Maine. (6362).   FIG. 311.—California. (21873).   FIG. 312.—California. (7117).

All ½.

FIGS. 309–312.—Stone sinkers.

Fig. 309.—An object of limestone, rather rudely worked, and slightly compressed in the longitudinal direction. Both extremities contract and show traces of asphaltum. The line evidently encompassed both ends. From Santa Rosa Island. Sent by Mr. G. W. Harford.

Fig. 310.—This sinker is made of a chloritic pebble, of which the pecking has not entirely removed the original surface. A cross-section through the middle, therefore, would not present a circular but an irregular form. The upper end shows a slight expansion, barely sufficient to afford a hold to the line when tied around it. Obtained near the Saint Croix River, Maine, and presented by Mr. G. A. Boardman.

Fig. 311.—A specimen of kindred form, but larger, and perfectly symmetrical in shape. The surface of this object, which consists of serpentine, shows distinct striæ, produced by the tool with which it was finished. Found on Santa Cruz Island by Mr. Schumacher.

Fig. 312.—Another Californian specimen with a more considerable bulge and a very slender neck, terminating in a hardly perceptible enlargement. The material of this well-worked, but not polished, sinker is hornblende-schist. Sent by Dr. L. G. Yates.

---

* Messrs. Squier and Davis figure on p. 235 of "Ancient Monuments of the Mississippi Valley" a specimen exhibiting a greater bulge and more elaborate workmanship. The comparatively small upper end is grooved; the lower end terminates in a conoid. No special mention of this object is made in the text of their work.

SINKERS. 177

The sinkers which next claim our attention are perforated at the upper extremity.

Fig. 314.—Louisiana. (34406).   Fig. 313.—California. (26403).   Fig. 315.—Arkansas. (9942).

Figs. 313–315.—Stone sinkers.

Fig. 313.—A well-worked, but not polished, small specimen of potstone, with a hole drilled from both sides, and therefore bi-conical in shape. Though of the sinker form, the object is rather small, and possibly may have served as an ornament. Perhaps it belonged to the fishing-tackle of a juvenile angler. Obtained on San Miguel Island by Mr. Bowers.

Fig. 314.—One of the series of fine polished sinkers from Morehouse Parish, in Louisiana, presented by Mr. Brodnax. It consists of specular iron. The hole is bi-conical, and drilled with great precision.

Fig. 315.—This sinker, of very regular shape and well polished, is made of amygdaloid. The perforation has a cylindrical form, and below it are seen two incised ornamental lines. Found in Arkansas, and presented by Mrs. R. L. Stuart.

Fig. 316.—California.   Fig. 317.—Illinois.

Figs. 316 and 317.—Stone sinkers.

R 23

Nearly of this shape, but more slender in the neck, are the drilled stone and ivory sinkers still made by the western Eskimos. Some of their sinkers are provided with a hole at each end, as an example will show hereafter.

Fig. 316 (on page 177).—A very good specimen from San Miguel Island, made of greenish-gray, slightly porous stone, apparently of volcanic origin. The perforation, near the *blunt* end, is bi-conical. This sinker and that represented in Fig. 317 belong to the extensive collection of the late Mr. W. S. Vaux, of Philadelphia, and were kindly loaned to me by his brother, Mr. George Vaux, of that city.

Fig. 317 (on page 177).—A well-polished sinker of coarse-grained syenite. The portion above the bi-conical hole is somewhat damaged by fracture. It formed the less pointed end of the object. From Chester, Randolph County, Illinois.*

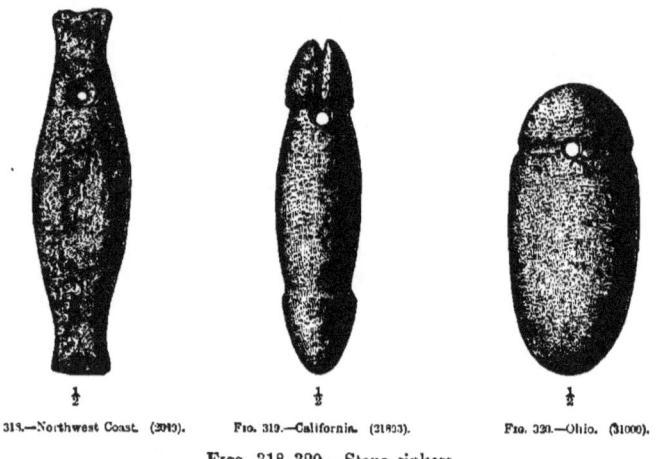

Fig. 318.—Northwest Coast. (2043).   Fig. 319.—California. (21803).   Fig. 320.—Ohio. (31000).

Figs. 318–320.—Stone sinkers.

Fig. 318.—A specimen made of gneiss, presenting a rather rough appearance, but nevertheless symmetrical in form. The bulging part is slightly flattish, and both ends exhibit a still more compressed shape. The bi-conical perforation is one inch distant from the upper end, which shows an insignificant depression in the middle. Obtained on the Northwest Coast during Lieutenant Wilkes's exploring expedition.

Fig. 319.—Marked as a cast of a specimen in the collection of the Cali-

---

* I have the upper half of a well-made drilled stone sinker, which, significantly enough, was found in the Richland Creek, near Belleville, Saint Clair County, Illinois.

fornia Academy of Sciences, at San Francisco. The object, to judge from its imitation, is well worked. The upper end shows a deep groove, running vertically from one aperture of the bi-conical hole to the other. I cannot state of what material the specimen is made, and from what special locality in California it is derived. My inquiries led to no definite result. A cast of another Californian sinker of the same shape was sent by Mr. R. E. C. Stearns to the National Museum (No. 30110). The original, consisting of dark slate, was found in Solano County.

Fig. 320.—This specimen is made of a flattish pebble of fine-grained sandstone, to some extent modified by grinding. A well-ground horizontal groove passes through the apertures of the cylindrical perforation. The object has the appearance of a sinker; but, nevertheless, may have been designed for another use. From Cleveland, Ohio. Presented by General J. T. Wilder.

FIG. 321.—Eskimo stone sinker. Alaska. (24702).

Fig. 321.—A well-made Eskimo sinker of greenish porphyry, having at both ends perforations which still hold cords of thong and sinew-remnants of the line and of a strip to which the hook was attached. The perforations run in opposite directions. Obtained on Ukivok or King Island, Alaska, by Mr. L. M. Turner.

In concluding my account of North American stone sinkers, I present on page 180 two illustrations of such articles, which should have been noticed in their proper connection with others of similar character. The figures, however, show the objects exceptionally in natural size, being printed from blocks not specially prepared for this work, but already used in an official report.[*] The

---

[*] Norris: Fifth Annual Report of the Superintendent of the Yellowstone National Park; Washington, 1881; Fig. 7 on p. 33, and Fig. 8 on p. 34.

originals, moreover, were both found near the Yellowstone Lake, in the Yellowstone Park, Wyoming, and sent to the National Museum by Mr. P. W. Norris.

Fig. 322.—A grooved sinker, made of a syenite pebble of somewhat compressed shape. The pecked groove seems to be its only artificial modification.

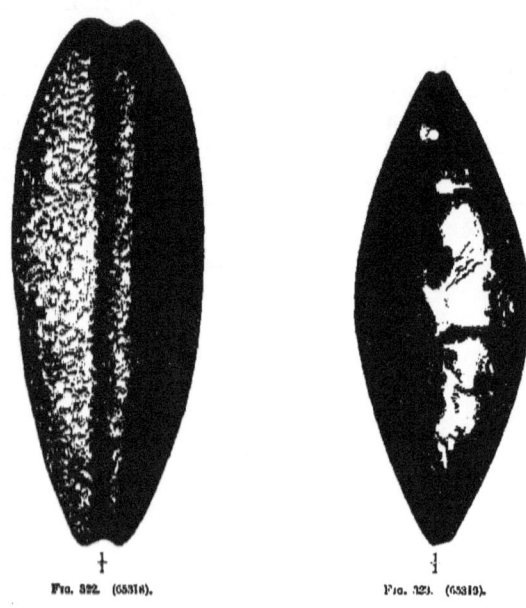

FIGS. 322 and 323.—Stone sinkers. Wyoming.

Fig. 323.—This very fine and carefully polished sinker consists of whitish quartz, variegated with black spots. The hole is regularly drilled from both sides.

On a preceding page allusion was made to sinkers of native copper. As this metal would have furnished an excellent material for sinkers, the small number of copper articles of this kind hitherto discovered must excite some surprise. Indeed, I know only of two specimens, representations and descriptions of which are here given.

Fig. 324.—A sinker of beaten native copper, approximately round in the cross-section, and provided with a groove for the attachment of the line. The object is not quite regularly shaped, and shows several cracks, into one of which, at the lower end, a thin piece of beaten native silver is inserted. The original was found, in June, 1819, with a number of other relics, in a mound at Marietta,

Ohio. This mound and its contents have been minutely described by Dr. S. P. Hildreth in a letter addressed to Mr. Caleb Atwater.* The full-size figure is made after the original, which belongs to the collection of the American Antiquarian Society, at Worcester, Massachusetts, but was kindly loaned to me through the mediation of Mr. Stephen Salisbury, Jr., of the same place.†

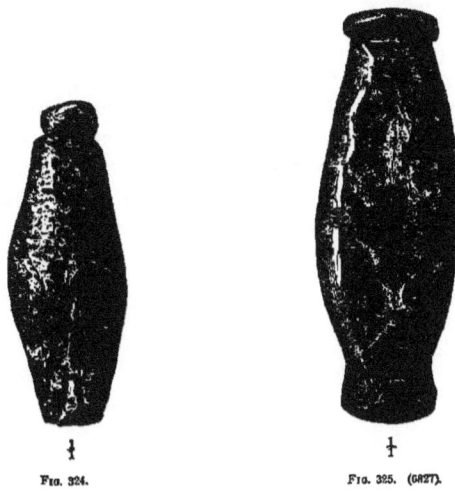

Fig. 324.   Fig. 325. (6827).

Figs. 324 and 325.—Copper sinkers. Mounds in Ohio.

Fig. 325.—This sinker, presented by General J. H. Devereux, is carefully hammered from a solid piece of native copper, of good, though not entirely symmetrical, shape, and smooth on the surface, which shows some slight cavities. The upper part terminates in a compressed knob, sufficiently projecting to afford a firm hold to the line, and the lower end, without forming a knob, shows a somewhat similar shape. The object is not round, but flattened throughout, measuring about half an inch in thickness. A cross-section through the middle would almost resemble a rectangle with strongly rounded angles.

---

* Archæologia Americana; Vol. I, 1820; p. 168, etc. The wood-cut on p. 173 (Fig. 5) bears only a distant resemblance to the object.

† Since the above was written, Professor F. W. Putnam has published in the "Proceedings of the American Antiquarian Society" (New Series, Vol. II; p. 349-363) an article relating to the objects discovered in the mound at Marietta. He thinks the specimen, which I call a sinker, has been made by pounding together an arborescent mass of native copper containing native silver. The peculiar occurrence of these two virgin metals in the Lake Superior district is well known, and before having examined the specimen in question, I entertained the view expressed by Professor Putnam. But upon close inspection it appeared to me as though the piece of silver in the sinker showed traces of beating, and hence my statement. After all, the matter is not of great importance.

General Devereux informed me that he obtained this specimen, in the summer of 1852, from the family of the finder. It had been exhumed, some years previously, from a tumulus in Painesville Township, Lake County, Ohio. He had not the opportunity of personally visiting the site and remains of this mound, which, from the description given of it, was of no unusual size or shape. It had been gradually leveled by the plough, during which process large quantities of detached human bones as well as many distinct skeletons had come to light; and also implements and ornaments of stone, together with the copper article—the only one made of that metal. The family of the discoverer had displaced or lost everything of the find, excepting the copper relic, which happily had been carefully preserved as possessing unusual value.

In a valuable treatise on North American prehistoric copper articles, Dr. Emil Schmidt has described this object as an ornament.* Its weight and form militate against this view, whereas it has all the characteristics of a sinker, and probably was employed as such. It is a reproduction in copper of a certain type of stone sinkers, of which the specimen represented in Fig. 298 may serve as an example.

In the next group I finally present designs of four specimens made of shell, three of which correspond in shape more or less to certain objects of stone brought to the reader's notice, which I consider as sinkers.

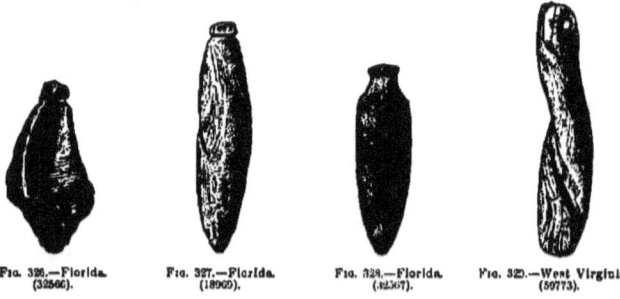

Fig. 326.—Florida. (32566). Fig. 327.—Florida. (18969). Fig. 328.—Florida. (32567). Fig. 329.—West Virginia. (59773).

All ½.

Figs. 326–329.—Shell sinkers.

Fig. 326.—Cast of a modified shell of *Strombus pugilis*, found in Florida, and sent to the National Museum for reproduction in plaster, by Mr. J. W. Velie, of Chicago. The edge-portion of the wall of this shell has been removed until its more solid part was reached; the end of the beak is ground off, and below the

---

* Schmidt: Die prähistorischen Kupfergeräthe Nordamerikas; Archiv für Anthropologie; Vol. XI, 1878; p. 88.

small plane thus formed it is encircled by a groove. It appears probable that this prepared shell served as a sinker.

Fig. 327.—An object made of the columella of *Pyrula perversa*. Its great resemblance to a class of stone sinkers justifies the opinion that it also was a sinker. From Sarasota Bay, Florida. Presented by Mr. J. G. Webb.

Fig. 328.—Cast of another specimen of shell, worked into the form of a sinker. Original likewise found in Florida, and loaned to the National Museum by Mr. Velie.

Fig. 329.—Columella of *Pyrula perversa*, carefully brought into shape, and perforated at one end. This specimen was found in a shell-heap on Blennerhassett's Island in the Ohio River, two miles below Parkersburg, West Virginia, and belongs to a collection of relics from that island sent to the National Museum by Mr. J. P. MacLean.* It would have done excellent service as a sinker for a fishing-line; but as the shell out of which it is made occurs only on the southern coasts of the United States, it doubtless was deemed valuable by the inhabitants of the interior country, and hence it may have been designed for an ornamental rather than a practical purpose.

Fish-cutters.—Any one acquainted with the types of North American stone implements is aware of the existence of smoothed or polished cutting-tools of slate, which generally exhibit a semi-lunar shape, having a curved cutting-edge and a straight or nearly straight back, thick and projecting for greater convenience in handling. One of these cutters is figured by Squier and Davis, and they are thus alluded to :—"Another variety is occasionally found in the Eastern States. They are sometimes composed of slate, and are of various sizes, often measuring five or six inches in length. They are very well adapted for flaying animals, and other analogous purposes."† They were afterward noticed by myself,‡ and more minutely described by Professor Putnam § and Dr. Abbott.‖ The above-quoted statements are correct, excepting the remark that these cutters occur *occasionally* in the Eastern States. They are, in fact, rather frequent in the Northern Atlantic States, but apparently confined to that region. The specimens in the National Museum were obtained in New Hampshire, Massachusetts, Connecticut, New York, and Pennsylvania. According to Dr. Abbott, they are common in New Jersey.

Fig. 330, on the following page, shows the form of one of the smaller specimens of this class, composed of a greenish-gray slate. The back is in the middle

---

* His description of the shell-deposits on that island will be found in another section of this work.

† Squier and Davis: Ancient Monuments; p. 215, etc.

‡ The Archæological Collection of the United States National Museum; No. 287 of Smithsonian Contributions to Knowledge; Washington, 1876; p. 24.

§ Putnam: Bulletins of the Essex Institute, Vol. V, April and May, and July, 1873; p. 80, etc.; p. 126.

‖ Abbott: Primitive Industry; p. 63, etc.

three-eighths of an inch thick, but, as in other specimens of the same kind, becomes gradually thinner toward the ends. It has a tolerably sharp cutting-edge. The specimen was found at Blackstone, Worcester County, Massachusetts, and belongs to the series of New England relics acquired from Mr. J. H. Clark.

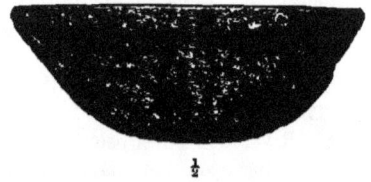

FIG. 330.—Stone fish-cutter. Massachusetts. (17938).

The original of Fig. 331 is in possession of Mr. F. Roulet, of Newark Valley, Tioga County, New York, and the illustration was made after an exact cast taken by one of the modelers of the National Museum. This specimen, which consists of a reddish-brown, mottled, ferruginous slate, was found on the flats of Owego Creek, near Newark Valley. It probably had originally a greater depth, which gradually became less by grinding. The cutting-edge is beveled from both sides. The back is in the middle half an inch thick, and afforded, like that of the first-described specimen, a convenient handle.

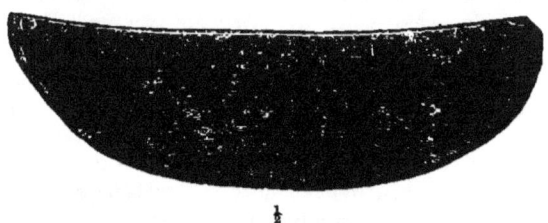

FIG. 331.—Stone fish-cutter. New York. (58520).

Fig. 332 represents a large, unfortunately defective, cutter of gray slate, found on the bank of the Schuylkill, near Norristown, Montgomery County, Pennsylvania, and presented to the National Museum by Mr. J. H. McIlvaine. In this specimen the back is only five-sixteenths of an inch thick in the middle, and, considering the size of the implement, which measured more than nine inches in length when complete, is too insignificant to afford a firm grasp. It is therefore obvious that the blade was originally inserted, or intended to be inserted, into a separate handle, probably of wood. A slit cut in longitudinally below the projecting upper part, and not placed in the middle, but nearer one end of the blade (for a reason to be explained very soon) facilitated the connection of the two parts by means of a ligature. Professor Putnam and Dr. Abbott figure in their before-cited publications a specimen from Massachusetts, showing three longitudinal holes below the back, which in that instance forms a thin edge.

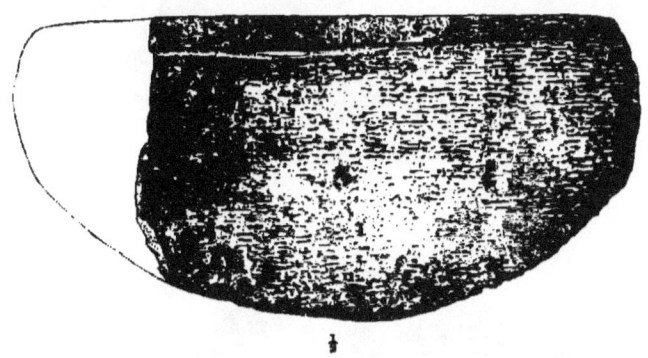

Fig. 332.—Stone fish-cutter. Pennsylvania. (8025).

I have called these implements "fish-cutters," not for conveying the idea that they were exclusively used for the purpose indicated by that name, but because I believe that the cutting of fish was one of their chief applications. There are in the National Museum handled cutting-implements of the same shape, and partly of the same material, obtained from Innuits and Indians of the Northwest Coast, and these tools are generally designated by those who sent them from that region as "fish-knives," "knives for splitting fish," "halibut-knives," etc., and it is sometimes stated that they are chiefly used by women. I will give a few examples.

Fig. 333, on the next page, shows a large, well-polished, and sharp-edged slate knife, designed to be inserted into a handle. It was obtained by Mr. E. W. Nelson from Eskimos of Norton Sound, Alaska. He calls it "a woman's fish-knife," and draws special attention to the absence of the handle.

In Fig. 334, also on the following page, I represent another slate knife, sent from the same locality by Mr. L. M. Turner. It is set in a massive semi-lunar handle of pine-wood. A ligature of whalebone passing through a hole in the blade and fitting into a groove in the handle keeps both parts firmly united. The cutting-edge of this tool is quite sharp. It will be noticed that the hole in

R 24

the blade is not in the middle, but nearer one of its corners, just as in the original of Fig. 332. It was probably intended to exert a greater pressure on one side.

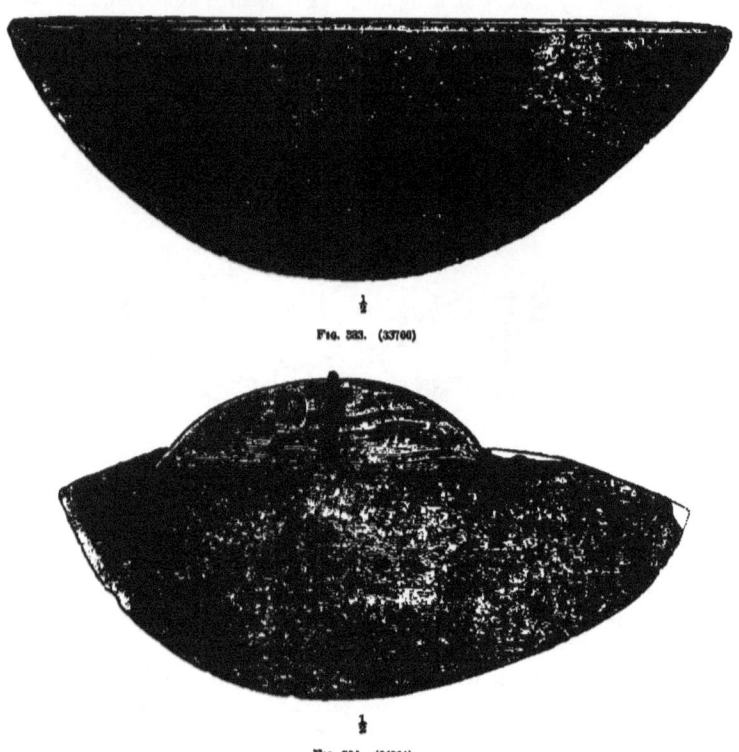

FIGS. 333 and 334.—Stone fish-cutters. Eskimos, Norton Sound, Alaska.

Fig. 335 presents the form of a "halibut-knife" used by the Makah Indians of Neah Bay, Washington Territory, and sent by Mr. James G. Swan. The blade consists of a thin piece of iron, and is inserted into a slightly-curved, rather thick handle of pine-wood. The two holes in the blade have no significance; they were originally in the piece of sheet-iron obtained from the whites, which was afterward utilized in the manufacture of a knife.

Another Makah knife from Neah Bay sent by him consists entirely of slaty stone. It has, as Fig. 336 shows, a semi-circular cutting-edge and a massive, rudely-shaped back without shoulders. In this uncouth, but very characteristic, implement only the cutting-edge is ground. Mr. Swan calls it an "*ancient knife for splitting fish.*"

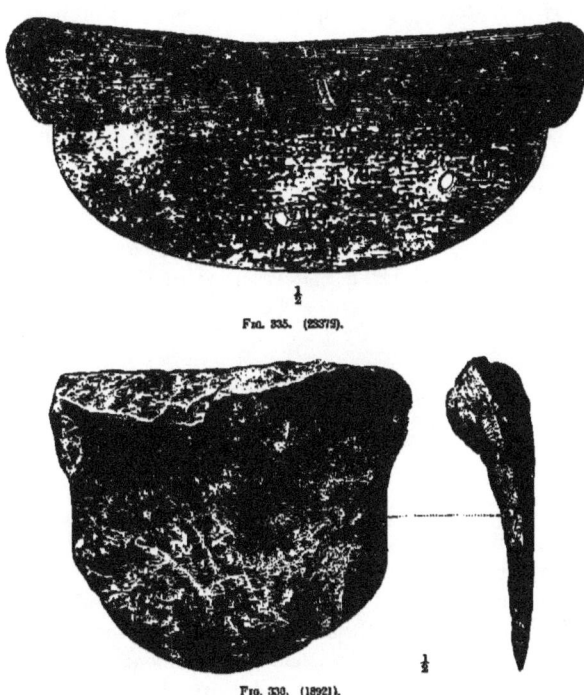

Fig. 335. (23379).

Fig. 336. (18921).

Figs. 325 and 336.—Fish-cutters of iron and stone. Makah Indians, Neah Bay.

The Greenland Eskimos, more especially the women, use at present a semi-circular iron cutting-tool (called *ooloo*), which is hafted like a saddler's knife; but formerly, before they obtained iron from Europeans, they employed knives with blades of slate,* as did also the eastern Innuits south of Greenland.

The resemblance between the modern cutters denominated "fish-knives" and the older slate knives described by me is really striking, and hence it will be deemed justifiable that I have claimed an analogous use for the latter, and have mentioned them in connection with prehistoric fishing.

* Sometimes of meteoric iron.

In commenting on these tools, Dr. Abbott observes:—"As these semi-lunar knives are more abundant in New England than in the Middle States, and do not appear to have been in use among the southern coast-tribes, it is probable that the pattern is derived from the Eskimos, with whom the northern Algonkins were frequently in contact."* This appears to me entirely probable.

BOATS AND APPURTENANCES.

Boats.—The simple craft of the Indians are alluded to in the earliest works on North America, but very little of a descriptive character is given, excepting in the first volume of De Bry, which contains an account of the manufacture of boats hollowed out of stems of trees.† It does not seem that in this country circumstances have favored the preservation of boats for a considerable time, the only case known to me being that recorded by Colonel Charles C. Jones. He says:—

Fig. 337.—Boat, exhumed near Savannah.

"In 1845, while digging a canal on one of the rice-plantations on the Savannah River, located only a few miles distant from the city of Savannah, at a depth of three feet and a half below the surface of the swamp, the workmen came upon a canoe embedded in the soil. It answered to the description of what is familiarly known as a *dug-out*, and had been fashioned from the trunk of a cypress-tree. About eleven feet long and thirty inches wide, its depth was scarcely more than ten inches. Both bow and stern were strengthened, each by a wooden brace kept in position by wooden pins passing through the sides of the canoe and entering the braces at either end. This boat curved upward at either end, so that the bow and stern rose above the middle portion. Located about three feet from the stern was a seat nine inches wide, consisting of a rude cypress-plank. For its reception the sides of the canoe had been notched three inches below the gunwales, and it was further kept in position by four wooden pins—two on each side—driven through the boat and entering the seat at either end, as in the case of the bow and stern braces.

"The bottom was flat, the sides rounding. No effort had been made to form

---

* Abbott: Primitive Industry; p. 64.
† See "Extracts."

a keel. The bow and stern were both pointed, and not unlike in their general outlines, the latter being more blunt than the former. At the top the sides were rather more than half an inch in thickness, increasing, however, as they descended and curved below the water-line.

"When cleaned and dried, this canoe weighed sixty pounds, and could be transported with the greatest facility by a single individual. The agency of fire had obviously been invoked in the construction of this little boat. While there were no marks of sharp cutting-tools, the evidence appeared conclusive that the charred portions of the wood, both within and without, had been carefully removed by rude incisive implements, probably of shell or stone. The plan of felling the tree and of hollowing out the log, as perpetuated in one of De Bry's illustrations, seems to have been observed in this instance. Regarding the regularity with which the outlines and the relative thicknesses of the sides of this boat had been preserved, one could but admire the care and skill with which that dangerous element, fire, had been made subservient to the uses of the primitive boat-builder. It is entirely probable that the ordinary stone celts, chisels, gouges, scrapers, or simple shells, were the only implements at command for the removal of the charred surface, as the cypress-tree was by degrees converted into the convenient *dug-out*. — — —

"This canoe had evidently lain for a very long time in its present position, and seemed to have settled gradually. There was an accumulation of forty inches of mud and soil above it, and around lay the rotting trunks, arms, and roots of forest-trees, which, during the lapse of years, had died and become intermingled with the *débris* of the swamp. Above the spot were growing cypress-trees as large and seemingly as old as any in the surrounding forest.

"It is difficult to form a satisfactory estimate of the age of this relic. That embedded cypress is, for an almost indefinite period, well-nigh indestructible by ordinary agencies, is capable of proof. We have but to instance the salt-marshes along the line of the Georgia coast, in not a few of which, at the depth of several feet below the surface, may still be found the clearly-defined and well-preserved traces of cypress-forests, consisting of limbs, trunks, knees, and roots. In former years, at least some of these salt-marshes must have been fresh-water swamps; and, without the violent intervention of some marked convulsion of nature, of which we have no record, and for which no plausible reason can be assigned, centuries must have elapsed before a gradual settling of the coast could have occurred to such an extent as to have admitted the influx of tidal waves converting cypress-swamps into extensive, uniform salt-marshes, destroying the original growth, and finally covering the fallen forests with mud to the depth of several feet.

"We are not aware that a sufficiently accurate record has been kept of the annual deposit of mud from the overflowing waters of the Savannah River, to enable us to derive from this source a plausible conjecture as to the age of this canoe. So many uncertainties enter into calculations of this character, that in most instances all attempts to arrive at definite results fall far short of satisfactory conclusions. All we know is, that this Indian canoe is old—older than the barge which conveyed Oglethorpe up the Savannah, when he first selected the home of the Yamacraws as a site for the future commercial metropolis of the colony of Georgia—more ancient, probably, than the statelier craft which carried the fortunes of the discoverer of this Western Continent.

"So far as our information extends, this is the first and only well-authenticated instance of the exhumation of an ancient canoe in this country. It is in just such a locality that we might have anticipated with greatest confidence the existence of such a relic. The general employment of bark and skin in the manufacture of their canoes by Northern Indians precludes all reasonable hope of finding ancient specimens made of such perishable materials."*

This canoe, Colonel Jones informs me, gradually yielded to decay after its exhumation.

Fig. 338.—Wooden toy-boat. Santa Cruz Island. (18178).

During his exploration of graves in California, Mr. Paul Schumacher discovered some wooden objects which I consider as toy-boats. Fig. 338 represents the best-preserved and smallest of them, which was found on Santa Cruz Island. It is a miniature flat-bottomed dug-out, measuring nearly seven inches in length, and showing at one end a perforation, evidently designed to receive the line by which the little canoe was guided. This specimen is a very creditable sample of Indian wood-carving.

Bailing-scoops.—In a former publication I have designated another wooden object, likewise obtained by Mr. Schumacher on Santa Cruz Island, as a bailing-vessel, because its form and material suggested that use.

Fig. 339 represents the specimen in question. It is skillfully cut out of one piece of wood, including the handle, and has a capacity of about one pint. The outline of this vessel, which is eight inches long with the handle, resembles that of an irregular rectangle with strongly-rounded angles. The upper edge opposite the handle is curved downward, as if by wear—a feature which led me

---

* Jones: Antiquities of the Southern Indians; p. 53, etc.; figure of canoe on p. 53. Colonel Jones kindly loaned me the cut.

to believe that the utensil served for bailing. While the bottom is sufficiently flat to allow the object to stand, the lower part of the excavation has a curved (concave) form. Like the toy-canoe just described, this vessel consists apparently of cedar-wood, the material having become very light in both instances— almost as light as the wood of the utensils extracted from the sites of lacustrine settlements in Switzerland. Unfortunately I am unable to state whether these two relics were found associated with manufactures of Caucasian origin or not.

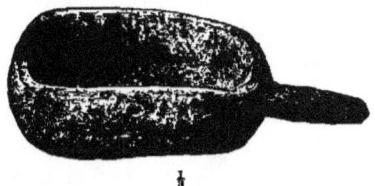

Fig. 339.—Wooden bailing-scoop (?). Santa Cruz Island. (18326).

Though I have called the original of Fig. 339 a bailing-scoop, I would by no means assert that it was used as such. It may have been a ladle or dipper.

Paddles.—Through the kindness of Mr. W. Wallace Tooker, referred to on page 126 of this publication, I am enabled to record the discovery of a fragmentary Indian paddle. It was extracted in the winter of 1880 from the mud of a creek at Canoe Place, Long Island, by a man engaged in eel-fishing.

Canoe Place (Niamuck in the Indian language) is a low, narrow isthmus between Peconic and Shinnecock Bays, and so called because the Indians were in the habit of hauling their canoes across it from bay to bay. Such operations are also performed by whites. Mr. Tooker has seen quite large sail-boats and smacks drawn across the isthmus on wheels, its narrowest part being less than half a mile in width.

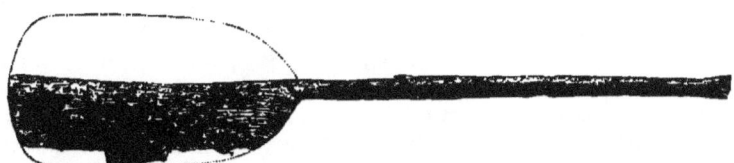

Fig. 340.—Paddle. Long Island.

As Fig. 340 shows, this paddle, which is thirty-four inches and one-fourth long, and made of one piece of oak, has lost one-half of its blade; but a restoration in dotted lines has been attempted. The relic belongs to Mr. Tooker, to whom I am indebted for the description and a photograph, after which the illustration was made.

I am not aware that other paddles have been found under similar circumstances in this country.

Anchor-stones.—Many years ago, while spending some days at Nanuet, a post-village in Rockland County, New York, I saw in a store, kept by a man who was in a small way a collector of aboriginal relics, two boulders of good size, each encircled by a groove around the middle. I had not seen such stones before, but concluded at once that they had served as anchors, not knowing any other use to which they could have been applied. These objects, I believe, are now generally considered as weights which were attached to strong lines (probably thongs) of the proper length, and used as primitive anchors to moor canoes to the shores, or to arrest, if need required, their drifting in mid-water. Yet smaller stones of this kind, too heavy for net-sinkers, may have been employed as weights to keep set-nets in place.

"Large angular pebbles or boulders, with deep encircling grooves," says Dr. Abbott, "have been frequently found in the Delaware River as well as in many of the larger creeks flowing into it. These grooved boulders, I believe, were used as anchoring-stones.

"One of these so-called anchors, found in the bed of Crosswick's Creek, near Bordentown, New Jersey, is a compact sandstone boulder, nearly a cube in shape, and weighs forty pounds. The groove divides the stone into equal parts, is evenly worked, and measures uniformly one inch in width and three-fourths of an inch in depth.

"This specimen was found embedded in mud, at a depth of nearly three feet from the present surface. Near it were found a dozen notched pebbles, a grooved stone axe, and several fragments of pottery.

"The circumstances under which this grooved boulder was found clearly indicate that it was used as an anchor; and its being associated with a small series of notched pebbles is as interesting as it is suggestive. Unlike the large notched pebbles referred to from the Water Gap,[*] this specimen could not have been used as an attachment to a net, but at once suggests the use of a boat; and as we know that these boats were in almost daily use, it is not probable that they were always drawn from the water when not in use."[†]

Two remarkable anchor-stones were sent, in 1882, to the National Museum

---

[*] See note on p. 158 of this publication.
[†] Abbott: Primitive Industry; p. 242, etc.

by Mr. John B. Wiggins, of Waverly, Tioga County, New York. Fig. 341 shows the form of one of them. It is made of a flattish boulder of fine-grained sandstone, more than three inches in thickness. The groove, which runs parallel with the longer sides of the boulder, is over an inch deep on the face shown in the illustration, and ground out its whole length, but much shallower on the opposite one, and there it seems to be a natural, yet artificially modified, depression in the boulder. This specimen, which weighs eighteen pounds and three-quarters, was discovered in August, 1881, near the middle of the Susquehanna River, in the neighborhood of Sayre, Bradford County, Pennsylvania, by Mr. Benjamin F. Coolbaugh, while engaged with a party in spearing fish. Seeing the object by the light of the torch, in passing over the place where it lay, he returned and secured it.

Fig. 341.—Anchor-stone. Found in the Susquehanna River, Pennsylvania. (59108).

The other specimen, somewhat smaller, and weighing not more than sixteen pounds and a half, is almost identical in shape with the one just described, and consists of the same kind of fine-grained sandstone. It was also obtained in 1881 by Mr. Coolbaugh, at Sayre, where it came to light while laborers, employed by a railroad-company, were clearing away the ground with a steam-shovel, to prepare a place for erecting machine-shops. The stone lay imbedded in gravel and sand ten feet below the surface.

Fig. 342 on the following page, representing an anchor-stone of another form, is made after a drawing sent to me by its owner, Dr. J. F. Snyder, mentioned on page 126 of this work. It was found, some years ago, in the bed of the

Illinois River, near the mouth of the Sangamon (Illinois), while United States engineers were engaged in dredging-operations. This stone consists of compact carboniferous sandstone of yellow color, and weighs thirty-four pounds and a half. Its dimensions, as given by Dr. Snyder, are as follows:—

Diameter	12 inches.
Thickness in the middle	6½ "
Width of groove	1¼ inch.
Depth of groove	¾ "

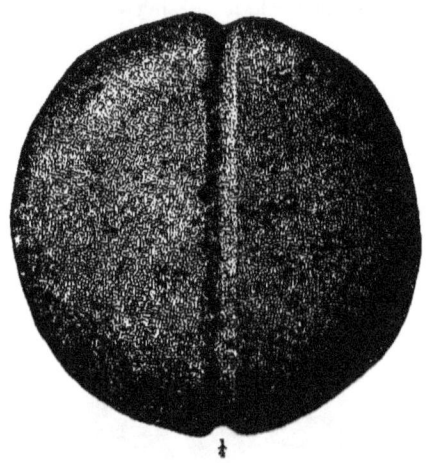

FIG. 342.—Anchor-stone. Found in the Illinois River, Illinois.

"The anchor-stone of which you have a drawing," observes Dr. Snyder, "is altogether a work of art. It is not smooth, but 'pecked' all over, probably with a sharp-pointed flint. It evidently has been worked to its present dimensions and shape from a rough block of sandstone by long-continued, patient labor. The groove in it is neatly cut, and also shows the traces of pecking.

"I have secured two other anchor-stones from the banks of the Illinois River, since I sent you the drawing of this one; but neither of them is as symmetrically shaped. The largest of the two is unfinished, and consists of the same kind of sandstone. The angles of the rough block have been only partially pecked down, and the groove is not deep. I did not weigh it; but I think it will bear down forty-five or fifty pounds.

"The other one is apparently natural in its form: a smooth, water-worn river-rock, two inches and a half in thickness, twelve in diameter, and slightly concavo-convex; it is nearly circular, with rounded edges. Across one of its faces runs a groove, an inch or more wide, but not deep; sufficient, however, to indicate its use. It is a white stone, of silicious character, I think, and harder than the sandrock. This object was exhumed from an old Indian grave, or rather from a low, flat sand-mound, on the bank of the Illinois River, near Beardstown, in this county (Cass). The enclosed skeleton was very much decayed, extended at full length, with the head to the east, and the back of the skull lying in the concave surface of the stone, which seemed to have been placed as a pillow under the occiput of the corpse. Under each shoulder and each hip, and under each heel of the skeleton was found a common, smooth water-worn pebble as large as a hen's egg. A few flint arrow-points and three scales of the alligator-gar completed the sepulchral deposit. I have not weighed this stone, but judge that it will not exceed twenty-five pounds."

In another communication Dr. Snyder speaks of an anchor-stone, now destroyed, which was also found in the same neighborhood in the bed of the Illinois River, and was similar to that here figured. "It was," he says, "almost an exact copy of mine, in material, dimensions, and weight."

Very large notched pebbles and perforated stone slabs might have been used as anchor-stones; but specimens thus modified, to which I could assign that application with any degree of positiveness, have not fallen under my notice.

Stones are still employed instead of anchors for small craft in Europe as well as in North America, and probably all over the world. With regard to North American anchor-stones, therefore, some discrimination is required to discover whether an object of this class is a relic of the former inhabitants or of their white successors, and there may be cases in which a proper distinction becomes well-nigh impossible. Our fishermen on the great lakes and rivers almost universally use stones in lieu of anchors. On the Susquehanna, I am informed, they employ an unaltered stone slab of an elongated, approximately rectangular form, preferring one which is naturally indented or inwardly curved on one of its longer sides, in order to give a firm hold to the line. Such stones weigh, according to the current in which they are used, from twenty-five to fifty pounds.

For the following information, bearing on the employment of anchor-stones in Virginia, I am indebted to Professor Otis T. Mason:—

"In response to your inquiry concerning the use of anchor-stones by the negroes of Virginia, I would state that I have many a time gone out in a dug-out canoe with negroes or 'poor whites' to catch the white cat-fish found only in the running water of the middle bed, or channel, of the streams. The fisherman was provided with two strong cedar-poles, a clothes-line, a number of hooks on short lines, and a square slab of stone attached to about twenty feet of rope for an anchor. This stone weighed fifteen pounds or more, and its form was modified only sufficiently to secure the crosswise attachment of the rope. The poles were stuck in the mud on either side of the channel, and the clothes-line stretched between. The baited hooks were distributed along the line at convenient distances, and the dug-out anchored to await results. Shortly a tugging at the line would indicate business, and the stern of the canoe would be poled to the vicinity of the excited hook. The fish secured and the hook rebaited, the sportsman lay by for a new conquest. I am quite sure anchor-stones were employed also in the little boats used on plantations near salt water, to catch oysters for home consumption."

The New England fishermen, also, in order to avoid expenses, replace anchors by stones, as shown in the following examples.

FIG. 343.—"Underrunning rock." Massachusetts. (54346).

I represent in Fig. 343 one of the so-called "underrunning rocks," which are attached to the end of trawl-lines, to sink them to the bottom. The object here figured is a granite boulder of an ovoid form, showing no other alteration by art than a drilled hole for receiving a grooved wooden pin to which the rope is attached. Obtained at Gloucester, Massachusetts.

Fig. 344 presents the form of a New England "killick," used as an anchor for a fishing-boat, and also for mooring gill-nets, fish-traps, and trawl-lines. It is an artificially-prepared, grooved granite slab of square outline, firmly set into a somewhat anchor-like wooden structure, terminating in flukes at the base—a curious combination of the anchor-stone and the anchor. From Rockport, Massachusetts.

FIG. 344.—"Killick." Massachusetts. (54417).

PREHISTORIC STRUCTURES CONNECTED WITH FISHING.

Fish-preserves.—Colonel Charles C. Jones, in his account of the mounds in the State of Georgia, draws attention to artificial excavations occurring in the immediate vicinity of some of the earthworks, and assigns to these excavations the character of fish-preserves. He first notices the earthworks located upon the right bank of the Etowah River, on the plantation of Colonel Lewis Tumlin, a few miles from Cartersville, in Bartow County. I reproduce on page 198 his plan of the works as Fig. 345, and quote his statements relative to them:—

"Viewed as a whole," he says, "this group is the most remarkable within the confines of the State. These mounds are situated in the midst of a beautiful and fertile valley. They occupy a central position in an area of some fifty acres, bounded on the south and east by the Etowah River, and on the north and west by a large ditch or artificial canal, which at its lower end communicates directly with the river. This moat (*G G*) at present varies in depth from five to twenty-five feet, and in width from twenty to seventy-five feet. No parapets or earth-walls appear upon its edges. Along its line are two reservoirs (*D D*), of about an acre each, possessing an average depth of not less than twenty feet, and its upper end expands into an artificial pond (*P*), elliptical in form, and somewhat deeper than the excavations mentioned.

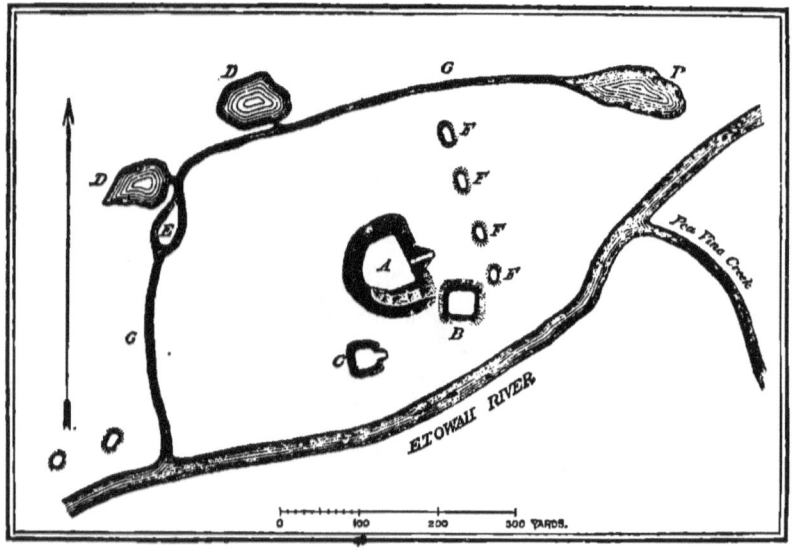

Fig. 345.—Earthworks in the Etowah Valley.

"Within the enclosure formed by this moat and the river are seven mounds. Three of them are pre-eminent in size, the one designated in the accompanying plan by the letter *A* far surpassing the others both in its proportions and in the degree of interest which attaches to it. — — —

"The central tumulus rises about sixty-five feet above the level of the valley. It is entirely artificial, consisting wholly of the earth taken from the moat and the excavations, in connection with the soil collected around its base. It has received no assistance whatever from any natural hill or elevation.

"In general outline it may be regarded as quadrangular, if we disregard a slight angle to the south. That taken into account, its form is pentagonal. — — — On its summit this tumulus is nearly level. Shorn of the luxuriant vegetation and tall forest-trees which at one time crowned it on every side, the outlines of this mound stand in bold relief. Its angles are still sharply defined. The established approach to the top is from the east. Its ascent was accomplished through the intervention of terraces, rising one above the other—inclined planes leading from the one to the other. These terraces are sixty-five feet in width, and extend from the mound toward the southeast. Near the eastern angle a pathway leads to the top; but it does not appear to have been intended for very general use. May it not have been designed for the priesthood alone, while, assembled upon the broad terraces, the worshipers gave solemn heed to the religious ceremonies performed upon the eastern summit of this ancient temple?

"East of this large central mound—and so near that their flanks meet and mingle—stands a smaller mound about thirty-five feet high, originally quadrangular, now nearly circular in form, and with a summit diameter of one hundred feet. From its western slope is an easy and immediate communication with the terraces of the central tumulus. This mound is designated in the plan by the letter B. Two hundred and fifty feet in a westerly direction from this mound, and distant some sixty feet in a southerly direction from the central mound, is the third (C) and last of this immediate group. Pentagonal in form, it possesses an altitude of twenty-three feet. It is uniformly level at the top. — — —

"East of this group, and within the enclosure, is a chain of four sepulchral mounds ($F\ F\ F\ F$), ovoidal in shape. Little individual interest attaches to them. Nothing, aside from their location in the vicinity of those larger tumuli and their being within the area formed by the canal and the river, distinguishes them from numerous earth-mounds scattered here and there throughout the length and breadth of the Etowah and Oostenaula Valleys.

"The artificial elevation E, lying northwest of the central group, is remarkable for its superficial area, and is completely surrounded by the moat which, at that point, divides with a view to its enclosure. The slope of the sides of these tumuli is just such as would be assumed by gradual accretions of earth successively deposited in small quantities from above."

Having expressed, in the next paragraph, his opinion that the central mound served as a temple of the sun, Colonel Jones continues:—

"In the true relation of the vicissitudes which attended the Governor Don Hernando de Soto, and some nobles of Portugal in the discovery of the Province of Florida, we are informed by the Gentleman of Elvas that 'on Wednesday, the nineteenth day of June, the Governor entered Pacaha, and took quarters in the town where the Cacique was accustomed to reside. It was enclosed, and very large. In the towers and the palisade were many loopholes. There was much dry maize, and the new was in great quantity throughout the fields. At the distance of half a league to a league off were large towns, all of them surrounded with stockades. Where the Governor stayed was a great lake near to the enclosure; and the water entered a ditch that well-nigh went round the town. From the River Grande to the lake was a canal, through which the fish came into it, and where the Chief kept them for his eating and pastime. With nets that were found in the place, as many were taken as need required; and however much might be the casting, there was never any lack of them. — — — The Cacique of Casqui many times sent large presents of fish, shawls, and skins."*

"While the earth removed in the construction of the ditch and excavations was primarily employed in the erection of the tumuli within the enclosure, while they may in one sense be regarded as the sources of the mounds, and while their sizes and depths were, to a certain extent, regulated by the supply of material requisite for the completion of the projected truncated pyramid and its dependent mounds, we are of opinion that, during the progress of the entire work, direct reference was had to the final use of these excavations, and of this canal as fish-preserves, whence the priests, caciques, and noted personages of the nation, who probably dwelt within the enclosure formed by the moat and the river, could at all seasons derive an abundant supply of fish. The canal leading from the artificial pond in which it takes its rise communicates directly with both reservoirs, and, after passing them, empties into the Etowah. Through this canal fishes could have been readily introduced from the river into all three of these artificial lakes, and there propagated. Cane or wooden wears—in such common use among the Southern Indians during the sixteenth century—would have prevented all escape, and thus these reservoirs would have answered the purposes of *fish-preserves*. Such we believe them to have been."†

Somewhat similar excavations accompanying tumular erections were seen by Colonel Jones in other parts of Georgia, namely, in the neighborhood of two mounds lying close to the left bank of the Savannah River, on the Mason plantation, twelve or fifteen miles below the city of Augusta; and on the site of the "Messier Mound," located on Messier's plantation in Early County, about twelve miles east of the Chattahoochee River.‡ Yet in these instances they present less marked features than in the case of the mound-group in the Etowah Valley.

I am not aware that excavations bearing the distinct character of fish-preserves have been noticed in connection with the numerous mounds and mural earthworks in Ohio.

Fish-pens.—I am indebted to my esteemed correspondent, Mr. William L.

---

* Narratives of the Career of Hernando de Soto, etc.; p. 112, etc.

† Jones: Antiquities of the Southern Indians; p. 186, etc.

‡ Ibid.; p. 152, etc.; p. 166, etc.

PREHISTORIC STRUCTURES CONNECTED WITH FISHING. 201

Stone—the well-known author—for the following account of a stone structure, evidently a fish-pen, in the State of New York:—

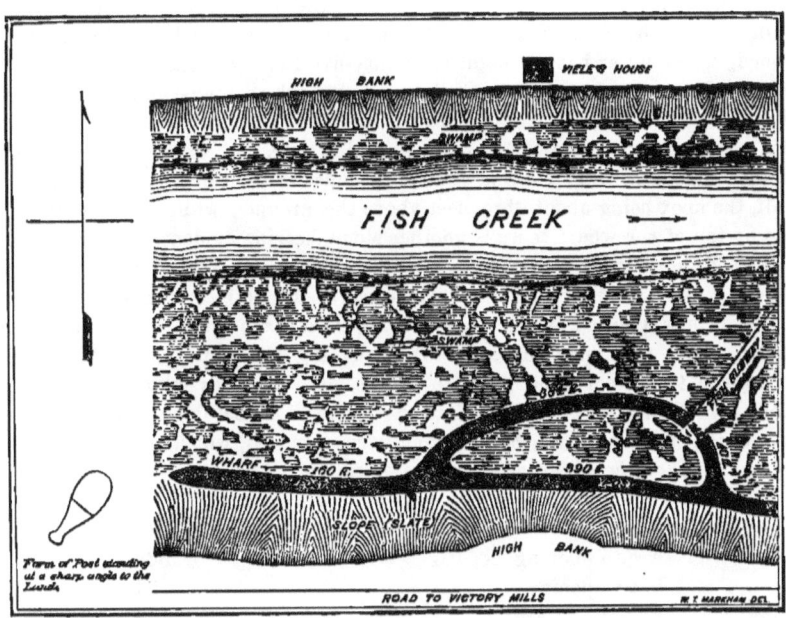

FIG. 346.—Stone fish-pen. Saratoga County, New York.

"When at Saratoga Springs, in the summer of 1879, Mr. Benjamin R. Viele, who resides on the left or north bank of Fish Creek (the outlet of Saratoga Lake, running into the Hudson), called my attention to what he considered an ancient Indian work; and accordingly, the following day, in company with Mr. James M. Andrews, Jr., I drove over to his house. Mr. Viele took us in a boat across Fish Creek to the spot he had described; and the afternoon was spent in a careful investigation of the work. At a point directly opposite the Viele farm-house, between the creek and the high slate bank on the top of which runs the road to Victory Mills, there is a large, open swamp. In this swamp, extending in an irregular semi-circular form from the high bank, is a solid wall built of cobble-stones, regularly laid up and ranging in width from six to eight feet, and enclosing an area of about half an acre. On each side of the wall a pole can be run down in the marshy muck from sixteen to twenty feet. In shape it is, as

R 26

before stated, nearly a semi-circle, both ends resting on, or rather terminating at, the bank, the latter forming the base of a segment, or a chord of a circle. It is continuous save toward its eastern extremity, where there is a break or gap of twenty-four feet. Connecting the ends of the semi-circle is a straight wall built close to the shore, and at the foot of the slate bank or bluff already mentioned, which latter has a height of twenty-five feet. Beyond the curve to the west, and connected with this straight stone work, extends another wall, the object of which is not apparent, unless it served as a wharf. Near the centre of this shore wall, or chord of the arc, within the weir, and standing on the edge of the embankment, is a stone post of curious form, deeply embedded in the wall, the apex being about three feet above the ground; while near the middle and on top of the wharf there is another stone, bearing evidence of having long withstood the ravages of time. It is two feet long, with a small round knob as a head, worn smooth by friction. Its broad pedestal is surrounded by large stones, deeply planted, which hold it firmly at a sharp angle to the land. A glance at the accompanying map, drawn by my friend, Mr. W. T. Markham, will make this description plain to the reader. The day following my visit, Hon. J. P. Butler and Professor Henry McGuier, of Saratoga Springs, drove over to the spot, and took the following measurements, which may prove valuable to the scientific delver after archæological data:—

Descriptive.	Feet.
Arc to opening	384
Weir opening	24
Remaining arc	40
Chord of arc (stone or shore wall)	390
Axis of arc	84
Wharf	160

"The cobble-stones have all been brought from a field three-fourths of a mile distant.

"This structure is evidently not the work of whites, as may be conjectured from the facts that the oldest settler has no record or tradition regarding it, and that there are directly upon the top of the wall, in different places, stumps of white oak betokening a growth of several centuries. The wall has so much sunk that it is at present but two feet above the water of the swamp. It does not appear to have been the work of the aborigines inhabiting the country when discovered; for had it been, those Indians would have had a tradition regarding its origin, and would not have failed to communicate it to the early settlers, by whom, in turn, it would have been transmitted to their children and grandchildren, many of the latter of whom are yet living. Yet that it was meant to serve some important purpose is evident from the great labor involved in its construction. To a nomadic people, accustomed to depend almost entirely on the uncertainties of the chase for support, the question of food for use in their warlike expeditions was of the first consequence.

"Now, the plan pursued by the Iroquois in hunting deer and other wild animals, as described by a Jesuit missionary, Father Brulé, who lived among them in the seventeenth century, was as follows:—

'On the borders of a neighboring river twenty-five of the Indians had been busied ten days in preparing for their annual deer-hunt. They planted posts interlaced with boughs in two straight, converging lines, each extending more than half a mile through forests and swamps. At the angle where they met was made a strong enclosure, like a pound. At dawn of day the hunters spread themselves through the woods, and advanced with shouts and clattering of sticks, driving the deer before them into the enclosure, where others lay in wait, to dispatch them with arrows and spears.'

"Our belief, therefore, is that the same plan was followed by the builders of the work in the taking of fish, and that this enclosure was designed simply as an immense trap in which to catch large quantities of that game, to be afterward smoked and laid aside for the year's food. It is a well-known fact that in colonial times, before the mills and dams were erected at Schuylerville by General Philip Schuyler in 1760, herring and shad in enormous shoals were in the habit of running in the spring up the Hudson into Fish Creek (hence the name), and thence through Saratoga Lake and the Kayaderosseras Creek even to Rock City Falls.* At this season of the year the swamp along the sides of the creek is overflowed to the depth of several feet. Is it then not possible, probable even, that the Indians at this time of the year, in their canoes, beat the creek, until, approaching nearer and nearer, large quantities of herring and shad would be driven through the gap in the wall into the enclosure? And this appears the more reasonable when it is remembered that fish, season after season, have their 'run-ways' as well as deer. Observation had shown the Indians that the fish, at this part of the creek, came across from the north to the south bank; and hence the opening left directly opposite this angle of the stream—thus affording the more easy driving of the fish into the enclosure. Then having driven the fish into this immense 'eel-pot' and closed the gap with brush, they could at their convenience either scoop them up, or, awaiting the subsidence of the water, capture the fish, thus left high and dry, an easy prize.

---

* Mr. Henry Wagman, of Old Saratoga, informs me that when his grandmother (one of the very earliest settlers) first came into the country, she and her neighbors were in the habit of scooping up in their aprons out of Fish Creek quantities of these fish.

"Nor is it necessary to assume that high water, then as now, covered the swamp in the spring. The lay of the land and the observations of the settlers for the last seventy-five years clearly show that the creek formerly washed the high bank seen in the accompanying sketch, and that it gradually has been filling in. Indeed, every few years the Victory Mills Company are obliged to dredge out the creek to keep the supply of water from failing. This tallies also with my own observation; for a spot in the middle of the creek over which, fifteen years since, my old schoolmate, W. S. Mersereau, and myself anchored our boat in ten feet of water, has now become a bank of mud rising a foot above the water. The rapidity of this filling-in process would seem to show that when the wall was erected, it was built in the shallow water of the stream—a supposition which makes the use to which the enclosure was put, as above hinted, still more probable.

"The singular stones briefly described suggest by their positions the purposes they served. The one last mentioned was probably the post to which the Indians made fast their chain of canoes stretching diagonally across the stream, when engaged in beating back and preventing the fish from running up and past the opening in the weir (see map). The other larger stone (within the weir) may have been used by the Indians in time of war or alarm, to secure and protect their fleet of war-canoes, by attaching them with thongs to this firmly-imbedded rock. Thus these works would secure their fleet from sudden attack or surprise, until their forces could rally from the hill and prevent their capture—the high bluffs, covered with large oaks, securing protection to the defenders of the weir. This work, therefore, may have served a double purpose, viz., to catch fish during peace, and as a harbor and place of protection for their canoes in time of war. When, however, the slate reefs were worn away below in the bed of the creek, and the water gradually subsided to its present limits, these works became useless and were consequently abandoned. There are abundant evidences to show that at one time Saratoga Lake (the source of Fish Creek) was twenty to thirty feet higher.

"I offer these suggestions because, in the present stage of archæological investigation, any fact that throws light upon the customs and habits of the former inhabitants of this country must be of value."

There are probably similar structures in this country, which have not yet attracted the attention of observers.

REPRESENTATIONS OF FISHES, AQUATIC MAMMALS, ETC.

In the first part of this work I have reproduced a series of designs of fishes and aquatic mammals, executed by the cave-men of Europe, and bearing witness to their artistic bent as well as to their appreciation of the advantages they derived from these denizens of the water. It may not be out of place if I give some account of corresponding productions of the former inhabitants of this country, who seem, however, to have preferred in similar imitations the plastic to the graphic mode of execution, all specimens to which I can refer being either pipes, or simply representations in stone or shell, or clay vessels of a fish-form.

Pipes.—I am not aware that there is among the many so-called "platform-pipes," exhumed from tumuli in Ohio and other western states, a single one which exhibits a fish as principal object, while such imitations of birds, quadrupeds, and even amphibians, are by no means rare. Many pipes of this description, all made of stone, were obtained by Messrs. Squier and Davis, in the course of their exploration of earthworks in Ohio, from mounds within an embankment of earth close to the Scioto River, four miles north of Chillicothe. This enclosure, somewhat in the shape of a square with strongly-rounded angles, comprises an area of thirteen acres, over which twenty-three mounds are (or were) scattered without much regularity. It has been called "Mound City," from the great number of mounds within its precinct. In digging into the mounds, the explorers discovered in many of them hearths, which furnished a great number of relics; and from one of the hearths nearly two hundred of the above-mentioned pipes were taken, not all entire, but partly cracked by the action of fire, or otherwise damaged. In two of these pipes fishes are represented, but merely as accessories to the principal figures, which form the receptacles of the smoking-material.

Fig. 347. Fig. 348.

Figs. 347 and 348.—Stone pipes representing a heron feeding on a fish, and an otter with a fish in its mouth. Mound near Chillicothe.

Fig. 347 shows the imitation of a tufted heron in the act of striking a fish. It is a very good carving, composed of a brownish, speckled stone of no great hardness.* The other pipe, Fig. 348, is carved in the shape of the fore-part of

---

* Squier and Davis: Ancient Monuments; p. 259.

an animal with a fish in its mouth. Squier and Davis call this animal an otter;[*] Mr. Stevens, however, supposes it to be the lamantin, manatee, or sea-cow (*Trichechus manatus*, Lin.), a mammal not met in the higher latitudes of North America, but only on the coast of Florida.[†] The latter is a herbivorous animal, and hence the artist probably would not have carved its likeness with a prey befitting a carnivore. The first suggestion, therefore, may be the correct one.[‡] This specimen consists of a material analogous to that composing the heron-pipe, and both are now in the Blackmore Museum, at Salisbury, England.

FIG. 349.—Clay pipe in the shape of a fish (?). Chattanooga.

The original of Fig. 349 is a pipe of burned clay, found at a considerable depth below the surface, near Chattanooga, Tennessee, and belonging to Dr. J. B. Nicklin, of that place. It is moulded in the form of what appears to be a fish with widely-opened mouth, feebly-expressed fins, and unforked tail. The eyes are indicated by roundish incisions, and the body is marked on both sides with two rows of rudely-engraved lines, meeting in a median line. The form of the fish appears to be altogether conventional, as none of the experts in ichthyology whom I consulted was able to determine its character.[§]

Imitations in Stone and Shell.—Prehistoric carvings in stone or other material, exhibiting the forms of fishes and aquatic mammals, it appears, have not frequently been discovered in this country. Such as have fallen under my notice, directly or indirectly, are here described.

Fig. 350 represents a rude imitation of a fish, preserved in the National Museum. It consists of a rough, flat piece of greenish-gray slate, not quite half an inch in thickness, and ground (even polished) around the edge; the indenta-

---

[*] Squier and Davis: Ancient Monuments; p. 257.
[†] Stevens: Flint Chips; p. 429.
[‡] There are among the pipes of "Mound City" several thought to be imitations of the lamantin.
[§] The pipe has even been thought to represent the head of a snake.

tion of the tail, however, is produced by the process of pecking. Mouth and eyes are indicated on both sides by incised lines. This specimen was obtained by Lieutenant F. W. Ring from shell-heaps on the Stikine River, Alaska, which Mr. Dall ascribes to a pre-Indian Innuit population. It remains uncertain whether this rude relic was a mere trinket, or had some significance as an amulet or a charm.

FIG. 350.—Piece of slate worked into the likeness of a fish. Alaska. (9796).

Similar doubts exist with regard to the object represented in Fig. 351. It is a rather thin piece of iridescent *Haliotis*-shell, cut with some skill into the shape of a fish. The specimen, found by Mr. Schumacher on San Nicolas Island, may have been a charm, or simply an ornament, if, indeed, it was not designed for a more practical use, namely, that of an artificial bait employed in fishing with a line. However, in view of its uncertain character, I have deemed it preferable to refer to it merely as a fish-representation.

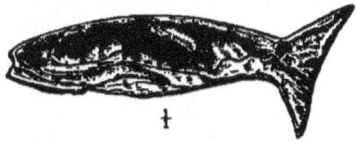

FIG. 351.—Fish-shaped object of *Haliotis*-shell. San Nicolas Island. (20429).

The original of Fig. 352 on page 208, first brought to notice by Professor Putnam, was dug out of the ground in a garden at Ipswich, Essex County, Massachusetts. The neighborhood of this place is mentioned as one particulary rich in stone relics. I give Professor Putnam's description of the object in full:—

"This stone was evidently carved with care for the purpose of being worn as an ornament, and was probably suspended from the neck. It is of a soft slate, easily cut with a sharp, hard stone. The markings left in various places by the carver, showing where his tool had slipped, indicate that no very delicate instrument had been used, while the several grooves, made to carry out the idea of the sculptor, indicate as plainly that the instrument by which they were made had what we should call a rounded edge, like that of a dull hatchet, as the grooves are wider at the top than at the bottom, and the striæ show that they were made by a sort of sawing motion, or a rubbing of the instrument backwards and forwards. In fact, the carver's tool might have been almost any stone implement, from an arrow-head to a skin-scraper, or any piece of hard, roughly-chipped stone.

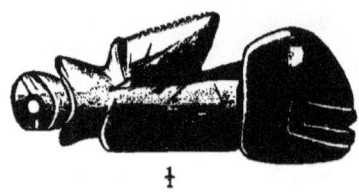

FIG. 352.—Stone-carving representing a fish. Ipswich.

"The figure represents the stone of natural size, its total length being two and a half inches. It is of general uniform thickness, about one-fifth of an inch, except where the angles are slightly rounded off on the front of the head and on the abdominal outline, and the portion representing the forked tail, or caudal fin, which is rapidly and symmetrically thinned to its edges, as is the notched portion representing the dorsal fin.

"The carving was evidently intended to represent a fish, with some peculiar ideas of the artist added and several important characters left out. The three longitudinal grooves in front represent the mouth and jaws, while the transverse groove at their termination gives a limit to the length of the jaw, and a very decided groove on the under side divides the under jaw into its right and left portions. The eyes are represented as slight depressions at the top of the head. The head is separated from the abdominal portion by a decided groove, and the caudal fin is well represented by the forked portion, from the centre of which the rounded termination of the whole projects. In this part there is an irregularly made hole of a size large enough to allow a strong cord to pass through for the purpose of suspension. The portion of the sculpture rising in the place of a dorsal fin is in several ways a singular conception of the ancient carver. While holding the position of a dorsal fin, it points the wrong way, if we regard the portion looking so much like a shark's tooth as intended to represent the fin as a whole. It is very likely that the designer wished to show that the fin was not connected with the head, and, as he was confined by the length of the piece of stone, after making the head so much out of proportion, he was forced to cut under the anterior portion of the fin, in order to express the fact. If we regard it in this light, the notches on the upper edge may be considered as indicating the fin-rays; but the figure best shows the character of the sculpture, and persons interested can draw their own conclusions.

"The symmetry of the whole carving is well carried out, both sides being alike, with the exception that the raised portion at the posterior part of what I have called the dorsal fin is a little more marked on the left side than on the right, and the edge on the same side is surrounded by a faint, irregularly-drawn line.

"The carving was, I think, unquestionably made by an Indian of the tribe once numerous in this vicinity, and, as it was almost beyond a doubt cut by a stone tool of some kind, it must be considered as quite an ancient work of art, probably worn as a 'medicine,' and possibly indicated either the name of the wearer or that he was a noted fisherman."*

This specimen is probably still in possession of the finder.

Professor Putnam has also given an account of a stone-carving representing a cetacean animal, preserved in the collection of the Amesbury Natural History Club. It is here represented in two views as Fig. 353. I describe it in his own words, merely changing the past into the present tense:—

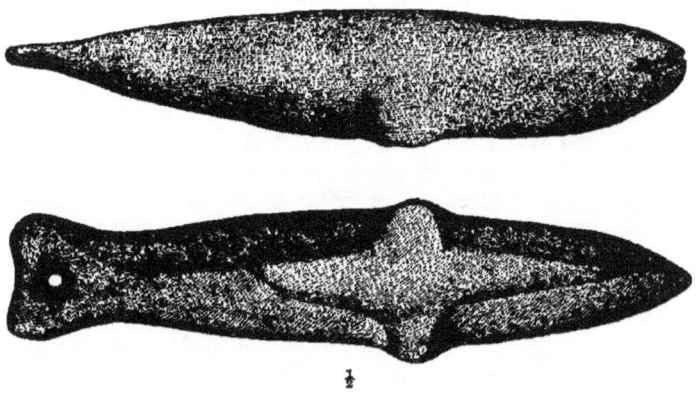

Fig. 353.—Stone-carving in the form of a cetacean. Seabrook.

"It rudely represents a porpoise, or, still better, a white whale or *Beluga*, as it has no protuberance representing the dorsal fin of the porpoise, and the

---

* Putnam: Description of an Ancient Indian Carving, found in Ipswich, Mass.; Bulletin of the Essex Institute, Vol. IV, No. 11.

Beluga is without the fin. The flippers or pectoral fins are represented by the protuberances on the sides, and the mouth is cut in and well indicated. The broad horizontal tail is decidedly cetacean in character, and the whole carving, though rudely done by picking the syenitic rock, from which it is made, with stone implements, is yet so characteristic as to indicate at once that a porpoise or Beluga was intended. A hole through the portion representing the tail shows that the object was suspended, but the stone is so large and heavy that it can hardly be classed as a personal ornament, though it is probably to be regarded as a totem. It measures ten inches in length by about two in depth at the pectoral fins, and is about two and a quarter inches wide across the pectorals as measured on the under side. This interesting specimen was found at Seabrook, New Hampshire, and it is said that two other similarly worked stones have been found at the same place. The figures here given represent the 'totem' in profile and from the under side."*

Among the relics collected by Mr. Schumacher on the Santa Barbara Islands is a series of curious stone-sculptures, in some of which certain animals can be recognized, while others are so conventional in execution that it requires much fancy to ascribe to them any definite character. It is probable, at any rate, that they represent charms, perhaps designed to insure the capture of the animals they are intended to imitate. M. Léon de Cessac likewise obtained a number of such objects on San Nicolas Island, and he has described them with great precision.† He calls them fetiches; but I hardly think this term here applicable in its English acceptation.

I give representations of two specimens found by Mr. Schumacher on San Nicolas Island, and both carved from a greenish-gray steatitic material.

The original of Fig. 354 seems to be a conventional representation of some cetacean animal, the identification of which would be a difficult task. The maker, perhaps, thought of the fin-back (*Balænoptera*) or killer (*Orca*). The base of the figure measures one inch from fin to fin, insomuch that it will stand when placed on a level surface.

The other specimen, shown in Fig. 355, is an imitation of a seal, the general contour of the figure and the distinct flippers leaving no doubt as to its character. This object is much weathered all over by exposure, and the original of Fig. 354 on the side not seen in the illustration. Both are evidently old.

---

* Putnam : Description of a Carved Stone representing a Cetacean, found at Seabrook, N. H.; Bulletin of the Essex Institute; Vol. V, June, 1873.

† De Cessac : Observations sur des Fétiches de Pierre sculptés en forme d'Animaux, découverts à l'Île de San Nicolas (Californie); Revue d'Ethnographie, publiée sous la Direction de M. le Dr. Hamy; Vol. I, Paris, 1882; p. 30, etc.

Many carvings of ivory, bone, and stone, in the shape of fishes, whales, seals, etc., derived from Indians and Innuits of the Northwest Coast, are exhibited in the National Museum. Some of these specimens probably represent

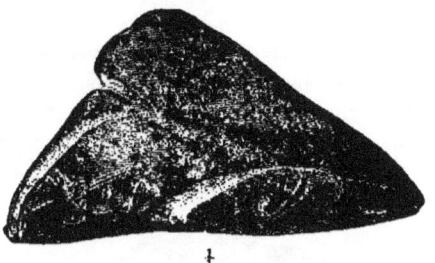

FIG. 354.—Stone-carving representing a cetacean. San Nicolas Island. (20426).

charms, while others, perhaps, have a totemic or mythological significance; not a few may be nothing but trinkets. I have not at present sufficient data for a proper characterization.

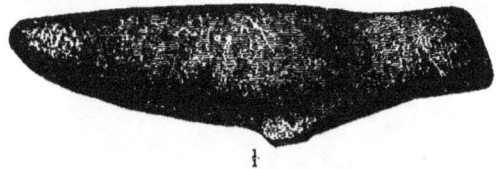

FIG. 355.—Stone-carving in the shape of a seal. San Nicolas Island. (20428).

Clay Vessels.—There are in the National Museum a few of the fish-shaped vessels to which allusion was made. The most characteristic among these objects, which were obtained from mounds and burial-grounds in the Mississippi Valley, is represented in Fig. 356 on the following page.

It was presented by General J. H. Devereux, with several other specimens of pottery, which had been exhumed from a burial-site adjacent to the Mississippi, nearly nineteen miles (measured with the stream) below Helena, in Phillips County, Arkansas.* The object seen from above, as in the illustration,

---

* For the following communication relative to the discovery of this burial-place and its character, I am indebted to General Devereux:—

"The specimens were procured during the year 1859, and under the following circumstances, as related to me by Mr. Jerome B. Pillow, a brother of General Gideon J. Pillow. Mr. Pillow's plantation was to be protected by a levee, and he had undertaken to build it.

"In constructing the levee across the two lakes, called Long Lake and Old Town Lake, a large quantity of

presents the form of a fish, in which ichthyologists have recognized the sun-fish (*Pomotis*), an inhabitant of the Mississippi River. Its distinctive features are said to be rendered with sufficient faithfulness to permit identification. The neck of this interesting piece of pottery, which consists of grayish clay with a slight admixture of pounded shells, measures a little more than an inch in height; its lower part is rounded like that of a bowl, and terminates in a flat base on which the vessel can stand. The height from the bottom to the rim of the neck is exactly four inches. The other clay vessels of this form on exhibition in the National Museum likewise seem to be intended to represent the sun-fish; but they are less expressive in character than the object here figured.

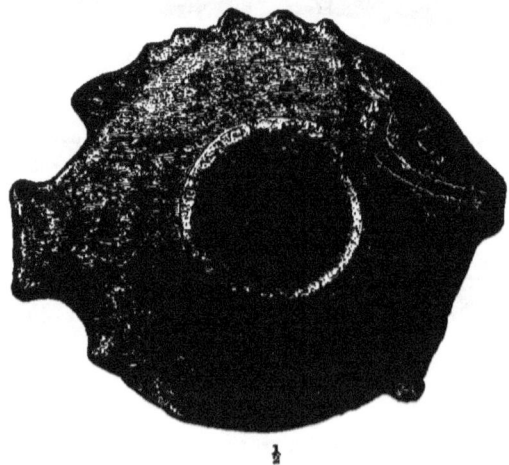

FIG. 356.—Clay vessel made in imitation of the sun-fish. Arkansas. (7293).

earth was needed, to procure which Mr. Pillow commenced removing the material from what turned out to have been the site of an ancient cemetery of great extent. Hundreds of human skeletons of all ages and both sexes were exhumed, and generally some article of pottery was found near each skeleton. The bodies had been buried in a sitting posture, and were found from three to ten feet below the surface, the bones being in all cases in a perfect state of preservation. Trees from three to five feet in diameter were growing near the human remains, and, as indicative of the antiquity of the burial-place, one of the trees particularly noted and described by Mr. Pillow was a sassafras-tree, which, having attained the diameter of five feet, had passed from maturity into natural and gradul decay, until withered and wasted away; only its roots were then sound.

"There had been no previous knowledge or record of this ancient cemetery; but a legend of the early settlers had located at or near this spot the camp in which De Soto wintered in ascending the Mississippi. It is the highest elevation of land for many miles along the river.

"Mr. Pillow secured at least fifty perfect specimens of pottery, of which I procured several which are now in the Smithsonian Institution. Some of the finest of the vessels I could not obtain. One of them, in the shape of a quadruped, and of a capacity of several quarts, was of great interest to me, because I had seen a similar vessel taken from a grave in Egypt."

REPRESENTATIONS OF FISHES, AQUATIC MAMMALS, ETC.   213

Fig. 357 represents a fish-shaped vessel found during the explorations of aboriginal burial-places in Southeastern Missouri, in the region where New Madrid is situated. These explorations, as known, brought to light a large number of clay vessels. The figure is copied from a quarto volume prepared under the auspices of the Archæological Section of the Saint Louis Academy of Science.* The vessel is thus described:— "A very neat specimen of baked ware; the color is a pale yellow, and the curves denoting the scales are painted in white." My endeavors to learn under what special circumstances it was found, and where it is preserved, proved fruitless.

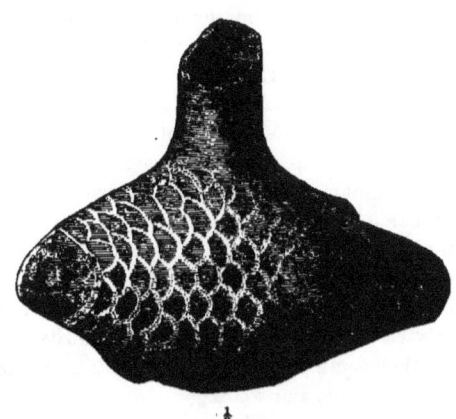

FIG. 357.—Fish-shaped clay vessel. Missouri.

This specimen of pottery bears much resemblance to a certain class of fish-shaped Peruvian vessels, of which mention will be made in the appendix to this work.

Delineations.—The notched stone sinker represented in Fig. 261 on page 160 is the only object in the National Museum, which has a bearing on prehistoric fishing in the present territory of Mexico. Upon inquiry, I learned from Sr. Don Gumesindo Mendoza, Director of the *Museo Nacional* of Mexico, that relics illustrative of fishing as practised by the inhabitants of the Aztec empire are wanting in that institution. Yet, the Mexicans undoubtedly acquired a great part of their subsistence by fishing, and this is confirmed by the early authors treating of their affairs. Fish-ponds in Mexico and other places of the country are

---

* Contributions to the Archæology of Missouri; Part I. Pottery (by Dr. Ed. Evers); Salem, Mass., 1880; Fig. 4 on Plate 9.

repeatedly mentioned by them; Cortés himself, in one of his letters to the emperor Charles the Fifth, speaks of these tanks. He also states there that great quantities of fish—fresh, salt, uncooked, and cooked—were sold in the market of Tenochtitlan.* Montezuma's table, it is even said, was frequently provided with fish from the Gulf of Mexico, brought to the capital by runners, twenty-four hours after their capture. The name of Michoacan, one of the Mexican provinces, means "the place where possessors of fish live." Opochtli received homage as the patron of Mexican fishermen. "The god Opochtli," says Sahagun, "was placed among the number of the Tlaloques, which signifies inhabitants of the terrestrial paradise; yet people generally were convinced that he was only a man. They ascribed to him the invention of fishing-nets and of an implement called *minacachalli*, used in killing fish, and resembling a fork armed with three prongs, like a trident. It was also used in hunting birds. He had likewise invented bird-snares and paddles.† According to the Abbé Clavigero, it appears that he was known under different names. "In Cuitlahuac, a city upon a little island in the lake of Chalco," says that author, "there was a god of fishing highly honored, named *Amimitl*, who probably differed from Opochtli no otherwise than in name."‡

Notwithstanding these different data evidencing the importance of fishing among the Mexicans, I have in the course of my reading found but little that would serve to elucidate the methods employed by them in that pursuit. Clavigero, a comparatively recent, but acknowledged, authority, confines himself to the observation that they commonly made use of nets in fishing, but that they also employed hooks, harpoons, and weirs.§

Some designs in the collection of Mexican pictographs, called the Mendoza Codex, show that the male youth in Mexico received at an early age instruction in fishing. These pictures were executed by native artists shortly after the conquest, during the administration of the viceroy, Antonio de Mendoza, and sent by him, with interpretations in Aztec and Spanish, as a present to the emperor Charles the Fifth. A copy of this codex in the Bodleian Library at Oxford has been reproduced in the first volume of Lord Kingsborough's "Mexican Antiquities" (London, 1831). The codex consists of three parts, treating, respectively,

---

* "Venden mucho pescado fresco, y salado, crudo, y guisado."—*Lorenzana: Historia de Méjico, escrita por su Esclarecido Conquistador, Hernan Cortés*; New York, 1828; p. 150.

† Sahagun: Histoire Générale des Choses de la Nouvelle-Espagne; traduite et annotée par D. Jourdanet et Remi Siméon; Paris, 1880; p. 36.—Bernardino de Sahagun, a Franciscan, came to Mexico in 1529 and died there in 1590. He is the chief authority on Mexican mythology.

‡ Clavigero: The History of Mexico; translated by Charles Cullen; Philadelphia, 1817; Vol. II, p. 22.— The Italian original of Clavigero's work was published at Cesena, in 1780.

§ Ibid.; Vol. II; p. 187.

REPRESENTATIONS OF FISHES, AQUATIC MAMMALS, ETC. 215

of the history of Mexico, of the tributes paid to its rulers, and of the social state, including education, among the Mexicans.

Figs. 358 and 359.—Fac-simile delineations illustrating Aztec navigation and fishing. From the Mendoza Codex.

On the sixty-first plate, which is the third of the last part, several groups illustrating the training of boys and girls are drawn. One of the groups (Fig. 358) shows a father, seated and speaking (as indicated by a symbol before his mouth), and two boys of thirteen years. One of them carries reeds or sticks to a canoe already partly loaded, and the other stands in it, handling a paddle. The age of the boys is denoted by thirteen circles or dots, and two connected ovals marked with small dashes indicate that they were allowed two cakes or tortillas for a meal. In the other group (Fig. 359 on the preceding page) a father superintends the fishing of his son of fourteen years, who stands in the canoe, dropping into it a fish, or fishes, caught with a scoop-net. The meal of the boy still consists of two tortillas.

Though the boats here figured are unproportionally small, we learn at least how they were shaped. We also become cognizant of the fact that the Aztecs used scoop-nets.

Some other designs relating to fishing, in the Codex Borgianus (College of the Propaganda at Rome) and the Codex Vaticanus, both reproduced in the third volume of Kingsborough's work, are not sufficiently illustrative to warrant reproduction in this place.

ARTIFICIAL SHELL-DEPOSITS.

Introductory Notices.—The accummulations of shells owing their origin to human agency, which, as formerly stated, occur in various places on the North American sea-coasts, correspond in many respects to the Danish kjökkenmöddings described in the first part of this work; but, while the period of abandonment of the latter is lost in the dawn of history, some of those found in this country were doubtless still in the process of formation in recent times; for modes of life, which had long ago ceased to exist in Europe, continued to prevail among certain tribes of North America.

Cabeza de Vaca was the first to allude to North American shell-deposits. He sojourned as a prisoner on an island (*Isla del Malhado*) in the Gulf of Mexico, watched by a number of Indians, who, on account of a famine on that island, were compelled to leave it. They proceeded to *terra firma*, visiting the neighboring bays, which abounded in oysters. "For three months," the Spanish author says, "they subsist on these shell-fish, and drink very bad water. Wood is there very rare, and the country full of mosquitoes. They construct their cabins of mats, and erect them on heaps of oyster-shells, upon which they sleep naked."*

The Jesuit missionary, Father Isaac Jogues, refers incidentally to shell-heaps which he noticed in 1643 on Manhattan Island:— "There are some houses built of stone. Lime they make of oyster-shells, great heaps of which are found here, made formerly by the savages, who subsist in part by that fishery."†

---

* Cabeza de Vaca: Naufragios; p. 16.—" Sus Casas son edificadas de Esteras, sobre muchas Cascaras de Hostiones, i sobre ellos duermen encueros."

† Jogues: Narrative of a Captivity among the Mohawk Indians, a Description of New Netherland in 1642–3, and other Papers. With a Memoir of the Author, by John Gilmary Shea; New York, 1857; p. 57.—In the original:— " Il y a quelques logis bastys de pierre; Ils font la chaux avec des coquilles d'huistres dont il y a de grans monceaux faits autrefois par les sauvages, qui vivent en partie de cette pesche."

The artificial deposits of shells attracted the attention of the Swedish traveler, Professor Peter Kalm, who arrived in North America in 1748, and he makes repeated mention of them.* "Some *Englishmen*," he states, "asserted that near the river *Potomack*, in *Virginia*, a great quantity of oyster-shells were to be met with, and that they themselves had seen whole mountains of them. The place where they are found is said to be about two *English* miles distant from the seashore. The proprietor of that ground burns lime out of them. This stratum of oyster-shells is two fathom and more deep. Such quantities of shells have likewise been found in other places, especially in *New York*, on digging in the ground; and in one place, at the distance of some *English* miles from the sea, a vast quantity of oyster-shells and of other shells was found. Some people conjectured that the natives had formerly lived in that place, and had left the shells of the oysters which they had consumed in such great heaps. But others could not conceive how it happened that they were thrown in such immense quantities all into one place."† This shows at least that the origin of North American shell-heaps was a matter of speculation more than a century ago.

Professor Kalm also draws attention to the existence of deposits of fluviatile shells, which indicate the places where the aborigines feasted on fresh-water mollusks. In one of his notes, dated Raccoon, New Jersey, March 2, 1749, he says:— "*Mytilus anatinus*, a kind of muscle-shells, was found abundantly in little furrows, which crossed the meadows. The shells were frequently covered on the outside with a thin crust of particles of iron, when the water in the furrows came from an iron mine. The *Englishmen* and *Swedes* settled here seldom make any use of these shells; but the *Indians* who formerly lived here broiled them and eat the flesh. Some of the *Europeans* eat them sometimes."‡

According to Dr. D. G. Brinton, the artificial character of many of these deposits was first brought prominently before the scientific public by Mr. Lardner Vanuxem, in the "Proceedings of the American Association of Geologists and Naturalists" for 1840–'42 (page 21, etc.). I have not seen his article, which, as Dr. Brinton states, refers to shell-heaps on the shores of the Chesapeake and its affluent streams, on the Jersey shore, and Long Island.§

During his second visit to the United States Sir Charles Lyell observed shell-accumulations on the coasts of Massachusetts and Georgia, notably on Saint Simon's Island, near the mouth of the Altamaha River. His account of what he saw on that island is so concise and characteristic that I cannot refrain from quoting it in this place:—

---

* His notice of shell-deposits in the neighborhood of New York is given in the "Extracts."
† Kalm: Travels into North America; translated by John Reinhold Forster; London, 1772; Vol. I, p. 76.
‡ Ibid.; Vol. I, p. 374.—The place formerly called Raccoon is now Swedesborough in Gloucester County.
§ Brinton: Artificial Shell-Deposits of the United States; Smithsonian Report for 1866; p. 356.

"We landed on the northeast end of Saint Simon's Island, at Cannon's Point, where we were gratified by the sight of a curious monument of the Indians, the largest mound of shells left by the aborigines in any one of the sea-islands. Here are no less than ten acres of ground, elevated in some places ten feet, and on an average over the whole area five feet, above the general level, composed throughout that depth of myriads of cast oyster-shells, with some mussels, and here and there a modiola and helix. They who have seen the Monte Testaceo, near Rome, know what great results may proceed from insignificant causes where the cumulative power of time has been at work, so that a hill may be formed out of the broken pottery rejected by the population of a large city. To them it will appear unnecessary to infer, as some antiquaries have done, from the magnitude of these Indian mounds, that they must have been thrown up by the sea. In refutation of such an hypothesis, we have the fact that flint arrow-heads, stone axes, and fragments of Indian pottery have been detected throughout the mass."*

Shortly after Sir Charles Lyell's visit to this country, the reports on Danish kjökkenmöddings by Messrs. Forchhammer, Steenstrup, and Worsaae (published in 1850-'56) became known on this side of the Atlantic, and, of course, stimulated naturalists and antiquaries to a closer examination of similar refuse-heaps along our sea-boards. Indeed, since then such investigations and printed accounts of them have become so numerous that I can barely refer in this publication to a number of examples sufficient to illustrate the character of deposits of shells, both of marine and fluvial origin, in different parts of North America. I avail myself of the copious literature on the subject as well as of several written communications setting forth the results of personal observation.

Greenland.—Having found no references to shell-heaps in Greenland, either in Egede's or in Cranz's descriptions of that country—the subject, as stated, being one which has only in later years attracted the attention of investigators—I will record here some of the observations made by the distinguished scientist, Baron A. E. Nordenskiöld:—

"As a Greenlander now seldom resides at any distance from the Danish trading-stations, one finds in numberless places along the coast old deserted dwelling-places. They are recognizable at a distance by the lively verdure arising from the rich vegetation, which the remnants of fishing and hunting-prey scattered round the cottages or tents have produced. On taking a few spadefuls of earth, or on examining the walls of the new houses,—generally built with turf taken from these spots,—one everywhere finds the earth and grass-roots mixed with the bones of the animals which the Greenlanders hunt. The animals

---

* Sir Charles Lyell: A Second Visit to the United States of America; New York, 1849; Vol. I, p. 252.

killed by the men are in fact cleansed by the women beside or in the cottage itself, and the refuse after the cleansing or the meal is thrown away—seldom far from the cottage-door. Even now, in the course of years, a heap is frequently collected as truly circular as if it had been drawn with a pair of compasses round the door as a centre. On examining its contents, it is found to consist of a black, fat earth, formed of decayed refuse—frequently bits of bone gnawed asunder and broken, shells, especially those of *Mytilus*, lost or broken household-goods, etc. This bone-mixed earth most likely contains, like guano, not only considerable quantities of phosphoric acid, but also ammoniac salts, and it may happen that the trade of Greenland may find in this a valuable article of export.

"As the kitchen-midden dates from the stone age in Greenland,—which undoubtedly extended beyond the epoch at which the whalers first began to visit these coasts,—we find in it arrow-heads, skin-scrapers, and other instruments of various kinds in stone, and especially a quantity of stone flakes knocked off in forming the instruments, easily recognizable, not only by their form, but by their consisting of stones—chalcedony, agate, and especially green jasper (called by the Greenlanders 'angmak')—not met with in the gneiss-formation, but only at certain spots in the basalt-region of Disko or the peninsula of Noursoak. One sometimes finds smaller instruments of clear quartz, also half-wrought crystals of the same mineral. Everything shows that the material was carefully chosen among such minerals as united the necessary hardness with absence of cleavage and a flat conchoidal fracture. Among minerals, in general, the different varieties of quartz (rock-crystal, agate, chalcedony, flint, and jasper) are the only ones which fully satisfy these conditions; and it is therefore almost exclusively these minerals that the various races of man have chosen for making their chipped (not ground) stone instruments.

"The two largest of the old house-sites, among which we were now resting (near the ice-fjord of Jakobshavn, West Greenland), lay so near the sea that their bases were washed by the water. A small stream had found its way through one of them, and had thus not only exposed a section of the kitchen-midden, but also subjected a part of it to a washing-process, in consequence of which bits of bone and other heavier objects lay clean-washed at the bottom of the channel and in the hollows of the gneiss-slabs of the shore. These were carefully examined, and a number of stone instruments and stone chips were collected. There were no traces of iron; but we found a small oval perforated piece of copper, which had evidently once served as an ornament. At the largest site a tolerably thick circular stone wall, eight or ten feet high, and twenty-six in section, was still distinguishable, divided into two unequal portions by a party-wall. The entrance seems to have led into the larger of these areas, judging from the extensive kitchen-midden just outside it. In one of the other heaps of bones a flat stone was found, so large as to require the united efforts of several Greenlanders to turn it. They declared that the workshop for the fabrication of stone instruments must have been situated on that spot, and expected accordingly to find a great quantity of chips in its vicinity, which, however, the result of their searches did not confirm.

"The kitchen-midden outside the large cot rested on a low slab of gneiss, separated from it by a thin layer of turf, in which was no trace of any piece of bone, and which had therefore been formed before the place was inhabited. In other respects this turf, of which specimens were taken away, was perfectly like the earth which was mixed with bones and stone chips. Here there were no *Mytilus*-shells, though these are everywhere else found around Greenland dwellings: an indication that formerly the inhabitants were not obliged to have recourse to this species of famine-food.

"To discover the various animal forms that had here been the prey of the hunter, Dr. Öberg collected a quantity of bones, in which work the Greenlanders took a lively interest, usually determining with great certainty the species to which the pieces of bone had belonged.

"The following species could be ascertained: *Cervus tarandus, Ursus maritimus, Trichechus rosmarus, Cystophora cristata, Phoca barbata, Phoca grœnlandica, Phoca hispida, Phoca vitulina, Delphinapterus leucas.*

"Even if we suppose that this spot was first inhabited shortly after the Eskimos entered Greenland by Smith's Sound, its age will be scarcely more than five hundred years, a period generally too short to show marks of the slow but continuous changes to which the organic world is subjected. Neither do the kitchen-middens of Kaja* contain any other forms of animals than those still living on the coast of Greenland. Nevertheless we obtain here an interesting confirmation of the changes that the ice-fjord has undergone. The walrus, *Phoca barbata,* and *Cystophora cristata* no longer venture into this long ice-blockaded fjord; and even the bear has now become so scarce in the colonies of North Greenland south of the Waigat that most of the Danes resident in those parts have never seen it. The remnants of bones in the kitchen-middens, on the other hand, prove that these animals were abundant there formerly, and are consequently an evidence that the fjord at Jakobshavn was less filled with ice than now."†

Dr. Emil Bessels makes the following statements concerning the formation of refuse-heaps in Greenland:—

---

* Name of the place.

† Nordenskiöld: Account of an Expedition to Greenland in the year 1870; Manual of the Natural History, Geology, and Physics of Greenland and the Neighboring Regions, etc.; edited by Professor T. Rupert Jones; London, 1875; p. 412, etc.

"The Eskimo throws bones, shells, fishes, skins which have become useless, in short everything that is of no value to him for the moment, before his hut, in consequence of which a rich vegetation springs up, noticeable from afar by its fresh verdure. A short time suffices to discover in these kjökkenmöddings traces of nearly all usable vertebrate animals of the Greenlandic coast, and in many cases it would not be difficult to determine the season of the year in which these layers were formed; for sometimes the remains of birds predominate; sometimes those of fishes; or there are strata almost exclusively composed of *Mytilus*-shells."*

Nova Scotia.—Mr. J. M. Jones, President of the Nova Scotian Institute of Natural History, at Halifax, communicated in 1863 to the "London Athenæum" a brief report of the examination of a shell-heap on the shore of Saint Margaret's Bay, distant about twenty-two miles from Halifax, the capital of Nova Scotia. This account was reprinted in the Smithsonian Report for 1863. The shell-deposit chiefly noticed lies, some twenty feet above high-water mark, on the shore of one of the smaller bays or coves, that has a sandy beach, where canoes could be hauled up without difficulty. The deposit, about fifty yards or more in length, by eight yards in breadth, but only eighteen inches deep, forms part of a farm, and is covered with two or three inches of soil, producing grass and common field-plants. The shells themselves, perfect and broken, form a compact layer, which was found to inclose bones of quadrupeds, birds, and fishes, large and small teeth, flint and quartz arrow and spear-heads, bone awls, and many fragments of rudely-made pottery, dark-colored, and containing grains of granitic sand, and mica in quantity. Pebbles, about the size of a man's fist, and bearing traces of having undergone the action of fire, occurred in the deposit, and also charcoal. Rounded granitic boulders lying scattered on the heap are supposed to have served as seats, and on digging around them, greater masses of shells and more evident traces of fire were discovered. The deposit consisted chiefly of shells of the quahaug or hard-shell clam (*Venus mercenaria*) and soft-shell clam (*Mya arenaria*). There were also found the shells of the scallop (*Pecten islandicus*), boat-shell (*Crepidula fornicata*), and mussel (*Mytilus edulis*), those of the latter in a very friable state. Vertebræ of two or three species of fishes came to light, and some well-preserved opercular spines of the Norway haddock (*Sebastes norvegicus*), which probably were used as piercing-tools. The moose, bear, beaver, and porcupine, represented by broken bones and teeth, constituted the mammalian fauna; and the presence of birds, belonging to several species, could likewise be traced by their bones, which were partly broken, one in particular having been opened down the side by means of a cutting-instrument.

No object betokening a connection with the whites occurred in this deposit.†

---

* Bessels: Die Amerikanische Nordpol-Expedition; Leipzig, 1879; p. 47.
† Smithsonian Report for 1863, p. 370, etc.

New Brunswick and New England.—Between the years 1869 and '73, Professor S. F. Baird made several visits to New Brunswick and New England, during which he examined a number of shell-deposits in those districts; but the notes in which he details his observations have but lately been published. I will single out some of the more important localities visited by him.

The largest shell-mound was seen at Oak Bay, a narrow fjord extending northward from Passamaquoddy Bay, New Brunswick. The total thickness of the bed, which consisted of a number of distinct layers, amounted to five feet. "A striking feature in this mound is the abundance of spikes and shells of Echini, which evidently constituted a large portion of the food of the aborigines. A careful examination of the ashes indicated that they were derived, for the most part, from eel-grass (*Zostera marina*), and it is suggested that the cooking of the shells was done by wrapping them up in dry eel-grass and setting fire to it. This would probably cook the animals sufficiently to enable them to be readily withdrawn from the shell."* The principal shells here found were *Buccinum plicosum, Natica heros, Pecten tenuicostatus, Pecten cardium, Mya arenaria, Mytilus,* and *Helix alternata.*

Another interesting bed was seen on Frye's or Cailiff's Island, New Brunswick. "Here the shell-bed was a very large one, about fifteen feet above the present high tide, and seemed to have been torn up by the tide and restratified by the water, so that articles of the same kind and specific gravity were usually found in association."

Other points in New Brunswick and several localities in Eastern Maine were examined. Resuming his observations, Professor Baird says:— "They are characterized in some cases by large beds of shells of the soft clam (*Mya arenaria*)—never of the quahaug or *Venus mercenaria*—with a little admixture of earth; in others the shells are in a much decomposed condition, with black earth scattered among them; again, by the association of large bones, especially of the moose and caribou, with but little mixture of anything else. Occasionally these beds alternated with pure shell or pure bone, possibly the shells being aggregated in summer and the bones of mammals in winter. Everywhere the bones of the great auk were found, as also those of the beaver."†

At Damariscotta, Lincoln County, Maine, the extensive beds consist almost entirely of oysters. They cover many acres to a depth of from five to fifteen or twenty feet. The oysters are large, and generally narrow or slipper-shaped. Very few are now found living in the vicinity.

---

* Baird: Notes on certain Shell-Mounds on the Coast of New Brunswick and of New England; Proceedings of the United States National Museum; Vol. IV, Washington, 1882; p. 292.

Remains of the *Zostera marina*, it will be remembered, also occurred in the Danish kjökkenmöddings, where this sea-plant is supposed to have been used in the production of salt. See p. 85 of this work.

† Ibid.; p. 296.

ARTIFICIAL SHELL-DEPOSITS.

The shell-beds at Eagle Hill, Ipswich, Massachusetts, are of considerable extent, and consist largely of the *Mya arenaria*, a species still abounding in the neighborhood. It forms an important article of commerce, being used as bait for codfish. Bones of the great auk* were frequent at this place.

On the whole, stone implements were found to be comparatively rare in the shell-deposits of Southern Massachusetts.

The collections made on these occasions (shells, bones, chipped and ground stone implements, and fragments of pottery) are on exhibition in the National Museum.

In company with a number of associates, Professor Jeffries Wyman examined in 1867 some shell-heaps on the coasts of Maine and Massachusetts, and published in the following year an account of his explorations in the "American Naturalist" for 1868. It has already been quoted in this work.

He examined deposits on Frenchman's Bay, between the main-land and Mount Desert Island, and on Crouch's Cove, situated on Goose Island, Casco Bay, in Maine. His explorations in Massachusetts were confined to deposits at Ipswich (Eagle Hill), Salisbury, and Cotuit Port in the township of Barnstable (Cape Cod). The mammalian fauna of these shell-accumulations represents seventeen species, all still living, and including man, whose presence was only indicated by the discovery of a bone of the foot at Cotuit Port. The bird-remains were referable to the great auk, razor-bill, duck (three species), wild turkey, and heron. Two kinds of tortoise have been met with. The fish-remains are those of the shark, cod (*Morrhua americana*), and goose-fish (*Lophius americanus*); and of shell-fish, the whelk (*Buccinum undatum*), two species of conch (*Pyrula carica* and *Pyrula canaliculata*), oyster (*Ostrea borealis*), clam (*Mya arenaria*), quahaug (*Venus mercenaria*), mussel (*Mytilus edulis*), scallop (*Pecten tenuicostatus* and *Pecten islandicus*), and hen-clam (*Mactra*) are mentioned. These mollusks probably were all used as food; several other species, likewise found in the shell-deposits, are supposed to have been accidently introduced. The bones of deer and of birds were the most numerous, and of the former "not one was whole, all having been broken up for the double purpose of extracting the marrow, a custom almost world-wide among savages, and often practised by hunters, and of accommodating them to the size of the vessel in which they were cooked."† In the bird-bones the ends had mostly disappeared, and many bore traces of having been gnawed by animals. The discovery of fire-places is repeatedly mentioned.

Fragments of pottery and stone implements were rare, but articles of bone (piercers, harpoon-heads) of more frequent occurrence.‡

---

* Now considered as entirely extinct. See p. 36 of this publication.

† Wyman: An Account, etc.; p. 575.

‡ Fig. 221 on p. 142 and Fig. 242 on p. 150 represent bone dart-heads found at Crouch's Cove.

Concerning the age of these shell-deposits, Professor Wyman remarks:—

"The shell-heaps we have here described yield nothing which indicates as high an antiquity as those of the old world. The materials of them present some variety in the degree of decomposition which has resulted from time and exposure, the lower layers being much more disintegrated and friable, the shells, in fact, falling to pieces, while those of the upper ones generally preserve their original firmness. That there was a difference in time in which these layers were deposited is further indicated by the fact that, in two of the heaps, a stratum of earth is interposed between the earlier and later deposits, as if the locality had been abandoned as a camping-place, and then after a prolonged absence of the natives had been reoccupied. Each heap, too, is covered with a deposit of earth and vegetable mould, of variable thickness, and in some cases, as at Frenchman's Bay, supporting a growth of forest-trees, though these were nowhere of such size as to indicate that they had lived a century. —— ——

"On the other hand, it may be safely said that there is nothing in the condition of these heaps which is inconsistent with the hypothesis that they were begun many centuries ago. The examinations at Crouch's Cove, Eagle Hill, and Cotuit Port were sufficiently extended to enable us to obtain a fair representation of the objects they contain; but in no case was there found, nor have we been able to learn that there had been previously found, a single article which could be regarded as having been made by, or derived from, the white man, nor did we obtain any evidence that these particular heaps had been materially added to since the European has occupied these shores. Had intercourse with Europeans been once fairly established, it were a reasonable presumption that we should have found at least a glass bead, a fragment of earthenware, or an instrument of some sort indicative of the fact, especially when we bear in mind that it would be in just such places, where the savages collected around their fires and seething-pots to cook and eat, that such objects might be expected to be broken or lost."

In addition, there seems to be historical evidence that a heavy growth of trees was found on the deposits of clam-shells near Mount Desert Island by the first settlers.[*]

Quite recently Professor Putnam has explored shell-heaps on Muscongus Sound and the neighboring Damariscotta River, both inlets of the sea extending into Lincoln County, Maine. These localities have been previously mentioned in this publication, and the latter was noticed just now in connection with Professor Baird's examination of shell-deposits. The substance of a lecture on these shell-heaps by Professor Putnam was published in the "Boston Evening Transcript" of November 13, 1882.

---

[*] Wyman: An Account, etc.; p. 571, etc.

A shell-deposit at Keene's Point, on Muscongus Sound, is four or five feet thick on the water's edge, and extends several hundred feet along the shore and a hundred feet inland. The shells here found are those of the soft-shell clam, which enters most largely into the formation of the heap, the quahaug (hard-shell clam), scallop, whelk (*Buccinum*), and cockle (*Natica*). "Although the bones of mammals were most often those of the moose, deer, bear, wolf, fox, and beaver, yet there were also found bones of the otter, skunk, raccoon, woodchuck, seal and porpoise. Bones of several species of birds occurred, also some bones of the turtle, while fishes were represented by the cod, flounder, and great goose-fish, giving with the mollusks quite an extended bill of fare. The bones and shells were broken with hammer-stones, which are found scattered through the heap." Stone implements occurred rather frequently, and from the presence of numerous chips it has been inferred that the former were made on the spot. Bone implements were also met with.*

"The discovery of the art of pottery," the lecturer stated, "seems to have been made during the immense time these heaps were being formed, as I have not found fragments of pottery in the lower portions of the older and larger heaps, while such fragments are common in the upper beds and in the more recent heaps."

The extensive deposits at Damariscotta and Newcastle, situated opposite each other on either side of the Damariscotta River, consist almost wholly of oyster-shells. These oysters are slender and long ("slipper-shaped," as Professor Baird calls them), many measuring fourteen inches in length, and now hardly ever found of this shape and size on the coast of New England. "Old men at Damariscotta say that their fathers have sometimes seen one, but it has probably never been abundant since the time of the earliest settlement, so that we must believe that these great heaps were formed long before that time."

In the shell-heap at Newcastle a human skeleton was found a few years ago, and Messrs. A. T. Gamage and A. I. Phelps discovered portions of five skeletons in a shell-heap on Fort Island, in the Damariscotta River.

New York.—Allusion has been made on a preceding page to shell-heaps on the coasts of New York. They are particularly numerous on Long Island, and those in the neighborhood of Sag Harbor, on Gardiner's Bay, in the eastern part of the island, have been specially examined by Mr. W. Wallace Tooker, a resident of that place. He has kindly communicated to me the following description:—

---

* The bone dart-heads represented in Fig. 226 on p. 143 and Figs. 236 and 237 on p. 146, it will be remembered, were found by Messrs. Gamage and Phelps in the course of their examination of shell-heaps on Damariscotta River and Muscongus Sound.

"Careful examination has disclosed the fact that shell-heaps, or kitchen-middens, of greater or less extent abound upon the banks or shores of nearly every body of water or swamp indenting or dotting Long Island.

"Different authors have at various times mentioned these shell-heaps, yet without attempting any description, probably for the reason that no thorough examination of these deposits had been made at the time they wrote. Prime speaks of 'the immense shell-banks on the shores of Long Island';[*] Gardiner of the 'many places whitened with the shells of clams around Gardiner's Bay and Three Mile Harbor.'[†]

"The shell-heaps found on that part of Long Island which lies between Montauk Point and Canoe Place are more extensive and numerous, and have been more carefully examined than others; but as they do not differ materially, a description of a few of these will suffice for the rest. To show how numerous these deposits are, the writer would state that he has located more than twenty-five separate shell-heaps within a radius of two miles from Sag Harbor.

"These heaps consist of the shells of oysters, soft and hard-shell clams, scallops, periwinkles, and mussels, mingled with ashes, charcoal, bones of mammals, birds, and fishes, stone and bone implements, fragments of pottery, and other refuse that would naturally accumulate in and around the dwelling of a savage. West of the Otter Pond at Sag Harbor is a large heap, covering nearly three acres. On its surface have been found hundreds of stone arrow-points and other implements. A part of the deposit is still hidden under the leaves and soil of the woods, and has never been disturbed. Along the cove beyond, for a distance of about a mile and a half, is one almost continuous shell-heap. Back on the southern slopes of the hills, near swamps and springs, are others, some being an acre in area. At Payne's Creek is one of the largest and most compact shell-heaps on this part of Long Island. At the time the shells were accumulating, the creek evidently flowed in front of the deposit, but now it is filled up, and a sandy country-road extends along its front. This deposit covers about three acres, and is fully four feet in depth. There have been found in it bones of the raccoon, bear, otter, fox, deer, and rabbit, a great variety of stone implements, bone awls, and a large fish-hook of bone.[‡] This shell-heap is being rapidly destroyed by the march of improvement, and will soon disappear.[§]

"About a mile from this shell-heap, on Little Hog-Neck, facing the narrows and cove, is a good-sized shell-heap, covered by alluvium. It has been ploughed over many years; but the deposit underneath has not been disturbed to any

---

[*] History of Long Island.
[†] Chronicles of East Hampton, Long Island.
[‡] Figured on p. 127.
[§] Almost the same description of the shell-heaps near Otter Pond and Payne's Creek was furnished by Mr. Tooker to Dr. Abbott, who has published it on p. 439–40 of "Primitive Industry."

great extent. It is from one to four feet deep, two hundred and fifty feet in length, and extends back the same distance. In this deposit ashes seem to predominate, although in some places the shells are packed so closely that excavating becomes difficult. The sand below the shells and ashes shows the effect of fire very plainly. In a space ten feet square the writer found five bone perforators, many notched sinkers, hammer-stones, sharpening-stones, broken celts, a few arrow-points, quartz-chippings, nearly a peck of pottery fragments, a perforated piece of a potstone vessel, and various other objects. Bones of birds and mammals—those of deer and bear predominating—and fin-bones of fishes, were scattered through the whole mass. Under all appeared a hearth of stones, showing the effects of fire.

"Triangular arrow-points of quartz are far more numerous in the various shell-heaps than those of other forms or material. No human bones suggesting cannibalism or sacrifices have been found. Many of these shell-heaps were camping-places after the settlement of the island, as shown by the presence of gun-flints, leaden bullets, brass buttons, brass arrow-points, glass beads, and bottles, which are found from time to time in the upper layers."

I was informed by Mr. J. Carson Brevoort, of Brooklyn, that shell-heaps are numerous along Rockaway Beach, in the southeastern part of the island. It does not seem that they have thus far been examined.

Mr. F. Lewis, Jr., in an article on the Long Island coasts, speaks of "many Indian shell-heaps, all of them now surrounded by meadows. Some of them, six or more feet deep, near the margin of the ocean, are covered by every tide. These are probably very old, and were formed originally at the uplands."* As will presently appear, similar indications of a littoral subsidence have been observed in New Jersey.

New Jersey.—The shell-heaps of New Jersey have been noticed by Drs. G. H. Cook and C. C. Abbott, Mr. C. F. Wolley, and by myself. According to Dr. Abbott, they occur along the greater part of the New Jersey coast, from Cape May to Keyport.† My own investigations, made in the summers of 1863 and '64, relate to shell-deposits in the neighborhood of the last-named place, a post-town situated in Monmouth County, on Raritan Bay, and noted for its trade in oysters and other edible mollusks. In the following résumé I avail myself of an article contributed by me to the Smithsonian Report for 1864.

There are several places in the vicinity of Keyport, and one even within the precincts of the town, where the soil is covered with shells, among which Indian relics occur; but the principal shell-heap lies on Poole's farm, a mile and a half

---

* Popular Science Monthly; Vol. X, 1877; p. 436, note.

† Abbott: Primitive Industry; p. 439.

northeast of Keyport, and about three-quarters of a mile south of a small projection of the coast, known as Conasconck Point.

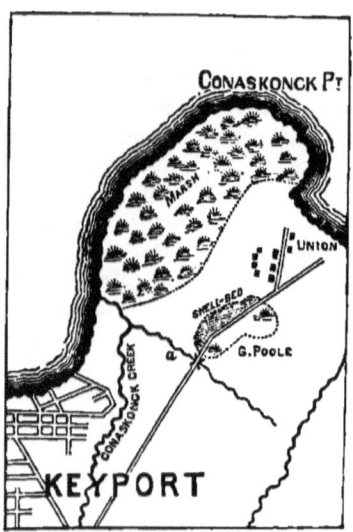

Fig. 360.—Plan showing the location of the principal shell-deposit at Keyport.

The road leading from Keyport to the village of Union passes through the farm-land and borders the shell-bed, indicated by a dotted space on the accompanying plan. It spreads over an area of six or seven acres, and forms several extensive heaps or ridges, on an average five feet high. The accumulations consist of shells, mostly imbedded in sand, and intermingled with innumerable pebbles, representing a great variety of mineral substances. The oyster and hard-shell clam are here, as elsewhere in the neighborhood, the prevailing species; but I found also, though not very frequently, shells of *Pyrula*, both *canaliculata* and *carica*, which doubtless were eaten by the aborigines. I collected only a few valves of the soft-shell clam, and none of the mussel, the last-named bivalve occurring but sparingly in the neighborhood. In addition, there were a few broken valves of the scallop, and some specimens of *Nassa obsoleta*, the latter doubtless accidentally brought to the place. The few bones noticed by me were so much decayed that they almost crumbled to pieces when handled, and their condition rendered identification impossible. The non-conservative quality of the surrounding sand accounts for their destruction.

"That considerable time was required to heap up these shells, is evident, and, moreover, indicated by the chalky, porous appearance and fragility of many of the valves; but those that were cast away at later periods exhibit these signs of decay in a far less degree, and are even sometimes as sound as though they had but lately been left on the shore by high water. A great number of the shells are broken, especially those of clams, which seem to be more brittle than oyster-shells. This breaking into fragments is caused by the sudden changes of temperature, in consequence of which the valves crack and ultimately fall to pieces. Concerning the depth of this deposit, I learned that about twelve years ago several hundred loads of shells were taken away from a certain spot for making a road. The excavation thus produced reached about eight feet downward, and the mass was found to consist throughout that depth of shells, sand, and pebbles. My own diggings, which were, however, of a more superficial character, led to the same result. This shell-bed is about half a mile distant from the shore at low tide, and the intervening area consists chiefly of so-called salt-meadow. In transporting the shell-fish to the camping-place it is probable that the aborigines availed themselves of a small nameless creek (marked a on the plan) running toward the sea, west of the shell-bed, and not very distant from it. This creek, though rather narrow, is sufficiently deep for canoe-navigation during high water, and joins the more considerable Conaskonck Creek, which flows into the beach. There was, consequently, a water-connection between the sea and the camp. The space enclosed by a dotted line on the accompanying plan indicates the continuation, or rather the running out, of the shell-bed just described; for here the shells are by far less numerous, and form no longer heaps, but lie thinly scattered over the ground, which is partly under cultivation, and swampy in some places, as marked in the sketch, by which it is only intended to show approximately the location and extent of the deposit."*

My search for aboriginal artefacts among these shell-heaps and in the adjacent fields was very successful; for I obtained a considerable number of arrow-heads, cutters, etc., of flint, quartz, and other materials, grooved axes of sandstone and greenstone, and many fragments of a rude, dark pottery, frequently mixed with coarse sand, yet sometimes bearing ornamental lines and notches. I also found a piece of a large potstone vessel. No bone implements were met with.

The great number of flint articles, especially arrow-heads, and of remnants of clay vessels, found at this place—not to speak of the quantity and appearance of the shells—indicates its long-continued use as a camping-ground. Arrow-heads, etc., were made on the spot. This became evident not only from the abundance of flint chips which lie scattered among the shells, but also from

---

* Artificial Shell-Deposits in New Jersey; Smithsonian Report for 1864; p. 372.

the not unfrequent occurrence of unfinished arrow-heads, which had been thrown aside as useless, on account of a wrong crack or some other defect in the stone. There can be no doubt that the material was here furnished, to a great extent at least, in the shape of uncountable pebbles of silicious character; for nearly all the unfinished arrow-heads picked up by me still exhibit portions of the smooth, water-worn surface of the pebbles from which they were made. Among the collected objects I specially mention two scrapers of brown jasper, worked into a spoon-like form, which lay on the shell-covered ground, a short distance from each other, and were perhaps made by the same hand.*

At the time of my sojourn at Keyport old people still remembered that Indians annually visited the neighborhood for catching shell-fish, which they dried for consumption during winter. These Indians are said to have belonged to the Narragansett tribe, which may be true, but seems somewhat improbable, as they might have been able to obtain their supplies of mollusks in the more northern, sea-bordered district inhabited by them.

Some interesting data concerning shell-heaps in New Jersey have been furnished by Dr. Cook. "There are," he says, "immense deposits of shells found at different places along the sea-shore. They are the marks of the aborigines who came down here to gather their supplies of clams and oysters, and left the shells in piles as we now see them. Some of them are the remains of shells which have been broken up to make wampum. Large piles of these broken shells have been met with at Manahawkin, at Tuckerton, at Leed's Point, at Beesley's Point, and they have been heard of at several other places.

"They are applied directly on the soil, and soon begin to show their good effects. They may be used with safety in almost any quantity, and will be found a lasting fertilizer."†

Dr. Cook noticed that in several places of the New Jersey coast the salt-marsh had encroached upon the shell-heaps and grown several feet around them. According to his opinion, the Atlantic coast of North America has been for several hundred years past, and still is, in a state of slow subsidence.‡ The origin of these shell-heaps evidently dates back to a time when their sites lay higher, and were free from salt-meadow.

Delaware.—Mr. Francis Jordan, Jr., of Philadelphia, has published through the Numismatic and Antiquarian Society of Philadelphia an account of an aboriginal encampment at Rehoboth, a watering-place on the coast of Delaware, five miles south of the town of Lewes, and nineteen miles from Cape May, which

---

* One of them is figured on p. 400 of the Smithsonian Report for 1872.
† Cook: Geology of New Jersey; Newark, New Jersey, 1868; p. 501.
‡ Ibid.; p. 362.

lies diagonally opposite. The camping-ground is situated directly in the rear of what is now called Rehoboth Beach, and not more than five hundred feet distant from the sea.

"The present dimensions of the encampment," says Mr. Jordan, "are, in length, three-quarters of a mile, running in a direct line north and south, parallel with and, as I have said, distant from the ocean some four or five hundred feet, and protected from it by a sand-bluff rising six or eight feet above high-water mark, and extending from Rehoboth Beach to Cape Henlopen. The width of the encampment varies from one hundred to five hundred feet. A ridge of sand-hills intersects its length, dividing it into nearly equal parts, and as the southern section is on a higher plane, the two form what might be called an upper and a lower encampment.

"Lying a quarter of a mile south, stretches out the famous Rehoboth Bay, once the habitation of clams and oysters, and whose shallow waters still teem with a great variety of fish and myriads of hard and shedder crabs. Skirting a portion of the western boundary, we behold one of those phenomenal freaks of nature rarely met with on our coast, namely, three lakes whose waters are perfectly fresh and clear as any in our northern latitudes, although within a few hundred feet of the salt sea. The largest covers some fifty acres of land and has a mean depth of five feet. The quantity of water in each remains nearly the same in all seasons, the constant exhaustion from evaporation being supplied by hidden springs.

"In selecting this spot as the site for an encampment, the Indians displayed a keen appreciation of its unsurpassed natural advantages. Here they had every comfort their savage natures could wish for. Game, fish, and oysters in abundance and easily obtained: an inexhaustible supply of fresh water at their very threshold; and the adjacent forest of white oak harbored the deer and bear, and furnished them with fuel, and lumber to construct their sea-canoe.

"Hitherto for many centuries they annually came to escape the enervating heat of the inland villages, and probably remained far into the autumn, or until the geese and ducks, with which the bay and lakes are stocked at this period, deserted those placid waters for a warmer climate. Hence it is that I call this an encampment, in contradistinction to their permanent abiding-places. The evidences of their sojourn—their domestic habits—are many, and even to the unscientific observer are unmistakable in the conclusions they point to. The character of the ground is in itself a revelation, and contributes to the belief that its level and compact surface—almost as solid as a macadamized road, whereon no vegetable growth is visible—is not entirely the result of nature's handiwork, but that the foot of man assisted in producing it. It seems to have been so pounded down by the tread of the successive generations of its periodical visitors that vegetation is rendered impossible, whereas one step across its limits brings you to a luxuriant growth of heather and such other grasses as usually flourish contiguous to the sea in this latitude, and springing from a soil into which the feet sink several inches. — — —

"Scattered throughout its precincts at irregular intervals are the remains of several hundreds of what I shall call camp-fires—small conical elevations composed of clam, oyster, and mussel-shells, mingled with charcoal. These mounds vary in size and in seeming entirety. Some appear to have successfully resisted the force of the elements, and retained their original form almost intact, whilst others have partially succumbed to the wash of the winter-tides that have occasionally gained access through apertures in the sand-bluffs and submerged a part of the surface. There are still others that have been entirely effaced from the same cause, and their positions are only distinguishable by the chalky appearance of the ground, and the presence of myriads of broken shells that have bleached by centuries of exposure. — — —

"At the Rehoboth encampment there are no large mounds, and presumably never have been, as the number and positions of those extant preclude such a supposition.

"The positive evidence of their origin is found in the fact that in the immediate vicinity as well as mingled with the mollusks are fragments of pottery in large quantities, celts, arrow-heads, and a variety of other stone implements and ornaments; the bones of animals, and many pieces of calcined stone that once played an important part in the construction of their long since extinct fire-places. Indeed, in almost every stone picked up within the confines of the camp-ground can be traced the fragment of an implement of domestic use, the chase, or war. It should be borne in mind that stones are not found in this part of Delaware."

The remainder of the account treats more specially of the artefacts discovered at this place of encampment, such as the fragments of clay vessels, celts, hammer-stones, etc. "Large quantities of flint chips," the author says, "and unfinished and broken arrow-heads, as well as numerous perfect specimens are to be found wherever a mound is to be seen, and lead to the opinion that the manufacture of these implements was largely engaged in by the camp-dwellers. The prevailing form is the triangular variety without the notched base, which distinguishes those usually obtained from Pennsylvania and New Jersey."

It must be considered as fortunate that Mr. Jordan has recorded the existence of this camping-place, as its vestiges will soon be obliterated. "Even as I write," he says, "embryo streets traverse its domain in every direction, and in the space of perhaps only a few months lofty hotels and comfortable cottages will rise upon the site of the Indian wigwam, and every trace of the aboriginal character of the spot will have disappeared before the march of improvement."*

Mr. Jordan has kindly communicated to me in writing the results of further explorations of shell-deposits in Delaware, and I herewith give his account in his own words:—

"The little bays and inlets of the Lower Delaware, famous for the abundance and fine quality of oysters and other mollusks, were especially attractive to the Indians. The artificial shell-deposits—some of them of considerable magnitude—that occur in the vicinity of Cape Henlopen and elsewhere along the coast of Delaware, and which furnish in their construction the evidence of their aboriginal character, testify to their appreciation of a locality possessing numerous eligible encamping-sites as well as a remarkably equable climate and inexhaustible fisheries. It is difficult to arrive at an accurate computation of the age of these deposits; but from their extent and the nature of their formation, it is fair to assume that they represent the accumulations of centuries. It is a well-ascertained fact that the aborigines visited the coast periodically, and hence these remains are the débris of their temporary encampments, and are generally to be found on the banks of an estuary which gave their occupants safe connection with the open sea.

"Three miles north of Rehoboth, and a mile and a half west of Cape Henlopen, is Long Neck Branch, a narrow strip of land, as its name implies, which, within the memory of living inhabitants, projected into a shallow inlet of the sea, where now only an immense salt-meadow exists, that may be safely crossed on foot. On this peninsula, which is triangular in shape, half a mile long and about a quarter of a mile wide at its base, and on an elevation far removed from inundating tides, are shell-heaps which occupy the entire length of the neck, and form, with one or two trivial breaks, a continuous mound. In the narrowest parts of the peninsula the shell-deposits completely cover the surface, but elsewhere their average width is thirty feet. A large portion of the deposit is covered with a grove of pine-trees, which must have sprung up since the place was deserted, as in many instances they have taken root directly upon the summits of the heaps; and among them are a number whose cortical rings denote an age of two centuries. The trees and undergrowth have largely contributed to the preservation of the deposit, and where the roots have arrested disintegration and kept the mass compact, the composition of the accumulations can be studied as accurately as if their abandonment had been a recent event. Numerous excavations established their depth to be from two to six feet, but did not reveal characteristics differing materially from those observed in the deposits at Rehoboth. They consist of hard-shell clam, oyster, and conch-

---

* Jordan: The Remains of an Aboriginal Encampment at Rehoboth, Delaware; Philadelphia, 1880; p. 2, etc.

shells, the bones of animals that have been split for the purpose of extracting the marrow, fragments of pottery, and charcoal. The latter formed a prominent constituent of the mass, and is so free from extraneous substances, that it was difficult to realize the fact that these aboriginal fire-places had remained undisturbed for at least two centuries. Under the roots of a lofty pine tree, where the cinders were especially abundant, I dug up pieces of earthenware of extraordinary size and quite black, either from usage or contamination with the charcoal in which they were buried. Wherever excavations were made at Long Neck Branch, the quantity of broken pottery was greater and the sherds in a more perfect condition than on the unprotected sands of Rehoboth and Lewes. In ornamentation, however, and in the composition of the clay, which has an admixture of sand and pounded shells, the specimens are identical. From a careful measurement of the curved lines of these fragments, the vessels of which they were once a part could not have contained more than two or three quarts of liquid, and both in design and dimensions show very little variation.

"The results of my investigations at Long Branch Neck were not as satisfactory as I had reason to expect. I was led to anticipate a valuable addition to my collection, on account of the situation of the deposit in an unfrequented section of country where its existence and prehistoric character being almost unknown, it had been left undespoiled by the relic-hunter; but, besides the pottery, I only obtained a number of rough hammer-stones and flint knives, some finished and unfinished arrow-heads, and an abundance of calcined beach-stones. My researches did not yield a single specimen of the larger and finer class of stone tools, or an ornament of any description. With a view of ascertaining a cause for so unlooked for a disappointment, I made a close survey of the surroundings, and finally reached the conclusion that the remains were simply those of a fishing-post lying midway between the two great encampments of Rehoboth and Lewes. There was insufficient space for the comfortable accommodation of a large community, which in a measure may explain the remarkable absence of the ordinary stone implements.

"An interesting discovery here was that of a well-defined trail through the glades connecting the shell-heaps with two miniature lakes of fresh water, where the Indians doubtless obtained their supply.

"There was no evidence that any part of the deposit had been converted into a place of sepulture.

"A far more extensive series of irregular heaps can be traced for over a mile on the downs in front of the town of Lewes, where they first become visible about half a mile from the bay-shore. After running parallel with the latter for some distance, in the direction of Cape Henlopen, they make a rather excentric curve to the southeast, from which, and other indications, it was supposed they followed the bed of a dried-up water-course. I consulted the old map of

Delaware Bay and River, prepared in 1654–'55 by Peter Lindström, Royal Swedish engineer attached to Menewe's expedition. This map, now in the Swedish archives, shows a sheet of water of considerable size, called Flower River, that corresponds precisely with the present line of the mounds, and confirms the theory that the ground they occupy was selected for an encampment on account of the facilities offered by this inlet as an exit into the bay. The northern end of the great sand-dune, spoken of as lying between the cape and Lewes, has in its progress inland buried from view several hundred feet of the deposit near its southeastern terminus. Emerging thence, they continue, and enter the pine-forest northwest of the cape, where they terminate.

"Half a century ago some portions of these accumulations were from fifteen to twenty feet high, and the dazzling whiteness of the bleached shells made them a conspicuous object far at sea. Now, they have an altitude that in places will scarcely measure as many inches, except where sheltered by the timber. Atmospheric action has done much to produce this change; but the great factor in the work of demolition has been utilitarian man, by whom tons of the decomposed valves have been carted away for fertilizing purposes, and the elements are gradually obliterating the remainder.

"I made many excavations among the shell-hills at Lewes; but in respect to the number of implements found therein, they were as unproductive as the mounds at Long Neck Branch. I dug out in one place, two feet below the surface, three boulders of sandstone, which, from their relative position and calcined appearance, I infer were once hearth-stones. Near these stones I found a chisel of exquisite workmanship and two tubes of banded slate; also a portable corn-mill of conglomerate rock, weighing thirty-six pounds. On the surface of the sand, however, near the accumulations, I picked up a large number of specimens, comprising several axes, a well-polished gouge of serpentine, arrow and spear-heads, scrapers, many hammer-stones, and a flat piece of granite, on which there are three perfectly-executed grooves converging to a point, three inches long, an eighth of an inch deep, and the same in width.

"In conclusion, I desire to say to future explorers that if, in making excavations directly among the shells, their object is the discovery of stone tools, their search will by an unrequited one. My experience has taught me that articles of real archæological value are only to be found at some distance from the mounds, where one would suppose the habitations of the Indians were placed."

Maryland.—Dr. Elmer R. Reynolds, of Washington, D. C., kindly placed at my disposition a large manuscript, descriptive of extensive explorations of shell-heaps, carried on by him along the Maryland side of the estuary of the Potomac River. But feeling reluctant to avail myself of this ample material, which Dr. Reynolds intends to utilize himself in an elaborate account of these shell-deposits,

I returned the manuscript, expressing the desire to be furnished by him with an abstract of it. He very obligingly complied with my request, and communicated to me the following data:—

"The region about to be considered was occupied by the *Wicomico* or *Yoacomico* Indians prior to 1633. At this time they sold their lands to Lord Baltimore, and, drifting northward, thereafter lost their tribal identity. These Indians are said to have been of a pacific disposition, and were chiefly devoted to agriculture, hunting, and fishing. All that is known about them is found in Father Andrew White's 'Relatio Itinineris in Marylandiam.'

"The shell-mounds and shell-fields of the Potomac region are both numerous and of large extent. They were first observed on Nanjemoy Creek, where the water is of a brackish character. Thence they are found at frequent intervals on both sides of the Potomac. The most interesting, however, are located at Pope's Creek, fifty-eight miles south of Washington. The deposits at this place are two in number, the larger being situated on the northern side of the creek, near its junction with the Potomac. This mound rests on a high bank which faces the creek on the south and also extends northward parallel with the Potomac. It spreads over several acres of ground, and is partially concealed by an overlying stratum of earth. The shells vary in depth from one to seven and a half feet. They are mostly those of the common oyster (*Ostrea virginiana*), still found in this vicinity. Among them are also occasionally found shells of the quahaug or hard-shell clam (*Venus mercenaria*), and carapaces of the tortoise. The shells themselves, while showing traces of approaching disintegration, are still in a sound condition, excepting, however, those near the substratum, where time and enormous pressure have conduced to their decomposition.

"Only a few fragments of bones have thus far been observed.

"Pits containing ashes and charcoal are occasionally met with in the southern margin of the mound, where the shells have been removed for lime-making. The shells do not appear to have been much broken during the process of opening, probably because the mollusks were cooked in the fire prior to opening.

"Stone implements of a rude character are quite frequent. They consist mostly of hammer-stones, axes, celts, broken arrow and spear-points, and net-sinkers. Fragments of plain and ornamented pottery are also found in all parts of the deposit.

"The southern mound is much smaller than the one just mentioned. It is eleven feet in height, but its superficial extent cannot be determined with accuracy, inasmuch as the shells are mostly concealed by earth and vegetation. These shells are also of the common oyster. The implements, although similar in character, are not so numerous as in the other mound.

"The shell-fields which exist south of this place, are of great extent, and in many places of such a depth as to prevent the cultivation of the soil. The first field is situated near Blenheim Manor; the next is at the Ferry House; the third at Lower Cedar Point. A mile further south is a very large shell-field on the Hungerford estate, at Waverly. The estate called Banks of the Dee contains a shell-field nearly two miles in extent. It follows the Potomac from Piccowaxton to Cuckhold's Creek. A large shell-pile is situated in the Potomac southwest of the Banks of the Dee. Simm's Island in the mouth of Cuckhold's Creek is covered with a deposit of shells more than a foot in depth. Other large fields are found at Bachelor's Hope and Swan Point. A shell-mound is found at Lancaster's Landing, on the Wicomico River, two miles east of its junction with the Potomac. Shell-fields have been examined at Charleston Creek and Stoddard's Wharf. All the localities thus far mentioned in this paragraph are situated in Charles County. They also occur at Plowden Manor and Chickahominy in Saint Mary's County.

"Oysters were formerly common in the vicinity of Nanjemoy Creek, but they are now rarely found above Port Tobacco River. They are said to have disappeared almost entirely about 1779, and again during the first quarter of the present century. Fishermen say that the oyster-beds in shoal water are frequently destroyed during long-continuing storms, when the wind blows from the shore, and the small streams carry down sand and detritus, which cover the oysters.

"Shells of the hard-shell clam, as stated, have been met with in the northern mound at Pope's Creek; but these mollusks are not found at present in the same locality.

"Shell-fields occur on the Virginia shore as far north as Mathias Point, in King George County. They are also said to exist on the same side thence to Chesapeake Bay, but in smaller number than on the Maryland shore.

"As to the age of the shell-deposits at Pope's Creek, it seems evident to the writer that they antedate the Columbian era. This belief is based upon the fact that when Lord Baltimore's colonists arrived in 1633-4, these mounds were concealed from view by a thick stratum of earth which sustained a large forest. This forest remained standing until about 1740, when the soil was prepared for cultivation. At this date minor shell-heaps were found above the stratum of earth which concealed the ancient shell-deposit."

In another part of Maryland shell-heaps were explored by Mr. Joseph D. McGuire, of Ellicott City, in Howard County, of that state. I am indebted to him for the following communication:—

"In several visits, extending through a period of ten years or more, I have examined quite a number of shell-heaps at and near the mouth of South River, in Anne Arundel County, Maryland. Oysters of a good quality are found in the neighborhood at the present day, and a large number of persons gain their livelihood as oystermen in the waters adjacent to the shell-heaps. The latter are invariably composed of shells of the common oyster. No one can doubt that these heaps are aboriginal deposits. Within a radius of three miles from Mayo's Island, which is at the mouth of South River near its southern bank, there are as many as twenty-five distinct shell-heaps, possibly four times that number; for I have never yet passed a day in that vicinity without finding at least one new camping-place. The largest deposit, however, is on a property, about two miles up the river, belonging to a Mr. Brewer. At this place there is a point of land projecting into the river, with a well-sheltered little bay on its southern side, forming an excellent location for a camp. The shells cover, I should judge, from ten to twenty acres, and in places are as much as five feet in thickness, thinning out by degrees. Unless a shell-deposit is carefully examined, especially on a hill-side, one is very apt to be misled, and to imagine it to be deeper than it really is.

"On the Brewer property I found the depressions common to shell-heaps, not only in North America, but also in Denmark, to be more distinct than elsewhere in this vicinity. These depressions are elliptical in shape, but occasionally round, and from eighteen inches to two feet deep in the centre. As a rule, they measure from four to six feet in the smaller, and from eight to ten in the larger diameter. They are evidently the sites of habitations, partly filled by the freezing and thawing of centuries, which causes the shells to break down as we see stone walls falling and forming accumulations totally unlike walls. On the Brewer property the hollows are certainly twice as large as I have noticed them elsewhere, probably because they were the sites of larger habitations.

"One of the heaps on Mayo's Island is about one-fourth of a mile in length, and extends back not more than thirty feet; but as it reaches to the water's edge, forming there a precipitous bank at least six feet high, it evidently has been partly worn away. One heap, four or five hundred feet long, which crops out along the bluff on the south side of the river, and rises from six to fifteen or more feet above tide, has within ten years been reduced to half its size, and in a few years more will have entirely disappeared. Another heap on the west side of the river is little, if at all, above the present high-water line, and I think it possible that the surface has subsided.

"As to the age of these heaps, it would be most difficult to offer even a conjecture other than that, as a rule, they are pre-Columbian. Theories with the strongest arguments (apparently) in their favor are often in a moment destroyed. I instance the heap on the south side of the river, which I have said was disappearing. In one place this heap is covered by at least five feet of superimposed earth, which I considered a fair indication of great age, until on one of my visits

I removed from the bank a piece of an iron pot. Afterward I discovered that this thick layer of earth had been gradually washed down from the neighboring hill.

"Trees of three or four feet in diameter have grown on the tops of the heaps. The contents of these accumulations, as may be imagined, are various; but one circumstance is peculiar, namely, that stone implements are exceedingly rare. I have found on several occasions hearths composed of rounded pebbles; also, in one instance, wood-ashes amounting to a cart-load. Charcoal is quite common. Pieces of pottery occur in all the heaps, and are often perforated with holes, apparently for the purpose of mending the broken vessels. Sometimes, but not commonly, this pottery exhibits rude decorations; in color it varies from white to black and red in all shades. It is invariably mixed with pounded shells, and differs in this respect from that found a few miles inland, which nearly always contains triturated quartz instead of shell. English clay pipes of early date are often found in and near these heaps.

"Fish-bones, so common in the New England shell-heaps, I never discovered in those of Maryland; but bones of birds and mammals and turtle-shells are numerous, and such remains as I had identified are those of the duck, goose, swan, wild turkey, squirrel, rabbit, deer, black bear, and terrapin (diamond-back)."

West Virginia.—Deposits of fresh-water shells on Blennerhassett's Island, a locality familiar to the student of North American history, have lately been examined by Mr. J. P. MacLean, of Hamilton, Ohio, and a collection made by him during his exploration is in the United States National Museum. It consists of *Unio*-shells, human and animal bones, arrow-heads, celts, pestles, implements of shell and bone, and fragments of pottery. I am indebted to Mr. MacLean for the following account of the locality and of the character of the deposits:—

"Blennerhassett's Island is situated in the Ohio River, two miles below Parkersburg, West Virginia, and less than two miles west of the mouth of the Little Kanawha. It extends east and west, and is of peculiar form, being narrow in the middle, broad near the centre of either half, and coming to a point at the lower extremity. The length of the island is over three miles, and it embraces two hundred and ninety-seven acres. It contains five refuse-heaps—principally composed of shells of the *Unio*—which afford a fine field for the study of the domestic life of the prehistoric aborigines.

"The first impression that strikes the observer is the favorable situation which the island offered for a safe and convenient home suited to the requirements of the savage. Its natural surroundings afforded him sufficient shelter against the sudden incursions of enemies—besides granting him the advantage of a fertile soil for producing maize, while the broad Ohio, surrounding him on all sides, would furnish an abundance of food. On the Virginia side of the river the banks are almost perpendicular, being elevated to a height of more than five hundred feet, thus presenting a natural barrier against the inroads of foes from that direction. On the opposite side the plain of Belpre ranges from fifteen to seventy feet higher than the island, thus giving protection on the north, although less than that on the south. An additional security consisted in the distance between the shores of the island and those of the main-land, because it is so great as to be practically beyond the range of any primitive weapon of offense.

"The largest shell-heap is located on the eastern point of the lower half of the island. Its present shape is that of a triangle, conforming to the natural contour of the ground, and being eleven hundred and twenty-five feet long by two hundred feet at its western and three feet at its eastern extremity. Originally it was much larger, for within the last forty years a strip seventy feet in width, and extending the whole length of the deposit, has been carried away on the north side by the constant erosion of the river. How much more than this has been torn off cannot now be determined. At the present time the shell-heap is under cultivation, excepting a very narrow road-way along its northern brink. The plough has turned out the shells of the *Unio* and the bones of the deer (*Cervus virginianus*), and the surface is almost covered with these remains. Among the bones the lower jaw of the deer predominates. Bones of other mammals occur; also of birds, but not in abundance. These osseous remains are generally in a very good state of preservation. Chips of chert are scattered over the ground, and may be picked up almost everywhere.

"Under the road-way (where the shells have not been disturbed by the plough) the vegetable mould covering the deposit varies from six to thirty inches in depth. The deposit averages six inches in thickness, and is composed of a compact layer of *Unio*-shells, cemented, as it were, with a sediment of sand and vegetable mould. On exposure the sharp edges of the shells rapidly crumble. Some of them are slightly calcined, proving that they had been placed on coals, either for being cooked, or for facilitating the extraction of the meat. Others are broken, in consequence of a forcible separation of the valves, and many again, which bear no such marks, probably were opened by placing them in hot water. Intermingled with these shells are found the bones of various animals, and there also occur among them vestiges of fire-places. The aboriginal relics here found consist of arrow and spear-heads of chert and hornstone, stone axes, pestles, tubes, pipes, circular stones, bone needles, bodkins, and beads, ornaments of shell and cannel-coal, and fragments of pottery. There is an abundant yield of such articles.

"The shell-heap next in size is located on the upper half of the island, and faces the Virginia shore. It covers an area of about half an acre. When first noticed, it was enclosed by a nearly square wall composed of surface-material. This deposit does not afford as fine an exposure as the one first described, because it has been longer under cultivation, and the shells have mostly crumbled into dust. The yield of this deposit is in variety the same as that of the other, but less abundant.

"The three remaining refuse-heaps are very small, but present the same general features as the last one.

"Within these deposits and in close proximity to them have been found many human skeletons. Some of the skulls do not show the flattening of the occiput so characteristic of the red race.

"The island, at the time of its discovery, was overgrown with forest-trees, hiding the shell-heaps as well as the rest of the land. When Blennerhassett first began to cut down the wood, he found antiquities in the form of pottery, but probably was not aware of the existence of shell-deposits."

Ohio.—As early as 1822, Mr. Caleb Atwater noticed the existence of heaps of cast-away fluviatile shells, intermingled with bones, and inclosing fire-places, near the mouth of the Muskingum River, opposite Marietta. He regards them as very old.*

Tennessee.—Dr. D. G. Brinton, while attached to the Army of the Cumberland during the late civil war, noticed the prevalence of shell-heaps along the Tennessee River and its affluents. "They are very frequent at and above the Muscle Shoals, and are composed almost exclusively of the shells of the freshwater muscle. Close to the famous Nick-a-jack Cave is the railway-station of Shell-Mound, so called from an uncommonly large deposit of shells, probably left by the Cherokees, who so long used this spot as one of their headquarters. It was taken by our troops as a military post, and embankments were thrown up around the summit of the mound. The excavations made for this purpose abundantly proved its wholly artificial origin. In all instances I found the shellheaps close to the water-courses, on the rich alluvial bottom-lands. The mollusks had evidently been opened by placing them on fire. The Tennessee muscle is margaritiferous, and there is no doubt but that it was from this species that the early tribes obtained the hoards of pearls which the historians of De Soto's expedition estimated by bushels, and which were so much prized as ornaments."†

I learned from Dr. Brinton that the mussels of the Tennessee River were occasionally eaten "as a change" by the soldiers of the above-named army-corps, and pronounced no bad article of diet.

Iowa.—Accumulations of fresh-water shells were observed during five years

---

* Archæologia Americana; Vol. I, Worcester, Massachusetts, 1822; p. 225.

† Brinton: Artificial Shell-Deposits in the United States; Smithsonian Report for 1866; p. 357.

(beginning in 1868) by Dr. C. A. White, now of the United States National Museum, along the Mississippi and its tributaries in Minnesota, Iowa, Illinois, Missouri, and Indiana. "In general character," he states, "these fresh-water shell-heaps resemble those of marine coasts, but they are usually not so extensive. They vary in extent from a few bushels of shells to accumulations from fifty to a hundred yards long, four or five yards broad, and from a few inches to a yard or two in thickness. They are usually located upon the immediate bank of the river, sometimes a little below, and sometimes above the reach of the highest floods."

The three most interesting shell-heaps were found by him near the villages of Keosauqua, Sabula, and Bellevue, in Iowa; the first upon the bank of the Des Moines River, and the other two upon that of the Mississippi. The shells constituting these heaps represented fourteen species of *Unio* and one of *Paludina*, all still inhabiting the neighboring water. Among them occurred remains of the cat-fish and sheep's-head, snapping and soft-shelled turtle, wild goose, buffalo, and common deer. The artefacts consisted of flint flakes and arrow-heads, one greenstone axe (found at Keosauqua), and fragments of a coarse kind of pottery.

Both at Sabula and Bellevue Dr. White noticed in the ground small pits, showing the action of fire, and now filled with shells and bones. "The earth had evidently been heated by building a fire in the pits; the mollusks and other food were then placed in them, then covered, and the contents allowed to cook by the retained heat."

Concerning the age of these heaps, Dr. White thinks "that the entire absence of all articles of civilized manufacture, even those that savages most eagerly secure, seems to be very good evidence that they are older than the date of the discovery." He also found oak and elm-trees from two to two and a half feet in diameter growing in the soil that had accumulated upon the shell-heaps, and he ascribes to the latter an age of not less than two hundred years.[*]

Georgia.—The shell-deposit on Saint Simon's Island, briefly but graphically described by Sir Charles Lyell,[†] may serve as a type of artificial accumulations of marine shells in Georgia. Concerning deposits of fluviatile shells, Colonel Charles C. Jones remarks that they are found upon the banks of most of the rivers in Georgia. He further says:—

---

[*] White: Artificial Shell-Heaps of Fresh-Water Mollusks; Proceedings of the American Association for the Advancement of Science; Twenty-second Session, held at Portland, Maine, August, 1873; Salem, 1874; p. 183, etc.—A short notice relating to the same subject had previously appeared in the "American Naturalist" (Vol. III, 1870, p. 54), and also an article of wider range, "Kjœkkenmœddings de l'Amérique du Nord," in the Compte-rendu of the Fifth Session of the International Congress of Prehistoric Anthropology and Archæology, held at Bologna in 1871 (Bologna, 1873, p. 379, etc.).

[†] See p. 218 of this volume.

"As an illustration of their frequency and extent — — — we may instance those on the right bank of the Savannah River, above the city of Augusta. Only one need be specifically mentioned, and this will be found in Columbia County, near the confluence of the Great Kiokee Creek and the Savannah River. Here, opposite a succession of rapids in the river—a locality which would have afforded marked facilities for successful fishing in the manner adopted by the Indians of this region—upon a bold bluff is an accumulation of fresh-water shells covering the surface of the ground to a depth varying from two to four feet, and extending nearly one hundred yards in length, and more than a quarter of that distance in width. Intermingled with them may still be found the bones of large fishes, deer, turkeys, raccoons, bears, bison, turtles, squirrels, rabbits, and other animals and birds, and also fragments of pottery, arrow and spear-points, soapstone net-sinkers,* crushing-stones, axes, chisels, rude mortars and other implements, and various ornaments of clay and soapstone. Here, then, was one of the favorite camping-grounds of the Indians. Hither they resorted for centuries, feeding upon fish, mussels, and game. This is but one of many extensive refuse-heaps of a similar character which have attracted the notice of the writer along the banks of fresh-water rivers not only in Georgia, but also in Florida, Carolina, Alabama, and Tennessee. In these relic-beds no two parts of the same shell are, as a general rule, found in juxtaposition. The hinge is broken, and the valves of the shell, after having been artificially torn asunder, seem to have been carelessly cast aside and allowed to accumulate at the very doors of the lodges, where, mixed with the *débris* of the encampment, in the course of time they became heaped up to such an extent as to form these large shell-banks.†

Cast shells, both marine and fluviatile, were also used in the construction of burial-mounds by the aborigines of Georgia. "Shell-mounds," says Colonel Jones, "formed the common graves of the Indians occupying the coast. They abound upon all the sea-islands, and are thickly congregated upon the outer bluffs and along the banks of salt-water streams. The admixture of shells imparted a permanency to many small mounds which, otherwise, would long since have been entirely obliterated. Most of them contain more than one skeleton, the bones being generally disposed in a horizontal position. In a few instances the dead were inhumed in a sitting posture. Only occasionally do the human bones found in these tumuli indicate the action of fire. — — — The drift-shells—collected by the action of the tides into ridges so common along the coast—were also employed in the construction of these tumuli."‡

Florida.—The fresh-water shell-heaps abounding along the banks of the Saint John's River have been specially studied since 1860 by the late Professor

---
* Noticed on p. 165.
† Jones: Antiquities of the Southern Indians; p. 483, etc.
‡ Ibid.; p. 195, etc.

Jeffries Wyman, and the results of his investigations are contained in a handsome memoir published by the Peabody Academy of Science, at Salem, Massachusetts. It is thus far the most conspicuous treatise on shell-heaps issued in this country. Professor Wyman's field of investigation extended a considerable distance along the river, from Forrester's Point, some miles above Palatka, to the Salt Lakes; but he found the deposits most abundant between Lakes George and Harney. He is of opinion that these heaps were the dwelling-places of the first inhabitants of the region through which the Saint John's River flows.*

"The shell-deposits on the river," he says, "are entirely different as to their characteristics from the mounds of the sea-coast. The last extend around the shores of the whole peninsula of Florida, and in certain places, as at Turtle Mound, Charlotte Harbor, and Cedar Keys, are of gigantic proportions. They are composed exclusively of marine species, mostly of oysters on the Atlantic, but on the Gulf coast of several species belonging to different genera, as *Ostrea, Bysicon, Strombus, Fasciolaria, Cardium*, etc.

"The mounds of the river, on the contrary, consist exclusively of fresh-water species, viz.: *Ampullaria depressa*, Say, *Paludina multilineata*, Say, and *Unio Buckleyi*, Lea. The Paludina forms by far the largest portion of every mound, and with a few Unios the whole of some. Either of the above-mentioned species, however, instead of being promiscuously mingled with the rest, as is generally the case, may be found forming considerable deposits by themselves, without the admixture of the others, as if at certain times they had been exclusively used for food. At Old Town we have seen large deposits of Ampullariæ alone in one part, and of Unios in another. Other shells, as Melaniæ and Helices, are occasionally found, but are too small and too few to justify the supposition that their presence was other than accidental.

"As far as known to the writer, the fresh-water shell-mounds on other rivers of the United States, understanding by the word shell-mound a dwelling-place, consist almost exclusively of Unios. Those of the Saint John's are therefore peculiar, and are the only, or certainly the chief, instances in which the Ampullariæ and Paludinæ just mentioned have become to so large an extent articles of food. There is not a single mound on the Saint John's composed exclusively of Unios. — —

"The most of the mounds are in the form of long ridges parallel to the shore, though a few are nearly circular. The limits of all are sharply defined, and at a few feet from the base shells cease to be found. Rising somewhat abruptly from their foundations, they are mostly surmounted with a nearly level area."† The larger ones sometimes cover several acres, and rise to the height of fifteen, twenty, or twenty-five feet.

---

* Wyman: Fresh-Water Shell Mounds on the Saint John's River, Florida; Fourth Memoir of the Peabody Academy of Science; Salem, Mass., 1875; p. 3.

† Ibid.; pp. 9 and 10.

Professor Wyman examined in all forty-eight shell-heaps, which, of course, cannot be singly referred to in this place. The shells composing them have already been mentioned; the list of mammals, birds, amphibians, and fishes, represented in the heaps by broken bones, teeth, shells, etc., comprises the bear, raccoon, hare, deer, otter, opossum, turkey, several undetermined species of birds, the alligator, four species of turtles, the cat-fish, gar-pike, whiting, and another species of fish not determined. Professor Wyman also met with bones and teeth of extinct mammals (mastodon, elephant, etc.); but their remains had undergone changes, from which he concluded that these animals had not been contemporaneous with the people who left the mounds. These accumulations also contain "human bones, broken up in the same manner as the bones of edible animals, and believed to be the remains of cannibal feasts." As may be imagined, fire-places were noticed.

Stone implements occurred rarely in the mounds themselves, and they are classed by the author of the memoir as flakes or chips, hammer-stones, arrow-heads, and worked pieces resembling somewhat the implements of the Saint-Acheul type. These artefacts generally present a very rude appearance. Better implements, however, occur in some abundance on the surface and in the neighborhood of the heaps, and are thought to have originated with the Creeks and other Indian tribes, which, coming from South Carolina and Georgia, overran East Florida more than a century ago, and, having conquered the natives of the country, formed afterward the Seminole nation. Implements of bone, mostly piercers, were of more frequent occurrence in the heaps than stone artefacts, and there were likewise found bones and parts of antlers, to be made into implements, as shown by the marks of sawing on them. Not unfrequent were chisels and gouges made of the shell of *Strombus gigas*, *Pyrula perversa*, and *Pyrula carica*. Drinking-vessels made of the first-named Pyrula, which were found on or a little below the surface of the shell-heaps, are not considered as coeval with them, but of later origin. The author also mentions among the objects obtained by him during his exploration shells of the *Pyrula carica*, wrought in a certain manner for a purpose not known to him. They are apparently the club-heads described by me a year after the appearance of his memoir,[*] and may have replaced to a certain extent the grooved stone axes, none of which were found by Professor Wyman in or upon the shell-heaps. Ornaments were almost entirely wanting, and not a single pipe came to light. No objects of copper, gold, silver, or other metal were discovered by him. Fragments of a rude kind of pottery occurred in the later but not in the oldest shell-heaps.

The author concludes his interesting memoir with a résumé, embodied in

---

[*] The Archæological Collection of the United States National Museum; No. 287 of Smithsonian Contributions to Knowledge; Washington, 1876; p. 66.—The modified shells, however, are mostly those of *Pyrula perversa*.

the present abstract, excepting the last three paragraphs, which I give in his own words:—

"Though the absolute age of the mounds cannot be determined, a minimum age of several hundred years has been approximately ascertained, justifying the conclusion that some of them were essentially finished two or three centuries before the arrival of the white man, as shown by the age of the trees growing upon them. Other, but not exact, signs of age are to be found in the changes of the channel since the mounds were built, the greater or less destruction of the mounds by the river, the growth of swamps and the consolidation of the shells through the agency of percolated water charged with lime.

"Only a single skull of the builders has been found; this differs from the skulls of the burial mounds in being longer, with the ridges and processes more pronounced. There are bones from other parts of the body from two individuals, in both of which there was the flattening of the tibia. A second collection of human bones was found embedded in sandstone, under a shell-heap at Rock Island, Lake Monroe. Only a part of the skull was found; the tibiæ were flattened, but no other peculiarities were observed.

"Whether the builders of the mounds were the same people as those found there by the Spaniards and the French is uncertain. The absence of pipes in all and of pottery in some of the mounds, and the extreme rarity of ornaments, are consistent with the conclusion that they were a different people. To those may be added the negative fact that no indications have been found that they practised agriculture."*

The coasts of Florida, as has been stated, are lined with vast accumulations of marine shells cast away by the former population of the peninsula. I will make special mention of those located on and near Tampa Bay, on the Gulf Coast, which have been examined and described by Mr. S. T. Walker, connected with the United States Commission of Fish and Fisheries.

"The materials of which the shell-heaps are composed," he remarks, "are indicated by the name applied to them, shells constituting by far the larger portion of the mass, differing only in the species composing them; and here I will state that, after diligent search, I have never discovered a shell in these heaps belonging to a species that is not common in Tampa Bay to-day. The kinds of shell that predominate are those which are most abundant in the immediate vicinity. Thus, if the mound be located near oyster-bars, as on bayous, or near the mouths of creeks or rivers, we find that shell constituting the mass of the structure. If on or near sand-flats, we find conchs, clams, scallops, etc., predominating. Intermingled with the shell, but forming only a small part of

---

* Wyman: Fresh-Water Shell Mounds; pp. 86, 87.

the mass, are crabs' claws, and the bones of the turtle, shark, drum-fish, deer, and sea-birds, occurring as named, the bones of the turtle being most plentiful. Broken pottery of a very thick, heavy pattern, without ornament, is scattered about the sites of former fires. Stone ornaments and arrow-heads are sometimes found on the surface, but never, to my knowledge, in the interior of these mounds."*

Very large shell-heaps were seen by Mr. Walker at Shaw's Point, on the mouth of Manatee River. They extend five hundred and sixty-four feet along the shore, and are from fifteen to twenty feet in altitude at the highest points. The sea having encroached on one side of a heap, a perpendicular section was presented, enabling Mr. Walker to distinguish the old fire-places, which were gradually brought to a higher level, proportionate to the increase of the heap. A representation of this section, accompanying his report, shows this very plainly.†

Not the least interesting observations made by Mr. Walker are those relating to the gradual progress in the manufacture of pottery found in the shell-heaps of Florida. He presents a diagram (reproduced on the following page), showing a section of a shell-heap at Cedar Keys, which he thinks a fair representation of the interior of Floridian shell-deposits in general, if the unusually thick layer of soil near the middle of the mass is excepted. This section was produced by cutting through the mound in opening a street. Fragments of pottery are pretty uniformly distributed throughout the heap from the bottom to the top; but an entire vessel, to Mr. Walker's knowledge, has never been found in any of the shell-heaps of Florida. The three stages marking the progress in the ceramic art are thus characterized by Mr. Walker:—

"In all the large shell-heaps examined hitherto I have invariably found pottery in the lowest stratum of shell, and, in many instances, in the soil beneath the foundations, which I regard as conclusive evidence that the aborigines were acquainted with the art of fabricating earthenware pots long before they began these vast accumulations of shell. The art, however, was in its rudest state. The fragments are thick, heavy, and coarse, the composing clay often containing a mixture of coarse sand or small pebbles. The utensils were of large size, as shown by the curves of the fragments, and rudely fashioned, and they were destitute of all attempt at ornament. The rims were plain, and were not thickened or re-enforced to increase their strength. This style is found generally for about three or four feet in height, and may be said to represent the first stage. Above this a gradual change is perceptible, the two styles overlapping, so that it is difficult to say where one begins and the other ends.

---

* Walker: Report on the Shell-Heaps of Tampa Bay, Florida; Smithsonian Report for 1879; p. 418.
† Ibid.; p. 416, etc.

SECTION OF SHELL-HEAP AT
CEDAR KEYS.

Six inches of modern soil.
(Later stage). Fine thin pottery, beautifully ornamented. Neatly-made implements of bone, shell, etc. Axes, arrow and spear-heads of stone; also stone beads and objects of stone used in games. Three feet.
Two feet of soil containing a few fragments of pottery.
(Middle stage). Better pottery, rudely ornamented. Primitive implements of bone and shell. Four feet.
(Earlier stage). Rude, heavy pottery, destitute of ornament. Three feet.

"The second stage, however, as we ascend, soon becomes plainly marked. The walls of the utensils become thinner. The rims are turned outward and slightly thickened. Dots and straight lines are cut into the sides of the vessel by way of ornament, and the thickened rims are sometimes 'pinched' like pie-crust with the fingers. During this stage the savage artist first began to mould his wares in rush-baskets, which were subsequently burned away, leaving the vessel curiously checked as though it had been pressed, while wet, with coarse cloth. The use of sand or gravel is totally abandoned during this stage, and the quality of the pottery is in every way improved. Implements of shell and bone are sometimes found; but they are generally few in number and rude in manufacture.

"This brings us to a portion of the shell-heap corresponding in position with the two-feet stratum of soil shown in the diagram, and that stratum marks the transition-period between the middle and modern styles of Indian pottery. Immediately below this layer of soil we find the curved line introduced in ornamental designs on the utensils, and a few fragments of the rims of pots show that ears began to be attached to them for the convenience of suspension, and that the thickness of the ware was reduced by the employment of better materials. Immediately over the stratum of soil all the fragments show improvement on those below. New patterns are introduced, and we begin to find fragments of dishes, bowls, cups, as well as those of jars and pots, many of them of elegant design and of a superior quality of ware. Stone axes, arrow-heads, bone and shell implements are of frequent occurrence.

"As we approach the top, marks of improvement are numerous. All the larger pots are furnished with numerous ears, through which strings might be run for suspension. Vessels are sometimes furnished with handles, and all the finer wares are elaborately ornamented with zigzag-lines, curves, dots, and, in rare cases, with figures of men and animals. The finest wares are invariably found on or near the surface, and among them we find the first attempt of the aborigines at coloring their work."

Mr. Walker tries to determine the time needed for the accumulation of the different strata, and attributes, as the result of his calculations, an age of one thousand years to the oldest shell-heaps. Yet, he is far from making any positive assertion. "There are so many possibilities to be encountered," he says, "that the question of age is lost among them. The growth of a shell-heap depended, of course, upon the number of people living in the vicinity, the circumstance whether their residence was continuous or occasional, the abundance or scarcity of shell-fish, and many other accidents too numerous to mention. Layers of soil in different parts of the same heap show that portions of the mass ceased to grow for long periods of time, while thick strata of clean shell indicate the rapid and continuous growth of other portions. Future investigations may throw more light on this subject, at present involved in doubt and mystery."*

Alabama.—Among other shell-heaps on the coasts of the Gulf of Mexico, I will only refer to those on the Mobile River, Alabama, described by Messrs. A. S. Gaines and K. M. Cunningham.

They allude to the great number of such deposits on the banks of that river, especially upon Simpson Island, which forms the delta between the mouths of the Mobile and Tensas Rivers. "Many of them are the sites of market-gardens, and the shells from those most accessible to the water have been utilized in paving the stock-yards of the railroads, and the grounds around the cotton warehouses in Mobile. The one chiefly examined is about nineteen miles above Mobile, on the land of the Mobile and Ohio Railroad, and two hundred feet from the water's edge. The heaps are composed almost entirely of clam-shells, although a few specimens of *Arca incongrua, Neritina, Melania,* and *Fusus cinereus* are met with."†

There were also found portions of fourteen human skeletons, pointed bone implements, thousands of fragments of pottery, and even five entire vessels, now in the National Museum.

California and Oregon.—Mr. Paul Schumacher's reports on explorations of shell-heaps and village-sites on the coasts of California and Oregon, and on the Santa Barbara Islands‡ are known to all who take an interest in North American archæology. In view of the many facts presented by the explorer, it would be a rather laborious task to give a résumé of his results. Fortunately, however, Mr. Schumacher himself has published in German a short article—"Observa-

---

* Walker: The Aborigines of Florida; Smithsonian Report for 1881; p. 677, etc.
† Gaines and Cunningham: Shell-Heaps on Mobile River; Smithsonian Report for 1877; p. 290.
‡ See p. 119, note.

tions on the Ruined Aboriginal Villages on the Pacific Coast of North America"*—which fully answers that purpose, and is here reproduced in an unabridged, though somewhat free, translation:—

"The shell-heaps on this coast mark the sites of former villages of the aborigines. In some cases, however, the accumulations of shells were caused by occasional visits to places where edible mollusks are found in large quantities. In such temporary camping-grounds, which, as a rule, are unfavorably situated for permanent settlements, the mollusks were extracted from the shells, in order to be transported with greater facility to the distant village. By this process, and by the innumerable meals taken, for centuries, on the spot during such visits, shell-beds, often of vast extent, were formed. We notice in these temporary camping-places no indications of the former existence of huts; there are no flint flakes—nothing that betokens the manufacture of weapons and domestic utensils; and graves, likewise, are wanting. All we find are small heaps of cobble-stones, about the size of a hand, and bearing distinct marks of the action of fire; and, accompanying these, charcoal and ashes—additional proofs that they represent old fire-places. The shells in these temporary camping-grounds are always those of mollusks occurring in the neighborhood. We see, for instance, upon the downs which extend for a distance of twelve miles between Point San Luis and Point Sal (Southern California) several of such shell-beds composed almost exclusively of a species of *Lucina*, while they contain but a small number of the *Venus mercenaria*, and other edible kinds; bones of small land-animals and fishes are proportionally very rare. At Point Sal, on the other hand, where we observed the remains of a permanent settlement, there are found not only the shells of all mollusks which prosper on the rocks of the neighboring sea, *Mytilus californianus* predominant among them, but also those of such as occur on the sand-banks near the temporary camping-grounds, together with an abundance of the bones of various land and sea-animals. It would be difficult to determine whether such places were considered as neutral, or whether the mollusks there caught reached the inhabitants of the interior in the way of exchange for other products; but there can be no doubt that they obtained them, for we discovered their remains farther north on the Santa Maria River.†

"The view, sometimes expressed, that the shell-heaps were built up by the aborigines for burial-purposes, and were gradually increased by mortuary feasts, etc., is wrong. On the contrary, it is proved beyond doubt that they indicate the places of ancient settlements, and are the kitchen-refuse heaped up during long periods, and, further, that they inclose graves only in cases when the ground is

---

* Schumacher: Beobachtungen in den verfallenen Dörfern der Ureinwohner an der pacifischen Küste in Nordamerika; Mittheilungen der Anthropologischen Gesellschaft in Wien; Vol. VI, 1876, p. 287-293.

† Northern boundary of Santa Barbara County.

rocky, and resisted the primitive implements of the natives. We find not only the whole mass of the kjökkenmöddings intermingled with fragments of domestic utensils, implements, and weapons, but also discover on the surface, as evidences of permanent settlements, round depressions, generally still surrounded by a circular embankment, which mark the spots where the huts formerly stood. As further evidences we may mention the working-places, where arrow-heads, knives, etc., were made, as is shown by the presence of flakes of chalcedony, jasper, flint, quartz, obsidian, and similar kinds of stone, as well as by the frequent occurrence of broken and half-finished arrow-heads, and of rough-hewn discs, about as large as a hand, in which shape those mineral-substances, which do not occur on the islands, and are also mostly wanting along the coast, were imported by way of barter. Finally, there are round stones, upon which, by means of hammer-stones of harder substance, weapons and piercing-tools were brought into a rudimentary shape, to be finished afterward with a bone implement.

"The traces of a village of the aborigines, especially when occurring in grassy or solid ground, remind the observer of a group of enlarged mole-hills, sunk in, but having a raised circumference or embankment. The digging into one of these cavities reveals the subterranean part of a hut, which reached about four feet below the surface. The floor is recognizable by a harder layer, in the midst of which we find the fire-place and charcoal and ashes. The sides of the hut sometimes can still be traced by the presence of split boards running horizontally, and by vertical posts. Though the under-ground part is quadrilateral in most cases—about ten feet square—we find, nevertheless, that the pit as now seen (rarely deeper than two or three feet, though often very steep) presents a roundish cavity, owing to the circular form of the embankment and the action of the elements in the process of filling a depression in loose ground. In Oregon we found exceptionally several sites of huts inclosed by a quadrilateral projection of earth; such, however, doubtless date from the period of white immigration, and form, as it were, the transition from Indian to trappers' huts, such as we have noticed among the present Klamath Indians. As a proof thereof we find in these cases the wood shaped with the axe, while in the old sites of huts it is split* and charred at the ends. The subterranean part of a hut is pretty much the same along the whole coast, and is only exceptionally of a round form; but in the inner arrangement differences are observable.

"In excavating, for instance, several sites of huts in the deserted chief settlement of the Tu-tu-to-ni, on the right bank of Rogue River, about five miles distant from its mouth (Oregon), we found the hearth-cavity placed on one of the sides, and above it a draft-passage worked from below the embankment

---

* With wedges of elk-horn, which occur quite frequently among the débris.

upward to the surface (Fig. 361). At Chetl-e-shin, near the mouth of Pistol River (likewise in Oregon), we also found the hearth on one side, but without a draft-passage. At other places in Oregon the fire was kept in the centre of the earth-hut, and we made the same observation on the Californian coast, south of San Francisco.

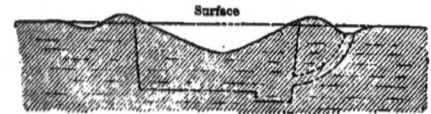

Fig. 361.—Section of the under-ground part of a hut. Oregon.

"The superstructure of the hut doubtless corresponded to the form of the embankment: being circular, and probably terminating conically. On the Island of San Nicholas, in the Santa Barbara Channel,* we found in the course of our explorations in the interest of the Smithsonian Institution that the framework of the huts consisted of colossal whale-ribs, which were so placed that, owing to their curvature, the superstructure assumed a conoidal form, and thus bore some resemblance to a bee-hive. It was only on the islands that we sometimes saw whale-bones used instead of wood in the construction of the huts.

"There are numerous indications that much of the work of the former inhabitants was performed in the open air. Thus we find all places where arrowheads, beads, fish-hooks, mortars, etc., were made, located between the sites of the huts. Arms, knives, drills, and other objects of the flinty material, which, as stated, had to be acquired by importation, were manufactured in all permanent settlements; and so were the numerous mortars and pestles, which consist either of sandstone or basalt. In these latter artefacts not only the material varies according to localities, but we also notice different degrees of skill in their make; while flint points from different places vary but little, if made of equally good material. In some districts the mortars are of masterly workmanship, beautifully formed, and often richly decorated with inlaid pieces of shell, or even with well-executed raised sculpture; but in other localities, where the stone-cutter was

---

* San Nicolas Island is a desert, like San Miguel and San Clemente Islands, for nothing thrives there but a little grass and a few low plants peculiar to the coast; the soil consists of sandstone and banks of sand. No other but drift-wood, therefore, is obtainable. Water is found on all the green islands, though sparingly on some of them. Santa Rosa is grassy, but has no trees. On Santa Cruz Island mountain-willows and scrub-oaks grow in some spots, and there is near the landing a small fir-wood, perhaps the southernmost natural growth of that kind on the coast. Santa Catalina and Santa Cruz are the finest islands in the channel; the former is likewise tolerably well grown with scrub-oak and mountain-willow. Of all the eight islands—Anacapa and Santa Barbara are rocks and without water—Santa Cruz alone has a brook, while on the others water is found in springs. The climate is delightful, more especially that of Santa Catalina. The islands are not inhabited, and merely utilized for cattle-raising.

less practised in his trade, these objects are clumsy, of unelegant shape, and exhibit a shallow cavity. Shell beads and other ornaments of shell were abundantly made on the islands, and probably served as articles of trade. The fine cooking-vessels of potstone, usually globular, and wrought with great skill, appear to have been important objects of barter. The material of which they are composed has thus far not been discovered *in situ* on this coast, though there are indications that it occurs in Southern California. The pots, cut out of a solid piece, must have passed into commerce in a finished state; for, being usually very capacious, the raw material of the larger ones cannot have weighed less than several hundred pounds; and they present, moreover, so much similarity in shape and execution, that their distribution from *one* centre of manufacture appears highly probable. There is hope that the quarry of the aborigines will be discovered; and if that happens, and in confirmation of our supposition, a manufacturing-place has there existed, we shall gain an interesting insight into the methods employed by the natives of this coast in one of their mechanical arts.*

"As the implements used in digging the ground consisted at best only of stone, it follows that a rocky condition of the ground hindered the laying out of a village, and therefore required the deposition of a stratum of a more yielding substance, which was presented in the sand, everywhere plentiful on the coast. If, therefore, a natural, easily-worked ground was wanting in a locality otherwise favorably situated for a settlement, it became necessary to cover the surface with a layer of sand, corresponding to the extent of the village and the depth of the huts. Upon this the latter were built, and the kitchen-refuse began to accumulate, gradually forming what are now shell-heaps. In thus prepared village-sites we find the graves always in the artificial sand-bank, or—what is the same—the shell-heaps. If, however, the soil is sandy, or otherwise of a yielding character, we have to look for the graves outside of the area of the village. They consist in the southern part of California of a communal excavation, about five feet deep, in which the skeletons are placed in narrow compartments, formed either of slabs of limestone (common on this coast) or of whale-bones. They generally are deposited in layers, one above the other, lying on the back, and having the knees drawn up. But this position is often disturbed by the repeated opening of the graves. In order to convey an idea of the limited space allowed to the defunct Californian, we will state that a cemetery extending over an area of six hundred square feet inclosed nearly four hundred skeletons. In Oregon the hut of a dead native was used as his grave, after it had been burned down; but interment in single graves also took place."

---

* Mr. Schumacher discovered afterward potstone-quarries and pot-factories on Santa Catalina Island. His account is contained in the "Eleventh Annual Report of the Trustees of the Peabody Museum of American Archæology and Ethnology," 1878; p. 258, etc.

I am under obligations to Major J. W. Powell for the following notice of shell-heaps in the vicinity of San Francisco, which were examined by him:—

"The shores of San Francisco, San Pablo, and Suisun Bays, in California, were formerly occupied by a tribe or a number of tribes of Indians, who, to a large extent, subsisted upon shell-fish, which abound in the adjacent waters. The shore-line following all of their indentations must be several hundred miles in length. In the neighboring hills are many beautiful springs, and wherever such a spring or any small pond of fresh water is found, a mammoth shell-heap, or sometimes a group of them, can now be seen, so that altogether many thousands of them still exist, and are now held to be valuable sources of fertilizing-material. One of the mounds examined by myself—not the largest that I have seen by any means—was three hundred yards in length and eighty yards in width, and a shaft sunk through the shells to the virgin earth below was sixty-two feet in depth. In the heap were found, besides the shells, many bones of mammals, birds, reptiles, and fishes, showing that the people had a great variety of animal food. Among the many implements found were stone mortars and pestles, doubtless used, as the Indians of that country now use them, chiefly for grinding acorns, and perhaps also other seeds to some extent. The adjacent hills are covered with the oaks of the Pacific Coast, which furnish a great abundance of acorns."

Mr. Dall informs me that the most common mollusks in those waters are *Schizothærus Nuttallii*, Conr., *Tapes staminea*, Conr., *Macoma nasuta*, Conr., and *Saxidomus aratus*, Gould. As less frequent he mentioned *Chiton tunicatus*, Wood, *Chiton lineatus*, Wood, *Purpura saxicola*, Val., *Cryptochiton Stelleri*, Midd., and *Platyodon cancellatus*, Conr. All the species here named, he thinks, were eaten by the aborigines.

Shell-heaps near Cape Mendocino, Humboldt County, California, were explored, in the interest of the National Museum, by Mr. John J. McLean, of the United States Signal Office, and until lately stationed at Cape Mendocino. He communicated, in October, 1883, the following description of these deposits:—

"About a mile south of a small creek which empties into the Pacific, and from which the Cape Mendocino light-house can be plainly seen, there are a large number of aboriginal shell-heaps. Their site covers an area extending about one-quarter of a mile north and south between sand-dunes parallel to the ocean beach, and about fifty yards in average width. Forty-two distinct heaps, great and small, are scattered about within this limited space. There is no regularity in their distribution, as they were formed as it happened to suit the convenience of the shell-fish eating Indians.

"Nine of these heaps have been built up in a conical form by successive layers of shells, bones, and charred timber. Numerous smaller heaps are scattered around generally, prolonged or flattened out under the lee of the contiguous sand-dunes.

"Not more than a dozen varieties of shells appear in the remains. Very large specimens of mussel-shells seem to predominate. Next in point of frequency are the common clam and cockle-shell. The common sea-snail frequently occurs. A conical shell is also quite numerously represented. A univalve with spiral curve, very thick and semi-transparent, comes next in abundance. The latter is generally broken at the side, the aperture forming a hole through the centre at right angles with its mouth. This mutilation is noticed in nearly all of the spiral-curved shells, and was probably made for the purpose of extracting the mollusk; but the shells may have had a subsequent use for ornamental purposes by stringing them together. A great many fragments of the abalone-shell (*Haliotis*) are also found. The mussel and snail-shells, especially the former, are very much broken up, and exceedingly friable when found whole.

"Numerous portions of whale-skeletons are met with, the jaw-bones of one, fully fifteen feet high, forming an arch to the entrance of the Ocean House Hotel. It was carried from the shell-heaps to its present position. There are no specimens of pottery found in or in the vicinity of the shell-heaps.

"This locality was not only resorted to for capturing and consuming the daily food, but was also a workshop of the aborigines, where their implements of war and the chase were manufactured, as numerous flint chips and imperfect arrow and spear-heads prove. Within the radius of a mile these specimens are to be found, more than a thousand of them having been picked up by the writer. Business and pleasure must have been combined in no small degree by these ancient coast-dwellers. Thousands of Indians must have helped to add to the height of this immense mass of débris through many generations.

"Several of the mounds were carefully examined. A trench was dug across the apex, and then another at right angles with the first cutting. The largest heap thus explored showed a combination of shells, bones of animals, and charred timber to the depth of four feet. The shells and bones fell in pieces upon being exposed to the air. Other mounds showed a similar combination of material, differing slightly in the depth of the layers.

"There are no shells of any description found along the beach for five miles southward and three miles northward, excepting those on and in the mounds. Careful examination of the rocks opposite the heaps at low tide only shows one kind of shell-fish, namely, the conical-shaped univalve.

"The flint chippings and arrow and spear-heads are not confined to the immediate vicinity of the heaps, but may be found at numerous places for five miles along the beach in a southerly direction, especially on the sheltered side of a sand-dune or bluff. It would seem that the Indian sat down to manufacture his implements wherever the material was most convenient and abundant. None of the larger implements, such as axes, hammers, pestles, or mortars have been found, excepting one, a weather-worn axe of soft stone. The latter was found near the mouth of the creek."

The collection of stone objects sent to the National Museum by Mr. McLean comprises chips, flakes, rude implements, broken leaf-shaped implements, scrapers, and arrow-heads, of green, brown and yellowish jasper, and other silicious material. The shells taken from these heaps were identified by Mr. Dall as those of *Mytilus californianus*, *Purpura crispata*, *Purpura saxicola*, *Acmœa pelta*, *Acmœa spectrum*, *Acmœa mitra*, *Tapes staminea*, *Pholas californica*, *Fissurella aspera*, *Chrysodomus dirus*, *Haliotis rufescens*, *Chlorostoma funebrale*, *Chlorostoma brunneum*, and *Helix Townsendiana*. There were further found plates of *Cryptochiton Stelleri* and of an undetermined species of *Chiton*, a fragment of an *Echinus*-shell, and some teeth of canine animals.

Alaska.—In describing a number of bone dart-heads, obtained by Mr. W. H. Dall from shell-heaps on the Aleutian Islands, I briefly indicated, in accordance with his statements, the general character of those deposits, and presented also some of the conclusions therefrom derived by him.[*]

It will be remembered that he found the shell-heaps on the islands to consist of three successive deposits, which, he thinks, mark different stages in the development of the population that had formed them. The earliest or *littoral period* is characterized by the echinus-layer, which, resting on the natural soil, consists almost exclusively of the broken, or rather pulverized, tests and spines of *Echinus Dröbachiensis*, Agass., the only species of its kind found in that region, and eaten raw by the present Aleuts. This layer is sparingly intermixed with shells of still living mollusks, among which those of *Modiola vulgaris*, Fleming, *Mytilus edulis*, Lin., *Purpura lima*, Martyn, and *Purpura decemcostata*, Midd., may be mentioned as being most frequent. This bed, varying from two to three feet in thickness, contained no other bones of vertebrates, but some fish-bones, and these in very rare instances. There were no traces of the use of fire observable, and no implements or weapons of bone or stone occurred, excepting rude hammer-stones with indentations on the broad sides. These stones served for cracking the echini and shells. No remains bearing on navigation occurred, though Mr. Dall thinks that rafts or rude canoes of some kind must have been in use. The people who left this layer, the explorer conjectures, lived in an extremely low stage of human development, and he thinks they were addicted to cannibalism, though he has found no confirmatory evidence of this practice in the deposit. He is inclined to assign no less than a thousand years to the accumulation of the stratum.

---

[*] See p. 144 of this work.

Upon this echinus-layer follows one composed of fish-bones, intermixed with shells of mollusks, few bird-bones, and traces of echinus-shells and spines. The chief mass of this bed, however, consists of fish-bones, compacted to such a degree that bar and pick-axe were required in making excavations. It characterizes what Mr. Dall calls the *fishing-period*. The thickness of this stratum varies from one to three feet in different localities. The fish-remains found in it (mostly heads and vertebræ) represent two kinds of salmon, the cod, halibut, and several species of herrings, sculpins, and flounders. Among the artefacts may be mentioned some net-sinkers in the shape of pebbles notched on opposite sides. These, however, appear, according to Mr. Dall, "on the uppermost surface of the echinus-layer, indicating that to the primitive hand-nets or scoop-nets, with which the echinus-eaters might have secured their food, had been added the larger, more elaborate, and more effective seine."* There are mentioned, as occurring in the fish-bone layer, somewhat rude knives of the kind denominated "fish-knives," stone dart-heads, and, in the upper portion of the stratum, harpoon-heads of bone. It is thought probable that skin-boats came into use during this period. Mr. Dall is careful to note the progress which the presence of the above-named objects implies; yet he lays some stress on the absence of charcoal in the deposit, and of those peculiar stone lamps in which fish-oil could have been burned as fuel. The fish, he thinks, were eaten raw, which, to some extent, still is the custom of the Aleuts. The people of this period are supposed to have lived in huts of mats or skins, leaving no traces behind them.

The *hunting-period*, finally, is represented by the uppermost or mammalian layer. "The sharp line of definition between the echinus-layer and the fish-bone layer, which suggested an incursion of fishermen upon the echinophagi, is not paralleled in the line between this and the mammalian stratum. The distinction is readily marked in an actual section of a shell-heap, but the uppermost portion of the fish-bone bed contains some mammalian bones, and the mammalian bed throughout, but particularly at its base, contains a fair proportion of fish-bones. In fact, the change is what we might expect in the progress of a race stimulated by new invention or application of means which placed new, valuable, and eagerly-accepted powers within their reach."† Mr. Dall found the mammalian layer varying from two or three to eight or ten feet in thickness, and the extent of the deposits of this period denotes a considerable increase of the population. "If we allow a thousand years for the duration of the littoral period, or deposition of the echinus-layer (and I am disposed to do so), then I think that fifteen hundred or two thousand years is not an excessive estimate for the duration of the fishing and hunting-periods."‡

---

* Dall: On Succession in the Shell-Heaps of the Aleutian Islands; p. 56.
† Ibid.; p. 62.
‡ Ibid.; p. 73.

Mr. Dall gives a long list of the mammals and birds represented by their remains in the three strata into which he divides the deposit of the hunting-period. Among them are various phocine and cetacean animals, and many kinds of birds, such as puffins, gulls, auks, several species of eiders and other ducks, etc. "Remains of houses of the half-underground type, afterward so universal, appear only in the middle stratum, showing that not until then had the population so multiplied and mutual confidence sufficiently matured, for the more ancient, temporary, above-ground houses to begin to be supplanted by more substantial and comfortable structures."*

During this period some cooking was done in the open air, as evidenced by the discovery of stone hearths still bearing the marks of fire. A great improvement is perceivable in the articles fashioned by the hand of man, and even attempts at ornamentation are not wanting. There were found in this deposit lance-heads of stone and bone, or both combined, bone harpoon-heads† of better make than those discovered in the fish-bone layer, wedges, skin-dressers, and awls, all of bone, stone fish-knives, dish-shaped lamps of stone, and perforated articles of bone or ivory belonging to kayaks, and designed to make paddles and darts fast to them. These last-named accessories to boats occurred in the upper part of the mammalian layer, in which were also found bone handles for dishes or baskets, bone spoons, and other articles similar to those used by the present Aleuts.

Mr. Dall's memoir is undoubtedly of great interest; yet some of his conclusions have not passed unchallenged. I would be guilty of an omission if I failed to allude to the diverging views expressed by Mr. Ivan Petroff, himself for several years an explorer in those regions.

Mr. Petroff agrees with Mr. Dall that the theory of an Asiatic influx of population over the Aleutian chain of islands is entirely untenable, and that they were peopled from the east, but he does not think that this migration took place before the invention of the kayak, considering that there is no timber on the islands, excepting drift-wood, which he considers entirely unfit for the manufacture of canoes, or even for the construction of rafts. "The assumption," he says, "that the earliest inhabitants of the Aleutian Islands were without a kayak or boat of some kind is based upon researches in the shell-heaps of abandoned village-sites on those islands; but a kayak with a whale-bone or even a wooden frame without its modern ornaments of ivory and bone, contained no material that would withstand decay and final absorption. The skin-covering, when worn out and unfit for use as such, was, no doubt, then as now, cut up into straps and patches, or served as food in time of famine, while the frame could be utilized

---

* Dall : On Succession, etc.; p. 75.

† I refer to Figs. 224, 225, 288, 234, 235, 238, 243, 244, and 245, representing bone dart-heads from the fish-bone and mammalian layers.

in many ways that would leave no trace behind. The mere absence from the lower strata of shell-heaps of anything pointing to the existence of the kayak can scarcely be considered as proof conclusive of its non-existence. My personal observations have led me to believe that the remains of former villages and dwellings found on the Aleutian Islands and the continental coast of Alaska are not of the antiquity ascribed to them. Wherever I had the opportunity to observe such localities at long intervals of time, I was astonished at the rapidity with which nature extinguished the traces of man by a growth of sphagnum and other vegetation, giving to the site of the village abandoned but a few years every appearance of great antiquity.

"The absence of stone and bone implements of more delicate construction from the lower strata of the shell-heaps can easily be attributed to the same cause that explains the absence of iron implements from the upper layers that must have accumulated within historic times. Such articles were the product of much labor, and consequently too precious to be lost. At every successive removal from one dwelling-place to another all such products of their ingenuity were carefully collected and removed by the ancient Aleuts, just as it is done now with regard to iron by the natives of the present day. — —

"In the settlements remote from the trading-centres the people of Innuit stock live to-day as they did probably centuries ago, in a manner not at all inconsistent with the remains found in the lower strata of shell-heaps. Even the presence of stone and bone arrow and spear-heads is no true indication of age, as they are manufactured at the present day, as I had an opportunity to witness frequently during my travels in remote regions.

"The time required for the formation of a so-called layer of 'kitchen-refuse' found under the sites of Aleutian or Innuit dwellings I am also inclined to think less than indicated by Mr. Dall's calculations. Anybody who has watched a healthy Innuit family in the process of making a meal on the luscious echinus or sea-urchin, would naturally imagine that in the course of a month they might pile up a great quantity of spinous débris. Both hands are kept busy conveying the sea-fruit to the capacious mouth; with a skillful combined action of teeth and tongue the shell is cracked, the rich contents extracted, and the former falls rattling to the ground in a continuous shower of fragments until the meal is concluded. A family of three or four adults, and perhaps an equal number of children, will leave behind them a shell-monument of their voracity a foot or eighteen inches in height after a single meal. In localities in Prince William Sound I had an opportunity to examine the camp-sites of sea-otter hunters on the coast contiguous to their hunting-grounds. Here they live almost exclusively upon echinus, clams, and mussels, which are consumed raw, in order to avoid building fires and making smoke, and thereby driving the sensitive sea-otter from the vicinity. The heaps of refuse created under such circumstances during a single season were truly astonishing in size. They will surely mislead the ingenious calculator of the antiquities of shell-heaps a thousand years hence."*

---

* Petroff: The Limit of the Innuit Tribes on the Alaska Coast; American Naturalist, 1882; p. 571, etc.

Mr. Dall, after having read at my request the preceding extracts from his work and from Mr. Petroff's article, communicated to me the following statements, which I take pleasure in making known:—

"Knowing at the time Mr. Petroff's article was published that he had no practical knowledge of shell-heaps, and that he had never resided or remained for any length of time in the Aleutian Islands, and, furthermore, finding the contents of the article to consist chiefly of opinions rather than facts, I did not deem it worth the extended consideration necessary to correct its misconceptions and errors. However, as the latter appear likely to pass into serious literature, I have availed myself, by the kind permission of Dr. Rau, of the present opportunity of rectifying one or two of them. Referring to my work on the Aleutian shell-heaps, Mr. Petroff ascribes to me the assumption 'that the earliest inhabitants were without a kyak or boat of some kind,' etc. On page 56 of my paper I state 'they must have had rafts or rude canoes of some kind, but no trace of them is left.' He considers drift-wood unfit for making canoes or even rafts; but I have myself seen the present Aleuts constructing the frames of their canoes of it. In fact, nearly all the boats and canoes (not made of bark) of Northern Alaska are made of drift-wood, both on the Yukon and the coast. This happens because the drift-wood comes from the southeastern coast or the heads of rivers to the southward, and is of larger size than the wood growing nearer the northern coast.

"Mr. Petroff believes that the remains of villages on the Aleutian Islands and the continental coast are not of the antiquity (I have) ascribed to them. He speaks of his astonishment at the rapidity with which sphagnum 'and other vegetation' extinguished the traces of man. This may be true for the continental coast, where he has resided, and to which I did not refer; it is certainly untrue for the Aleutian Islands, where it is a matter of notoriety that the remains of villages abandoned before the Russian advent are distinguishable at the present day as far as the eye can reach; even the paths formerly used by the inhabitants remain nearly free from vegetation, and over the village-sites sphagnum is almost unknown, as they are nearly all comparatively high and tolerably well drained. As to their antiquity, I state (l. c., p. 62) that 'even the most lax hypothesis will not permit us to attempt any computation of the length of time' which it has taken to form the layers indicating village-sites (fish-bone and mammalian layers), though I have shown that, given certain stated and not inherently improbable conditions, the earliest (echinus) layer might have been formed within certain computable limits. All beyond this I distinctly state 'is only an assumption.' Mr. Petroff's opinion that shell and bone-heaps eight or ten feet in thickness 'must have accumulated within historic times' it is not necessary to characterize, if by 'historic times' he means since the Russian advent in 1742. If he means the limits of written history of the civilized world, I have nowhere claimed anything equal in length to that period. It must be remembered that within fifty years after their first exploration the Aleuts were reduced by disease, massacre, and starvation to about their present population, not more than three thousand souls, who occupy altogether less than a dozen villages; less, in fact, than existed on a single bay of Unalashka Island previously.

"It would hardly be worth while to continue tedious explanations for the benefit of readers who are supposed to know something of anthropology. If any such, after studying with care the facts collected in my article on the Aleutian shell-heaps, shall find a more satisfactory and coherent explanation for them, I shall not regret it."

EXTRACTS FROM VARIOUS WRITINGS

OF THE

SIXTEENTH, SEVENTEENTH, EIGHTEENTH, AND NINETEENTH CENTURIES,

IN WHICH REFERENCE IS MADE TO

ABORIGINAL FISHING IN NORTH AMERICA.*

Egede (Hans): Beschreibung und Natur-Geschichte von Grönland; übersetzt von Dr. J. G. Krünitz; Berlin, 1763.—Translation: "In fishing the Greenlanders use iron hooks, and in their absence hooks made of the breast-bone of the bird called *auk*. Their fishing-lines are thin and narrow strips of whalebone tacked together at the ends. With such lines they will draw up a hundred fish to one which our people take with their hempen lines. But for catching halibut they use lines made of seal-skin, and also our hempen lines." (Page 130).

Crantz (David): The History of Greenland: including an Account of the Mission carried on by the United Brethren in that Country; London, 1820.†—"A few of the common salmon have been seen in certain places (of Greenland), but they fall greatly short of those of Norway and other countries in size. The Greenlanders catch these fishes under the stones with their hands, or strike them with a prong of bone or iron. At the season when the salmon ascend from the sea into the rivers, the natives build a wear of stones across the mouth of the stream at low water; over these the fish pass with the tide, and are left in the shallows by the ensuing ebb. — —

"The ordinary food of the Greenlanders is the *Angmarset*, or Greenland Salmon, *Salmo Grœnlandicus*. The Newfoundland men call these fishes Capelins.

---

* This section is far from embodying all early and later notices of fishing, as practised by the North American Indians and Innuits. The copious literature bearing on the natives of the northern half of America might have enabled me to increase the given material to a considerable extent; but it is doubtful whether more extracts would have added much to the reader's information. Even in those here presented iteration is not wanting. I have arranged the extracts geographically, beginning with Greenland and ending with Alaska, following the plan adopted in my account of North American shell-heaps.

† The first edition of the German original of this work was published at Barby (Prussian Saxony) in 1765, and it was for the first time translated into English in the following year. The author's name was not Crantz, but *Crans*.

They are about half a foot long. — — — They do not spawn till May and June, at which time the Greenlanders lade out whole boat-loads of them with hoop sieves strung with sinews: they dry them on the rocks in the open air, and store them up in leathern sacks, or cast-off clothes, for their winter provision. — — —

"The most common food of the Greenlanders, next to the Capelin, is the Lasher Bullhead, or *Ulke, Scorpius Cottus*, Lin. This fish may be found at any season of the year in all the inlets of the coast in deep water, and is caught most plentifully in winter, by poor women and children, with a line of whalebone or feathers thirty or forty fathoms long. A blue stone is fastened to the end of this line to sink it, and a white bone, or a glass bead, or a bit of red cloth serves as a bait for the hook. — — —

"The common flounder is seen on these coasts, but seldom taken. But at certain seasons the Greenlanders catch great numbers of the Holibut, *Pleuronectes Hypoglossus*, with large fish-hooks fastened to whale-bone or seal-gut thongs, from a hundred to a hundred and twenty fathoms in length; the largest are a yard and an half or two yards in length, about half as broad, and a full span thick; they weigh from a hundred to two hundred pounds and upwards." (Vol. I, page 88, etc.).

"Of the whale-fishery of the Greenlanders, it is to be observed that the proper whale and Narwhal are only caught in the north; the Cachalot and smaller species in the south also. Their method of taking the Greenland whale is as follows: all the natives who engage in the pursuit put on their best clothes; for, according to a saying of their sorcerers, if any one of the company wore a dirty dress, especially one contaminated by a dead body, the whale would fly their approach, and even though killed would sink to the bottom. The women are forced to accompany the expedition, partly in order to row, partly to mend the men's clothes and boats, should they get torn or damaged. They assail the whale courageously in their boats and kajaks, darting numerous harpoons into his body. The large seal-skin bladders tied to these weapons prevent him from sinking deep in the water. As soon as he is tired out they despatch him with short lances. The men then creep into their fishing dress, which is composed of seal-skin, and has shoes, stockings, gloves and cap, all in one piece. Thus equipped they jump upon the whale, or even stand in the water by his side, buoyed up by their swollen dress. They cut off the blubber with their uncouth knives, and though provided with such poor instruments, are very expert in extracting the whalebone from the jaws. The former operation is a scene of the utmost confusion. Men, women, and children, armed with pointed knives, tumble over each other's backs, every one striving to be present at the sport, and to have a share in the spoil. It is a matter of wonder to a spectator how they avoid wounding each other more frequently. However, the scuffle seldom ends without bloodshed. The smaller species of whales they catch like seals, or drive them into bays, till they run aground." (Vol. I, page 120).

"They (the boats) are of two kinds, the greater and smaller. The great or women's boat, *Umiak*, is commonly from six to eight or nine fathoms long, from four to five feet broad, and three deep. It is narrowed to a point at each extremity, with a flat bottom. It is made of slender laths, about three fingers broad, fastened down by whalebone, and covered with tanned seal-skin. Two ribs run along the sides parallel to the keel, meeting together at the head and stern. Across these three beams, thin spars are mortised in. Short posts are then fitted to the ribs to support the gunwale; and as they are liable to be forced outwards by the pressure of the transverse benches for the rowers, of which there are ten or twelve, they are hooped in on the outside by two gunwale ribs. The timbers are not fastened by iron nails, which would soon rust and fret holes in the skin coating, but by wooden pins or whalebone. The Greenlander performs his work without line or square, taking the proportions by his eye, which he does with great accuracy. The only tools which he employs for this and every other kind of work, are a small saw, a chisel, which when fastened on a wooden handle serves for a hatchet, a small gimlet, and a sharp-pointed pocket-knife.* As soon as the skeleton of the boat is completed, the woman covers it with thick seals' leather, still soft from the dressing, and calks the interstices with old fat, so that these boats are much less leaky than wooden ones, the seams swelling in the water. They require however a new coating almost every year.

"They are rowed by the women, commonly by four at a time, while one manages the helm. It would be scandalous for a man to interfere, except he were warranted to snatch the oars by a case of extreme danger.

"The oars are short with a broad palm like a shovel, and they are confined to their places on the gunwale by leathern grooves. At the head of the boat, they spread a sail of gutskins sewed together, two yards high and three broad. Rich Greenlanders make their sails of fine white linen striped with red. But they can only sail with the wind, and even then cannot keep up with an European boat. They have however this advantage, that they can make way with their oars much faster in contrary winds or a calm. In these boats they undertake voyages of from four to eight hundred miles north and south along the coast, with their tents and all their goods, besides a complement of ten or twenty persons. The men however keep them company in kajaks, breaking the force of the waves when they run high, and, in case of necessity, holding the sides of the

---

* These, of course, are not the original Eskimo tools, which were those of a stone-age people. Yet they worked meteoric iron into instruments. The "Compte-rendu du Congrès International d'Anthropologie et d'Archéologie Préhistoriques, 6ᵐᵉ Session, Bruxelles, 1872," "contains an interesting article by Professor J. S. Steenstrup on the subject. It is entitled "Sur l'Emploi du Fer Météorique par les Esquimaux du Grœnland."

boat in equilibrium with their hands. They commonly sail thirty miles a day. — — —

"The small man's boat, or *Kajak*, is six yards long, and shaped like a weaver's shuttle. The middle is not a foot and a half broad, and scarcely a foot in depth. It is constructed of long laths with cross hoops, secured by whalebone, and is cased in seal-skin leather. Both the ends of the boat are capped with bone, on account of the friction to which they are exposed amongst the rocks. In the middle of the leathern covering of the kajak is a round hole with a ring of wood or bone. In this the Greenlander squats down upon a soft fur, the hoop or margin reaching up to his hips, and tucks his water-pelt or great coat so tightly round him, that no water can penetrate into the boat. This water-coat is also fastened close round his neck and arms, by bone buttons. The harpoon-dart is strapped to the kajak at his side. Before him lies the line rolled up, and behind him the bladder. He grasps with both hands the middle of his *Pautik*, or oar, which is made of solid deal plated with metal at the ends, and with bone along the sides, and strikes the water quickly and evenly, beating time. Thus equipped, he sets out to hunt seals or sea-fowl, with spirits as elate as the commander of the largest man-of-war." (Vol. I, page 137, etc.).

"There are three methods of taking the seal; either singly with the bladder, or in company, by the clapper hunt, or in the winter on the ice. — — —

"The customary method is that in which the harpoon and bladder are employed. The Greenlander seated in his kajak with all his accoutrements, no sooner perceives a seal than he approaches, if possible, to leeward of him, with the sun on his back, lest he should be seen or scented by the animal. Concealing himself behind a wave, he darts swiftly but softly forward, till he arrives within the distance of five or six fathoms, taking care meanwhile, that the harpoon, string, and bladder, lie in proper order. He then takes the paddle in his left hand, and seizing the harpoon in his right, lances it by the casting board at the seal. If the harpoon sinks deeper than the barbs, it immediately disengages itself from the bone joint, and that again from the shaft, while the string is wound from its roller in the kajak. The Greenlander, the moment he has struck the seal, which dives down with the velocity of an arrow, throws the bladder after him into the water. He then picks up the floating shaft, and restores it to its groove in the kajak. The bladder, which displaces a body of water of more than a hundred pounds weight, is frequently dragged down by the seal; but the animal is so wearied by this encumbrance, that he is obliged to reappear on the surface in about a quarter of an hour to draw breath. The Greenlander, on perceiving the bladder, rows up to it, and as soon as the seal makes his appearance, wounds him with the great barbless lance; and this he repeats as often the animal emerges above water, till it is quite exhausted. He then despatches it with the small lance, and ties it to the left side of the kajak, after inflating the cavity under the skin, that the body may float more lightly after him. — — — This solitary method of seal-catching only succeeds with the stupid attarsoak.

"Several in company pursue the cautious kassigiak and the attarsoit, in what is called the Clapper-hunt, surrounding and killing them in great numbers at certain seasons. In autumn these animals generally shoal together in the creeks, particularly into *Nepiset Sound* in Baal's River, a narrow firth upwards of four miles in length. There the Greenlanders cut off their retreat, and drive them under water by shouting, clapping, and throwing stones. The seals not being able to remain long without respiration, are soon exhausted, and at last continue so long on the surface that they may be conveniently surrounded and killed by the *Aglikak*, or missile dart. This hunt also affords the Greenlanders ample scope for displaying their address. Their manœuvres are not unlike those of a body of hussars. When the seal emerges, they all rush upon him like falcons with deafening cries, and on the animal's diving, which he is quickly compelled to do, the whole party retire in an instant to their posts, watching to see at what spot he will rise next. This is generally half a mile from the former place. If the seal has the range of a sheet of water four or five miles square, he will keep the huntsmen in play for two hours before he is totally exhausted. Should he retire to the land in his distress, he is assailed with sticks and stones by the women and children, while the men strike him in the rear. This is a very lucrative as well as lively diversion to the Greenlanders. A single man sometimes receives nine or ten seals for his share in a day.

"The third method of seal-catching, on the ice, is principally practised in Disko, where the firths are frozen over in winter. They are taken in several ways. The Greenlander posts himself near a breathing hole which the seal has made, sitting upon a stool, with his feet resting on another lower one, to prevent the effects of the cold. When a seal comes and puts its nose to the hole, he immediately strikes it with his harpoon; then enlarging the opening, he draws out his prize and kills it outright. At other times he lies upon his belly on a kind of sledge, near one of the holes at which the seals come forth to bask in the sun. A smaller aperture is made not far from the large one, into which another Greenlander puts a harpoon with a very long shaft. He that lies on the ice, watches at the great hole till he perceives a seal coming towards the harpoon. He then makes a signal to his companion, who forcibly drives down his harpoon into the seal.

"When the hunter descries a seal basking near his hole on the ice, he crawls towards it on his belly, wagging his head and imitating its peculiar grunt. The incautious animal, mistaking him for one of its companions, suffers him to approach near enough to throw his lance.

"Again, when the current has made a large opening in the ice in spring, the

Greenlanders, planting themselves round it, wait till the seals approach in droves to the brink for air, and kill them with their harpoons. Many of these creatures likewise meet with their death while sleeping and snoring in the sun." (Vol. I, page 142, etc.).*

Lloyd (T. G. B.): On the Beothucs, a Tribe of Red Indians, supposed to be extinct, which formerly inhabited Newfoundland; Journal of the Anthropological Institute of Great Britain and Ireland; Vol. IV, 1875.†—" The *Canoe* (Plate III; here Fig. 362) peculiar to these Indians comes next to be considered. The principle on which the Red Indian's canoe is constructed is perhaps nowhere else to be met with. It has in a way no bottom at all, the side beginning at the very keel, and from thence running up in a straight line to the edge or gunwale. A transverse section of it at any part whatever makes an acute angle, only that it is not sharpened to a perfect angular point, but is somewhat rounded to take in the slight rod which serves by way of a keel. This rod is thickest in the middle (being in that part about the size of the handle of a common hatchet), tapering each way, and terminating with the slender curved extremities of the canoe. The form of the keel will, then, it is evident, be the same with the outline of the longitudinal section, which, when represented on paper, is nearly, if not exactly, the half of an ellipse, longitudinally divided. Having thus drawn the keel, whose two ends become also similar stems to the canoe, the side may easily be completed after this manner: perpendicular to the middle of the keel, and at two-thirds the height of its extremities, make a point; between this central and the extreme points, describe each way a catenarian arch, with a free curve, and you will have the form of the side, as well as a section of the canoe, for their

Fig. 362.—Canoe of the Beothucs, Newfoundland.

---

* Many of the details here given by Cranz are contained in Hans Egede's earlier work on Greenland. I have preferred quoting from Cranz, because his descriptions are more elaborate.

† The substance of this article is taken from a written narrative of an expedition to the district inhabited by the Beothucs, undertaken in the year 1768 by Captain John Cartwright. His original manuscript was in 1875 in the possession of the Protestant Bishop of Newfoundland. Mr. Lloyd obtained permission to transcribe as much of the document as served his purpose. He gives no account of fishing as practised by the Beothucs, probably because Captain Cartwright's manuscript contains none; but, as I have included in this work descriptions of boats, I thought it proper to insert here that of the remarkable canoes in use among the natives of Newfoundland.—The extract from De Laet following next refers to the same subject.

difference is so very slight as not be discernible by the eye, which will be clearly comprehended on recollecting that the side, as I before said, begins at the keel. The coat, or shell, of the canoe is made of the largest and fairest sheets of birch bark that can be procured, its form being nothing more than two sides joined together, where the keel is to be introduced. It is very easily sewn together entire. The sewing is perfectly neat, and performed with spruce roots, split to the proper size. The portion along the gunwale is like our neatest basket-work. The seams are payed over with a sort of gum, which appears to be a preparation of turpentine, oil, and red ochre, which effectually resists all the effects of the water. The sides are kept apart, and their proper distance preserved, by means of a thwart of about the thickness of two fingers, whose ends are looped on the rising points above mentioned in the middle of the gunwale. The extension caused when this thwart is introduced lessens in some degree the length of the canoe by drawing in still more its curling ends; it also fixes the extreme breadth in the middle, which is requisite in a vessel having similar stems, and intended for advancing with either of them foremost, as occasion may require, and by bulging out their sides gives them a perceptible convexity, much more beautiful than their first form. The gunwales are made with tapering sticks, two on each side, the thick ends of which meet on the rising points of the main thwart, and, being moulded to the shape of the canoe, their smaller ends terminate with those of the keel rod in the extremities of each stem. On the outside of the proper gunwales, with which they exactly correspond, and connected with them by a few thongs, are also false gunwales, fixed there for the purpose of fenders. The inside is lined entirely with sticks, or ribs, two or three inches broad, cut flat and thin, and placed lengthwise, over which again others are crossed, which, being bent in the middle, extend up each side to the gunwale, where they are secured, serving as timbers. A shut thwart near each end, to prevent the canoe from twisting or being bulged more open than proper, makes it complete. It may readily be conceived, from its form and light fabric, that, being put into the water, it would lie flat on one side, with the keel and gunwale both at the surface, but, being ballasted with stones, it settles down to a proper depth in the water, and then swims upright, when a covering of sods and moss being laid on the stones, the Indians kneel on them, and manage the canoe with paddles. In fine weather they sometimes set a sail on a very slight mast, fastened to the middle thwart, but this is a practice for which their delicate and unsteady barks are by no means calculated. A canoe about fourteen feet long is about four feet wide in the middle." (Page 26, etc.).

De Laet (Joannes): Novvs Orbis seu Descriptionis Indiæ Occidentalis Libri XVIII; Lvgd. Bat., 1633.—Translation: [The inhabitants of Newfoundland, their condition and manners]. "Their boats are made of the bark of trees, at most twenty feet long, about five feet wide, and in the form of a half-moon, being raised and curved at both ends; they carry five persons at the most. By means of these very light vessels they cut the waves with great velocity, and they carry them on their shoulders in case of need; for, having no fixed dwelling-places, they roam about like nomads, and very often change their abodes, either on the spur of necessity, or when it appears convenient to them." (Page 34).*

De Champlain (Le Sieur): Voyages et Descovvertvres faites en la Novvelle France, depuis l'année 1615. iusques à la fin de l'année 1618 ; Paris, 1619; Œuvres de Champlain publiées par l'Abbé C.-H. Laverdière ; Vol. IV, Québec, 1870.— Translation: [Hurons]. "The men make the nets to capture fish in summer as well as in winter, when they generally fish, reaching their prey even below the ice, either with the line or the seine.

"They perform this kind of fishing by making several holes in a round through the ice, that by which they have to draw up the seine being some five feet long and three feet wide. At this opening they begin to let down their net, which is attached to a wooden pole from six to seven feet long, and having brought it under the ice, they move this pole with the net from hole to hole, where it is seized by a man or two through the holes; and this they continue until the opening of five or six feet is reached. This done, they let go the net, which sinks to the bottom of the water by means of certain small stones attached to the end; and afterward they draw it up by its two ends, and thus secure the fish caught in it. This is in short the method they employ in fishing during winter." (Page 101).†

Sagard Theodat (Le F. Gabriel): Histoire du Canada et Voyages que les Frères Mineurs Recollects y on faicts pour la Conuersion des Infidelles, etc.; Paris, 1636 ; Paris reprint of 1866.—Translation: [Hurons]. "From the cordage which the women and girls have prepared, the men, during winter, make nets and seines for catching fish even under the ice, by means of holes cut in different places,

---

* [Incolæ Terræ Novæ, eorum habitus & mores]. "Cymbæ ipsis ex corticibus arborum compositæ, viginti ut plurimum pedes longæ, quinque aut circiter latæ & semilunæ in modum, ad proram atque puppim erectæ atque incurvæ, quinque ad summum vectorum capaces; illis utpote levissimis undas summa velocitate secant, easdem quum opus fuerit humeris gestant; nam ne statis quidem sedibus se continent, sed vagi Nomadum instar sæpius habitationes mutant, prout illos aut necessitas cogit, aut commoditas invitat."

† "Les hommes font les rets pour pescher, & prendre le poisson en esté comme en hyuer, qu'ils peschent ordinairement, & prennent le poisson iusques soubs la glace à la ligne, ou à la seine.

"Et la façon de ceste pesche est telle, qu'ils font plusieurs trous en rond sur la glace, & celuy par où ils doibuent tirer la seine a quelque cinq pieds de long, & trois pieds de large, puis commançent (sic) par ceste ouuerture à mettre leur filet, lesquels ils attachent à vne perche de bois, de six à sept pieds de long, & la mettent dessoubs la glace, & font courir ceste perche de trou en trou, où vn homme, ou deux, mettent les mains par les trous, prenant la perche où est attaché vn bout du filet, iusques à ce qu'ils viennent ioindre l'ouuerture de cinq à six pieds. Ce faict, ils laissent couller le rets au fonds de l'eau, qui va bas, par le moyen de certaines petites pierres qu'ils attachent au bout, & estans au fonds de l'eau, ils le retirent à force de bras par ces deux bouts, & ainsi amenent le poisson qui se trouue prins dedans. Voila la façon en bref comme ils en vsent pour leur pesche en hyuer."

proceeding in the following way: by heavy blows with an axe they make a hole of sufficient size in the ice of a lake or river; they make smaller ones at a certain distance from each other, and by means of a pole they pass a string from hole to hole below the ice; this string, as long as the net to be extended, reaches to the last hole, and by drawing it forward the whole net attached to it is stretched out in the water. To examine the net, it is drawn through the largest opening, and the fish taken out. Afterward it is only necessary to draw back the string for stretching the net again, the pole simply serving for passing the string the first time." (Vol. I, page 245).*

"We found in the bellies of several large fishes hooks made of a piece of wood and a bone, so placed as to form a hook, and very neatly bound together with hemp; but the line being too weak for drawing on board such large fishes, the result was the loss of the labor of the fishermen, and of the hooks thrown into the sea by them; for, in verity, there are in this fresh-water sea sturgeon, assihendos, trout, and pike of such monstrous size, that larger ones cannot be seen anywhere else, not to speak of several other kinds of fish there caught, which are here (in Europe) unknown." (Vol. III, page 588).†

"As for the fishes found in the rivers and lakes in the country of our Hurons, and particularly in the fresh-water sea, the principal are the Assihendo, of which we have spoken elsewhere, and trout, called Ahouyoche by them, which are mostly of extraordinary size, insomuch that I have not seen there any that were not bigger than the largest we have on this side; their flesh is ordinarily red, though in some of a yellow or orange color, yet of excellent taste.

"The pike, called Soruissan, which they catch here also with the sturgeon, called Hixrahon, astonish people, for some are of marvelous size, and more palatable than any of our species of fish. —— —— Some weeks after the season for catching large fish, they pursue the capture of the Einchataon, a kind somewhat

---

* "Pendant l'Hyuer, du filet que les femmes & filles ont disposé, les hommes en font des rets & seines pour pescher & prendre le poisson iusques sous la glace, par le moyen des trous qu'ils y font en plusieurs endroits, dont en voicy la methode.

"Ils font à grands coups de hache un trou assez grandelet dans la glace d'un lac ou de la riuiere; ils en font d'autres plus petits d'espaces en espaces, & auec des perches ils passent une ficelle de trous en trous par dessous la glace; ceste ficelle aussi longue que les rets qu'on veut tendre, se va arrester au dernier trou, par lequel on tire, & on estend dedans l'eau toute la rets qui luy est attaché. Quand on les veut visiter, on les retire par la plus grande ouuerture, pour en recueillir le poisson, puis il ne faut que retirer la ficelle pour les retendre, les perches ne seruans qu'à passer la premiere fois la ficelle."

† "Nous trouuasmes dans le ventre de plusieurs grands poissons, des ains faicts d'un morceau de bois accommodé auec un os, qui seruoit de crochet & lié fort proprement auec de leur chanure, mais la corde trop foible pour tirer à bord de si gros poissons, auoit faict perdre & la peine & les ains de ceux qui les auoient iettez en mer, car veritablement il y a dans cette mer douce des esturgeons, assihendos, truittes & brochets, si monstrueusement grands qu'il ne s'en voit point ailleurs de plus gros, non plus que de plusieurs autres especes de poissons qu'on y pesche & qui nous sont icy incognus."

resembling our barbel, and about a foot and a half or a little less in length: this fish serves to give taste to their sagamité* during winter. — — —

"In another season they catch with the seine a certain kind of fish, which seem to correspond to our smallest herrings, and which they eat fresh or buccaned. — — — They also catch several other species of fish; but as they are unknown to us, and as similar ones are not found in our rivers, I make no mention of them. — — —

"Eel in the proper season is an invaluable article to our Montagnais. I have admired the extreme abundance of this fish in some of the rivers of our Canada, where every year uncountable hundreds are caught. They come just in time, for, were it not for this succor, one would be greatly embarrassed, more especially in some months of the year; the savages and the members of our orders use them as meat sent by Heaven for their relief and solace. They catch them in two ways: with a wicker basket, or with a harpoon during night by the light of fire. They construct with some ingenuity wicker baskets, long and wide, and large enough to hold five or six eels. When the sea is low, they deposit them on the sand in a suitable remote place, securing them in a manner that the tide cannot carry them off. At both sides they heap up stones, which extend like a chain or small wall on both sides, in order that the fish, which always seeks the bottom, in encountering this obstacle, may glide slowly toward the aperture of the basket to which the stones lead. When the sea has risen, it covers the baskets; and after it has subsided again, they are examined. Sometimes hundred or two hundred eels are found at one tide; sometimes more, and occasionally none at all, according to wind and weather. When the sea is agitated, many are caught; when it is calm, few or none; but then they have recourse to their harpoons.† — — —

"The savages cure fish in the following manner: they let them drip a little, and then cut off the heads and tails; they open them at the back, and having emptied them, they make incisions, to allow the smoke to penetrate them thoroughly; the perches in their huts are all loaded with them. When they are well buccaned, they bring them together, and make them into packages, each containing about a hundred." (Vol. III, page 693, etc.).‡

---

* Previously mentioned in Sagard's work. It was maize parched in the ashes and pounded, for making pulse.

† This account of eel-fishing and the succeeding description of fish-drying correspond almost literally with those given by Father Le Jeune in his "Relation" (published in 1635, from which the extract following next is made. Concerning the eel-traps, however, Father Le Jeune states they were large enough to hold five or six hundred eels (*capables de tenir cinq et six cens anguilles*), while Sagard speaks only of five or six (*capables de contenir cinq & six anguilles*).

‡ "Pour ce qui est des poissons qui se retrouuent dans les riuieres & lacs au païs de nos Hurons, & particulierement à la mer douce, les principaux sont l'Assihendo, duquel nous auons parlé ailleurs, & des Truictes, qu'ils appellent Ahouyoche, lesquelles sont de desmesurée grandeur pour la pluspart, & n'y en ay veu aucune qui ne soit plus grosse que les plus grandes que nous ayons par deça: leur chair est communement rouge, sinon à quelqu'unes qu'elle se voit iaune ou orangée, mais excellemment bonne.

EXTRACTS. 271

Le Ievne (Le P. Paul): Relation de ce qui s'est passé en la Nouvelle France sur le grand Fleuve de S. Laurens en l'année 1634;* Relations des Jésuites, etc.; Vol. I, Québec, 1858.—Translation: "This harpoon (for spearing eel) is an instrument consisting of a long stick, of the thickness of three fingers, to the end of which they fasten an iron spike,† which they arm on each side with a curved prong, both coming nearly together at the end of the iron point. In striking an eel with this harpoon, they drive the iron into it, and the two prongs, yielding to the force of the thrust, let in the eel, after which they contract again by themselves (having opened merely by the shock of the stroke), and prevent the speared eel from escaping.

"This fishing with the harpoon is ordinarily done only during the night: two savages sit in a canoe, one behind who steers and paddles, and the other ahead, seeking by the light of a bark torch, attached to the prow of the craft, his prey with the eyes, while gently moving along the bank of this great river. Perceiving an eel, he darts his harpoon without losing hold of it, pierces the eel as stated, and then throws it into his canoe. Some will catch three hundred, and many more, in a single night, but very few at other times." (Page 44).‡

"Les Brochets, appellez Soruissan, qu'ils y peschent aussi auec les Esturgeons nommez Hixrahon, estonnent les personnes, tant il s'y en voit de merueilleusement grands, & friands au delà de toutes nos especes de poissons. —— Quelques sepmaines apres la pesche des grands poissons, ils vont à celle de l'Einchataon, qui est un poisson vn peu approchant aux barbeaux par deça, long d'enuiron vn pied & demy, ou peu moins: ce poisson leur sert pour donner goust à leur sagamité pendant l'Hyuer. ——

"En autre saison ils y peschent à la seine une certaine espece de poissons, qui semblent estre de nos harangs, mais des plus petits, lesquels ils mangent frais & boucanez. —— Ils peschent aussi de plusieurs autres especes de poissons, mais comme ils nous sont incognus, & qu'il ne s'en trouue point de pareils en nos riuieres, ie n'en fais point aussi de mention. ——

"L'anguille en sa saison est une manne qui n'a point de prix chez nos Montagnais. I'ay admiré l'extreme abondance de ce poisson, en quelqu'unes des riuieres de nostre Canada, où il s'en pesche tous les ans vers l'Automne une infinité de centaines, qui viennent fort à propos, car n'estoit ce secours on se trouueroit bien souuent empesché en quelques mois de l'année principalement; les Sauuages & nos Religieux en usent comme viande enuoyée du Ciel pour leur soulagement & consolation. Ils la peschent en deux façons, auec une nasse, ou auec un harpon, ce qui se falot la nuict à la clarté du feu. Ils font des nasses auec assez d'industrie, longues & grosses, capables de contenir cinq & six anguilles: la mer estant basse, ils les placent sur le sable en quelque lieu propre & reculé, les assourent en sorte que les marées ne les peuuent emporter: aux deux costez ils amassent des pierres, qu'ils estendent comme une chaisne ou petite muraille de part & d'autre, afin que ce poisson qui va tousiours au fond rencontrant cet obstacle, se glisse doucement vers l'embouchure de la nasse où le conduisent ces pierres: la mer venant à se grossir, couure la nasse, puis se rabaissant, on la va visiter: par fois on y trouue cent ou deux cens anguilles d'une marée, quelquefois plus, & d'autres fois point du tout, selon les vents & les temps. Quand la mer est agitée, on en prend beaucoup, quand elle est calme, peu ou point, mais alors ils ont recours à leur harpon. ——

"Voicy comment les Sauuages font seicher de ces poissons. Ils les laissent un peu esgoutter, puis leur couppent la teste & la queuë, ils les ouurent par le dos, puis les ayant vuidés ils les taillandent, afin que la fumée entre par tout: les perches de leurs cabanes en sont toutes chargées. Estans bien boucanez, ils les accouplent & en font de gros paquets enuiron d'une centaine à la fois."

* Published at Paris in 1635.

† The iron mentioned by Father Le Jeune, of course, was furnished by whites. The armature of this gig in its original state consisted of bone or horn.

‡ "Ce harpon est vn instrument composé d'vn long baston, gros de trois doigts, au bout duquel ils attachent vn fer pointu, lequel ils arment de part et d'autre de deux petits bastons recourbés, qui se viennent quasi ioindre

Charlevoix (Father): Letters to the Dutchess (sic) of Lesdiguieres, etc.; London, 1763.—[Indians of Canada]. "These People have a wonderful Skill in striking Fish in the Water, especially in the Torrents. They fish also with the Sein, and they have an odd Ceremony before they use this Net. They marry it to two young Maids, and during the Wedding Feast they place it between the two Brides. They exhort it very seriously to take a great many Fish, and they think to engage it to do so by making great Presents to its pretended Fathers-in Law. — — — The Sturgeon here is a Sea and a fresh Water Fish; for they take it upon the Coasts of *Canada,* and in the great Lakes which cross the River *St. Laurence.* — — — The Savages take them in the Lakes in this Manner: Two Men are at the two Ends of a Canoe; he behind steers, and the other stands up, holding a Dart in one Hand, to which a long Cord is fastened, the other End is tied to one of the Bars of the Canoe. As soon as he sees the Sturgeon in his Reach, he throws his Dart, and endeavours to strike where there are no Scales; if the Fish is wounded it flies, and draws the Canoe also pretty swiftly, but after having swam about 150 Paces it dies, then they draw up the Cord and take it." (Page 86, etc.).

"The *Michilimakinacs* lived almost only by Fishing, and there is perhaps no Place in the World where there is such Plenty of Fish. The most common Fish in the three Lakes, and in the Rivers that flow into them, are the Herring, the Carp, the Gilt Fish, the Pike, the Sturgeon, the *Astikamegue,* or white Fish, and above all, the Trout. They take three Sorts of the last, among which some are of a monstrous Size, and in such Numbers, that a Savage with his Spear will sometimes strike fifty in three Hours Time. But the most famous of all is the White Fish: It is about the Bigness and Shape of a Mackerel; I know of no Kind of Fish that is better eating. The Savages say, that it was *Michabou* who taught their Ancestors to fish, that he invented Nets, and that he took the Notion of them from the Spider's Web. These People, as you see, Madam, do not give greater Honour to their God than he deserves, since they are not afraid of sending him to School to a vile Insect." (Page 194).

[Bark canoes]. "I believe that I have already told you that there are two Sorts of them, the one of Elm Bark, which are wider and more clumsily built, but commonly bigger. I know none but the *Iroquois* who have any of this Sort.

---

au bout de la pointe du fer: quand ils viennent à frapper vne anguille de ce harpon, ils l'embrochent dans ce fer, les deux bastons adjoincts, cedans par la force du coup, et laissans entrer l'anguille; puis se reserrans d'eux mesmes, car ils ne s'ouurent que par la secousse du coup, ils empêchent que l'anguille embrochée ne ressorte.

"Cette pesche au harpon ne se fait ordinairement que la nuict: ils se mettent deux Sauuages dans vn canot, l'vn derriere qui le gouuerne et qui rame, et l'autre est deuant, lequel à la faueur d'vn flambeau d'écorce, attaché à la prouë de son vaisseau, s'en va cherchant la proye de ses yeux, rodans doucement sur le bord de ce grand fleuue; appercevant vne Anguille, il lance son harpon sans le quitter, la perce comme i'ay dit, puis la iette dans son canot; il y en a tel qui en prendra trois cens en vne nuict, et bien dauantage, quelquefois fort peu."

The others are of the Bark of Birch Trees, of a Width less in Proportion than their Length, and much better made: It is these that I am going to describe, because all the *French*, and almost all the Savages use them.

"They lay the Bark, which is very thick, on flat and very thin Ribs made of Cedar: These Ribs are confined their whole Length by small Cross-Bars, which separate the Seats of the Canoe; two main Pieces of the same Wood, to which these little Bars are sew'd, strengthen the whole Machine. Between the Ribs and the Bark they thrust little Pieces of Cedar, which are thinner still than the Ribs, and which help to strengthen the Canoe, the two Ends of which rise by Degrees, and insensibly end in sharp Points that turn inwards. These two Ends are exactly alike; so that to change their Course, and turn back, the Canoe-Men need only change Hands. He who is behind steers with his Oar, working continually; and the greatest Occupation of him who is forward, is to take Care that the Canoe touches nothing to burst it. They sit or kneel on the Bottom, and their Oars are Paddles of five or six Feet long, commonly of Maple; but when they go against a Current that is pretty strong, they must use a Pole, and stand upright. One must have a good deal of Practice to preserve a Ballance in this Exercise, for nothing is lighter, and of Consequence easier to overset, than these Canoes; the greatest of which, with their Loading, does not draw more than half a Foot Water.

"The Bark of which these Canoes are made, as well as the Ribs and the Bars, are sew'd with the Roots of Fir, which are more pliable, and dry much less than the Ozier. All the Seams are gum'd within and without, but they must be viewed every Day, to see that the Gum is not peeled off. The largest Canoes carry twelve Men, two upon a Seat; and 4000 l. Weight. Of all the Savages, the most skilful Builders of Canoes are the *Outaouais;* and in general the *Algonquin Nations* succeed herein better than the *Hurons*. Few *French* as yet can make them even tolerably; but to guide them, they are at least as safe as the Savages of the Country." (Page 117).*

Henry (*Alexander*): *Travels and Adventures in Canada and the Indian Territories, between the years 1760 and 1776; New York, 1809.*—"The white-fish is taken (at Michilimakinac) in nets which are set under the ice. To do this,

---

* Father Lafitau gives a similar account of the building of bark canoes, bestowing much praise on those made by the Algonkin nations, which he calls the master-pieces of savage art, but speaking disapprovingly of the Iroquois canoes.

"The Iroquois," he says, "make no canoes of birch bark, but buy them from other nations, or make in their stead canoes of elm bark. These latter scarcely serve for more than one voyage, as they are less solid than the others, and can easily be replaced in case of loss. They consist of one piece, and are made with all possible inaccuracy and clumsiness."—*Mœurs des Sauvages Amériquains;* Paris, 1724; Vol. II, p. 213, etc.

By far the best description of modern manufacture of bark canoes among the Ojibways is that by J. G. Kohl, who devotes to the subject a whole chapter (or letter) in his work entitled "Kitschi-Gami oder Erzählungen vom Obern See," published at Bremen in 1859 (Vol. I, p. 41, etc.).—This work has been translated into English by L. Wraxall, under the title "Kitchi Gami. 'Wanderings round Lake Superior" (London, 1860).

R 35

several holes are made in the ice, each at such distance from that behind it, as that it may be reached, under the ice, by the end of a pole. A line, of sixty fathoms in length, is thus conveyed from hole to hole, till it is extended to the length desired. This done, the pole is taken out, and with it one end of the line, to which the end is then fastened. The line being now drawn back by an assistant, who holds the opposite extremity, the net is brought under, and a large stone is made fast to the sinking-line at each end, and let down to the bottom; and the net is spread in the water, by lighters on its upper edge, sinkers on its lower, in the usual manner. The fish, running against the net, entangle their gills in the meshes, and are thus detained till taken up." (Page 55).

"These *rapids* (of Sault de Sainte-Marie) are beset with rocks of the most dangerous description; and yet they are the scene of a fishery in which all their dangers are braved and mastered with singular expertness. They are full of white-fish, much larger and more excellent than those of Michilimakinac, and which are found here during the greater part of the season, weighing, in general, from six pounds to fifteen.

"The method of taking them is this: each canoe carries two men, one of whom steers with a paddle, and the other is provided with a pole, ten feet in length, and at the end of which is affixed a scoop-net. The steersman sets the canoe from the eddy of one rock to that of another; while the fisherman in the prow, who sees through the pellucid element the prey of which he is in pursuit, dips his net, and sometimes brings up, at every succeeding dip, as many as it can contain. The fish are often crowded together in the water in great numbers; and a skilful fisherman, in autumn, will take five hundred in two hours.

"This fishery is of great moment to the surrounding Indians, whom it supplies with a large proportion of their winter's provision; for, having taken the fish in the manner described, they cure them by drying in the smoke, and lay them up in large quantities." (Page 58, etc.).

Hearne (Samuel): A Journey from Prince of Wales's Fort in Hudson's Bay, to the Northern Ocean. Undertaken by Order of the Hudson's Bay Company, for the Discovery of Copper Mines, a North West Passage, &c. In the years 1769, 1770, 1771, & 1772; London, 1795.—"The track of land inhabited by the Northern Indians is very extensive, reaching from the fifty-ninth to the sixty-eighth degree of North latitude; and from East to West is upward of five hundred miles wide. It is bounded by Churchill River on the South, the Athapuscow Indians' Country on the West; the Dog-ribbed and Copper Indians' Country on the North, and by Hudson's Bay on the East. — — —

"The many lakes and rivers with which this part of the country abounds, though they do not furnish the natives with water-carriage, are yet of infinite advantage to them; as they afford great numbers of fish, both in Summer and

Winter. The only species caught in those parts are trout, tittameg, (or tickomeg,) tench, two sorts of barble, (called by the Southern Indians Na-may-pith,) burbot, pike, and a few perch. The four former are caught in all parts of this country, as well the woody as the barren; but the three latter are only caught to the Westward, in such lakes and rivers as are situated among the woods; and though some of those rivers lead to the barren ground, yet the three last mentioned species of fish are seldom caught beyond the edge of the woods, not even in the Summer season. — — —

"The only method practised by those people to catch fish either in Winter or Summer, is by angling and setting nets; both of which methods is attended with much superstition, ceremony, and unnecessary trouble; but I will endeavour to describe them in as plain and brief a manner as possible.

"When they make a new fishing-net, which is always composed of small thongs cut from raw deer-skins, they take a number of birds' bills and feet, and tie them, a little apart from each other, to the head and foot rope of the net, and at the four corners generally fasten some of the toes and jaws of the otters and jackashes. The birds' feet and bills made choice of on such occasions are generally those of the laughing goose, wavey, (or white goose,) gulls, loons, and black-heads; and unless some or all of these be fastened to the net, they will not attempt to put it into the water, as they firmly believe it would not catch a single fish.

"A net thus accoutred is fit for setting whenever occasion requires, and opportunity offers; but the first fish of whatever species caught in it, are not to be sodden in the water, but broiled whole on the fire, and the flesh carefully taken from the bones without dislocating one joint; after which the bones are laid on the fire at full length and burnt. A strict observance of these rules is supposed to be of the utmost importance in promoting the future success of the new net; and a neglect of them would render it not worth a farthing.

"When they fish in rivers, or narrow channels that join two lakes together, they could frequently, by tying two, three, or more nets together, spread over the whole breadth of the channel, and intercept every sizable fish that passed; but instead of that, they scatter the nets at a considerable distance from each other, from a superstitious notion, that were they kept close together, one net would be jealous of its neighbor, and by that means not one of them would catch a single fish.

"The methods used, and strictly observed, when angling, are equally absurd as those I have mentioned; for when they bait a hook, a composition of four, five, or six articles (all animal substances) by way of charm, is concealed under the bait, which is always sewed round the hook. In fact, the only bait used by those people is in their opinion a composition of charms, inclosed within a bit of fish-skin, so as in some measure to resemble a small fish. — — —

"They have also a notion that fish of the same species inhabiting different parts of the country, are fond of different things; so that almost every lake and river they arrive at, obliges them to alter the composition of the charm. The same rule is observed on broiling the first fruits of a new hook that is used for a new net; an old hook that has already been successful in catching large fish is esteemed of more value than a handful of new ones which have never been tried." (Page 326, etc.).

Mackenzie (Alexander): Voyages from Montreal, etc., to the Frozen and Pacific Oceans; in the years 1789 and 1793; London, 1801.—[Slave and Dogrib Indians]. "They always keep a large quantity of the fibres of willow bark, which they work into thread on their thighs. Their nets are from three to forty fathoms in length, and from thirteen to thirty-six meshes in depth. The short deep ones they set in the eddy current of rivers, and the long ones in the lakes. They likewise make lines of the sinews of the rein-deer, and manufacture their hooks from wood, horn, or bone. — — — Their canoes are small, pointed at both ends, flat-bottomed and covered in the fore part. They are made of the bark of the birch-tree and fir-wood, but of so slight a construction, that the man whom one of these light vessels bears on the water, can, in return, carry it over land without any difficulty. It is very seldom that more than one person embarks in them, nor are they capable of receiving more than two. The paddles are six feet long, one half of which is occupied by a blade, of about eight inches wide." (Pages 37, 39).

[Indians of Peace River District]. "Their nets and fishing-lines are made of willow-bark and nettles; those made of the latter are finer and smoother than if made with hempen thread. Their hooks are small bones, fixed in pieces of wood split for that purpose, and tied round with fine watape.* — — — They have spruce bark in great plenty, with which they make their canoes, an operation that does not require any great portion of skill or ingenuity, and is managed in the following manner:— The bark is taken off the tree the whole length of the intended canoe, which is commonly about eighteen feet, and is sewed with watape at both ends; two laths are then laid, and fixed along the edge of the bark which forms the gunwale; in these are fixed the bars, and against them bear the ribs or timbers, that are cut to the length to which the bark can be stretched; and, to give additional strength, strips of wood are laid between them; to make the whole water-tight, gum is abundantly employed. These vessels carry from two to five people." (Page 206, etc.).†

---

* Wattap: a kind of thread made of the small roots of the spruce-tree.

† In the course of his narrative, Mackenzie describes other appliances for fishing (weirs, fish-traps); but he fails to state by what tribes they were constructed.

Williams (Roger): A Key into the Language of America, or an Help to the Language of the Natives in that Part of America called New-England; London, 1643. Reprinted as Vol. I of the " Collections of the Rhode Island Historical Society;" Providence, 1827.—" Missúckeke-kéquock, Basse. The Indians (and the English too) make a daintie dish of the Uppaquontup, or head of this Fish; and well they may, the braines and fat of it being very much, and sweet as marrow.

"Kaúposh-shaûoog, Sturgeon. Obs: Divers part of the Countrey abound with this Fish; yet the Natives for the goodnesse and greatnesse of it, much prize it, and will neither furnish the English with so many, nor so cheape, that any great trade is like to be made of it, untill the English themselves are fit to follow the fishing.

"The Natives venture one or two in a Canow, and with an harping Iron, or such like Instrument sticke this fish, and so hale it into their Canow; sometimes they take them by their nets, which they make strong of Hemp.

"Ashòp, their nets. Which they will set thwart some little River or Cove wherein they kill Basse (at the fall of the water) with their arrows, or sharp sticks, especially if headed with Iron, gotten from the English, &c. — — —

"Mishcùp-paûog, Sequanamáuquock, Breame. Obs: Of this Fish there is abundance, which the Natives drie in the Sunne and smoake; and some *English* begin to salt, both wayes they keepe all the yeere; and it is hoped it may be as well accepted as Cod at a Market, and better, if once knowne. — — —

"Pótop-paúog, Whales. Which in some places are often cast up; I have seene some of them, but not above sixtie foot long: The Natives cut them out in severall parcells, and give and send farre and neere for an acceptable present, or dish. — — —

"Sickíssuog, Clams. Obs: This is a sweet kind of shellfish, which all Indians generally over the Countrey, Winter and Summer delight in; and at low water the women dig for them: this fish and the naturall liquors of it, they boile, and it makes their broth and their Nasaûmp (which is a kind of thickened broth) and their bread seasonable and savoury, in stead of Salt: and for that the English Swine dig and root these Clams wheresoever they come, and watch the low water (as the Indian women do) therefore of all the English Cattell, the Swine (as also because of their filthy disposition) are most hatefull to all Natives, and they call them filthy cut throats, &c.

"Séqunnock, Poquaûhock, A Horse fish.* Obs: This the English call Hens, a little thick shell fish which the Indians wade deepe and dive for, and after they have eaten the meat there (in those which are good) they breake out the shell, about halfe an inch of a blacke part of it, of which they make their Suckaûhock, or blackmoney, which is to them pretious.

---

* The hard-shell clam (*Venus mercenaria*, Lin.).

"Meteaûhock, The Periwinkle. Of which they make their Wómpan or white money, of halfe the value of their Suckáwhock, or blacke money. — — —

"The Natives take exceeding great paines in their fishing, especially in watching their seasons by night; so that frequently they lay their naked bodies many a cold night on the cold shoare about a fire of two or three sticks, and oft in the night search their Nets; and sometimes goe in and stay longer in frozen water." (Page 102, etc.).*

"Obs: Mishoòn, an Indian Boat, or Canow made of a Pine or Oake, or Chesnut-tree: I have seene a Native goe into the woods with his hatchet carrying onely a Basket of Corne with him, and stones to strike fire when he had felled his tree (being a Chesnut) he made him a little House or shed of the bark of it, he puts fire and followes the burning of it with fire, in the midst in many places: his corne he boyles and hath the Brook by him, and sometimes angles for a little fish: but so hee continues burning and hewing untill he hath within ten or twelve dayes (lying there at his worke alone) finished, and (getting hands,) lanched his Boate; with which afterward hee ventures out to fish in the Ocean.

"Mishoonémese, A little Canow. Some of them will not well carry above three or foure: but some of them twenty, thirty, forty men. — — —

"Obs: It is wonderfull to see how they will venture in those Canoes, and how (being oft overset as I have myselfe been with them) they will swim a mile, yea two or more safe to Land: I having been necessitated to passe Waters diverse times with them, it hath pleased God to make them many times the instruments of my preservation; and when sometimes in great danger I have questioned safety, they have said to me: Feare not, if we be overset I will carry you safe to Land." (Page 98, etc.).

(*Johnson* [*Captain Edward*]): *A History of New-England. From the English planting in the Yeere 1628. untill the Yeere 1652; London, 1654.*—"They are very good marks-men with their Bowe and Arrows. Their Boyes will ordinarily shoot fish with their Arrowes as they swim in the shallow Rivers, they draw the Arrow halfe way putting the point of it into the water, they let flye and strike the fish through." (Page 227).

Ogilby (*John*): *America: being the Latest and most Accurate Description of New-England, etc.; London, 1671.*—"In the Trade of Fishing they are very expert, being experienc'd in the knowledge of all Baits for several Fishes, and divers Seasons; being not ignorant likewise of the removal of Fishes, knowing when to Fish in Rivers, and when at Rocks, when in Bays, and when at Seas: Since the *English* came they are furnish'd with *English* Hooks and Lines; for before

---

* In the same chapter Roger Williams gives the Narragansett words for fishing-line, hooks in general, small hooks, large hooks, bait, net, two kinds of eel-pots, etc.

they made them of Hemp, being more curiously wrought, of stronger Materials than ours, and hook'd with Bone-Hooks; but laziness drives them to buy, more than profit or commendations wins them to make of their own. They make likewise very strong Sturgeon-nets, with which they catch Sturgeons of twelve, fourteen, and sixteen, and some eighteen Foot long in the daytime, and in the nighttime they betake themselves to their Birchen *Canoos*, in which they carry a fortyfathom Line, with a sharp-bearded Dart fastened at the end thereof; then lighting a Torch made of Birchen Rinds, they wave it to and again by their *Canoo* side, which the Sturgeon much delighted with, comes to them tumbling and playing, turning up his white Belly, into which they thrust their Lance, his Back being impenetrable; which done, they hale to the Shore their strugling Price. They have often recourse into the Rocks whereupon the Sea beats, in warm Weather, to look out for sleepy Seals, whose Oyl they much esteem, using it for divers things. In Summer they Fish any where, but in Winter in the fresh Water onely, and Ponds; in frosty Weather they cut round Holes in the Ice, about which they will sit like so many Apes with their naked Breeches upon the cold Ice, catching of Pikes, Pearches, Breams, and other sorts of fresh-Water Fish. ― ― ― Their Cordage is so even, soft, and smooth, that it looks more like Silk than Hemp. Their Sturgeon Nets are not deep, nor above thirty or forty Foot long, which in ebbing low Waters they stake fast to the Ground where they are sure the Sturgeon will come, never looking more at it till the next low Water. Their *Canoos* are made either of Pine-trees, which before they were acquainted with *English* Tools, they burn'd hollow, scraping them smooth with Clam-shells and Oyster-shells, cutting their out-sides with Stone Hatchets. These Boats are not above a Foot and a half, or two Foot wide, and twenty Foot long. Their other *Canoos* be made of thin Birch Rinds, close Ribb'd, and on the in-side with broad, thin Hoops, like the Hoops of a Tub; these are made very light, a Man may carry one of them a Mile, being made purposely to carry from River to River, and from Bay to Bay, to shorten Land-passages. In these cockling Flyboats, wherein an *English*-man can scarce sit without a fearful tottering, they will venture to Sea, when an *English* Shallop dare not bear a Knot of Sail, scudding over the over-grown Waves as fast as a wind-driven Ship, being driven by their Paddles, being much like Battle-doors; if a cross Wave (which is seldom) turn her Keel up-side down, they by swimming free her, and scramble into her again." (Page 157, etc.).*

Josselyn (*John*): *An Account of Two Voyages to New-England; London,* 1674.
―" Their fishing followes in the spring, summer and fall of the leaf. First for

---

* After having made the preceding extract from Ogilby's quarto work, I discovered that he had taken the whole of it almost literally from Chapters XVI and XVII of William Wood's "New England's Prospect" (London, 1635). I prefer, however, retaining Ogilby's text, the latter being less barbarous in the spelling than the original one, which appeared thirty-six years earlier.

Lobsters, Clams, Flouke, Lumps or *Podles*, and *Alewives;* afterwards for *Bass, Cod, Rock, Blew-fish, Salmon,* and *Lampres,* &c.

"The *Lobsters* they take in large Bayes when it is low water, the wind still, going out in their *Birchen-Canows* with a staff two or three yards long, made small and sharpen'd at one end, and nick'd with deep nicks to take hold. When they spye the *Lobster* crawling upon the Sand in two Fathom water, more or less, they stick him towards the head and bring him up. I have known thirty *Lobsters* taken by an *Indian* lad in an hour and a half, thus they take *Flouke* and *Lumps; Clams* they dig out of the *Clambanks* upon the flats and in creeks when it is low water, where they are bedded sometimes a yard deep one upon another, the beds a quarter of a mile in length, and less, the *Alewives* they take with Nets like a pursenet put upon a round hoop'd stick with a handle in fresh ponds where they come to spawn. The *Bass* and *Blew-fish* they take in harbours, and at the mouth of barr'd Rivers being in their *Canows*, striking them with a fisgig, a kind of dart or staff, to the lower end whereof they fasten a sharp jagged bone (since they make them of Iron) with a string fastened to it, as soon as the fish is struck they pull away the staff, leaving the bony head in the fishes body and fasten the other end of the string to the *Canow:* Thus they will hale after them to shore half a dozen or half a score great fishes: this way they take *Sturgeon;* and in dark evenings when they are upon the fishing ground near a Bar of Sand (where the *Sturgeon* feeds upon small fishes [like *Eals*] that are called Lances sucking them out of the Sands where they lye hid, with their hollow Trunks, for other mouth they have none) the *Indian* lights a piece of dry *Birch-Bark* which breaks out into a flame & holds it over the side of his *Canow*, the *Sturgeon* seeing this glaring light mounts to the Surface of the water where he is slain and taken with a fisgig. *Salmons* and *Lampres* are catch'd at the falls of Rivers." (Page 140, etc.).

"Ships they have none, but do prettily imitate ours in their *Birchen-pinnaces*, their *Canows* are made of *Birch*, they shape them with flat Ribbs of white *Cedar*, and cover them with large sheets of *Birch-bark*, sowing them through with strong threds of *Spruse-Roots* or white *Cedar*, and pitch them with a mixture of *Turpentine* and the hard rosen that is dryed with the Air on the outside of the Bark of *Firr-Trees*. These will carry half a dozen or three or four men and a considerable fraight, in these they swim to Sea, twenty, nay forty miles, keeping from the shore a league or two, sometimes to shorten their voyage when they are to double a Cape they will put to shore, and two of them taking up the *Canow* carry it cross the Cape or neck of land to the other side, and to Sea again; they will indure an incredible great Sea, mounting upon the working billowes like a piece of Corke; but they require skilful hands to guide them in rough weather, none but the *Indians* scarce dare to undertake it." (Page 144, etc.).

Van der Donck (Adriaen): A Description of the New Netherlands, etc.; (original printed at Amsterdam, 1656); Collections of the New-York Historical Society, Second Series, Vol. I, New-York, 1841.—" To hunting and fishing the Indians are all extravagantly inclined, and they have their particular seasons for these engagements. In the spring and part of the summer, they practise fishing. When the wild herbage begins to grow up in the woods, the first hunting season begins, and then many of their young men leave the fisheries for the purpose of hunting; but the old and thoughtful men remain at the fisheries until the second and principal hunting season, which they also attend, but with snares only. Their fishing is carried on in the inland waters, and by those who dwell near the sea, or the sea-islands. The latter have particular advantages. Their fishing is done with seines, set-nets, small fikes, wears, and laying hooks. They do not know how to salt fish, or how to cure fish properly. They sometimes dry fish to preserve the same, but those are half tainted, which they pound to meal to be used in chowder in winter." (Page 209).*

Kalm (Peter): Travels into North America, etc.; translated by John Reinhold Forster; London, 1772.—[New York, October, 1748]. "The *Indians*, who inhabited the coast before the arrival of the *Europeans*, have made oysters and other shell fish their chief food; and at present, whenever they come to a salt water, where oysters are to be got, they are very active in catching them, and sell them in great quantities to other *Indians*, who live higher up the country: for this reason you see immense numbers of oyster and muscle shells piled up near such places, where you are certain that the *Indians* formerly built their huts. This circumstance ought to make us cautious in maintaining, that in all places on the sea shore, or higher up in the country, where such heaps of shells are to be met, the latter have lain there ever since the time that those places were overflowed by the sea. — — — Among the numerous shells which are found on the sea-shore, there are some, which by the *English* here are called *Clams*, and which bear some resemblance to the human ear. They have a considerable thickness, and are chiefly white, excepting the pointed end, which both without and within has a blue colour, between purple and violet. They are met with in vast numbers on the sea shore of *New York*, *Long Island*, and other places. The shells contain a large animal, which is eaten both by the *Indians* and *Europeans* settled here. A considerable commerce is carried on in this article, with such *Indians* as live further up the country. When these people inhabited the coast, they were able to catch their own clams, which at that time made a great part of their

---

* The same volume contains translated extracts from John de Laet's "Nieuwe Wereldt" (Leyden, 1625). In Book III, Chapter X, this author, in giving Henry Hudson's account of the great river named after him, states that the navigator had seen the Indians "catching in the river all kinds of fresh-water fish with seines, and young salmon and sturgeon " (p. 300). This was in 1609. De Laet unquestionably had Hudson's journal before him. It is now lost, or, perhaps, buried in some Dutch archive.

food; but at present this is the business of the *Dutch* and *English*, who live in *Long Island* and other maritime provinces. As soon as the shells are caught, the fish is taken out of them, drawn upon a wire, and hung up in the open air, in order to dry by the heat of the sun. When this is done, the flesh is put into proper vessels, and carried to *Albany* upon the river *Hudson;* there the *Indians* buy them, and reckon them one of their best dishes. Besides the *Europeans*, many of the native *Indians* come annually down to the sea shore, in order to catch clams, proceeding with them afterwards in the manner I have just described." (Vol. I, pages 187, 189, etc.).

[Raccoon, New Jersey, January, 1749]. "When the *Indians* intended to fell a thick strong tree, they could not make use of their hatchets, but for want of proper instruments, employed fire. They set fire to a great quantity of wood at the roots of the tree, and made it fall by that means. But that the fire might not reach higher than they would have it, they fastened some rags to a pole, dipped them into water, and kept continually washing the tree, a little above the fire. Whenever they intended to hollow out a thick tree for a canoe, they laid dry branches all along the stem of the tree, as far as it must be hollowed out. They then put fire to those dry branches, and, as soon as they were burnt, they were replaced by others. Whilst those branches were burning, the *Indians* were very busy with wet rags, and pouring water upon the tree, to prevent the fire from spreading too far on the sides, and at the ends. The tree being burnt hollow as far as they found it sufficient, or as far as it could, without damaging the canoe, they took the above described stone-hatchets, or sharp flints, and quartzes, or sharp shells, and scraped off the burnt part of the wood, and smoothened the boats within. By this means they likewise gave it what shape they pleased. —— — A canoe was commonly between thirty and forty feet long." (Vol. I, page 340, etc.).[*]

"The *Indians* employ hooks made of bone, or bird's claws, instead of *fishing-hooks*. Some of the oldest *Swedes* here told me, that when they were young, a great number of *Indians* had been in this part of the country, which was then called *New Sweden*, and had caught fishes in the river *Delaware* with these hooks." (Vol. I, page 345).

Morgan (*Lewis H.*): *League of the Ho-dé-no-sau-nee, or Iroquois; Rochester, 1851.*—" In the construction of the bark canoe, the Iroquois exercised considerable taste and skill. The art appears to have been common to all the Indian races within the limits of the republic, and the mode of construction much the

---

[*] Professor Kalm describes very minutely (Vol. II, p. 129-33) the manufacture of a white-elm bark canoe, witnessed by him at Fort Ann, New York. The canoe was made according to Indian rules, though by whites. I insert the shorter account of Iroquois canoe-making given by Mr. Lewis H. Morgan, and relating to a special one which he figures.

same. Birch bark was the best material; but as the canoe birch did not grow within the home territories of the Iroquois, they generally used the red-elm and bitter-nut-hickory. The canoe figured in the plate is made of the bark of the red-elm, and consists of but one piece. Having taken off a bark of the requisite length and width, and removed the rough outside, it was shaped in the canoe form. Rim pieces of white-ash, or other elastic wood, of the width of the hand, were then run around the edge, outside and in, and stitched through and through with the bark itself. In stitching, they used bark thread or twine, and splints. The ribs consisted of narrow strips of ash, which were set about a foot apart along the bottom of the canoe, and having been turned up the sides, were secured under the rim. Each end of the canoe was fashioned alike, the two side pieces inclining towards each other until they united, and formed a sharp and vertical prow. In size, these canoes varied from twelve feet, with sufficient capacity to carry two men, to forty feet with sufficient capacity for thirty. The one figured in the plate is about twenty-five feet in length, and its tonnage estimated at two tons, about half that of the ordinary bateau. Birch bark retained its place without warping, but the elm and hickory bark canoes were exposed to this objection. After being used, they were drawn out of the water to dry. ——— For short excursions one person usually paddled the canoe, standing up in the stern; if more than two, and on a long expedition, they were seated at equal distances upon each side alternately. In the fur trade these canoes were extensively used. They coasted lakes Erie and Ontario, and turning up the Oswego river into the Oneida lake, they went from thence over the carrying place into the Mohawk, which they descended to Schenectady. They would usually carry about twelve hundred pounds of fur. At the period of the invasions of the Iroquois territories by the French, large fleets of these canoes were formed for the conveyance of troops and provisions. With careful usage they would last several years." (Page 367, etc.).

Loskiel (George Henry): History of the Mission of the United Brethren among the Indians in North America; translated from the German by Christian Ignatius La Trobe; London, 1794.—[Delawares and Iroquois]. "Little boys are even frequently seen wading in shallow brooks, shooting small fishes with their bows and arrows. The Indians always carry hooks and small harpoons with them, whenever they are on a hunting party; but at certain seasons of the year they go out purposely to fish, either alone, or in parties. They make use of the neat and light canoes made of birch-bark, as described above, for this purpose, and not only venture with them into spacious rivers, but even into the large lakes, and being very light, the waves do not break into them as easily as into European boats. They caulk them with the resinous bark of a species of elm, which they first pound, to prepare it for use. Another kind of canoes are made of the stems of large trees of light wood, chiefly cypress. These stems are excavated chiefly by fire, and finished with an hatchet. They look like long troughs, and are of various sizes.

"There is a particular manner of fishing,* which is undertaken in parties, as many hands are wanted, in the following manner: When the *Shad-fish* (clupea alosa) come up the rivers, the Indians run a dam of stones across the stream, where its depth will admit of it, not in a strait line, but in two parts, verging towards each other in an angle. An opening is left in the middle for the water to run off. At this opening they place a large box, the bottom of which is full of holes. They then make a rope of the twigs of the wild vine, reaching across the stream, upon which boughs of about six feet in length are fastened at the distance of about two fathoms from each other. A party is detached about a mile above the dam with this rope and its appendages, who begin to move gently down the current, some guiding one, some the opposite end, whilst others keep the branches from sinking by supporting the rope in the middle with wooden forks. Thus they proceed, frightening the fishes into the opening left in the middle of the dam, where a number of Indians are placed on each side, who standing upon the two legs of the angles, drive the fishes with poles, and an hideous noise, through the opening into the above-mentioned box or chest. Here they lie, the water running off through the holes in the bottom, and other Indians stationed on each side of the chest, take them out, kill them and fill their canoes. By this contrivance they sometimes catch above a thousand shad and other fish in half a day.

"In Carolina the Indians frequently use fire in fishing. A certain kind of fish will even leap into the boats, which have fire in them." (Part I, page 94, etc.).

De Bry (*Theodorus*): *Admiranda Narratio fida tamen, de Commodis et Incolarum Ritibus Virginiæ, etc., Francoforti ad Moenum, 1590.*—Translation: [XIII. The mode of fishing among the inhabitants of Virginia]. "They have also a remarkable method of fishing in the rivers: for, since they lack iron and steel, they fasten as a point on canes or long staffs the hollow tail of a certain fish resembling the sea-crab;† with these they transfix fishes in the night or during day-time, and bring them together in their boats: yet they also know how to use the spines and stings of other fishes. They likewise, by fixing sticks or rods in the water, construct wicker-work, which they entwine in such a manner as to make it gradually narrower, as the figure shows. There is never beheld among us such an excellent mode of catching fish, of which various kinds, differing from ours, yet of very good taste, are here found in the rivers."‡

---

* *Buschnetzfischerey* (bush-net fishing) in the German original, which was published at Barby in 1780.

† The king-crab or horse-shoe (*Limulus Polyphemus*, Latr.).

‡ [XIII. Incolarum Virginiæ piscandi ratio]. "Egregiam etiam habent piscandi in fluminibus rationem: cum enim ferro & chalybe careant, arundinibus aut oblongis virgis piscis cuiusdam cancro marino similis caudam

Fig. 363.—Methods of fishing practised by the Virginia Indians.
After De Bry.*

[XIV. Wooden hurdle on which they roast fishes]. "After a capture of plenty of fish, they proceed to the chosen place suitable for the preparation of victuals: having here fixed in the ground four forks marking a quadrangular space, they put on them four sticks, and across these others, thus forming a hurdle of sufficient height. When the fish have been placed upon the hurdle, they build a fire underneath it, in order to roast them; yet not according to the manner of the inhabitants of the Province of Florida, who only parch and harden them in the smoke that they may be kept during the whole winter; while these, laying by no store, roast and consume the whole; afterward, when needed, they roast or seethe fresh ones, as we shall see hereafter. In the meantime, when the hurdle cannot hold all the fishes, they suspend the remaining ones by the gills on little rods which they have stuck in the ground near the fire, and thus cook them: they also pay close attention that they are not burned. When the first

concauam pro cuspide imponunt, quibus noctu vel interdiu pisces figunt, & in suas cymbas congerunt: sed aliorum piscium spinis & spiculis vti norunt. Baculis etiam seu virgultis (sic) in aquam defixis tegetes conficiunt, quas intertexentes in angustum semper contrahunt, vt ex figura apparet. nunquam apud nos conspecta est tam subtilis pisces capiendi ratio, quorum varia genera istic in fluminibus reperiuntur, nostris dissimilia, & boni admodum succi."

* This design and the two following next are not taken directly from De Bry's volume, but from Beverly's "History of Virginia," which is illustrated with inverted, reduced, and here and there modified copies of De Bry's plates. I had some of Beverly's deviations corrected in accordance with the original engravings.

are roasted, they place fresh supplies on the hurdle, and repeat the cooking until they think they have a sufficiency of eatables."*

Fig. 364.—Virginia Indians smoking fish.
After De Bry.

[XII. The mode of making boats]. "The mode of manufacturing boats in Virginia is wonderful; for though they have neither iron implements nor others resembling ours, they nevertheless know how to make them not less convenient than our own, either for navigating rivers or for fishing. Having first selected a thick and high tree, corresponding to the size of the boat they intend to make, they light on the surface of the ground close to its roots, and all around it, a fire, using well-dried tree-moss, and rousing the fire gradually by means of chips of wood, lest the flame might ascend too high and diminish the length of the tree. When the tree is nearly burned and threatens to fall, they light a new fire, which they allow to burn until the tree comes down by itself. Having then burned away the top and the branches of the tree, in order to give the trunk the proper length, they deposit it on stems laid across forks, at a height

---

* [XIV. Crates lignea in qua pisces vetulant]. "Capta piscium abundantia, ad locum destinatum concedunt cibis parandis idoneum: illic defixis in terram quatuor furcis quadrangula area, quatuor ligna imponunt, atque his alia transuersa, cratis satis altæ instar. Crati piscibus impositis ignem substruunt, vt assentur, non incolarum Floridæ prouinciæ more, qui dumtaxat vetulant & fumo indurant, vt tota hieme adseruare possint: nam hi nihil seponentes omnia assant & absumunt, deinde cum opus habent, recentes assant aut elixant, vt postea videbimus. Cum vero cratis interdum omnes pisces capere nequeat, reliquos bacillis in terram apud ignem defixis per branchias appendunt, hac ratione cocturam absoluentes: diligenter autem obseruant ne adurantur. Primis assatis, alios recens allatos crati imponunt, subinde cocturam repetentes donec satis eduliorum se habere existiment."

convenient for their work; they now remove the bark with a certain kind of shells, and, using the less injured part of the trunk for its lower side, they light on the other side a fire all along the trunk, excepting its ends, and when they think that there has been enough burning, they extinguish the fire and commence scraping with shells; having made a new fire, they burn again, and thus continue in succession, alternately burning and scraping, until the boat is sufficiently hollowed out."*

FIG. 365.—Virginia Indians engaged in boat-making.
After De Bry.

Smith (Captain John): The General Historie of Virginia, New-England, and the Summer Isles, etc.; London, 1624.—[Indians of Virginia]. "Their fishing is much in Boats. These they make of one tree by burning and scratching away the coales with stones and shels, till they haue made it in forme of a Trough. Some of them are an elne deepe, and fortie or fiftie foote in length, and some

---

* [XII. Lintrium conficiendorum ratio]. "Mira est in Virginia cymbas fabricandi ratio: nam cum ferreis instrumentis aut aliis nostris similibus careant, eas tamen parare norunt nostris non minus commodas ad nauigandum quo lubet per flumina & ad piscandum. Primum arbore aliqua crassa & alta delecta, pro cymba quam parare volunt magnitudine, ignem circa eius radices summa tellure in ambitu struunt ex arborum musco bene resiccato, & ligni assulis paulatim ignem excitantes, ne flamma altius ascendat, & arboris longitudinem minuat. Pene adusta & ruinam minante arbore, nouum suscitant ignem, quom flagrare sinunt donec arbor sponte cadat. Adustis deinde arboris fastigio & ramis, vt truncus iustam longitudinem retineat, tignis transuersis supra furcas positis imponunt, ea altitudine vt commode laborare possint, tunc cortice conchis quibusdam adempto, integriorem trunci partem pro cymbae inferiore parte seruant, in altera parte ignem secundum trunci longitudinem struunt, præterquam extremis, quod satis adustum illis videtur, restincto igne conchis scabunt, & nouo suscitato igne denuo adurunt, atque ita deinceps pergunt, subinde urentes & scabentes, donec cymba necessarium alueum nacta sit."

will beare 40 men, but the most ordinary are smaller, and will beare 10, 20, or 30, according to their bignesse. In stead of Oares, they vse Paddles and stickes, with which they will row faster than our Barges. Betwixt their hands and thighes, their women vse to spin, the barkes of trees, Deere sinews, or a kinde of grasse they call *Pemmenaw*, of these they make a thread very even and readily. This thread serveth for many vses. As about their housing, apparell, as also they make nets for fishing, for the quantitie as formally braded as ours. They make also with it lines for angles. Their hookes are either a bone grated as they noch their arrowes in the forme of a crooked pinne or fish-hooke, or of the splinter of a bone tyed to the clift of a little sticke, and with the end of the line, they tie on the bait. They vse also long arrowes tyed in a line, wherewith they shoote at fish in the rivers. But they of *Accawmack* vse staues like vnto Iauelins headed with bone. With these they dart fish swimming in the water. They haue also many artificiall wires, in which they get abundance of fish." (Page 31, etc.).

(*Beverly* [*Robert*]): *The History of Virginia, in Four Parts;* London, 1722.— "Before the Arrival of the *English* there, the *Indians* had Fish in such vast Plenty, that the Boys and Girls would take a pointed Stick, and strike the lesser sort, as they swam upon the Flats. The larger Fish, that kept in deeper Water, they were put to a little more Difficulty to take; But for these they made Weirs; that is, a Hedge of small riv'd Sticks, or Reeds, of the Thickness of a Man's Finger, these they wove together in a Row, with Straps of Green Oak, or other tough Wood, so close that the small Fish cou'd not pass through. Upon High-Water Mark, they pitched one End of this Hedge, and the other they extended into the River, to the Depth of eight or ten Foot, fastening it with Stakes, making Cods out from the Hedge on one side, almost at the End, and leaving a Gap for the Fish to go into them, which were contrived so, that the Fish could easily find their Passage into those Cods, when they were at the Gap, but not see their Way out again, when they were in: Thus if they offered to pass through, they were taken.

"Sometimes they made such a Hedge as this, quite across a Creek at High-Water, and at Low would go into the Run, then contracted into a narrow Stream, and take out what Fish they pleased.

"At the Falls of the Rivers, where the Water is shallow, and the Current strong, the *Indians* use another kind of Weir, thus made: They make a Dam of loose Stone, whereof there is Plenty at hand, quite a-cross the River, leaving one, two, or more Spaces or Trunnels, for the Water to pass thro'; at the Mouth of which they set a Pot of Reeds, wove in Form of a Cone, whose Base is about three Foot, and perpendicular ten, into which the Swiftness of the Current carries the Fish, and there lodges them.

"The *Indian* Way of catching Sturgeon, when they came into the narrow part of the Rivers, was by a Man's clapping a Noose over their Tail, and by keeping fast his Hold. Thus a fish finding itself entangled, would flounce, and often pull the Man under Water, and then that Man was counted a *Cockarouse*, or brave Fellow, that would not let go; till with Swimming, Wading and Diving, he had tired the Sturgeon, and brought it ashore. These Sturgeons would also often leap into their Canoes, in crossing the River, as many of them do still every year, into the Boats of the *English*.

"They have also another Way of Fishing like those on the *Euxine* Sea, by the Help of a blazing Fire by Night. They make a Hearth in the Middle of their Canoe, raising it within two Inches of the Edge; upon this they lay their burning Light-Wood, split into small Shivers, each Splinter whereof will blaze and burn End for End, like a Candle: 'Tis one Man's Work to attend this Fire and keep it flaming. At each end of the Canoe stands an *Indian*, with a Gig, or pointed Spear, setting the Canoe forward with the Butt-end of the Spear, as gently as he can, by that Means stealing upon the Fish, without any Noise, or disturbing of the water. Then they with great Dexterity dart these Spears into the Fish, and so take them. Now there is a double Convenience in the Blaze of this Fire; for it not only dazzles the Eyes of the Fish, which will lie still, glaring upon it, but likewise discovers the Bottom of the River clearly to the Fisherman, which the Day-light does not." (Page 130, etc.).

Lawson (John): The History of Carolina; London, 1714.—[Indians of North Carolina]. "They are not only good Hunters of the wild Beasts and Game of the Forest, but very expert in taking the Fish of the Rivers and Waters near which they inhabit, and are acquainted withal. Thus they that live a great way up the Rivers practise Striking Sturgeon and Rock-fish, or Bass, when they come up the Rivers to spawn; besides the vast Shoals of Sturgeon which they kill and take with Snares, as we do Pike in *Europe*. The Herrings in *March* and *April* run a great way up the Rivers and fresh Streams to spawn, where the Savages make great Wares, with Hedges that hinder their Passage only in the Middle, where an artificial Pound is made to take them in; so that they cannot return. This Method is in use all over the fresh Streams, to catch Trout and the other Species of Fish which those Parts afford. Their taking of Craw-fish is so pleasant, that I cannot pass it by without mention. When they have a mind to get these Shell-fish, they take a Piece of Venison, and half-barbakue or roast it; then they cut it into thin Slices, which Slices they stick through with Reeds about six Inches asunder, betwixt Piece and Piece; then the Reeds are made sharp at one end; and so they stick a great many of them down in the bottom of the Water (thus baited) in the small Brooks and Runs, which the Craw-fish frequent. Thus the *Indians* sit by, and tend those baited sticks, every now and then taking them up, to see how many are at the Bait; where they generally find abundance; so take them off, and put them in a Basket for the purpose, and stick the Reeds down again. By this Method, they will, in a little time, catch several Bushels, which are as good, as any I ever eat. Those *Indians* that frequent the Salt-Waters, take abundance of Fish, some very large, and of several sorts, which to preserve, they first barbakue, then pull the Fish to Pieces, so dry it in the Sun, whereby it keeps for Transportation; as for Scate, Oysters, Cockles, and several sorts of Shell-fish, they open and dry them upon Hurdles, having a constant Fire under them. The Hurdles are made of Reeds or Canes in the shape of a Gridiron. Thus they dry several Bushels of these Fish, and keep them for their Necessities. At the time when they are on the Salts, and Sea Coasts, they have another Fishery, that is for a little Shell-fish, which those in England call Blackmoors Teeth. These they catch by tying bits of Oysters to a long String, which they lay in such places, as, they know, those Shell-fish haunt. These Fish get hold of the Oysters, and suck them in, so that they pull up those long Strings, and take great Quantities of them, which they carry a great way into the main Land, to trade with the remote *Indians*, where they are of great Value; but never near the Sea, by reason they are common, therefore not esteem'd. Besides, the Youth and *Indian* Boys go in the Night, and one holding a Lightwood Torch, the other has a Bow and Arrows, and the Fire directing him to see the Fish, he shoots them with the Arrows; and thus they kill a great many of the smaller Fry and sometimes pretty large ones. It is an establish'd Custom amongst all these Natives, that the young Hunter never eats of that Buck, Bear, Fish, or any other Game, which happens to be the first they kill of that sort; because they believe, if he should eat thereof, he would never after be fortunate in Hunting. The like foolish Ceremony they hold, when they have made a Ware to take Fish withal; if a big-belly'd Woman eat of the first Dish that is caught in it, they say that Ware will never take much Fish; and as for killing of Snakes, they avoid it, if they lie in their way, because their Opinion is, that some of the Serpents Kindred would kill some of the Savages Relations, that should destroy him." (Page 209, etc.).

Brickell (John): The Natural History of North Carolina; Dublin, 1737.— [Indians of North Carolina]. "They have *Fish-gigs* that are made of Reeds or *Hollow Canes*, these they cut and make very sharp, with two Beards, and taper at the Point like a *Harpoon;* being thus provided, they either wade into the Water, or go into their *Canoes*, and paddle about the Edges of the Rivers or Creeks, striking all the Fish they meet with in the depth of five or six Feet Water, or as far as they can see them; this they commonly do in dark calm Nights, and whilst one attends with a Light made of the *Pitch-pine*, the other with his *Fish-gig* strikes and kills the Fish: It is diverting to see them fish after this manner, which they sometimes do in the Day; how dexterous they are in striking, is admirable, and the great quantities they kill by this Method." (Page 365).*

Adair (James): The History of the American Indians; particularly those Nations adjoining the Mississippi, East and West Florida, Georgia, South and North Carolina, and Virginia, etc.; London, 1775.—" Their method of fishing may be placed among their diversions, but this is of the profitable kind. When they see large fish near the surface of the water, they fire directly upon them, sometimes only with powder, which noise and surprize however so stupifies them, that they instantly turn up their bellies and float a top, when the fisherman secures them. If they shoot at fish not deep in the water, either with an arrow or bullet, they aim at the lower part of the belly, if they are near; and lower, in like manner, according to the distance, which seldom fails of killing. In a dry summer season, they gather horse chesnuts, and different sorts of roots, which having pounded pretty fine, and steeped a while in a trough, they scatter this mixture over the surface of a middle-sized pond, and stir it about with poles, till the water is sufficiently impregnated with the intoxicating bittern. The fish are soon inebriated, and make to the surface of the water, with their bellies uppermost. The fishers gather them in baskets, and barbicue the largest, covering them carefully over at night to preserve them from the supposed putrifying influence of the moon. It seems, that fish catched in this manner, are not poisoned, but only stupified; for they prove very wholesome food to us, who frequently use them. By experiments, when they are speedily moved into good water, they revive in a few minutes.

"The Indians have the art of catching fish in long crails, made with canes and hiccory splinters, tapering to a point. They lay these at a fall of water, where stones are placed in two sloping lines from each bank, till they meet together in the middle of the rapid stream, where the entangled fish are soon drowned. Above such a place, I have known them to fasten a wreath of long grape vines together, to reach across the river, with stones fastened at proper distances to rake the bottom; they will swim a mile with it whooping, and plunging all the way, driving the fish before them into their large cane pots. With this draught, which is a very heavy one, they make a town feast, or feast of love, of which every one partakes in the most social manner, and afterward they dance together, singing *Halelu-yah*, and the rest of their usual praises to the divine essence, for his bountiful gifts to the beloved people. Those Indians who are unacquainted with the use of barbed irons, are very expert in striking large fish out of their canoes, with long sharp pointed green canes, which are

---

* The remainder of Brickell's account of Indian fishing in North Carolina is almost literally taken from Lawson's "History of Carolina."

well bearded, and hardened in the fire. In Savanah river, I have often accompanied them in killing sturgeons with those green swamp harpoons, and which they did with much pleasure and ease; for, when we discovered the fish, we soon thrust into their bodies one of the harpoons. As the fish would immediately strike deep, and rush away to the bottom very rapidly, their strength was soon expended, by their violent struggles against the buoyant force of the green darts: as soon as the top end of them appeared again on the surface of the water, we made up to them, renewed the attack, and in like manner continued it till we secured our game.*

"They have a surprising method of fishing under the edges of rocks, that stand over deep places of a river. There, they pull off their red breeches, or their long slip of Stroud cloth, and wrapping it round their arm, so as to reach to the lower part of the palm of their right hand, they dive under the rock where the large cat-fish lie to shelter themselves from the scorching beams of the sun, and to watch for prey: as soon as those fierce aquatic animals see that tempting bait, they immediately seize it with the greatest violence, in order to swallow it. Then is the time for the diver to improve the favourable opportunity: he accordingly opens his hand, seizes the voracious fish by his tender parts, hath a sharp struggle with it against the crevices of the rock, and at last brings it safe ashore. Except the Choktah, all our Indians, both male and female, above the state of infancy, are in the watery element nearly equal to amphibious animals, by practice: and from the experiments necessity has forced them to, it seems as if few were endued with such strong natural abilities,—very few can equal them in their wild situation of life.

"There is a favourite method among them of fishing with hand-nets. The nets are about three feet deep, and of the same diameter at the opening, made of hemp, and knotted after the usual manner of our nets. On each side of the mouth, they tie very securely a strong elastic green cane, to which the ends are fastened. Prepared with these, the warriors a-breast, jump in at the end of a long pond, swimming under water, with their net stretched open with both hands, and the canes in a horizontal position. In this manner, they will continue, either till their breath is expended by the want of respiration, or till the net is so ponderous as to force them to exonerate it ashore, or in a basket, fixt in a proper place for that purpose—by removing one hand, the canes instantly spring together. I have been engaged half a day at a time, with the old-friendly Chikkasah, and half drowned in the diversion—when any of us was so unfortunate

---

* Bartram describes the capture of a salmon trout of fifteen pounds' weight in a branch of Broad River, Georgia, by means of one of these harpoons:—

"The Indian struck this fish, with a reed harpoon, pointed very sharp, barbed, and hardened by the fire. The fish lay close under the steep bank, which the Indian discovered and struck with his reed; instantly the fish darted off with it, whilst the Indian pursued, without extracting the harpoon, and with repeated thrusts drowned it, and then dragged it to shore."—*Travels through South Carolina, Georgia, etc.;* Dublin, 1793; p. 44.

as to catch water-snakes in our sweep, and emptied them ashore, we had the ranting voice of our friendly posse comitatus, whooping against us, till another party was so unlucky as to meet with the like misfortune. During this exercise, the women are fishing ashore with coarse baskets, to catch the fish that escape our nets. At the end of our friendly diversion, we cheerfully return home, and in an innocent and friendly manner, eat together, studiously diverting each other, on the incidents of the day, and make a cheerful night." (Page 402, etc.).

Du Pratz (M. Le Page): Histoire de la Louisiane; Paris, 1758.—Translation: "Those who lived near rivers doubtless became desirous of eating fish, and tried to avail themselves of the victuals which the country offered. For the rest, it was only needed that a pregnant woman, having seen fine fishes, hankered after them: the complaisance of the husband on one hand, and his own inclination to eat them on the other, gave occasion for the manufacture of nets for catching fish.* These nets have meshes (*sont maillés*) like ours, and are made of the bark of the linden-tree. Large fish are shot with arrows.

"The nets usually serve for catching small fish; the natives also make use of them as bags for transporting fish. However, when they have many fishes, or have caught large ones with the line, they construct on the spot a make-shift for carrying them one or two leagues, or even farther, if required. For this purpose they take a green branch of pliable wood, an inch and a half in thickness, and bend it until both ends meet and it assumes the form of a racket on a large scale. Across this wood they stretch several strips of bark crosswise, and cover them with plenty of leaves, upon which they place the fish, covering them in the same manner. When the leaves and fishes are firmly tied to the frame, they attach their burden-strap to it, and carry it on the back like a basket." (Vol. II, page 179, etc.).

"They sometimes make arrows of thin, hard canes; but these only serve for shooting birds and fishes. — — —

"Their war-arrows are usually armed with a scale of the bony gar-fish (*Poisson-armé*); but if their arrows are designed for shooting carp or cat-fish (*Barbue*), which are large fishes, they attach to the shaft a bone pointed at both ends, in such a manner that one end forms the point of the arrow, while the other is a little distant from the shaft, and prevents the arrow from coming out of the body of the fish.† The arrow, moreover, is connected by a string with a piece of wood, which floats and does not allow the fish to go to the bottom or to escape." (Vol. II, page 168).

---

* Polite attention to women probably had little to do with the invention of fishing-nets, wherever it was made. Nets came into use, when populations increased, and the methods of spearing and angling proved insufficient for furnishing the necessary supplies of fish-food. Hunger, not gallantry, invented nets.

† Compare Fig. 43 on p. 47 in this volume.

"A pirogue is a trunk of a tree, more or less large, and hollowed out like a boat. Those of the natives will hold from two to ten persons. Before they knew the use of axes, which they have received from the French, they excavated them by means of fire, taking care to cover with mortar such portions as they wished to leave intact." (Vol. I, page 107, note).

Wyeth (Nathaniel J.): Letters addressed in 1848 to H. R. Schoolcraft, and published in his large work on "the History, Condition, and Prospects of the Indian Tribes of the United States;" Vol. I, Philadelphia, 1851.—[Shoshonees]. "The utensils originally used by the Indians of the valley of the Säaptin or Snake River, were wholly of stone, clay, bone or wood. So far as I observed, they possessed no metals. Their implements were the pot, bow and arrow, knives, graining tools, awls, root-diggers, fish-spears, nets, a kind of boat or raft, the pipe, mats for shelter, and implements to produce fire. — — —

"The fish-spear is a beautiful adaptation of an idea to a purpose. The head of it is of bone, to which a small strong line is attached near the middle, connecting it with the shaft, about two feet from the point. Somewhat toward the forward end of this head there is a small hole, which enters it ranging acutely toward the point of the head; it is quite shallow. In this hole the front end of the shaft is placed. This head is about two and a half inches long, the shaft about ten feet, and of light willow. When a salmon or sturgeon is struck, the head is at once detached by the withdrawal of the shaft, and being constrained by the string, which still connects it with the operator, turns its position to one crosswise of its direction while entering. If the fish is strong, the staff is relinquished, and operates as a buoy to obtain the fish when he has tired down by struggling. These Indians are very expert in the use of this instrument, and take many fish at all the falls and rapid waters, and construct, on small streams, barriers of stones or brush, to force the fish into certain places, where they watch for them, often at night with a light.

"Fish-nets are made with the outer bark of some weed which grows in the country, but I took no particular note of what it was, or how separated from the stalk. It makes a line stronger than any of those I had among my outfit, although they were selected from the best materials of an angling warehouse by myself, who profess to be a judge of such articles. The twine is formed by laying the fibre doubled across the knee, the bight towards to loft, and held between the thumb and finger of that hand, with the two parts which are to form the twine toward the right and a little separated; rolling these two parts between the knee and right hand, outwardly from the operator, and twisting the bight between the thumb and finger of the left hand, forms the thread. More fibre is added as that first commenced on diminishes in size, so as to make a continuous and equal line. In this way, excellent twine is made much more rapidly than could be expected. The nets are of two kinds: the scoop, which is precisely the same as is used in the United States; and the seine, which is also in principle exactly the same; and the knot used in netting also appears to me exactly the same: but in this I may be mistaken, as I have never seen the operation performed. The leaded line is formed by attaching oblong rounded stones, with a sunken groove near the middle in which to wind the attaching ligature. Reeds are used for floats.

"The navigation of this region appears to have been confined to crossing the streams when the water was too cold for comfortable swimming. The only apparatus used was little more than a good raft, made of reeds which abound on many of the streams. They are about eight feet long, and formed by placing small bundles of reeds, with the butt-ends introduced and lashed together, with their small ends outwards. Several of these bundles are lashed together beside each other, and in such a manner as to form a cavity on top. There is no attempt to make it tight; the only dependence is on the great buoyancy of the materials used. It is navigated with a stick, and almost entirely by pushing. This rude form of navigation, apparently, is the only one ever used in the country, in which, in fact, there is hardly timber enough for a more improved form." (Pages 211, 213, etc.).

Catlin (George): Letters and Notes on the Manners, Customs, and Condition of the North American Indians; New York, 1844.—"The skin canoes of the Man-

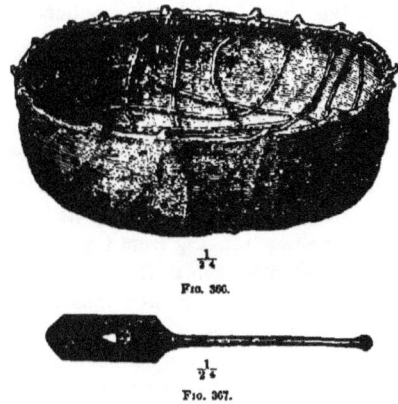

$\frac{1}{14}$

Fig. 366.

$\frac{1}{24}$

Fig. 367.

Figs. 366 and 367.—Bull-hide boat and paddle of poplar wood, made by Minnetarees at Fort Berthold, Dakota. (9785).*

---

* This boat, measuring in its present shrunken state five feet and four inches in diameter and two feet in depth, was sent to the National Museum in 1870 by Dr. Washington Matthews, U. S. A. It is made of buffalo-skin; but he informs me that the Indians are now beginning to employ ox-hide, owing to the increasing scarcity of buffalo.

dans (of the Upper Missouri) are made almost round like a tub, by straining a buffalo's skin over a frame of wicker work, made of willow or other boughs. The woman in paddling these awkward tubs, stands in the bow, and makes the stroke with the paddle by reaching it forward in the water and drawing it to her, by which means she pulls the canoe along with some considerable speed. These very curious and rudely constructed canoes are made in the form of the *Welsh coracle;* and, if I mistake not, propelled in the same manner, which is a very curious circumstance; inasmuch as they are found in the heart of the great wilderness of America, when all other surrounding tribes construct their canoes in decidedly different forms, and of different materials." (Vol. II, page 138).*

Powers (Stephen): Tribes of California; Contributions to North American Ethnology; Vol. III, Washington, 1877.—[The Yurok; Klamath River]. "As the redwood grows only along the Lower Klamath, the Yurok have a monopoly of making canoes, and they sell many to the Karok. A canoe on the Klamath is not pointed like the Chippewa canoe, but the width at either end is equal to the tree's diameter. On the great bar across the mouth of the river, and all along the coast for eighty miles, there are tens of thousands of mighty redwoods cast upon the strand, having been either floated down by the rivers or grubbed down by the surf. Hence the Indians are not obliged to fell any trees, and have only to burn them into suitable lengths. In making the canoe they spread pitch on whatever place they wish to reduce, and when it has burned deep enough they clap on a piece of raw bark and extinguish the fire. By this means they round them out with wonderful symmetry and elegance, leaving the sides and ends very thin and as smooth as if they had been sandpapered. At the stern they burn and polish out a neat little bracket which serves as a seat for the boatman. They spent an infinity of puddering on these canoes (nowadays they use iron tools and dispatch the work in a few days), two Indians sometimes working on one five or six months, burning, scraping, polishing with stones. When completed, they are sold for various sums, ranging from ten to thirty dollars, or even more. They are not as handsome as the Smith River or the T'sin-ŭk canoes, but quite as serviceable. A large one will carry five tons of merchandise, and in early days they used to take many cargoes of fish from the Klamath, shooting the dangerous rapids and surf at the mouth with consummate skill, going boldly to sea in heavy weather, and reaching Crescent City, twenty-two miles distant, whence they returned with merchandise. — — —

"In catching salmon they employ principally nets woven of fine roots or grass, which are stretched across eddies in the Klamath, always with the mouth

---

* These tub-shaped boats are also used to some extent by the Aricaras and Minnetarees. Mr. Catlin, it is well known, inclines to the view that the Mandans are partly descendants of the Welsh of Prince Madoc's expedition. The Welsh coracles and Mandan boats, at any rate, remind one of the curious circular skin-covered boats in use on the river Euphrates in the time of Herodotus (I, 194). Some of these latter, however, were of large size.

down-stream. When there is not a natural eddy they sometimes create one by throwing out a rude wing-dam. They select eddies because it is there the salmon congregate to rest themselves. At the head of the eddy they erect fishing-booths over the water, by planting slender poles in the bottom of the river, and lashing others over them in a light and artistic framework, with a floor a few feet above the water, and regular rafters overhead, on which brushwood is spread for a screen against the sun. In one of these really picturesque booths an Indian sleeps at night, with a string leading up from the net to his fingers, so that when a salmon begins to flounce in it he is awakened. Sometimes the string is attached to an ingenious rattle-trap of sticks or bones (or a bell nowadays), which will ring or clatter, and answer the same purpose.

"They also spear salmon from these booths with a fish-gig furnished with movable barbs, which after entering the fish spread open, and prevent the withdrawal of the instrument. Another mode they sometimes employ is to stand on a large bowlder in the main current where the salmon and the little skeggers shoot in to rest in the eddy when ascending the stream, whereupon they scoop them up in dip-nets. Again they construct a weir of willow-stakes nearly across the stream at the shallows, leaving only a narrow chute wherein is set a funnel-shaped trap of splints, with a funnel-shaped entrance at the large end. Ascending the stream the bold, resolute salmon shoots into this, and cannot get out. Sometimes the weir reaches clear across, the stakes being fastened to a long string-piece stretching from bank to bank. The building of one of these dams is usually preceded by a grand dance, and followed by a feast of salmon. The greater portion of the catch is dried and smoked for winter consumption. — — —

"Along the coast they engage largely in smelt-fishing. The fisherman takes two long slender poles which he frames together with a cross-piece in the shape of the letter A, and across this he stretches a net with small meshes, bagging down considerably. This net he connects by a throat with a long bag-net floating in the water behind him, and then, provided with a strong staff, he wades out up to his middle. When an unusually heavy billow surges in he plants his staff firmly on the bottom, ducks his head forward, and allows it to boom over him. After each wave he dips with his net and hoists it up, whereupon the smelt slide down to the point and through the throat into the bag-net. When the latter contains a bushel or so he wades ashore and empties it into his squaw's basket.

"About sunset appears to be the most favorable time for smelt-fishing, and at this time the great bar across the mouth of the Klamath presents a lively and interesting spectacle. Sometimes many scores of swarthy heads may be seen bobbing amid the surf like so many sea-lions. The squaws hurry to and fro across the bar, bowing themselves under their great conical hampers, carrying the smelt back to the canoes in the river, while the pappooses caper around stark naked, whoop, throw up their heels, and playfully insinuate pebbles into

R 38

each other's ears. After the great copper globe of the sun burns into the ocean, bivouac fires spring up along the sand among the enormous redwood drift-logs, and families hover around them to roast the evening repast. The squaws bustle about the fires while the weary smelt-fishermen, in their nude and savage strength, are grouped together squatting or leaning about, with their smooth, dark, clean-moulded limbs in statuesque attitudes of repose. Dozens of canoes laden with bushels on bushels of the little silver fishes, shove off and move silently away up the darkling river." (Page 47, etc.).

[The Henaggi; Smith River]. "The Henaggi deserve special mention on account of the handsome canoes which they fashion out of redwood. I saw one on Humboldt Bay, which had been launched by them on Smith River, and which had therefore demonstrated its sea-worthiness by a voyage of over a hundred miles. It was forty-two feet long and eight feet four inches wide, and capable of carrying twenty-four men or five tons of freight. It was 'a thing of beauty,' sitting plumb and lightly on the sea, smoothly polished, and so symmetrical that a pound's weight on either side would throw it slightly out of trim. Twenty-four tall, swarthy boatmen, naked except around the loins, standing erect in it, as their habit is, and with their narrow paddles measuring off the blue waters with long, even sweeps, must have been a fine spectacle." (Page 69).

[The Viard or Wiyot; Humboldt Bay, Eel River]. "Like all coast tribes the Viard depended largely on fishing for a subsistence, and the lower waters of Eel River yielded them a wonderful amount of rich and oleaginous eels. To capture these they constructed a funnel-shaped trap of splints, with a funnel-shaped entrance at the large end, through which the creature could wriggle, but which closed on him and detained him inside. Traps of this kind they weighted down so that they floated mostly below the surface of the water, and then tied them to stakes planted in the river bottom. Thus they turned about with the swash of the tide, keeping the large ends always against the current, that the eels might slip in readily." (Page 103).

[The Wailakki; western slope of the Shasta Mountains]. "In the hot and sweltering interior of the State the Indians generally leave their warm winter lodges as soon as the dry season is well established, and camp for the summer in light, open wickiups of brushwood, which they sometimes abandon two or three times during the summer for convenience in fishing, etc. Immediately on the coast this is scarcely done at all, because not necessary; but the Wailakki generally go higher up the little streams in the heated term, roaming and camping along where the salmon trout (*Salmo Masoni*) and the Coast Range trout (*Salmo irideus*) most abound. They capture these and other minnows in a rather ignominious and un-Waltonian fashion. When the summer heat dries up the streams to stagnant pools, they rub the poisonous soap-root in the water until the fish are stupefied, when they easily scoop them up, and the poison will not affect the tough stomach of the aborigines." (Page 116, etc.).

[The Makhelchel; Clear Lake]. "They construct boats of tule,* with indifferent skill. First, two or three long tule-stalks are sewed together for a keel, and hammered hard. Then others are laid alongside of them, each one overlapping the last a little in length, sewed on and beaten. When finished the bottom is twenty or thirty feet long, elliptical in shape, sharp at the ends, three or four layers of tule thick, and all hammered hard and water-tight. The sides are then built up perpendicular, but only one or two tules thick, and not ribbed. After being in the water awhile the thick bottom becomes water-logged, and if the boat is capsized it rights itself in an instant, like a loaded cork. One of these boats will last five years, and carry several men or a ton of merchandise in a heavy sea. The Makhelchel are bold watermen and skillful fishers. Yet they take most of their fish in the creeks in spring, which they frequently do by treading on them with their naked feet in the crevices of the rocks." (Page 215, etc.).

[The Wintūn; Upper Sacramento and Upper Trinity Rivers]. "They are as remarkable as all Californians for their fondness for being in, and their daily lavatory use of, cold water. They are almost amphibious, or were before they were pestered with clothing. Merely to get a drink they would wade in and dip or toss the water up with their hands. They would dive many feet for clams, remain down twice as long as an American could, and rise to the surface with one or more in each hand and one in the mouth. Though I have never given special attention to the singular shell-mounds which occur in this State, I have often thought they might have been originated by an ancient race of divers like these Wintūn. I am not aware that the latter accumulate the shells in mounds, but they are seen scattered in small piles about their riparian camps. In ancient times, two rival rancherias might have striven to collect each the larger heap of shells, as to-day two hunting or fishing parties will carry their friendly contention to the verge of fool-hardiness to secure the greater amount of game or fish.

"For a fishing-station the Wintūn ties together two stout poles in a cross, plants it in deep water, then lays a log out to it from the shore. Standing here, silent and motionless as a statue, with spear poised in the air, he sometimes looks down upon so great a multitude of black-backed salmon slowly warping to and fro in the gentle current, that he could scarcely thrust his spear down without transfixing one or more. At times, he constructs a booth out over the water, but it is not nearly so ingenious and pretty a structure as those on the Klamath. His spear is very long and slender, often fifteen feet in length, with a joint of

---

* Derived from the Aztec word *tullin*, signifying a bulrush.

deer's bone at the end, about three inches long, fashioned with a socket to fit on to the main spear-shaft, to which it is also fastened by a string tied around its middle. The Indian aims to drive this movable joint quite through the fish, whereupon it comes loose, turns crossways, and thus holds the fish securely, flouncing at the end of the string. The construction of this spear shows a good knowledge of the gamy, resolute salmon; the string at the end allows him to play and exhaust himself, while a stiff spear would be broken or wrenched out of him. A party of six Indians on McCloud's Fork speared over five hundred, in one night, which would at a moderate calculation give five hundred pounds to each spearman. In view of this, although an exceptional case, who can doubt that the ancient population of California may have been very great?" (Page 233, etc.).

[The Modok; formerly southern shore of Lower Klamath Lake, Hot Creek, Clear Lake, and Lost River]. "They formerly had 'dug-outs,' generally made from the fir, quite rude and unshapely affairs compared with those found on the Lower Klamath, but substantial, and sometimes capable of carrying a burden of 1,800 pounds. Across the bow of one of these canoes a fish-seine was stretched, bellying back as the craft was propelled through the water, until the catch was sufficiently large, when it was lifted up and emptied." (Page 255).

[The Yokuts; region of Tulare Lake]. "In the mountain streams which empty into Tulare Lake they catch lake trout, chubs, and suckers. Sometimes they construct a weir across the river with a narrow chute and a trap set in it; then go above and stretch a line of brushwood from one bank to the other, which they drag down stream, driving the fish into the trap. Another way is to erect a brushwood booth over the water, so thickly covered as to be perfectly dark inside; then an Indian lies flat on his belly, peering down through a hole, and when a fish passes under him he spears it. The spear is pointed with bone, and is two-pronged. Still another method is employed on Tule River and King's River. An Indian takes a funnel-shaped trap in his teeth and hands, buoys himself on a little log, and then floats silently down the rapids, holding the net open to receive the fish that may be shooting up. On Tulare Lake they construct very rude, frail punts or mere troughs of tule, about ten feet long, in which they cruise timidly about near the shore." (Page 376).

[The Palligawonap; Kern River]. "Tule is also the material from which they construct a rude water-craft. This is only about six feet in length, with the bow very long and sharp-rounded, and the stern cut nearly square across; sides perpendicular; a small tule keel running along the middle, dividing the bottom into two sides. It will carry only one man, and he has to be very careful when standing up to keep his feet one on each side of the keel, or the bobbing thing will capsize. It is used principally in fishing, for which purpose they employ a three-pronged gig pointed with bone. They show much more skill in balancing themselves in the boat than they do in making it." (Page 394).

Powers (Stephen): The Indians of Western Nevada; Manuscript in possession of the Bureau of Ethnology.*—[Pai-ute]. "A kind of balsa or raft is made of tule for fishing-purposes on Pyramid Lake. They select stalks which are ten or twelve feet long, and bind them firmly with willow-twigs into fusiform sheaves or bundles; two of these bundles make the outside of the raft, and between them is another one, smaller and of uniform thickness throughout. The ends of the raft are a little turned up, and sticks are thrust horizontally through the three bundles, to keep them stiff and level on the waves. This raft is propelled with a pole, which, when not in use, is retained on the raft by being thrust through loops in the willow-twigs. It will carry one or two men." — — —

" The Pai-Ute at Pyramid Lake are tribally named from the fish they chiefly eat—the *kú-yu-wi*, probably a species of carp, but commonly called by the Americans a sucker. It is caught in great quantities in the winter season, when ascending the Truckee River† to spawn. I have seen two Indians bring in, early in October, two large horse-loads—probably two hundred pounds—as the product of twenty-four hours' labor with a throw-line. A single Indian has been known to make twenty-five dollars a day, for a short period, catching these fish and selling them in Wadsworth. The night is a favorite time for fishing; the Indian sometimes lies on his face in a booth or on his tule raft, peering down into the water, and whenever he sees a fish glide over a white stone at the bottom, revealing itself plainly, he thrusts it through with a spear. But the spear is less employed than the hook, the net, and the throw-line. The hook, whether large or small, is made by lashing a sharp piece of bone to a shaft of grease-wood at a nearly right angle; this is baited with a minnow or a piece of flesh, and sometimes rubbed over with the aromatic seeds of a certain plant, powdered; and when the fish swallows it, the hook turns crossways in the throat. A number of these are fastened by snoods, at regular intervals, to a line with a sinker at the end, which is thrown out into the water, while the other end is tied to some object ashore, constituting what is known in the Western States as a throw-line or a ' trot-line.'‡

"Various kinds of nets are made of the fibre of the common milkweed (*Asclepias*), very ingeniously twisted on the thigh, and woven with a bobbin. Men and women both work in cutting up and drying the fish when a heavy catch has been made. The fish is cut open along the back, on both sides of the backbone, which is lifted out, but left attached at the head; the latter is not removed."

---

* This manuscript was kindly placed at my disposal by Major J. W. Powell.
† It flows into Pyramid Lake.
‡ Probably a corruption of " trawl-line."

Stone (*Livingston*): *Salmon-fishing among the McCloud River Indians in California.* Communicated in writing to the Author in June, 1882.—"The usual method practised by the McCloud River Indians for capturing salmon is spearing. Their spear is a very long and comparatively slender pole, thickest in the middle, and tapering toward both ends. I should say that twenty-five feet may be considered a fair average length of a McCloud River Indian's salmon-spear, and in the middle it is not far from an inch and a half or two inches in diameter. It is always painted black with a preparation of pitch.

"The anterior end of the spear terminates in a fork with two prongs, about fifteen inches in length, and likewise of wood. On the end of each of these prongs is loosely stuck a sharp-pointed piece of bone, made from the ankle of a deer. These bones are also firmly tied by a rope to the shaft of the spear. When preparing to strike the fish, the Indian poises the spear over his head, and throws it with great velocity at the victim. The moment the pointed bones pierce the salmon, he springs to get away, and pulls the bones off the ends of the prongs; but the pointed bones being ingeniously fastened to the rope near their middle, as soon as they are held only by the rope, change their direction nearly at a right angle, and now become laterally imbedded in the salmon's body. Thus the fish is firmly held and is soon pulled ashore.

"The Indians throw their spear with great dexterity, and are usually successful in getting salmon with it. They go spearing in the morning and evening, but usually in the morning, from daylight to sunrise. They capture with the spear nearly all the salmon that they eat fresh; but in the fall, when they are preparing to dry their winter's stock of fish, they catch them in another way. At this time they build an angular brush dam across or partly across the river, with the angle down stream, and at this angle they place a large coarse wicker basket. This is the season when hundreds and thousands of salmon are floating down the river in a dying condition at the close of the spawning season. These exhausted fish are trapped in great numbers in the wicker baskets, from which they are taken, split, and dried for winter use. Nearly all their supply for drying is obtained in this manner.

"The McCloud River Indians have a third method of fishing for salmon, by diving into the river themselves with nets; but this mode is only resorted to once or twice a year, and is made an occasion of festivities rather than a means of acquiring food. The whole year's supply of salmon is practically obtained by the first-mentioned two methods, viz., by the spear and the wicker basket. I should say, however, that since the United States Fish Commission has established a station on the river, the Indians derive a very large proportion of their daily and winter's supply of fish from the nets of the Commission."*

---

* Mr. Stone is Deputy U. S. Fish Commissioner for the Pacific Coast.

Dunn (John): The Oregon Territory, and the British North American Fur Trade; New York, 1845.—[Chinooks, etc.]. "The salmon season of those tribes towards the mouth of the Columbia commences in June: and its opening is an epoch looked forward to with much anxiety, and is attended with great formality. They have a public festival, and offer sacrifices. The first salmon caught is a consecrated thing; and is offered to the munificent Spirit who is the giver of plenty. They have a superstitious scruple about the mode of cutting salmon; especially at the commencement of the season, before they have an assurance of a plentiful supply. To cut it crosswise, and to cast the heart into the water, they consider most unlucky, and likely to bring on a scarce season. Hence they are very reluctant to supply the traders at the stations with any, until the season is advanced, and they can calculate on their probable stock; lest an unlucky cross cut by the white men may mar all their prospects. Their mode is to cut it along the back; they take out the back bone, and most studiously avoid throwing the heart into the water. The heart they broil and eat; but will not eat it after sunset. So plentiful is the fish, that they supply the white men with it in abundance." — — — "Their canoes vary in size and form. Some are thirty feet long, and about three feet deep, cut out of a single tree—either fir or white cedar—and capable of carrying twenty persons. They have round thwart pieces from side to side, forming a sort of binders, about three inches in circumference; and their gunwales incline outwards, so as to cast off the surge; the bow and stern being decorated, sometimes, with grotesque figures of men and animals. In managing their canoes, they kneel *two and two* along the bottom, sitting on their heels, and wielding paddles about five feet long; while one sits on the stern and steers, with a paddle of the same kind. The women are equally expert in the management of the canoe, and generally take the helm. It is surprising to see with what fearless unconcern these savages venture in their slight barks on the most tempestuous seas. They seem to ride upon the waves like sea-fowl. Should a surge throw the canoe upon one side and endanger its overturn, those to windward lean over the upper gunwale—thrust their paddles deep into the wave—apparently catch the water, and force it under the canoe; and by this action, not merely regain an equilibrium, but give the vessel a vigorous impulse forward." (Page 87, etc.).

"Sturgeon are caught by the Chinooks in the following manner. To the line—which is made from the twisted roots of trees—is attached a large hook, made of hard wood. This is lowered some twenty feet below the surface of the water. The canoes are not more than ten feet long; manned by never more than two, sometimes only by one; and slowly drift down the river with the current. When the sturgeon bites, and they have him fast, the line is hauled up gently until they get his head to the water's edge. He then receives a blow from a heavy wooden mallet, which kills him. The gunwale of the canoe is lowered to the verge of the water; and the sturgeon, though weighing upwards of three hundred pounds, is, by the single effort of one Indian, jerked into the boat." (Page 96).

"They are very ingenious in the construction of their nets, which are made of a sort of wild hemp, sometimes called silk-grass, found on the upper borders of the Columbia; or of the fibres of the roots of trees; or the inner ligaments of the bark of the white cedar. These nets are of different kinds, for the different kinds of fishery—the straight net for the larger fish in deep water; and the scooping or dipping-net for the smaller fish in the shallower waters. They also use a curious sort of many-pronged spear, for drawing up small fish. This is a pole set all round with numerous short wooden little spikes. This they work along against the current from the canoe, and against the small fish, that swim onwards in dense masses. At every take-up of this spear, which is done in quick succession, it is found filled with fishes impaled on those sharp spikes. In their nets they use stones in place of lead; and their superior usefulness and adaptation to the fishery of the Columbia, over the nets of the civilized white, may be shown from the following fact:— A Mr. Wyeth, of Boston, having heard much of the salmon fishery in the Columbia, and thinking it would afford a profitable trading speculation, chartered a vessel, in 1835; and on his way took a number of Sandwich Islanders as fishermen; supplying himself also with a cargo of fishing nets, and a great variety of other fishing apparatus, on the most approved principles. On arriving at the Columbia, he set vigorously to work, dead sure of making a fortune. But his nets were totally unfit for the occupation; and his exotic fishermen, notoriously familiar as they are with the watery element, were no match for the natives, pursuing their natural occupation in almost their indigenous element, and so familiar with the seasons, the currents, the localities, and all the many other circumstances that insure success." (Page 98, etc.).

Swan (James G.): The Northwest Coast; or, Three Years' Residence in Washington Territory; New York, 1857.—"The Chenook salmon commences to enter the river (Columbia) the last of May, and is most plentiful about the 20th of June. It is, without doubt, the finest salmon in the world, and, being taken so near the ocean, has its fine flavor in perfection. The salmon, when entering a river to spawn, do not at once proceed to the head-waters, but linger round the mouth for several weeks before they are prepared to go farther up. It has been supposed that they cannot go immediately from the ocean to the cold fresh water, but remain for a time where the water is brackish before they venture on so great a change. Be that as it may, one thing is certain, that the early salmon taken at Chenook are far superior in flavor to any that are subsequently taken farther up the river, and this excellence is so generally acknowledged that Chenook salmon command a higher price than any other. — — —

"The Chenook fishery is carried on by means of nets. These are made by the whites of the twine prepared for the purpose, and sold as salmon-twine, and rigged with floats and sinkers in the usual style. The nets of the Indians are made of a twine spun by themselves from the fibres of spruce roots prepared for the purpose, or from a species of grass brought from the north by the Indians. It is very strong, and answers the purpose admirably. Peculiar-shaped sticks of dry cedar are used for floats, and the weights at the bottom are round beach pebbles, about a pound each, notched to keep them from slipping from their fastenings, and securely held by withes of cedar firmly twisted and woven into the foot-rope of the net.

"The nets vary in size from a hundred feet long to a hundred fathoms, or six hundred feet, and from seven to sixteen feet deep.

"Three persons are required to work a net, except the very large ones, which require more help to land them. The time the fishing is commenced is at the top of high-water, just as the tide begins to ebb. A short distance from the shore the current is very swift, and with its aid these nets are hauled. Two persons get into the canoe, on the stern of which is coiled the net on a frame made for the purpose, resting on the canoe's gunwale. She is then paddled up the stream, close in to the beach, where the current is not so strong. A tow-line, with a wooden float attached to it, is then thrown to the third person, who remains on the beach, and immediately the two in the canoe paddle her into the rapid stream as quickly as they can, throwing out the net all the time. When this is all out, they paddle ashore, having the end of the other tow-line made fast to the canoe. Before all this is accomplished, the net is carried down the stream, by the force of the ebb, about the eighth of a mile, the man on the shore walking along slowly, holding on to the line till the others are ready, when all haul in together. As it gradually closes on the fish, great caution must be used to prevent them from jumping over; and as every salmon has to be knocked on the head with a club for the purpose, which every canoe carries, it requires some skill and practice to perform this feat so as not to bruise or disfigure the fish." — — —

"It was formerly the custom among the Chenook Indians, on the appearance of the first salmon, to have a grand feast, with dancing and other performances suited to the occasion; but the tribe has now dwindled down to a mere handful, and they content themselves simply with taking out the salmon's heart as soon as caught—a ceremony they religiously observe, fearful lest by any means a dog should eat one, in which case they think they can catch no more fish that season." (Page 103, etc.).

Swan (James G.): The Indians of Cape Flattery, at the Entrance to the Strait of Fuca, Washington Territory; Washington, 1869; No. 220 of Smithsonian Contributions to Knowledge.—"The principal subsistence of the Makahs is drawn from the ocean, and is formed of nearly all its products, the most important of which are the whale and halibut. Of the former there are several varieties which are taken at different seasons of the year. — — — The California gray is the kind usually taken by the Indians, the others being but rarely attacked.

"Their mode of whaling, being both novel and interesting, will require a minute description—not only the implements used, but the mode of attack, and the final disposition of the whale, being entirely different from the practice of our own whalemen. The harpoon consists of a barbed head, to which is attached a rope or lanyard, always of the same length, about five fathoms or thirty feet. This lanyard is made of whale's sinews twisted into a rope about an inch and a half in circumference, and covered with twine wound around it very tightly, called by sailors 'serving.' The rope is exceedingly strong and very pliable.

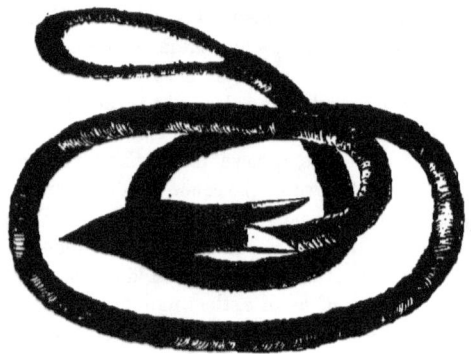

FIG. 368.—Makah harpoon-head and line.

"The harpoon-head is a flat piece of iron or copper, usually a saw-blade or a piece of sheet copper, to which a couple of barbs made of elk's or deer's horn are secured, and the whole covered with a coating of spruce gum. The staff is made of yew in two pieces, which are joined in the middle by a very neat scarf, firmly secured by a narrow strip of bark wound around it very tightly. I do not know why these staves or handles are not made of one piece; it may be that the yew does not grow sufficiently straight to afford the required length; but I have never seen a staff that was not constructed as here described. The length is eighteen feet; thickest in the centre, where it is joined together, and tapering thence to both ends. To be used, the staff is inserted into the barbed head, and the end of the lanyard made fast to a buoy, which is simply a seal-skin taken from the animal whole, the hair being left inwards. The apertures of the head, feet, and tail are tied up air-tight, and the skin is inflated like a bladder.

"When the harpoon is driven into a whale, the barb and buoy remain fastened to him, but the staff comes out, and is taken into the canoe. The harpoon which is thrown into the head of the whale has but one buoy attached; but those thrown into the body have as many as can be conveniently tied on; and, when a number of canoes join in the attack, it is not unusual for from thirty to forty of these buoys to be made fast to the whale, which, of course, cannot sink, and is easily despatched by their spears and lances. The buoys are fastened together by means of a stout line made of spruce roots, first slightly roasted in hot ashes, then split with knives into fine fibres, and finally twisted into ropes, which are very strong and durable. These ropes are also used for towing the dead whale to the shore. — — —

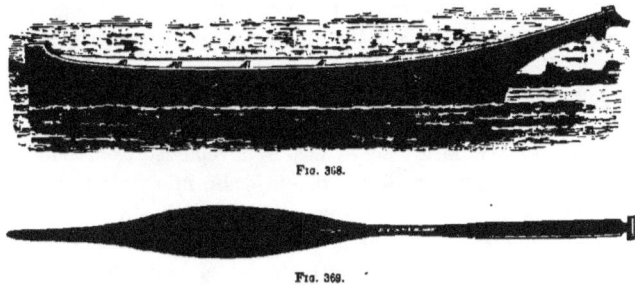

FIG. 368.

FIG. 369.

FIGS. 369 and 370.—Makah whaling-canoe and paddle.

"A whaling canoe invariably carries eight men: one in the bow, who is the harpooner, one in the stern to steer, and six to paddle. The canoe is divided by sticks, which serve as stretchers or thwarts, into six spaces. — — — When whales are in sight, and one or more canoes have put off in pursuit, it is usual for some one to be on the look-out from a high position, so that in case a whale is struck, a signal can be given and other canoes go to assist. When the whale is dead, it is towed ashore to the most convenient spot, if possible to one of the villages, and hauled as high on the beach as it can be floated. As soon as the tide recedes, all hands swarm around the carcass with their knives, and in a very short time the blubber is stripped off in blocks about two feet square. The portion of blubber forming a saddle, taken from between the head and dorsal fin, is esteemed the most choice, and is always the property of the person who first strikes the whale. The other portions are distributed according to rule, each man knowing what he is to receive. — — — The blubber, after being skinned, is cut into strips and boiled, to get out the oil that can be extracted by that process; this oil is carefully skimmed from the pots with clam shells. The blubber is then hung in the smoke to dry, and when cured, looks very much like citron. It is somewhat tougher than pork, but sweet (if the whale has been recently killed), and has none of that nauseous taste which the whites attribute to it. When cooked, it is common to boil the strips about twenty minutes; but it is often eaten cold and as an accompaniment to dried halibut." (Page 19, etc.).

"The principal articles manufactured by the Makahs are canoes and whaling implements, conical hats, bark mats, fishing-lines, fish-hooks, knives and daggers, bows and arrows, dog's hair blankets, feather capes, and various other articles. The largest and best canoes are made by the Clyoquots and Nittinats on Vancouver Island; the cedar there being of a quality greatly superior to that found on or near Cape Flattery. Canoes of the medium and small sizes are made by the Makahs from cedar procured a short distance up the Strait or on the Tsuess River. After the tree is cut down and the bark stripped, the log is cut at the length required for the canoes, and the upper portion removed by splitting it off with wedges, until the greatest width is attained. The two ends are then rough-hewed to a tapering form and a portion of the inside dug out. The log is next turned over and properly shaped for a bottom, then turned back and more chopped from the inside, until enough has been removed from both inside and out to permit it to be easily handled, when it is slid into the water and taken to the lodge of the maker, where he finishes it at his leisure. In some cases they finish a canoe in the woods, but generally it is brought home as soon as they can haul it to the stream. Before the introduction of iron tools, the making of a canoe was a work of much difficulty. Their hatchets were made of stone, and their chisels of mussel shells ground to a sharp edge by rubbing them on a piece of sandstone. It required much time and extreme labor to cut down a large cedar, and it was only the chiefs who had a number of slaves at their disposal who attempted such large operations. Their method was to gather round a tree as many as could work, and these chipped away with their stone hatchets till the tree was literally gnawed down, after the fashion of beavers. Then to shape it and hollow it out was also a tedious job, and many a month would intervene between the times of commencing to fell the tree, and finishing the canoe. The implements they use at present are axes to do the rough-hewing, and chisels fitted to handles; these last are used like a cooper's adze, and remove the wood in small chips. The process of finishing is very slow. A white carpenter could smooth off the hull of a canoe with a plane, and do more in two hours than the Indian with his chisel can do in a week. The outside, when it is completed, serves as a guide for finishing the inside, the workman gauging the requisite thickness by placing one hand on the outside and the other on the inside, and passing them over the work. He is guided in modelling by the eye, seldom, if ever, using a measure of any kind; and some are so expert in this that they make lines as true as the most skilful mechanic can. If the tree is not sufficiently thick to give the required width, they spring the top of the sides apart, in the middle of the canoe, by steaming the wood. The inside is filled with water which is heated by means of red-hot stones, and a slow fire is made on the outside by rows of bark laid on the ground, a short distance off, but near enough to warm the cedar without burning it. This renders the wood very flexible in a short time, so that the sides can be opened from six to twelve inches. The canoe is now strengthened, and kept in form by sticks or stretchers, similar to a boat's thwarts. The ends of these stretchers are fastened with withes made from tapering cedar limbs, twisted, and used instead of cords, and the water is then emptied out; this process is not often employed, however, the log being usually sufficiently wide in the first instance. As the projections for the head and stern pieces cannot be cut from the log, they are carved from separate pieces and fastened on by means of withes and wooden pegs. A very neat and peculiar scarf is used in joining these pieces to the body of the canoe, and the parts are fitted together in a simple and effectual manner. First the scarf is made on the canoe; this is rubbed over with grease and charcoal; next the piece to be fitted is hewn as nearly like the scarf as the eye can guide, and applied to the part which has the grease on it. It is then removed, and the inequalities being at once discovered and chipped off with the chisel, the process is repeated until the whole of the scarf or the piece to be fitted is uniformly marked with the blackened grease. The joints are by this method perfectly matched, and so neat as to be water-tight without any calking. The head and stern pieces being fastened on, the whole of the inside is then chipped over again, and the smaller and more indistinct the chisel marks are, the better the workmanship is considered.

FIG. 371.—Makah canoe showing method of scarfing.

"Until very recently it was the custom to ornament all canoes, except the small ones, with rows of the pearly valve of a species of sea-snail. These shells are procured in large quantities at Nittinat and Clyoquot, and formerly were in great demand as an article of traffic. They are inserted in the inside of the edge of the canoe by driving them into holes bored to receive them. But at present they are not much used by the Makahs, for the reason, I presume, that they are continually trading off their canoes, and find they bring quite as good a price without these ornaments as with them. I have noticed, however, among some of the Clallams, who are apt to keep a canoe much longer than the Makahs, that the shell ornaments are still used. When the canoe is finished, it is painted inside with a mixture of oil and red ochre. Sometimes charcoal and oil are rubbed on the outside, but more commonly it is simply charred by means of long fagots of cedar splints, set on fire on one end like a torch, and held against the side of the canoe. The surface is then rubbed smooth with a wisp of grass or a branch of cedar twigs." (Page 35, etc.).

Swan (James G.): The Haidah Indians of Queen Charlotte's Islands, British Columbia; Washington, 1874; No. 267 of Smithsonian Contributions to Knowledge.—" The Haidah Indians, living on an island separated from the mainland by a wide and stormy strait, are necessarily obliged to resort to canoes as a means of travel, and are exceedingly expert in their construction and management.

"Some of their canoes are very large and capable of carrying one hundred persons with all their equipments for a long voyage. But those generally used will carry from twenty to thirty persons; and in these conveyances they make voyages of several hundred miles to Victoria on Vancouver's Island, and from thence to the various towns on Puget Sound.

"These canoes are made from single logs of cedar, which attains an immense size on Queen Charlotte's Islands. Although not so graceful in model as the canoes of the west coast of Vancouver's Island and Washington Territory, which are commonly called Chenook canoes, yet they are most excellent sea boats, and capable of being navigated with perfect safety through the storms and turbulent waters of the Northwest Coast." (Page 2).*

Meares (John): Voyages made in the years 1788 and 1789, from China to the N. W. Coast of America, etc.; London, 1791.—[Inhabitants of Nootka Sound, Vancouver's Island]. " Vast quantities of fish are to be found, both on the coast and in the sounds or harbours.—Among these are the halibut, herring, sardine, silver-bream, salmon, trout, cod, elephant-fish, shark. dog-fish, cuttle-fish, a great variety of rock-fish, &c.—all of which we have seen in the possession of the natives, or have been caught by ourselves. There are, probably, a great abundance of other kinds, which are not to be taken by the hook, the only method of taking fish with which the natives are acquainted, and we had neither trawls or nets.

"In the spring, the herrings as well as the sardines, frequent the coast in vast shoals. The herring is from seven to eight inches long, and, in general, smaller than those taken in the British seas. The sardine resembles that of Portugal, and is very delicious: they are here taken by the people in prodigious quantities. They first drive the shoals into the small coves, or shallow waters,

---

* A canoe of this kind, procured through the agency of Mr. Swan, is in the National Museum. It attracted much attention during the Centennial Exhibition at Philadelphia, on account of its large size, being fifty-nine feet long, and eight feet wide by three feet and seven inches in depth amidships. It is made of a log of the yellow cedar (*Thuya gigantea*).

when a certain number of men in canoes keep plashing the water, while others sink branches of the pine with stones; the fish are then easily taken out with wooden troughs or wicker baskets. We have sometimes seen such numbers of them, that a whole village has not been able to cleanse them before they began to grow putrid.—After being cleaned, they are placed on rods, and hung in rows, at a certain distance, over their fires, that thay may be smoked; and when they are sufficiently dried, they are carefully packed up in mats, and laid by as a part, and a very considerable part, of their winter's provision. The season for taking these fish is in the months of July and August. Certain people, at this time, are stationed on particular eminences, to look for the arrival of the shoals, which can be very readily distinguished by the particular motion of the sea. The natives then embark in their canoes to proceed in their fishery. The sardine is preferred by them to every other kind of fish, except the salmon.

"In the months of July, August, and September, salmon are taken, though not in so great abundance as the other fish, but are of a very delicate flavour. They are split, dried, and packed up, as has already been described, and are considered as a great delicacy. The salmon of the district of Nootka are very different from those found to the Northward, which are of an inferior kind, and of the same species with those taken at Kamtschatka.

"During our stay in King George's Sound, we saw very few sharks or halibut; but the cod taken by the natives were of the best quality:—they are also prepared, like the rest, for the purpose of winter stores." (Vol. III, page 29, etc.).

"The occupations of the men of this coast were such as arose from their particular situation. Fishing, and hunting the land or larger marine animals, either for food or furs, form their principal employments.—The common business of fishing for ordinary sustenance is carried on by slaves, or the lower class of people:—While the more noble occupation of killing the whale and hunting the sea-otter, is followed by none but the chiefs and warriors.

"Their dexterity in killing the whale is not easily described, and the facility with which they convey so huge a creature to their habitations is no less remarkable. When it is determined to engage in whale-hunting, which the most stormy weather does not prevent, the chief prepares himself, with no common ceremony, for this noble diversion.—He is cloathed on the occasion in the sea-otter's skin; his body is besmeared with oil, and daubed with red ochre; and he is accompanied by the most brave, active, and vigorous people in his service.

"The canoes employed on this occasion are of a size between their war canoes and those they use on ordinary occasions; they are admirably well adapted to the purpose, and are capable of holding, conveniently, eighteen or twenty men.

"The harpoons which they use to strike the whale or any other sea-animal, except the otter, are contrived with no common skill. The shaft is from eighteen to twenty-eight feet in length; at the end whereof is fixed a large piece of bone cut in notches, which being spliced to the shaft, serves as a secure hold for the harpoon, which is fastened to it with thongs.—The harpoon is of an oval form, and rendered extremely sharp at the sides as well as the point; it is made of a large muscle-shell, and is fixed into another piece of bone, about three inches long, and to which a line is fastened, made of the sinews of certain beasts, of several fathoms in length; this is again attached to the shaft; so that when the fish is pierced, the shaft floats on the water by means of seal-skins filled with wind, or the ventilated bladders of fish, which are securely attached to it.

"The chief himself is the principal harpooner, and is the first that strikes the whale.—He is attended by several canoes of the same size as his own, filled with people armed with harpoons, to be employed as occasion may require. When the huge fish feels the smart of the first weapon, he instantly dives, and carries the shaft with all its bladders along with him. The boats immediately follow his wake, and as he rises, continue to fix their weapons in him, till he finds it impossible for him to sink, from the number of floating buoys which are now attached to his body. The whale then drowns, and is towed on shore with great noise and rejoicings. It is then immediately cut up, when part is dedicated to the feast which concludes the day, and the remainder divided among those who have shared in the dangers and glory of it.

"The taking of the sea-otter is attended with far greater hazard as well as trouble. For this purpose two very small canoes are prepared, in each of which are two expert hunters. The instruments they employ on this occasion are bows and arrows, and a small harpoon. The latter differs, in some degree, from that which they use in hunting the whale; the shaft is much the same, and is pointed with bone; but the harpoon itself is of a greater length, and so notched and barbed, that when it has once entered the flesh, it is almost impossible to extricate it. This is attached to the shaft by several fathoms of line of sufficient strength to drag the otter to the boat. The arrows are small, and pointed with bone, formed into a single barb. Thus equipped, the hunters proceed among the rocks in search of their prey.—Sometimes they surprise him sleeping on his back, on the surface of the water; and, if they can get near the animal without awakening him, which requires infinite precaution, he is easily harpooned and dragged to the boat, when a fierce battle very often ensues between the otter and the hunters, who are frequently wounded by the claws and teeth of the animal. The more common mode, however, of taking him is by pursuit, which is sometimes continued for several hours.—As he cannot remain under water but for a very short time, the skill in this chace consists in directing the canoes in the same line that the otter takes when under the water, at which time he swims with a degree of celerity that greatly exceeds that of his pursuers. They therefore separate, in order to have the better chance of wounding him with their arrows at the moment he rises; though it often happens that this wary and cunning animal escapes from the danger which surrounds him.

"It has been observed, in the account already given of the otter, that when they are overtaken with their young ones, the parental affection supersedes all sense of danger; and both the male and female defend their offspring with the most furious courage, tearing out the arrows and harpoons fixed in them with their teeth, and oftentimes even attacking the canoes. On these occasions, however, they and their litter never fail of yielding to the power of the hunters. The difficulty of taking the otter might indeed occasion some degree of surprise at the number of the skins which the natives appear to have in use, and for the purposes of trade. But the circumstance may be easily accounted for, by the constant exercise of this advantageous occupation: scarce a day passes, but numbers are eagerly employed in the pursuit of it.

"The seal is also an animal very difficult to take, on account of its being able to remain under water. Artifices are therefore made use of to decoy him within reach of the boats; and this is done in general by the means of masks of wood made in so exact a resemblance of nature, that the animal takes it for one of his own species, and falls a prey to the deception. On such occasions, some of the natives put on these masks, and hiding their bodies with branches of trees as they lie among the rocks, the seals are tempted to approach so near the spot, as to put it in the power of the natives to pierce them with their arrows. Similar artifices are employed against the sea-cow, &c. The otters, as well as some of the land animals, are, we believe, occasionally taken in the same manner.

"The very preparation for the business of hunting and fishing, requires no small portion of domestic employment. Their harpoons, lines, fish-hooks, bows and arrows, and other implements necessary in the different pursuits of peace and war, must make a very great demand upon their time. — — — The ingenuity of these people in all the different arts that is necessary to their support and their pleasure, is matter of just admiration to the more cultivated parts of the globe. Nature, that fond and bounteous parent to her children of every kind, has left none of them without those means which are capable of producing the relative happiness of all. But the most laborious, as well as most curious employment in which we saw the natives of Nootka engaged, (for we had no opportunity of seeing them construct one of their enormous houses,) was the making of their canoes; which was a work of no common skill and ability. These boats are, many of them, capable of containing from fifteen to thirty men, with ease and convenience; and at the same time are elegantly moulded and highly finished; and this curious work is accomplished with utensils of stone, made by themselves.

"They even manufactured tools from the iron which they obtained from us; and it was very seldom that we could pursuade them to make use of

R 40

any of our utensils in preference to their own, except the saw, whose obvious power in diminishing their labour, led them to adopt it without hesitation. In particular, they contrived to forge from the iron they procured of us, a kind of tool, which answered the purpose of hollowing out large trees much better than any utensil we could give them. This business they accomplished by main strength, with a flat stone by way of anvil, and a round one which served the purpose of an hammer; and with these instruments they shaped the iron from the fire into a tool bearing some resemblance to a cooper's adze, which they fastened to an handle of wood with cords made of sinews; and being sharpened at the end, was extremely well adapted to the uses for which it was intended.

"Their large war canoes were generally finished on the spot where the trees grew of which they are made, and then dragged to the water-side. We have seen some of them which were fifty-three feet in length, and eight feet in breadth. The middle part of these boats is the broadest, and gradually narrows to a point at each end; but their head or prow is generally much higher than the stern.

"As their bottoms are rounded, and their sides flam out, they have consequently sufficient bearings, and swim firmly in the water. They have no seats, but several pieces of wood, about three inches in diameter, are fixed across them, to keep the sides firm, and preserve them from being warped. The rowers generally sit on their hams, but sometimes they make use of a kind of small stool, which is a great relief to them. In the act of embarking they are extremely cautious, each man regularly taking the station to which he has been accustomed. Some of these canoes are polished and painted, or curiously studded with human teeth, particularly on the stern and the prow. The sides were sometimes adorned with the figure of a dragon with a long tail, of much the same form as we see on the porcelain of China, and in the fanciful paintings of our own country. We were much struck with this circumstance, and took some pains to get at the history of it; but it was among many other of our enquiries to which we could not obtain any satisfactory answer.

"After we had been some time in King George's Sound, the natives began to make use of sails made of mats, in imitation of ours. We had, indeed, rigged one of Hanna's large canoes for him, with a pendant, &c. &c. of which he was proud beyond measure; and he never approached the ship but hoisted his pendant, to the very great diversion of our seamen.

"The paddles are nicely shaped, and well polished with fish-skin: they are about five feet six inches in length; and the blade, which is about two feet long, is pointed like a leaf, and the point itself is lengthened several inches, and is about one broad. At the end of the handle there is a transverse piece of wood like the top of a crutch. These paddles the natives use in a most dextrous manner, and urge on the canoes with inconceivable swiftness.

"In no one circumstance of their different occupations do the natives of

Nootka discover more dexterity than in that of fishing. They however always preferred their own hooks, which were made from shells, or the bone of fish, to ours; nor indeed would they ever make use of the latter; but our lines they considered as very superior to those of their own manufacture. These are made from the sinews of the whale, which furnishes them with the materials of all their different cordage,—or from sea-weed, which grows on the coast in great abundance. This is split, boiled, and dried, when it forms a strong and very tough line.

"But, besides the common practice of angling, they have a very particular method of taking herrings, sardines, &c. This is managed with a stick or pole about eighteen feet long, with a blade of twelve or fourteen inches broad, and six feet long, on both sides of which are fixed a number of sharp pieces or points of bone, about three inches in length. When the shoal of fish appears, they strike this instrument into the water, and seldom fail of bringing up three or four fish at every stroke.—We have often seen a small canoe nearly filled with herrings, &c. in a very short time, by this easy method of fishing." (Vol. II, page 51, etc.).

Cook (Captain James) and King (Captain James): A Voyage to the Pacific Ocean, etc.; third edition; London, 1785, Vol. II.—[Inhabitants of Nootka Sound]. "Their canoes are of a simple structure, but, to appearance, well calculated for every useful purpose. Even the largest, which carry twenty people or more, are formed of one tree. Many of them are forty feet long, seven broad, and about three deep. From the middle, toward each end, they become gradually narrower, the after-part, or stern, ending abruptly or perpendicularly, with a small knob on the top; but the fore-part is lengthened out, stretching forward and upward, ending in a notched point or prow, considerably higher than the sides of the canoe, which run nearly in a straight line. For the most part, they are without any ornament; but some have a little carving, and are decorated by setting seal's teeth† on the surface, like studs; as is the practice on their masks and weapons. A few have, likewise, a kind of additional head or prow, like a large cut-water, which is painted with the figure of some animal. They have no seats, nor any other supporters, on the inside, than several round sticks, little thicker than a cane, placed across, at mid depth. They are very light, and their breadth and flatness enable them to swim firmly, without an out-rigger, which none of them have; a remarkable distinction between the navigation of all the American nations, and that of the Southern parts of the East Indies, and the Islands in the Pacific Ocean. Their paddles are small and light; the shape, in some measure, resembling that of a large leaf, pointed at the bottom, broadest in the middle, and grandually losing itself in the shaft, the whole being about five feet long.

---

* Vol. II is written by Captain Cook. The voyage was performed in the years 1776–'80.
† Mistaken for human teeth by Meares.

They have acquired great dexterity in managing these paddles, by constant use; for sails are no part of their art of navigation.

"Their implements for fishing and hunting, which are both ingeniously contrived, and well made, are nets, hooks and lines, harpoons, gigs, and an instrument like an oar. This last is about twenty feet long, four or five inches broad, and about half an inch thick. Each edge, for about two-thirds of its length (the other third being its handle), is set with sharp bone-teeth, about two inches long. Herrings and sardines, and such other small fish as come in shoals, are attacked with this instrument; which is struck into the shoal, and the fish are caught, either upon or between the teeth. Their hooks are made of bone and wood, and rather inartificially; but the harpoon, with which they strike the whales and lesser sea animals, shews a great reach of contrivance. It is composed of a piece of bone, cut into two barbs, in which is fixed the oval blade of a large muscle shell, in which is the point of the instrument. To this is fastened about two or three fathoms of rope; and to throw this harpoon, they use a shaft of about twelve or fifteen feet long, to which the line or rope is made fast; and to one end of which the harpoon is fixed, so as to separate from the shaft, and leave it floating upon the water as a buoy, when the animal darts away with the harpoon. — — — As to the materials, of which they make their various articles, it is to be observed, that every thing of the rope kind, is formed either from thongs of skins, and sinews of animals; or from the same flaxen substance of which their mantles are manufactured. The sinews often appeared to be of such a length, that it might be presumed they could be of no other animal than the whale. And the same may be said of the bones of which they make their weapons already mentioned; such as their bark-beating instruments, the points of their spears, and the barbs of their harpoons." (Page 327, etc.).

[Inhabitants of Prince William's Sound, present Territory of Alaska]. "Their boats or canoes are of two sorts; the one being large and open, and the other small and covered. I mentioned already, that in one of the large boats were twenty women, and one man, besides children. I attentively examined and compared the construction of this, with Crantz's description of what he calls the great, or women's boat in Greenland, and found that they were built in the same manner, parts like parts, with no other difference than in the form of the head and stern; particularly of the first, which bears some resemblance to the head of a whale. The framing is of slender pieces of wood, over which the skins of seals, or of other larger sea-animals, are stretched, to compose the outside. It appeared also, that the small canoes of these people are made nearly of the same form, and of the same materials with those used by the Greenlanders and Esquimaux; at least the difference is not material. Some of these, as I have before observed, carry two men. They are broader in proportion to their length than those of the Esquimaux; and the head or fore-part curves somewhat like the head of a violin.

"The weapons, and instruments for fishing and hunting, are the very same that are made use of by the Esquimaux and Greenlanders; and it is unnecessary to be particular in my account of them, as they are all very accurately described by Crantz. I did not see a single one with these people that he has not mentioned; nor has he mentioned one that they have not." (Page 371, etc.).

[Inhabitants of Oonalashka, Aleutian Islands]. "Political reasons may have induced the Russians not to allow these islanders to have any large canoes; for it is difficult to believe they had none such originally, as we found them amongst all their neighbors. The canoes made use of by the natives are the smallest we had any where seen upon the American coast; though built after the same manner, with some little difference in the construction. The stern of these terminates a little abruptly; the head is forked; the upper point of the fork projecting without the under one, which is even with the surface of the water. Why they should thus construct them is difficult to conceive; for the fork is apt to catch hold of every thing that comes in the way; to prevent which, they fix a piece of small stick from point to point. In other respects their canoes are built after the manner of those used by the Greenlanders and Esquimaux; the framing being of slender laths, and the covering of seal-skins. They are about twelve feet long; a foot and a half broad in the middle; and twelve or fourteen inches deep. Upon occasion, they can carry two persons; one of whom is stretched at full length in the canoe; and the other sits in the seat, or round hole, which is nearly in the middle. Round this hole is a rim or hoop of wood, about which is sewed gut-skin, that can be drawn together, or opened like a purse, with leathern thongs fitted to the outer edge. The man seats himself in this place; draws the skin tight round his body over his gut frock, and brings the ends of the thongs, or purse-string, over the shoulder to keep it in its place. The sleeves of his frock are tied tight round his wrists; and it being close round his neck, and the hood drawn over his head, where it is confined by his cap, water can scarcely penetrate either to his body, or into the canoe. If any should, however, insinuate itself, the boatman carries a piece of spunge, with which he dries it up. He uses the double-bladed paddle, which is held with both hands in the middle, striking the water with a quick regular motion, first on one side and then on the other. By this means the canoe is impelled at a great rate, and in a direction as straight as a line can be drawn. In sailing from Egoochshak to Samganoodha, two or three canoes kept way with the ship, though she was going at the rate of seven miles an hour.

"Their fishing and hunting implements lie ready upon the canoes, under straps fixed for the purpose. They are all made, in great perfection, of wood and bone; and differ very little from those used by the Greenlanders, as they are described by Crantz. The only difference is in the point of the missile dart; which, in some we saw here, is not above an inch long; whereas Crantz says, that those of the Greenlanders are a foot and a half in length." (Page 513, etc.).

APPENDIX.

NOTICES OF FISHING-IMPLEMENTS AND FISH-REPRESENTATIONS DISCOVERED SOUTH OF MEXICO.

Nicaragua.—Dr. J. F. Bransford, U. S. N., found during his explorations in Central America, undertaken in the interest of the National Museum, on the Island of Ometepec, in the Lake of Nicaragua, a number of sinkers made of lava pebbles or of fragments of clay vessels.

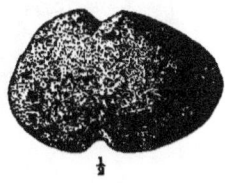

FIG. 372. (28846).   FIG. 373. (28830).

FIGS. 372 and 373.—Stone sinkers. Ometepec Island.

Figs. 372 and 373 represent two of the lava sinkers, which exhibit, respectively, the notched and the grooved type. They are made of dark-colored, massive pebbles, showing the cellules often characteristic of volcanic ejections.

The sinkers made of pieces of clay vessels are mostly notched on opposite sides, like the originals of Figs. 374 and 375 on the next page. The slight curve observable in these sinkers and their thickness (sometimes surpassing half an inch) indicate that they were made of fragments of large and strong vessels. The notches as well as the circumferences seem to have been ground, and the latter are not angular, but rounded. Some specimens still show the paint of the vessel. Similar sinkers, it will be remembered, have been found in Germany.*

Other objects from Ometepec Island, which, in all probability, served as sinkers, are made of parts of the thickened rims of vessels. These specimens generally present an elongated form, and are encircled with a groove near each

---

* See p. 62 of this work.

end, or simply provided in the same places with opposite notches. Fig. 376 shows the appearance of an object of the first kind, still covered with the reddish-brown paint of the vessel. It is ground into shape on the side formed by the fracture. Mr. Charles C. Nutting likewise procured for the National Museum a number of these specimens on Ometepec Island.

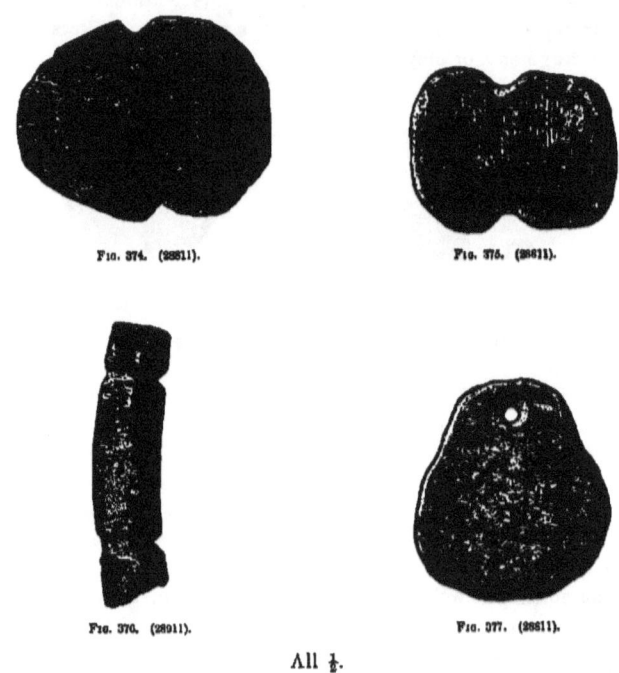

Fig. 374. (28611).   Fig. 375. (28611).

Fig. 376. (28911).   Fig. 377. (28611).

All ⅓.

FIGS. 374–377.—Sinkers made of fragments of clay vessels. Ometepec Island.

In Fig. 377, finally, I represent a sherd of somewhat pear-shaped outline, pierced for suspension near the narrower extremity. There seems to be little risk in classing it as a sinker.

Costa Rica.—The National Museum is indebted to Mr. M. C. Keith, connected with the Costa Rica Railway, which has its eastern terminus at Port Limon, for a large number of valuable relics discovered during the construction of that road. They consist of clay vessels, stone implements, and stone sculptures of various kinds.

APPENDIX. 321

Among the stone carvings is a somewhat rude and weathered specimen, to all appearance intended to imitate a fish. A handle rises from its back, as Fig. 378 shows. The object is flattish, about two inches thick in the middle, and nearly fourteen inches long. It weighs eight pounds and a half. The material is a rather compact, gray rock of volcanic origin. It is the only specimen of this kind sent by Mr. Keith, and I am unable to make any suggestion as to its use. It is probable, however, that it served a symbolic or ceremonial purpose. There is no trace of wear observable in any place.

FIG. 378.—Stone-carving in the form of a fish. Costa Rica. (60895).

Chiriqui, State of Panama, United States of Colombia.—It is now about twenty-five years that great excitement was caused by the discovery of large numbers of gold images in graves situated in the Chiriqui district, now belonging to the State of Panama. The cemetery, or *huacal*, which has furnished most of these interesting specimens of aboriginal art, is located in the parish of Bugaba, about twenty-five miles from David, the principal town in the district. It covers an area of twelve acres. The graves themselves were oval or quadrangular pits, lined with stones. They contained, in addition to the gold articles, well-formed clay vessels of various forms, animal-shaped clay whistles, stone celts and arrows, and metates of a highly ornamental character. The bodies, it appears, had altogether yielded to decay. The gold images alone, however, claim our attention in the present instance. They were evidently cast and afterward finished by beating, and their technical execution reflects credit on the skill of the manufacturers. Their forms were those of wild beasts, birds, reptiles, and fishes peculiar to the region; some represented men or semi-human monsters of hideous shape. They probably served as ornaments or charms, worn by the living and buried with the dead. It should be stated, however, that in most cases the gold composing them was not pure, but more or less alloyed with copper. In speaking of them, I have used the past tense, as I have reason to believe that most of these valuable relics were shipped to England, to be converted into bullion.

My attention was first directed to the Chiriqui discoveries by an article published in "Harper's Weekly," of August 6th, 1859, by Dr. F. M. Otis, then surgeon of the steamship "Moses Taylor." He had just returned from Panama, where he had gathered his information.

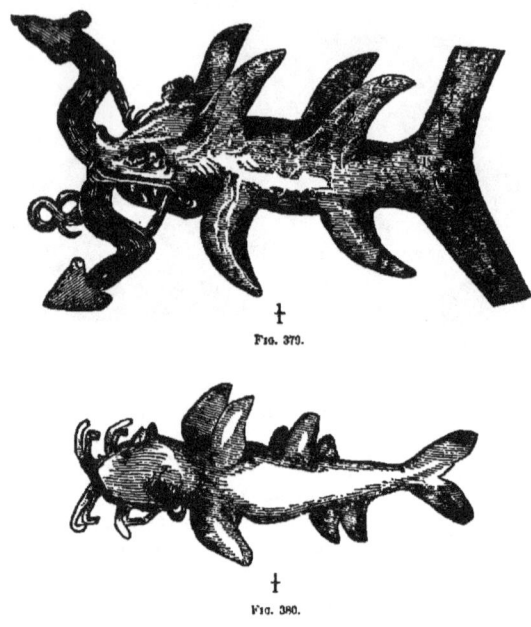

Figs. 379 and 380.—Fish-representations of gold. Chiriqui.

I present in Figs. 379 and 380 copies of two of the illustrations accompanying his article, which represent, as it appears, respectively, a shark holding a snake or snakes (?) in his jaws, and a species of cat-fish. These illustrations give a good idea of the character of the Chiriqui gold figures.*

State of Cauca, United States of Colombia.—In a small pamphlet published in 1870, and noticed in "Matériaux," Dr. L. Marchant states that M. Laurent

---

* A very good account of the Chiriqui graves, based on personal observation, is given by the late Dr. J. King Merritt in one of the bulletins of the American Ethnological Society, issued in 1860.

Rabut saw, in possession of the Abbé Tripier, three gold fish-hooks, obtained from a grave in New Granada.* No description of these hooks is given.

FIG. 381.—Gold fish-hook. Cauca.

Not long ago, Mr. Alexander C. Chenoweth, a civil engineer, showed me the gold fish-hook represented in Fig. 381. He discovered it on the 15th of June, 1882, in a mining-tunnel excavated under his direction on the property known as the Yacula gold-mine, situated in the State of Cauca, eighteen leagues distant from Barbacoas, on the Pacific Coast. The fish-hook was found in the ground, composed of gravel and drift-wood, together with two gold beads and several gold nuggets. These objects occurred at a depth of fifty feet from the surface, in the side of the mountain, which covered, in all probability, the ancient bed of the Yacula River, and it is Mr. Chenoweth's opinion that they cannot have been introduced, but must have lain in the place where they were discovered. I regret that I neglected asking the finder, now again abroad, concerning the elevation of the mountain. Other gold fish-hooks, he stated, had been found in the same district.

The hook, made of round, well-polished gold wire, is destitute of any contrivance for the attachment of a line.†

* Matériaux; Vol. VI, 1870; p. 348.—New Granada formerly embraced the present United States of Colombia.

† I found in the Washington "Sunday Post" of October 14, 1883, a short notice bearing on gold fish-hooks, which was taken from the "Arizona Citizen," published at Tucson. Mr. E. J. Smith, the County Coroner, it is stated in that notice, has in his possession four gold fish-hooks, acquired by him with others—now given away or lost—in 1866, while engaged in mining-operations in the State of Cauca. I wrote immediately to Mr. Smith, for the purpose of obtaining from him photographs of his gold fish-hooks and information as to their discovery; but I received no answer. I then addressed a letter to the editor of the "Arizona Citizen," Mr. S. Robert Brown, and he favored me with a reply, stating that he had spoken to Mr. Smith, and that the latter would send me the desired photographs without delay. My letter to Mr. Smith was afterward published as a part of an article, entitled "Prehistoric Fish Hooks," in the "Arizona Daily Star" (Tucson) of March 7, 1884. "The hooks, of which Mr. Smith has four," it is said, "are about one inch in length and somewhat thicker than a good-sized pin, and would in fishing be probably as effective as a barbless bent pin, which they much resemble. The shank to which the line was attached is bent in the shape of a small ring or eye, with a diameter of probably one-sixteenth of an inch. The hook is curved in a line parallel with the shank, and has been ground down to a point almost as sharp as that of a needle. The thirteen, which Mr. Smith at one time had, were, with one exception, of an almost uniform size and weight; the one excepted being much larger and heavier, but otherwise not different from the smaller ones.

"They were found in the State of Cauca, United States of Colombia, on the river Guava, about fifty leagues

Peru.—During his ten days' exploration of the ruins at Pachacamac, about twenty miles south of Lima, Mr. E. G. Squier examined a number of tombs, of one of which he gives a detailed description. It contained five desiccated human bodies, namely, those of a man of middle stature, of a full-grown woman, of a girl about fourteen years old, of a boy some years younger, and of an infant. Having mentioned the different wrappings shrouding the body of the man, Mr. Squier continues:— "Passing around the neck, and carefully folded on the knees, on which the head rested, was a net of the twisted fibre of the agave, a plant not found on the coast. The threads were as fine as the finest used by our fishermen, and the meshes were neatly knotted, precisely after the fashion of to-day. This seems to indicate that he had been a fisherman—a conclusion further sustained by finding, wrapped up in a cloth, between his feet some fishing-lines of various sizes, some copper hooks, barbed like ours, and some copper sinkers."*

I thought these articles were in the American Museum of Natural History at New York, this institution having acquired Mr. Squier's collection; but upon inquiry, I was informed that they are not there, and I am thus deprived of the opportunity of giving any additional account of them. I was particularly anxious to ascertain whether the hooks really were barbed, as stated by Mr. Squier; for all Peruvian specimens of this class seen by me were unbarbed, and I cannot remember having read any notice relating to barbed fish-hooks from Peru.

There are several single copper fish-hooks in the National Museum, and, moreover, two sets of angling-apparatus, which would be complete, if the rods were not wanting. These articles were but lately presented by Mr. G. H. Hurl-

---

from the city of Popayan, at which place Mr. Smith was, in conjunction with General O. Bando, mining for placer-gold in the year 1866. One of the hooks was in the possession of General Bando, and was by him exhibited as a curiosity at the time of Mr. Smith's going there. Another, taken from the bed of a river into which the Guava entered, was owned by a negro, and was by him also kept for the same purpose, showing therefore that even there the hooks were not common, and could not be obtained but by great labor in washing earth taken out many feet below the surface. The first hooks, three in number, found by Mr. Smith, were taken out ten feet below the river-bed. The river had, at great cost, been turned from its natural channel. Nine others were taken from a bar about two miles above the place where the first three had been found. The bar was the accumulation of centuries, and was covered by a thick growth of forest. The gold was generally distributed over the bar, and as the ground promised to be remunerative, it was adjudged best to sluice it entirely away. On the bed-rock, under a lime-tree fully two feet in diameter, at a depth of about fifteen feet, several more hooks were secured, and still others, at a like depth, in a crevice beneath an immense boulder that weighed probably twenty tons. The accumulated débris of the bar varied from eight to twenty feet in thickness.

"By the people of the neighborhood they were generally believed to be the handiwork of an extinct tribe of Indians, the remains of whose village were then to be seen six or seven leagues higher up, and near the source of the river. They had evidently been workers in gold, as several old arrastras and mining-shafts bore proof. Their graves have since been opened, and many trinkets of gold taken therefrom, lizards, fish and frogs being the most common devices."

Such is the account given in the above-named newspaper. Photographs of the hooks were sent by Mr. Smith; but they arrived too late for reproduction and utilization. This very note was already in type, and had to be modified to include the reference.

* Squier: Peru; Incidents of Travel and Exploration in the Land of the Incas; New York, 1877; p. 74.

APPENDIX. 325

but, son of the late minister of the United States in Peru. In 1881, these gentlemen sent out an inhabitant of Lima to procure antiquities. As the Chilians then invested the capital, it is probable that the relics acquired on that occasion were obtained in the vicinity of the city. More precise information as to their discovery has not been furnished. At any rate, there can be no doubt that they formed a part of a grave-deposit.

¼

Fig. 382.—Wooden mask with appended bags. Peru. (65376).

The most conspicuous, or central object, as it were—represented in Fig. 382—is a human face or mask with the neck indicated by a stem-like projection, the whole tolerably well carved in wood, which, though rather decayed, still bears traces of red paint. The eyes of this mask, which is somewhat larger than life-size, are made of shell, and it is provided at the top and sides with perforations serving for the attachment of various accompanying objects. The back part of the mask, in order to give the carving the appearance of a head, is bolstered by a netted bag filled with leaves, and covered with tow in imitation of hair. There are further to be mentioned a sort of head-dress of feathers and a cloth band around the top of the head. To this part of the head is attached a woven bag, which contained three stone sinkers, bits of copper, corn-husks inclosing earth, and other articles. Fastened to the left side of the mask is a bag of net-work in which were two reels of reed, with the lines wound around them, one of the reels having a copper fish-hook affixed to either end; also small nets filled with beans, gourd-seeds, etc. On the right side of the mask is attached a small, closely-woven pouch with long fringes at the lower edge, which contains small bundles of feathers, of wool, cotton, and various other substances.*

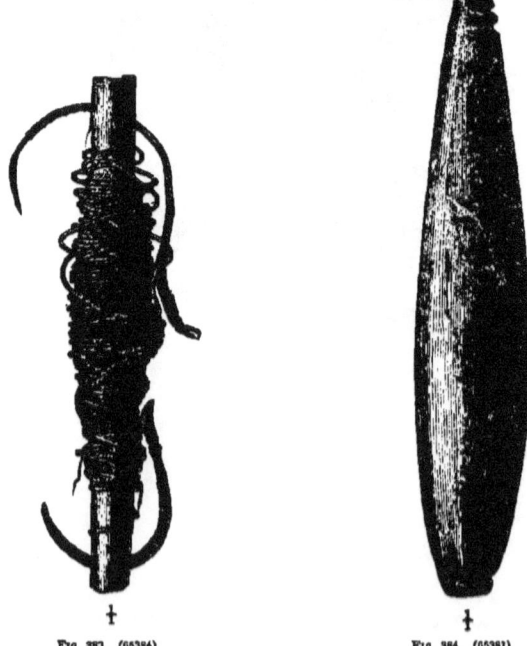

Fig. 383. (65384).   Fig. 384. (65381).

Figs. 383 and 384.—Reel with line and two copper fish-hooks, and stone sinker. Peru.

---

* Such masks are not unfrequently found in Peruvian graves. See Squier's "Peru," p. 90. Other authors on Peru likewise mention them.

APPENDIX. 327

Fig. 383 shows one of the pieces of reed with the line wound up. The latter consists of vegetable fibre, and is twisted with perfect regularity. The reel has at each end a split through which one of the copper fish-hooks is passed, as indicated in the illustration. The hooks are much corroded, and covered with verdigris. They are unbarbed, and the larger of them is provided with an eye for fastening the line, while the smaller one shows slight protuberances to facilitate that process. I have called them *copper* hooks, though there is a possibility that they may consist of bronze. They are rather frail, and an attempt to discover whether they consist of copper or an alloy might lead to their destruction.

Fig. 384 represents the largest and best-finished of the three sinkers, found separately from the hooks and reels, as stated. It is carefully made of dark argillite, well-smoothed, but not polished, and shows the striæ produced in fashioning it. A section through the middle would resemble an oval with one of the ends truncated. There are two grooves at one end, and only one at the other. These grooves are not entirely carried around, but terminate where they reach the flattened side of the sinker. The arrangement shown in the represented group conveys an impression of methodical order, perfectly in keeping with the habits of the Peruvians.

FIGS. 385–387.—Copper fish-hooks. Ancon.

In addition, I copy designs of three copper fish-hooks from Plate 81 of the yet unfinished splendid folio work by Messrs. W. Reiss and A. Stübel, entitled "The Necropolis of Ancon in Peru," which is published in German and English (Berlin and London) under the auspices of the Directors of the Berlin Royal Museum.* The authors devoted several years to the exploration of the burial-

---

* The appearance of this work was thus announced by the "London Times":—

"We have never seen anything finer in chromo-lithography, and the illustrations have all the appearance of being faithful reproductions of the originals. We have the strange-looking mummies themselves wrapped in their many particolored cloths, tied round with ropes, and the numerous articles that loving hands deposited beside

ground at Ancon, a small place situated on the sea-coast, a short distance north of Lima. The originals of Figs. 385, 386, and 387 on the preceding page differ in shape from the hooks shown in Fig. 383; the ends of the shanks are bent inwardly to facilitate the attachment of the line.

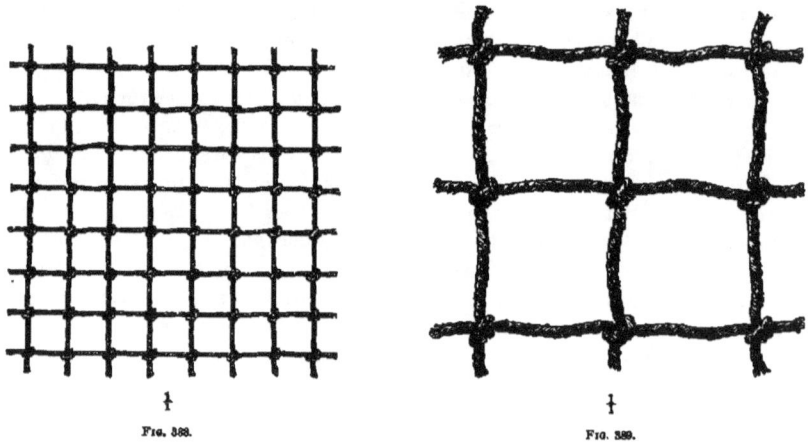

FIGS. 388 and 389.—Portions of nets. Ancon.

Net-making was practised to a great extent in Peru before the conquest of the country by the Spaniards, as the many netted articles found among grave-deposits testify. These nets, knotted exactly like ours, were not only made for purposes of fishing, but served also, in the form of bags, as the receptacles of various articles. Such bags with their contents have frequently been taken from Peruvian graves. The wrappings of the mummies, or rather desiccated bodies, are often externally encompassed by a net-work of bast or twisted straw.

Figs. 388 and 389 represent portions of nets found in graves at Ancon, and preserved in the Peabody Museum (Nos. 8789 and 7326). These nets differ in no way from those made at the present day. They are of a brownish color and the material is vegetable fibre, the character of which I am unable to determine.

It is well known that the former inhabitants of Peru excelled in the manufacture of pottery, producing vessels, which, by their peculiarities of form and

---

them for use on their endless journey. Then we have specimens of various kinds of woven garments, evidently of fine texture, and showing great taste in arrangement of color and elaboration of ornament. Spindles and work-baskets, clay figures, a view of the cemetery itself, and a panorama of the district in which it stands are among the other subjects illustrated. As the cemetery at Ancon was a common one, it is obvious that the objects contained in it will illustrate the life of the bulk of the people of Old Peru. This work is monumental in character, and its value to the archæologist will be of the highest."

APPENDIX. 329

ornamentation, generally can be distinguished without much difficulty from the ancient ceramic manufactures found in other parts of America. They often moulded their vessels in the form of the quadrupeds, birds, fishes, etc., of their country, or of human heads or entire human figures with various attributes, sometimes of unintelligible character. Indeed, it would be impossible to exhaust in a few words the range of conceptions expressed in their ceramic works. Figures of the character just alluded to also appear as the decorations of their more simple vessels, and these ornaments are either painted or worked in a kind of relief, their contour being brought out by the removal of the surrounding portion of the surface. Peruvian clay vessels imitating the form of a fish are not rare, and nearly every work treating of the antiquities of Peru refers to them. A fine fish-shaped vessel is figured on Plate XIII of the "Antiguëdades Peruanas" by M. E. Rivero and J. J. von Tschudi (Vienna, 1851), and one of similar, though somewhat simpler, form is preserved in the United States National Museum.

FIG. 390.—Fish-shaped clay vessel. Peru. (5341).

Fig. 390 represents it. The longitudinal axis measures a trifle more than ten inches, while the transverse middle diameter is only six inches in length. The two strongly bulging sides forming the fish-figure meet above and below under an obtuse angle, forming a blunt edge or ridge, which is interrupted by the neck and a flattish bottom, barely permitting the vessel to stand. It is coated

R 42

with a shining black color. The illustration renders further description superfluous. This specimen was brought from Peru, many years ago, by Captain Aulick, U. S. N.

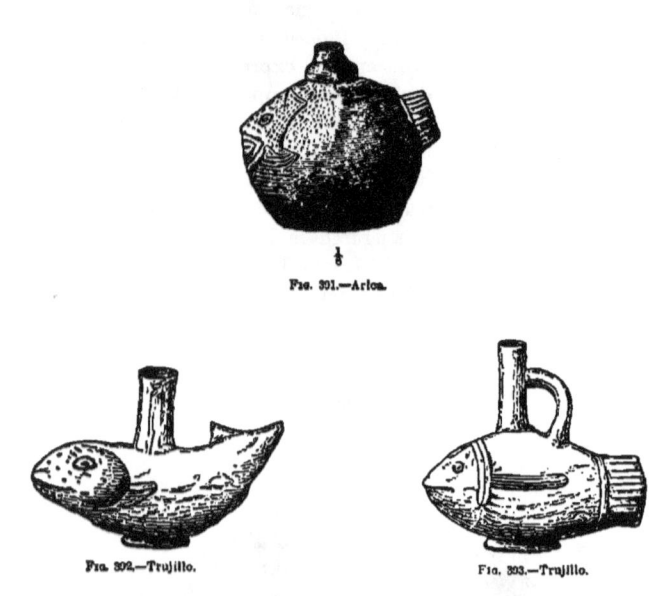

Fig. 391.—Arica.

Fig. 392.—Trujillo.   Fig. 393.—Trujillo.

Figs. 391–393.—Fish-shaped clay vessels.

Among the fish-formed vessels figured in M. Charles Wiener's work on Peru and Bolivia is one from Arica, which exhibits the same general character.[*] It is represented in Fig. 391. In Figs. 392 and 393 I present forms of clay vessels from Trujillo, belonging to Dr. José M. Macedo's collection of Peruvian antiquities, now on exhibition at Paris.[†]

In describing the fish-shaped vessel from Missouri, represented in Fig. 357 on page 213, I directed attention to its similarity to the corresponding class of Peruvian earthenware. I hardly need add that I draw no conclusions whatever from this resemblance.

I cannot remember having seen Peruvian vessels with fish-figures painted on them, and know of their existence only from descriptions. Dr. Macedo mentions in his catalogue several vessels ornamented with painted fish-designs, associated with other figures.

---

[*] Wiener: Pérou et Bolivie; Paris, 1880; p. 604.
[†] Hamy: Revue d'Ethnographie; Vol. I, 1882; p. 69, Figs. 57 and 61.

APPENDIX. 331

There are in the National Museum several vessels from Peru, showing fish-figures in relief. I give in Fig. 394 a representation of the most conspicuous among them—a black vessel of graceful form, with a handle in the shape of a monkey. There appears on each side a sort of panel showing the figures of two fishes and that of a long-billed bird between them. The background from which the figures stand out is marked with the raised dots often surrounding the relief-work on Peruvian earthenware. Fig. 395 shows the panel enlarged.

This fine specimen was presented to the National Museum by Mr. J. V. Norton.

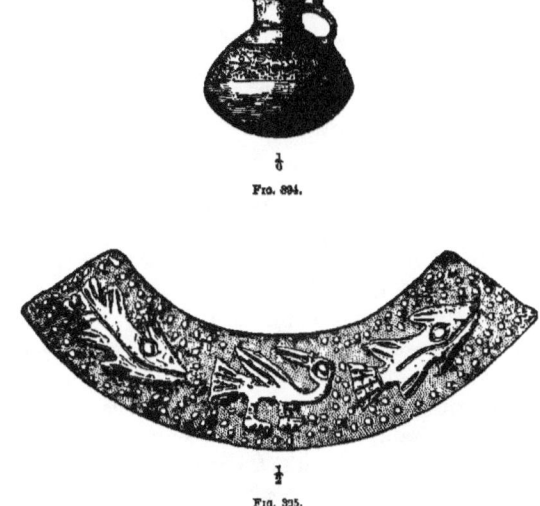

FIGS. 394 and 395.—Clay vessel and ornamentation on it enlarged. Peru. (17377).

Dr. Macedo mentions in his catalogue a small vase from Casma with an aperture in the form of a man's head and two animal-shaped handles. On the front part is represented in relief a man standing upright among fishes, and in the act of catching a large fish with a net.*

The progress in metallurgy which the Peruvians had made before the advent of the Spaniards is well known, and it would be foreign to my purpose to enlarge on the subject. Like all other indigines of America, I will simply state, they were unacquainted with the use of iron; but they worked copper and the precious metals, producing a great variety of tools, utensils, ornaments, and trinkets,

---

* Catalogue d'Objects Archéologiques du Pérou; Paris, 1881; p. 17, No. 261.

which often betoken a considerable degree of skill. Many objects were made of an alloy of gold and copper, called *champi*. They also used bronze. Imitations of living creatures in gold, silver, or champi are still in existence, though the gold objects, as may be imagined, have mostly been melted.

Mr. Squier represents a fish cast in solid silver, brought with other kindred articles from Peru;* but I refrain from copying his figure, being somewhat in doubt as to the genuineness of the original, which I have often seen. It is now in the American Museum of Natural History at New York.

In the year 1867 Mr. Squier received from Mr. Henry Swayne, then at Lima, a series of representations of fishes of various kinds, cut out from thin plates of silver. They are here shown in Figs. 396 to 403.† Mr. Squier considers them as "accurate representations of fishes actually found in Peruvian waters." I showed the illustrations for identification to Professor Theodore Gill, who pronounced them too conventional in execution for determining the different species. Concerning the circumstances of their discovery Mr. Swayne wrote as follows:—

"I avail myself of the first opportunity to send you a number of small silver fishes, which were taken out, by the captain of a coasting-vessel, a friend of mine, from the guano of the Chincha Islands, *thirty-two* feet below the surface. I think they will go far to establish the high antiquity of the aborigines of this country. This friend of mine, Captain Juan Pardo, an Italian, saw taken out of the guano, at the same time that these fishes were found, the body of a female, lacking the head, which, however, was discovered at some distance from the skeleton. The chest, breasts, and ribs were covered with thin sheets of gold, and the whole would have been a most valuable relic, had it been preserved as found. But the workmen divided the gold, part of which was sold to captains of ships loading guano, and the body thrown into the sea."‡

Mr. Squier is somewhat skeptic regarding the statements that artefacts have occurred at great depths in the guano. These accounts, he thinks, "are far too vague to be accepted, in this epoch of positive science, as the basis of rational speculation regarding the antiquity of man or his works on the shores of Peru. Articles may be found at considerable depths in *huanu*, where they have been buried. They may have been simply deposited at the surface and fallen down,

---

* Squier: Peru; p. 178.

† These illustrations appeared first in Frank Leslie's "Illustrated Newspaper" of October 19, 1867, accompanying an article by Mr. Squier. They were then again published by him in an essay in the "Journal of the Anthropological Institute of New York, Vol. I, New York, 1871-'72," p. 51; and finally found their way into his "Peru" (copyrighted in 1877). I am indebted to Messrs. Harper & Brothers for electrotypes of these illustrations as well as for that of Fig. 404, which likewise appeared both in the above-named journal (p. 54) and in the work on Peru.

‡ Squier: Antiquities from the Guano or Huanu Islands of Peru; Journal of the Anthropological Institute of New York; Vol. I, 1871-'72; p. 50, etc.

APPENDIX. 333

to an apparently great depth, with the disintegration or 'caving' down of the wall of the material in course of removal, and thus appear to have been deposited there. We must, however, exhaust the easiest modes of resolving a question before resorting to those that are complex."

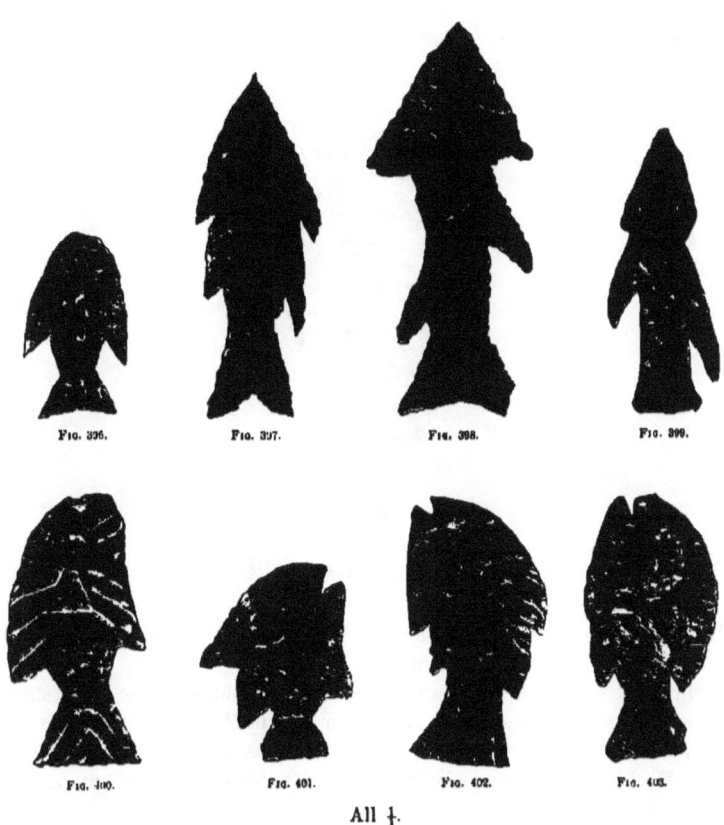

FIGS. 396–403.—Fish-shaped silver ornaments. From one of the Chincha Islands.

The silver fishes just described are in the American Museum of Natural History at New York. There can be little doubt that they were originally attached as ornaments to some article of dress, which has long yielded to decay

---

* Squier: Antiquities, etc.; p. 55.

in the covering deposit. This application appears the more probable as there is preserved among the antiquities of the New York Historical Society an ancient poncho, taken from a tomb at Gran Chimu, near Trujillo, upon which are sewed, in considerable number, silver fishes, not differing much from those sent by Mr. Swayne. On the head of the body with which the poncho was found rested a thin silver plate, cut out in a form which has been supposed to represent a skate, and having on it "struck-up" representations of three fishes resembling those attached to the poncho itself.

FIG. 404.—Fish-shaped silver ornament. Gran Chimu.

This fish-shaped ornament, shown in Fig. 404, measures nine and a half inches in greatest length, and five and a fourth inches in greatest breadth. Mr. Squier thinks it was inserted between the forehead and the fillet encircling it, and worn as a kind of aigrette.* Professor Gill is of opinion that this figure was not intended to imitate a skate, and thinks it resembles more the *Discopyge Tschudii*, Heckel (of the *Torpedo* family), a fish inhabiting the sea along the Peruvian coast.

The many textile fabrics rescued from Peruvian tombs bear witness to the skill in weaving and dyeing displayed by the former inhabitants, who used as materials cotton and the wool of the camel-like animals of their country (llama, alpaca, vicuña, and huanaco). Many of their stuffs show regular inwoven patterns, in the form of geometrical designs, or of fruits, reptiles, fishes, birds, quadrupeds, and men. These figures, owing to the difficulty of the process, are

---

* Squier: Antiquities, etc.; p. 52.

angular and of primitive appearance, yet, nevertheless, produce a pleasing effect.*

Fig. 405.—Piece of cloth with inwoven fish-designs. Pisco.

The reader, by this time accustomed to the conventional fish-representations of the Peruvians, will not fail to recognize one in the central design of Fig. 405, showing a portion of a piece of cloth, found at Pisco, one hundred and thirty miles south of Lima. The same figure, differently colored, is twice repeated at the lower edge of the fragment. The illustration is copied from page 637 of M. Wiener's "Pérou et Bolivie."

---

* "Il est intéressant de suivre ce que nous appellerions volontiers le développement des dessins dans la trame des étoffes. Les étoffes les plus simples ont pour ornements de simples lignes droites parallèles, d'autres des lignes croisées ; ce sont là les premiers modèles que nous retrouvons dans les nattes de paille. Cependant ces dessins se développent, le méandre remplace d'abord les lignes croisées, et puis petit à petit nous trouvons la reproduction de fruits, de poissons et d'animaux, pour nous élever finalement à la représentation de l'homme. Cependant les difficultés techniques empêchaient le libre développement de la ligne. La courbe est toujours remplacée par une ligne cent fois brisée et se mouvant suivant des angles droits. C'est ainsi que le crâne devient une pyramide à gradins, que l'œil devient un rhomboïde, le nez un triangle, la bouche un quadrilatère."—*Wiener: Pérou et Bolivie*, p. 636, etc.

INDEX.

Abbot, C. C., Trenton gravels, 114; bone fish-hook, Long Island, 126; sinkers, New Jersey, 157; fish-cutters, New Jersey, 183, 185; anchor-stones, New Jersey, 192; shell-heaps in New Jersey, 227.
Abundance of fish in North American waters, 117.
Adair, J., fishing of the Chikkasas and other Southern Indians, 291–293.
Age of kjökkenmöddings, 35; shell-heaps in Florida, 246; the Aleutian Islands, 256–260.
Aleutian Islands, shell-heaps in the, 256–260.
Amulets of the cave-men, 8; lake-dwellers, 42.
Anchor-stones of the neolithic age, 94; in North America, 192–196.
Animals and plants used by the lake-dwellers, 43–45.
Animal remains in the drift, 2, 115; Dordogne caves, 6; kjökkenmöddings, 35; lake-dwellings, 43; North American shell-heaps, 216–260, *passim*.
Antlers with incised figures in the reindeer-period, 27.
"Arpion," 51.
Arrow-heads of horn and flint in lake-dwellings, 56.
Art among the Dordogne cave-men, 6–8, 27.
Ash-pits in Ohio, 124.
Atwater, C., copper sinker, Ohio, 181; shell-heaps in Ohio, 241.
Aurochs, heads of, carved on antler, La Madelaine, 31.

Bailing-scoop, California, 190.
Baird, S. F., shell-heaps in New Brunswick and New England, 222.
Bait-holders of bone, Switzerland, 46; California, 119; of flint, Germany, 69; of bronze, Switzerland, 99; of stone, North America, 117.
Barbed points of bronze, Europe, 105.
Bark canoes of the Beothucs, Newfoundland, 266; Indians of Canada, 272; Iroquois, 273, 282; Northern Indians of British America, 276; New England Indians, 279, 280.
"Batons," in the reindeer-period, 27–31.
Beauchamp, W. M., fish-hook of deer-horn, New York, 128; harpoon-heads of deer-horn, New York, 145, 152.
Beothucs, of Newfoundland, 266.
Berlin Fishery Exhibition, bone fish-hooks, Switzerland, 48, 49; harpoon-head, Switzerland, 53; bait-holder of bronze, Switzerland, 99; bronze fish-hook, Switzerland, 103.
Bessels, E., flint-pointed fish-hook, Greenland, 121; formation of shell-heaps in Greenland, 221.

Beverly, R., aboriginal fishing in Virginia, 288.
Blood-grooves on Dordogne harpoon-heads, 17.
Boat found at Berneuchen, 91; near Savannah, 188.
Boats, from Robenhausen, 66; Saint Peter's Island, 66; Möringen, 67; Cudrefin, 105; Vingelz, 107; Mercurago, 108; found in Ireland, 91; the silt-beds of Scotland, 93; Denmark, 111; of the Greenland Eskimos, 268; natives of Nootka Sound, 314, 315; Prince William's Sound, 316; Unalashka, 317.
Boisbaudran, Lecoq de, unilateral barbs, 20.
Bone-and-flint harpoon-heads, Scania, 81; Prussia, 82.
Booths for fishing in California, 297, 299, 300.
Boucher de Perthes, drift-implements in France, 2.
Boys taught to fish in Mexico, 314.
Bransford, J. F., sinkers, Ometepec Island, 319.
Brickell, J., aboriginal fishing in North Carolina, 290.
Brinton, D. G., shell-heaps in the United States, 217; Tennessee, 241.
Broca, P., opinion concerning fishing in the reindeer-period, 10; definition of "harpoon," 19; absence of fishing-nets in the reindeer-period, 26; engraved design of the cave-dwellers, Laugerie Basse, 30.
Bronze, how brought into Europe, 96; in lake-settlements, 97; bronze age, 95, 111.
Brooks, Miss M., bone fish-hooks in shell-heaps, Rhode Island, V.
Bull-hide boats of the Mandans, etc., 295.
Butler, J. D., copper harpoon-heads, Wisconsin, 152.

Cabeza de Vaca, A. N., reference to nets of the Indians, 156; shell-heaps in North America, 216.
California, aboriginal fishing in, 296–301.
Canada, aboriginal fishing in, 268–274.
Cannibalism, signs of, in Florida shell-heaps, 245.
Canoes of birch-bark, how made, 266, 272, 273, 276, 279, 280, 282.
Carolinas, aboriginal fishing in the, 289–293.
Carp, remains of, in the Dordogne caves, 12.
Carvings of fish, Alaska and California, 207; Costa Rica, 321.
Cat-fish, catching of, by Southern Indians, 292.
Catlin, G., bull-hide boats of the Mandans, 295.
Cauca, gold fish-hooks from, 322.
Caves and rock-shelters in Europe, 4.
Caves of Dordogne, retreats of hunters and fishermen, 5.
Cazalis de Fondouce, P., fish-hook of antler, Norway, 72; stone anchor (?) from Bohusland, 94.
Cessac, L. de, carvings of cetaceans, etc., California, 210.
Champlain, Sieur de, fishing of the Hurons, 268.

Charlevoix, Father, aboriginal fishing in Canada, 272.
Charred objects in lake-dwellings, 41, 43, 44, 57.
Chenoweth, A. C., gold fish-hook, Cauca, 323.
Chinooks, salmon-fishing of the, 303.
Chiriqui, fish-shaped gold figures from, 321.
Christensen, bone fish-hook, Pomerania, 72; flint points for fish-hooks, Germany, 122.
Clams, how taken by the Wintūns, 299.
Clavigero, F. X., Mexican fishing, 514.
Clay cones in lake-dwellings, 60; rings in lake-dwellings, 62; vessels, fish-shaped, Arkansas, 211; Missouri, 213; Peru, 323.
Climate of Europe in the palæolithic age, 1; neolithic age, 32.
Cloth with inwoven fish-designs, Peru, 335.
Codfish-hooks of the Makahs, 15.
Collins, J. W., "devil's claw grapnel," 52.
Cook, J., boats and methods of fishing in Nootka Sound, Prince William's Sound, and Unalashka, 315–318.
Cook, G. H., shell-heaps in New Jersey, 230.
Copper, native, in North America, 138; working of, in North America, 138, 154.
Cortés, H., Mexican fish-ponds, etc., 213.
Costa Rica, fish-carvings from, 321.
Cox, J., bone fish-hooks, Ohio, 124, 127, 128; harpoon-head, Ohio, 147.
Cranz, D., fishing of the Greenlanders, 261.
Craw-fish, how caught by the North Carolina Indians, 289.
Curing fish, Indians of Canada, 270; Virginia, 285.
Cushing, F. H., bone fish-hook, New York, 125; sinkers, New York, 156.

Dall, W. H., harpoon-heads of bone, Alaska, 143, 147, 149, 151; Aleutian shell-heaps, 144, 256; copper-working in Alaska, 154; species of mollusks in Californian shell-heaps, 254, 256.
Dawkins, W. B., early man in America, VI; baton as arrow-straightener, 29; harpoon-head, Victoria Cave, 80.
Dawson, J. W., harpoon-head, Nova Scotia, VI.
De Bry, T., aboriginal fishing in Virginia, 284.
Decoys for seals, used by the natives of Nootka Sound, 313.
De Laet, J., boats in Newfoundland, 266.
Delaware and Iroquois fishing, 283.
Desor, E., lacustrine clay ring, 62; boats of the lake-dwellers, 67; on the bronze age, 98.
Devereux, J. H., copper sinker, Ohio, 181; fish-shaped vessel, Arkansas, 211.
"Devil's claw grapnel," 51.
Domestic animals, none in reindeer-period, 6; of the lake-dwellers, 44.
Drift, animals of the European, 2; the North American, 115.
Drift-implements in France and England, 1–4; North America, 114.
Driving fish, Delawares and Iroquois, 284; Southern Indians, 291.
Drying fish, Indians of North Carolina, 290.
Dug-out discovered near Savannah, 188.

Dug-outs in New England, 278, 279; of the Delawares, 283; Virginia Indians, 286, 287; California Indians, 296, 298, 300; Chinooks, 303; natives of Nootka Sound, 313, 315.
Dunn, J., salmon-fishing of the Chinooks, 303.
Dupont, E., baton from the cave of Goyet, 29.
Du Pratz, Le Page, aboriginal fishing in Louisiana, 293.

"Early Man in Europe," mentioned, VI.
Eel (?) traced on a baton, La Madelaine, 31; eel-fishing, aboriginal, in Canada, 270, 271; California, 298.
Egede, H., fishing of the Greenland Eskimos, 261.
Ellis, W., fish-hooks of the Society Islanders, 137.
Eskimos formerly further south, 115.
Evans, J., harpoon-heads from Kent's Cavern, 25; flint fish-hooks, Sweden and England, 70; sinkers, England and Scotland, 87; classification of bronze relics, 96; bronze fish-hook, Ireland, 109.
Evers, E., fish-shaped vessel, Missouri, 213.
Extinction of species in Europe, 2, 32, 36, 37, 43.

Fascine-works in Swiss lakes, 40.
Fauna of the European drift, 2; reindeer-period, 6; neolithic age, 32; North American drift, 115; North American shell-heaps, 220, 221, 222, etc.
Fellenberg, E. de, boats from the Lake of Bienne, 106.
Figuier, L., net-making in prehistoric times, 64.
Fire-places in kjökkenmöddings, 94; North American shell-heaps, 221, 227, etc.
Fire used in fishing, in the Carolinas, 284; Virginia, 280.
Fish, abundance of, in American waters, 117.
Fish carved on antler, La Madelaine, 27; on a bear's tooth, Duruthy Grotto, 28; on a reindeer-jaw, Laugerie Basse, 28; on a baton, cave of Goyet, 29.
Fish-cutters of stone, North American, 183.
Fish-hooks of horn, bone, etc., lake-dwellings, 47; of bone, Germany, 49, 72; Scania, 71; Dakota, 123; Arkansas, 125; Indiana, 125; New York, 125, 126; Illinois, 126; Ohio, 124, 126, 127, 128; California, 129; Greenland, 130; New Zealand, 137; of flint, Sweden, 69; of reindeer-horn, Norway, 72; Arctic America, 130; of bronze, Switzerland, 99–104, passim; Germany, 102, 110; Italy, 103; Savoy, 103; British Isles, 109; Denmark, 109; flint-pointed, Greenland, 120; Rügen, 121; of deer-horn, New York, 128; of shell (including mode of manufacture), California, 131–135; Salmon, 136; of turtle-shell, Serle Island, 136; of copper, Wisconsin, 138; Peru, 324; of cactus-spines, used by the Mohaves, how made, 139; of gold, Cauca, 323.
Fishing-arrows, Louisiana, 293.
Fishing-implements scarce in the European stone age, 68.
Fishing-scene on a scapula, Laugerie Basse, 29.
Fish-pen in New York, 200.
Fish-preserves in Georgia, 197.
Fish-rakes of the Chinooks, 304; natives of Nootka Sound, 315, 316.

Fish-remains in the Vézère caves, 10; kjökkenmöddings, 36; lake-dwellings, 45; North American shell-heaps, 218–260, *passim*.
Fish-shaped vessels, North America, 212; Peru, 329.
Floats for harpoons, 21; for lines and nets in lake-dwellings, 49, 63; none prehistoric in North America, 141; with arrows, Louisiana, 293.
Florida, aboriginal fishing in, 291.
Forging iron, natives of Nootka Sound, 314.
Friedel, E., bait-holders of flint, Prussia, 69; of bronze, Switzerland, 99; javelin-heads, Prussia, 82; anchor-stones, Prussia, 87, 94; boats, Prussia, 91, 110.
Frontispiece, note, 102.

Gaines, A. S., and Cunningham, K. M., shell-heaps in Alabama, 249.
Gastaldi, B., wooden anchor, Mercurago, 67; boat, Mercurago, 108.
Georgia, aboriginal fishing in, 291.
Gerucrd, J. M. M., stone sinkers, Susquehanna Valley, 157.
Gill, T., Peruvian fish-figures, 332, 334.
Glacial man, condition of, 1.
Goering, A., pile-dwellings in Venezuela, 38.
Gold figures, fish-shaped, Chiriqui, 321.
Goyet, cave of, 29.
Gratz, prehistoric net from Mammoth Cave (?), 156.
Greenland, fishing of the Eskimos in, 261–266.
Grewingk, C., harpoon-heads in marl of Estland, V.
Grooved sinkers, 59, 85–88, 89, 161–164, 319, 320.
Gross, V., harpoons of lake-dwellers, 55.

Haidahs, canoes of the, 310.
Halibut-hooks, Makahs, 14.
Haynes, H. W., Trenton gravels, 115.
Harpoon-arrows, La Madelaine, 23.
Harpoon-heads of reindeer-horn, France, 16, 18, 19, 23; England, 25; Switzerland, 25; of deer-horn, Switzerland, 52, 55; New York, 145, 150, 152; of bone, Switzerland, 54; Scania, 73; Soeland, 73, 77; Fünen, 77; Jütland, 77; Tierra del Fuego, 77; Victoria Cave, 80; in colonial times, 142; California, 143; Maine, 143, 144, 148, 151; Alaska, 144, 148, 149, 151; Puget Sound, 145; New York, 145, 150; Ohio, 147; Michigan, 147, 149; of ox-horn, Poland, 78; of stone, Europe, 83; North America, 141; of elk-horn, New York, 146; of copper, Wisconsin, 152; Alaska, 154.
Harpoons and fish-hooks, priority in time, 12, 141.
Harpoons of the cave-men, 16, 22; Eskimos and Northwest Coast Indians, 20; lake-dwellers, 52; Southern Indians, 291; Makahs, 306; natives of Nootka Sound, 311, 316.
Hearne, S., fishing of the Northern Indians, 274.
Henaggi Indians, dug-outs of the, 298.
Henry, A., aboriginal fishing in Michigan, 273.
Herring and shad, former spread of, in New York, 203.
Hoffman, W. J., bone fish-hook, Dakota, 123.
Horse-figure delineated on a baton, La Madelaine, 27; horse-heads traced on antler, La Madelaine, 31.

House-sites in Greenland shell-heaps, 219.
Hurons, aboriginal fishing of the, 268.

Ice-picks (?) of flint in the European drift, 4.
Implements of the drift, 2; reindeer-period, 6; neolithic age, 33; kjökkenmöddings, 35; lake-dwellers, 41.
Iroquois, fishing of the, 283.
Irving, W., pile-dwellings in Venezuela, 38.

Javelin-heads of bone with inserted flakes of flint, Scania, 81; Prussia, 82.
Jogues, I., shell-heaps in New York, 216.
Johnson, E., fish-shooting, New England Indians, 278.
Jones, C. C., stone sinkers, 165; dug-out exhumed near Savannah, 188; ancient fish-preserves in Georgia, 197; shell-heaps in Georgia, 242.
Jones, J. M., shell-heaps in Nova Scotia, 221.
Jones, S., fish-hooks of the Kutchin Indians, 122.
Jordan, F., shell-heaps in Delaware, 230.
Josselyn, J., aboriginal fishing in New England, 270.

Kalm, P., shell-heaps in the Atlantic States, 217; aboriginal fishing in New York and New Jersey, 281.
Kayaks of the Greenlanders, 264; Alaskans, 316.
Keith, M. C., carving of fish from Costa Rica, 320.
Keller, F., lake-dwellings, 37–68, 97–109, *passim*.
Kent's Cavern, 9; harpoon-heads from, 25.
Kesslerloch, 9; harpoon-heads from, 24.
"Killick," 196.
Kjökkenmöddings, or kitchen-middens, 33–37.
Klemm, G., flint sinkers and anchor-stones, Heligoland and Rügen, 87; flint-pointed fish-hook, Greenland, 120.
Knight of Elvas, Indian nets, 156.

Lake-dwellings, 37–68, 97–109; construction of, 40, 97.
Lake-settlements, age and duration of, 39, 98.
Lartet, E., and Christy, H., Dordogne caves, 5–32, *passim*.
Lartet, E., fishing of the cave-men, 10.
Lartet, L., and Duparc, C., exploration of Duruthy Grotto, 28.
Lawson, J., aboriginal fishing in North Carolina, 289.
Le Hon, H., bone arrow-head, Saint-Aubin, 47.
Le Jeune, Le P., aboriginal eel-fishing in Canada, 271.
Lewis, E., shell-heaps in Long Island, 227.
Lewis, H. C., age of the Trenton gravels, 114.
Lloyd, T. G. B., boats of the Boothucs, 266.
Looms of the lake-dwellers, 61.
Loskiel, G. H., fishing of Delawares and Iroquois, 283.
Louisiana, aboriginal fishing in, 293.
Lubomirski, J. T., fish-spear-heads, Poland, 78.
Lyell, Sir C., fauna of the Dordogne caves, 5; boats from the Scottish silt, 92; shell-heaps in Massachusetts and Georgia, 217.

Macedo, J. M., fish-shaped vessels, Peru, 331.
McGuire, J. D., shell-heaps in Maryland, 237.
Mackenzie, A., fishing of the Slave and Dogrib Indians, 276.

340 INDEX.

McLean, J. J. shell-heaps at Cape Mendocino, 254.
MacLean, J. P., shell-heaps on Blennerhassett's Island, 239.
Madsen, A. P., Danish harpoon-heads, 77; drawing of a Greenland fish-hook, 120.
Makahs, fishing of the, 305.
Makhelchels, tule boats of the, 299.
Mandans, bull-hide boats of the, 295.
Mann, C. L., copper fish-hook, Wisconsin, 138.
Marchant, L., gold fish-hooks, New Granada, 322.
Mask, ancient Peruvian, 325.
Mason, O. T., anchor-stones in Virginia, 195.
Massenat, E., rude tracing of a fishing-scene, Laugerie Basse, 29.
Meares, J., fishing of the natives of Nootka Sound, 310.
Mendoza Codex, delineations from the, 214.
Merk, K., harpoon-heads from the Kesslerloch, 24.
Michilimakinacs, fishing of the, 272.
Michoacan, "the place where possessors of fish live," 214.
Mitchell, A., Scottish stone sinkers, 84.
Modoks, fishing of the, 300.
Montezuma, fish-carriers of, 214.
Monuments of the neolithic age, 33.
Morgan, L. H., Iroquois canoes, 282.
Mortillet, G. de, fish-hooks (?) in the reindeer-period, 10; boat, Saint Peter's Island, 67; ancient boats discovered in France, 94.

Nelson, E. W., bird-capture of the Alaska Eskimos, 13.
Neolithic age, fishing in the, 33-95.
Nets not known (?) in the reindeer-period, 26; of the lake-dwellers, 57; from Mammoth Cave (?), 155; mentioned by early writers on America, 155; of the Canada Indians, 268; New England Indians, 279; Louisiana Indians, 293; Shoshonees, 294; California Indians, 296-301, *passim*; Pai-Utes, 301; from Ancon, 328; used as receptacles, Peru, 328.
Netting-needles (?) of the lake-dwellers, 64; modern, 65.
New England, aboriginal fishing in, 277-280.
New Jersey, aboriginal fishing in, 282.
New York, aboriginal fishing in, 281.
Nilsson, S., flint fish-hooks, Sweden, 69; bone harpoon-heads, Scania, 73; fish or bird-darts, Arctic America, 75; Scandinavia, 81; sinkers, Sweden, 90.
Nootka Sound, fishing of the natives of, 310-316.
Nordenskiöld, A. E., shell-heaps in Greenland, 219.
North Carolina, aboriginal fishing in, 289, 290, 291.
Notched sinkers, 59, 157-160, 319.

Ogilby, J., aboriginal fishing in New England, 278.
Opochtli, Mexican god, 214.
Ometepec Island, sinkers from, 319.
Ornaments, fish-shaped, of gold, Chiriqui, 321; silver, Peru, 332-334.
Otis, F. M., golden fish-figures, Chiriqui, 322.
Outaouais as canoe-builders, 273.

Pachacamac, tomb containing fishing-tackle, 324.
Paddles not found in the neolithic age, 94; prehistoric, in North America, 191; of the Makahs, 307; natives of Nootka Sound, 315.
Pai-Ute Indians, fishing of the, 301.
Palæolithic age in Europe, 1-32; in North America, 114.
Palligawonops, fishing of the, 300.
Palmer, E., cactus-spine fish-hooks, Mohaves, 139.
Peabody Museum, loan of lacustrine fishing-implements, VII.
Peace River Indians, fishing of the, 276.
Perforated sinkers, 59, 60, 88, 89, 165-167, 320.
Petroff, I., Aleutian shell-heaps, 258.
Phillips, B., eel-fishing in France, 46.
Pickering, C., turtle-shell (?) fish-hook, Serle Island, 136.
Pike, remains of, in the Dordogne caves, 12.
Pile-dwellings in Venezuela, Mexico, etc., 38.
Pirogues, Louisiana, 294.
Pliocene man in America, doubtful, 116.
Platform-pipes with fish-representations, Ohio, 205.
Plummets, 167.
Poisoning fish, Indians in the Southern States, 291; Wailakkis, 298.
Polynesian fish-hooks, 135.
Pottery probably unknown to palæolithic man, 1; of the neolithic age, 33, 42; kjökkenmöddings, 35; bronze age, 97, 98; North American shell-heaps, 221-249, *passim*; Florida shell-heaps, 247.
Powell, J. W., shell-heaps in California, 254.
Powers, S., aboriginal fishing in California, 296-301; Nevada, 301.
Pratt, W. H., bone fish-hook, Arkansas, 125.
Prehistoric America, meaning of the term, 113.
Prince William's Sound, fishing of the natives of, 316.
Prussia, sinkers of clay in, 91.
Putnam, F. W., remains from Mammoth Cave (?), 155; copper sinker, 181; slate fish-cutters, 183, 185; fish-carvings, 207; shell-heaps in New England, 224.

Races of the palæolithic age, 9.
Rafts of the Shoshonees, 295.
Refuse-accumulations in the Vézère caves, 5.
Reindeer-period, 4-10.
Reiss, W., and Stübel, A., "The Necropolis of Ancon," 327.
Reynolds, E. R., shell-heaps in Maryland, 285.
Roasting fish, Indians of Virginia, 285.
Rock-shelters in Europe, 4.
Runners carrying fish in Mexico, 214.

Sagard, T., fishing of the Hurons, 268.
Sahagun, B. de, Mexican god Opochtli, 214.
Salmon-fishing of the Chinooks, 303.
Salmon-spearing of the Shoshonees, 294; California Indians, 297, 299, 302.
Salmon, remains of, in the Dordogne caves, 11.
Sardine-fishing of the natives of Nootka Sound, 310.

INDEX. 341

Sauvage, H. E., fishing in the reindeer-period, 4, 11, 12.
Scarfing of canoes, Makahs, 309.
Schoolcraft, H. R., bone fish-hook, Cunningham's Island, 126.
Schumacher, P., bait-holder (?) of jasper, Oregon, 117; manufacture of shell fish-hooks, California, 134; shell-heaps in Oregon, 249.
Seal-figure traced on a bear's tooth, Duruthy Grotto, 32.
Seal-catching of the Greenlanders, 264; natives of Nootka Sound, 313.
Sea-otter-hunting of the natives of Nootka Sound, 311.
Shell-deposits, artificial, in Denmark, 33; North America, 216.
Shells, species of, in kjökkenmöddings, 36; North American shell-heaps, 216–260, *passim*.
Shoshonees, fishing of the, 294.
Silver fish-figures from one of the Chincha Islands, etc., 332.
Sinkers of stone, notched, Switzerland, 59; North America, 157–160; Nicaragua, 319; grooved, Switzerland, 59; Scotland, 85, 86; England, 87; Ireland, 88; Denmark, 89; North America, 161–164; Nicaragua, 319, 320; perforated, Switzerland, 59, 60; Ireland, 88, 89; North America, 165–167; Nicaragua, 320; of clay, Switzerland, 60; Germany, 62, 91; Nicaragua, 319; for fishing-lines, North American, of stone and other materials, smooth, incised, knobbed, perforated, etc., 167–183; of copper, Ohio, 180; of shell, North America, 182.
Skeletons, human, rare in lake-dwellings, 41.
Skin canoes of the Unalashkans, 317.
Slave and Dogrib Indians, fishing of the, 276.
Slaves employed to fish by the inhabitants of Nootka Sound, 311.
Sloan, J., bone fish-hook, Indiana, 125.
Smelt-fishing, aboriginal, in California, 297.
Smith, E. J., gold fish-hooks, Cauca, 326.
Smith, J., fish-hooks in Virginia, 122; aboriginal fishing in Virginia, 287.
Snyder, J. F., bone fish-hook, Illinois, 126; anchor-stones, Illinois, 193.
Social condition of the cave-inhabitants of the Vézère Valley, 9; Danish coast-dwellers, 35; Swiss lake-men, 41, 97.
Social rank in the reindeer-period, 8.
Squier, E. G., and Davis, E. H., sinker from Ohio, 164; plummets, 168; platform-pipes with fish-figures, Ohio, 205.
Squier, E. G., harpoon-head of bone, New York, 145; fishing-tackle from Pachacamac, 324; silver fish-figures from one of the Chincha Islands, 332.
Steaming of canoes, Makahs, 309.
Steenstrup, J. S., age of kjökkenmöddings, 35; use of meteoric iron in Greenland, 263.
Stevens, E. T., plummet in the Blackmore Museum, 173.
Stone implements in the palæolithic age, 2, 114; Dordogne caves, 6; neolithic age, 33; kjökkenmöddings, 35; lake-dwellings, 41; North American shell-heaps, 218–260, *passim*.
Stone, L., fishing of the McCloud River Indians, 302.

Stone, W. L., fish-pen in New York, 201.
Sturgeon-fishing, aboriginal, in New England, 279; Virginia, 289; of the Chinooks, 303.
Suckers, aboriginal fishing of, in Nevada, 301.
Superstitions connected with fishing, 272, 275, 290, 303, 305.
Swan, J. G., Makahs, fishing of the, 12, 14, 305; their halibut-hooks, 14; codfish-hooks, 15; Chinooks, fishing of the, 305; canoes of the Haidahs, 310.

Tertiary man, 1, 116.
Textile fabrics of the lake-dwellers, 43.
Tooker, W. W., shell-heaps in Long Island, 225.
Toy-boats, 67, 190.
Trenton gravels, 114.
Trill, C. F., artist, VII.
Troyon, F., harpoons of the lake-dwellers, 54; boats of the lake-dwellers, 67.
Tule boats (or rafts) of the Makhelchels, 290; Yokuts, 300; Pai-Utes, 301.
Twine-making of the Shoshonees, 294.

Umiak, of the Greenlanders, 263; Alaskans, 316.
Unalashka Island, canoes and fishing in, 317.
"Underrunning rock," 196.
Unilateral barbs, effects of, 20, 152.
United States Commission of Fish and Fisheries, V, VI.

Van der Donck, A., aboriginal fishing in the New Netherlands, 281.
Vézère River, caves on the, 5.
Viards, fishing of the, 298.
Victoria Cave, bone harpoon-head from, 80.
Village-sites in Oregon, 249.
Virchow, R., reference to clay sinkers in Prussia, 91.
Virginia, aboriginal fishing in, 284–289.
Vogt, C., extinction of the great auk, 36.
Voss, A., catalogue of German antiquities exhibited at Berlin, 68.

Wailakkis, fishing of the, 298.
Walker, S. T., shell-heaps in Florida, 246.
Wampum, New England, 277.
War-arrows, Louisiana, 293.
Weaving of the lake-dwellers, 61.
Weirs of the Greenlanders, 261; Virginia Indians, 285, 288; Yuroks, 297; McCloud River Indians, 302.
Whale-fishing of the Greenlanders, 262; Makahs, 306, 307; natives of Nootka Sound, 311.
Whales, uses of, among the Makahs, 307.
White, C. A., shell-heaps in Iowa, 241.
White-fish, Indian mode of catching, in Michigan, 273.
Wicomico Indians of Maryland, 236.
Wiener, C., fish-shaped vessels, Peru, 330; cloth with fish-designs, Peru, 335.
Wilde, Sir W., Irish sinkers, 88; boats, 91; bronze fish-hook, 109.
Williams, J. J., cave near Santo Domingo, Mexico, 100.
Williams, R., aboriginal fishing in New England, 277.
Wintūns, fishing of the, 299.

Wiyots, *see* Viards.
Women's boat, Greenland, 263; Alaska, 316.
Worsaae, J. J. A., kjökkenmöddings, age of, 85; Danish sinkers, 89; Asiatic origin of bronze, 96; bronze fish-hooks from Fünen, 109; coffin of the bronze age, 111.

Wyeth, N. J., fishing of the Shoshonees, 294.
Wyman, J., bone dart-heads, Maine, 148, 151; shell-heaps in New England, 223; Florida, 243.

Yarrow, H. C., explorations in Southern California, 119.
Yokuts, fishing of the, 800.

www.ingramcontent.com/pod-product-compliance
Lightning Source LLC
Chambersburg PA
CBHW020321240426
43673CB00039B/880